The First Generation
of Country Music Stars

ALSO BY DAVID DICAIRE
AND FROM MCFARLAND

*Jazz Musicians, 1945 to the Present* (2006)

*Jazz Musicians of the Early Years, to 1945* (2003)

*More Blues Singers: Biographies of 50
Artists from the Later 20th Century* (2002)

*Blues Singers: Biographies of 50
Legendary Artists of the Early 20th Century* (1999)

# The First Generation of Country Music Stars

*Biographies of 50 Artists Born Before 1940*

DAVID DICAIRE

McFarland & Company, Inc., Publishers
*Jefferson, North Carolina, and London*

LIBRARY OF CONGRESS CATALOGUING-IN-PUBLICATION DATA

Dicaire, David, 1963–
   The first generation of country music stars : biographies of 50 artists born before 1940 / David Dicaire.
      p.   cm.
   Includes bibliographical references and index.

   ISBN-13: 978-0-7864-3021-5
   softcover : 50# alkaline paper ∞

   1. Country musicians—United States—Biography.
I. Title.
ML394.D518   2007
781.642092'273—dc22   [B]                    2007018871

British Library cataloguing data are available

©2007 David Dicaire. All rights reserved

*No part of this book may be reproduced or transmitted in any form or by any means, electronic or mechanical, including photocopying or recording, or by any information storage and retrieval system, without permission in writing from the publisher.*

Cover photograph ©2006 Creatas

Manufactured in the United States of America

*McFarland & Company, Inc., Publishers*
   *Box 611, Jefferson, North Carolina 28640*
      *www.mcfarlandpub.com*

To my father,
who always had a cowboy song
in his heart

# Table of Contents

| | |
|---|---|
| *Preface* | 1 |
| *Introduction* | 3 |

### PART ONE: THE PIONEERS — 9

| | |
|---|---|
| Fiddlin' John Carson (1868–1949): The Virginia Reeler | 11 |
| Uncle Dave Macon (1870–1952): King of the Hillbillies | 14 |
| Dr. Humphrey Bate (1875–1936): The Possum Hunter | 17 |
| Vernon Dalhart (1883–1948): A Country Star | 20 |
| Gid Tanner (1885–1960): The Skillet Licker | 23 |
| A.P. Carter (1891–1960): Family Patriarch | 28 |
| Charlie Poole (1892–1931): North Carolina Rambler | 32 |
| E.V. "Pop" Stoneman (1893–1968): Country Patriarch | 35 |
| Riley Puckett (1894–1946): Blind Ambition | 39 |
| Jimmie Rodgers (1897–1933): The Singing Brakeman | 42 |

### PART TWO: COWBOYS AND RADIO STARS — 49

| | |
|---|---|
| Ken Maynard (1895–1973): Wagon Master | 51 |
| Roy Acuff (1903–1992): Wabash Cannonball | 54 |
| Wilf Carter (1904–1996): Montana Slim | 60 |
| Tex Ritter (1907–1974): Lone Star Cowboy | 63 |
| Gene Autry (1907–1998): The Singing Cowboy | 67 |
| Red Foley (1910–1968): The Mainstream Voice | 72 |
| Roy Rogers (1911–1998): Happy Trails Forever | 76 |
| Hank Snow (1914–1999): The Travelin' Canadian | 79 |

Merle Travis (1917–1983): The Individualist — 84
Eddy Arnold (1918–): The Tennessee Plowboy — 88

## Part Three: Western Swing/Bluegrass/Honky Tonk — 95

Bob Wills (1905–1975): The Western Swing King — 97
Bill Monroe (1911–1996): The Bluegrass Rambler — 104
Ernest Tubb (1914–1984): The Texas Troubadour — 112
Lester Flatt (1914–1979): Flat Pickin' — 118
Hank Williams, Sr. (1923–1953): Life to Legend — 123
Earl Scruggs (1924–): Dueling Banjoist — 132
Hank Thompson (1925–): Texas Swing — 137
Ray Price (1926–): Cherokee Cowboy — 141
George Jones (1931–): Honky Tonk Texan — 146

## Part Four: Women of Country Music — 157

Sara Carter (1899–1979): Wildwood Flower — 159
Maybelle Carter (1909–1978): Country Matriarch — 163
Dale Evans (1912–2001): Queen of the Cowgirls — 167
Kitty Wells (1918–): Queen of Country Music — 170
Molly O'Day (1923–1987): A Defining Role — 174
June Carter Cash (1929–2003): A Song in Her Heart — 177
Patsy Cline (1932–1963): A Country Music Treasure — 180
Loretta Lynn (1934–): Coal Miner Heartbreak — 187
Wanda Jackson (1937–): Country Music Heart — 192

## Part Five: Outlaws, Rebels and Superstars — 197

Chet Atkins (1924–2001): The Superpicker — 199
Marty Robbins (1925–1982): The Country Chameleon — 205
Buck Owens (1929–2006): Baron of Bakersfield — 212
Johnny Cash (1932–2003): The Man in Black — 218
Charlie Rich (1932–1995): The Silver Fox — 229
Glen Campbell (1936–): Rhinestone Cowboy — 234

Roy Clark (1933–): Lightning Fingers                240
Willie Nelson (1933–): Austin Outlaw                245
Conway Twitty (1933–1993): Uncrowned King           255
Waylon Jennings (1937–2002): Ladies Love Outlaws    262
Merle Haggard (1937–): Lonesome Fugitive            269
Kenny Rogers (1938–): The Gambler                   277

*Bibliography*                                      285
*Index*                                             289

# *Preface*

The subject of country music is an interesting one for many different reasons. The term—like blues, jazz, rock and roll, soul, R&B, folk and classical—encompasses many diverse branches. Since its humble beginnings in the old timey songs of the Appalachian practitioners, country music diversified into numerous themes and ideas.

The personalities that made the genre into a billion dollar industry illustrate the triumphs and the saddest aspects of life. The awards, the gold records, the money, the fame, the honorary degrees and epitaphs have been the goals of anyone who aspired to be a country artist. The alcoholism, plane crashes, divorces, heartache, and diseases that robbed many of their strength and vitality are the dark side.

The music and musicians are intermingled into a package that is rich in history and detail. Hundreds of books have been written, many words spilled onto the millions of pages to capture the power, glory, and beauty of the country sound. Its past reflects the growth of a nation, its struggles and victories.

Although my book is not a complete encyclopedia, it encompasses the diversity, personalities and history of country music from its humble beginnings to the 1970s. It is unique in scope because of its narrow focus on fifty of the most important characters, who cover the range of the genre.

The research for such an ambitious project includes reading biographies, autobiographies and listening to country music radio on a daily basis to put one in the mood. An already healthy love of country music certainly helped with the initial draft.

In the end, it is about the music and those who helped create it. I hope you like it.

# *Introduction*

The evolution of country music from its earliest, humble beginnings in rural America into a billion-dollar industry of international fame is a long, colorful tale. It is the story of the maturation of America as a nation from the very first settlements to its present diversity. To truly understand the transformation of country music, one must study its roots.

Those roots date back to the pre-Elizabethan period in England, Scotland, and Ireland. The folk-song culture thrived for hundreds of years in Great Britain and its surroundings, evolving slightly with each new generation. The music was mainly the songs of the white, mostly working class poor and it was this musical tradition that the first settlers brought with them to the New World. Because many of the peasants and laborers who adored the style were illiterate, the lyrics, melodies and harmonies were passed down verbally from one generation to another.

For two hundred years the style of the folk songs remained virtually unchanged with the exception of their content. The new lyrics reflected the growth and development of American culture to include the lore of lumberjacks, buffalo hunters, cowboys, as well as train drivers as the railroad spread across the country, opening up the Wild West for settlement. It was only after the Industrial Revolution arrived in America that the standard form of the simple folk song began to change.

The rapid development of communication and transportation systems helped spread the songs throughout the ever-expanding country. Boatmen carrying their goods up and down the Mississippi River and other waterways could be heard singing with loud, rich voices and served as important transmitters of the new songs that were being written at a frantic pace. Railroad workers were also keen on spreading the new music from one end of the blossoming nation to the other.

In the country's richest as well as humblest structures, families gathered around the piano and harmonized to their favorites. Many social gatherings featured singers, since music was an important part of all cultural events. In rural areas where the square or barn dance was the traditional form of entertainment, the fiddler was held in high esteem.

Arguably, the first true country musicians were the wandering minstrels—often blind—who earned a meager living travelling the countryside and performing the standard songs of the day. During this time many of the songs that had gone unchanged for hundreds of years underwent a drastic transformation. The minstrels adjusted the lyrics and style to fit the taste of each crowd they played to in order to gain a few extra pennies.

The minstrels eventually organized troupes that roamed from town to town. With a group of people instead of a solitary figure, they were able to perform a more complicated show. They produced a greater variety of entertainment and therefore earned a larger sum of money. When the large professional minstrel organizations broke up they were replaced by medicine shows.

The medicine shows usually consisted of a small group of three or four people. While others entertained the "medicine man" sold his cure-all. The potency of the concoction varied from doctor to doctor and from show to show. The medicine presentations were not restricted solely to country music; blues musicians also performed in these travelling venues.

Eventually, these shows gave way to vaudeville, which was larger in scope and included musicians, acrobats, dancers, and comics. Since the circuit was owned by theatre chains, these performers worked a planned route, unlike the minstrel and medicine wanderers who had followed the scent of money. The venue was also important because it brought the sounds of Tin Pan Alley to the South and took southern performers to the North and Midwest. By this period the earliest country music existed in three essential forms: commercial, folk traditions and sacred songs.

Other changes had a profound effect on the earliest country music. The most vital instrument for the first three hundred years of folk music in America was the fiddle. It was small, easy to carry around, and could be built with material indigenous to the surroundings of the southern people. Apple, maple or poplar wood was used to construct the solid body devices and horsehair for the bow. The old-time fiddler held a very high position in mountain folk society because of his musical ability; at the square dances he was revered.

Each distinct region—New England, southern Appalachia, the Ozarks, northern Georgia, and the Southwest—all had different styles. But the Great Revival that swept through Virginia, Kentucky, Tennessee and much of the backwoods South diminished the fiddle as the Devil's box, forcing many musicians to either play religious tunes or abandon their instruments altogether. Although the country violin had dominated the nineteenth century and would remain vital in the creation of American folk music, it would have to share its supremacy with a number of stringed instruments in the twentieth century.

The next string instrument to gain attention in the folk style was the banjo. It was of African origin and first played by slaves on the southern plantations, but gradually found its way to white folk music. The country banjo had one important distinguishing feature over its cousin the fiddle—it boasted a fifth string used for a thumb sound.

The guitar was the third instrument that formed the basic foundation of country music. It was scarce throughout much of the nineteenth century and it wasn't until the 1880s and 1890s that it began to make an impact on the folk music of white America. The explosion of the guitar's popularity, as well as that of its cousin the mandolin, fueled the creation of hundreds of string bands throughout the country.

The folk guitar drew inspiration from two main sources: Mexican music of the Southwest and the blues and ragtime of the South. During the Spanish-American War and World War I, southern soldiers were further exposed to the possibility of the instrument. Much of the picking that would form the basis of country music was learned from the black bluesmen.

From the very beginning country music was simple at its core, much like the blues. Both styles were about tradition, and their straightforward forms enabled the practitioners to explore endless possibilities. They also shared some of the same themes, melodies and songs. The blues and country musicians also experienced the same financial situation—they wallowed in poverty that fueled a heated passion in their music.

By the end of World War I, the seeds that had been planted for over a hundred years were ready to bloom and create a new art form called country music. The old British songs had been Americanized; semi-professional musicians had popularized the music of vaudeville, minstrels and medicine shows; and, the combination of the fiddle, banjo and guitar in a group setting was becoming standard practice.

The first recordings were rough and uneven. The invention and mass market production of the phonograph demanded that records be made. Blues, as well as jazz records, had already been available to the public; they sold in great numbers in the 1920s. The development of the country music recording industry was the first real step toward the commercialization of the style. Fiddlin' John Carson, Riley Puckett, Vernon Dalhart, the Carter Family, E.V. Stoneman and his kin, as well as Uncle Dave Macon were some of the early artists to put their songs on vinyl.

Radio was also to play an integral part in the popularization of the genre. It spawned the barn-dance program that featured primarily country material. It was one of these shows—on WSM in Nashville—that evolved into the *Grand Ole Opry* and became the heart and soul of country music.

George D. Hay was the announcer who first coined the term. Although the 1920s were a breakthrough for the hillbilly folk set, few made a decent living at it.

The Great Depression of the 1930s saw further expansion of country music through the radio. Because of the severe poverty among much of the audience that enjoyed the style, few could afford a phonograph, much less the records by their favorites. But the airwaves were free and every Saturday night the *Grand Ole Opry* invaded the homes of fans throughout the country. In Chicago, the *National Barn Dance* broadcasting on station WLS was essential; it satisfied the tastes of an eager audience that spanned the midwestern, Great Plains and southern territory.

The 1930s was also the decade of the singing cowboy in the movies. Many of the country artists that would achieve stardom on the big screen were first heard on radio—Gene Autry, Roy Rogers, Dale Evans and Tex Ritter, among others. This new breed of performer changed the genre forever, turning it from hillbilly music to country and western.

The 1940s were a decade of turbulence, confusion and further growth. World War II played a major role in deferring the explosive creativity and expansion that country music had enjoyed in the previous decades. The greatest change occurred in the shifting of focal points from Hollywood to Nashville. Hollywood (California) had been the greatest exponent of country music in the 1930s with its B-movies featuring the singing cowboys. But the decline in the making of these pictures rendered Tinsel Town a distant second. Chicago, another prime center, declined in popularity because of the failure of the radio show the *National Barn Dance*.

The growth of publishing companies and the recording industry in Nashville propelled it during the 1940s and 1950s into the number one center of country music. The *Grand Ole Opry* was also located there and it boasted the greatest talent the genre had to offer. The Tennessee center would eventually be dubbed Music City, USA.

It was also during the 1940s that country music branched off into different styles. The homespun, simple roots of the genre developed into western swing, a hard driving sound that was based on the dynamism between fiddle, guitar and banjo. Bob Wills was the prime architect of this style. In the hands of Bill Monroe, the simple core of country sounds turned into bluegrass. The arrival of Hank Williams, Sr., in 1949—the year he debuted on the *Grand Ole Opry*—ushered in honky tonk.

Hank Williams made enormous contributions to the genre in a very brief time. Perhaps his greatest achievement was to instill a desire for a purer, hard sound. Although he wasn't a hill singer, he influenced the direction of country music for the next few years and spurred the mountain sound revival. Later on, Marty Robbins expanded on what Williams had established and at the same time sparked a new era that saw the pure strain incorporated with other styles, including the emerging sound of rock and roll.

Rockabilly became all the rage. The combination of country music and rock and roll had its champions in Carl Perkins, Ronnie Hawkins, Johnny Cash, Jerry Lee Lewis and Wanda Jackson, among others. Early rock and rollers like Bill Haley and the Comets, and Elvis had strong roots in the country genre. To this day artists like Ronnie Hawkins continue to carry the rockabilly torch with pride.

The reign of rockabilly was short lived and gave way to the Nashville sound. This marked the beginning of the first period of modern country music as it is known today and many of the stars that emerged in the late 1950s and 1960s enjoyed great success for the next two decades. Although the genre had experienced both times of high popularity and periods of low public interest, it continued to forge on.

Despite the success of the Nashville Sound, there were those that felt it too constricting and a resistance movement began to swell, spreading far and wide. In Austin, Texas, Willie Nelson became the leader of the rebel group of country artists who turned their back on Music City U.S.A. In Bakersfield, California, Buck Owens developed his own style that included loud, amplified instruments and drums, in direct opposition to the more pop oriented product flowing out of Nashville.

The first era of country music faded away in the 1980s as a new breed of artists emerged with a new sound that was based on past exploits. The radio stations began to play the upstart artists, ignoring the older, more established stars.

This book is divided into five sections based on the significant branches of the music. The first section, The Pioneers, honors those who overcame many obstacles in order to present mountain music to a mass audience. The second section, Cowboys and Radio Stars, portrays those individuals who made radio the greatest means of communication of country music, as well as those who starred on the big screen. The third section, Western Swing, Bluegrass and Honky Tonk, focuses on how country music branched out in the 1940s and features the founders of each style as well as its main practitioners. The fourth section, Women of Country Music, reflects the major contributions that female artists have made since the genre's beginning. The fifth section, Outlaws, Rebels and Superstars, comprises a more modern country music sound that dominated the scene from the late 1950s to the mid–1980s.

This book champions the pioneers, the superstars, and the cult heroes born before 1940 and in some cases before the twentieth century. Although country music has endured many changes throughout its long history, it remains a dominant force. The flame continues to burn brightly.

Hundreds of semi-professional hill musicians had been playing some form of country music for years before the technology of records came along enabling them to supplement their meager incomes. However, for every star like Vernon Dalhart, there were dozens that never made it.

This section champions the most influential of the early country music pioneers.

Fiddlin' John Carson was the first authentic country musician to be recorded. A champion fiddler, he was a veteran of the marathon cutting contests that were a staple throughout the Southern hill region.

Uncle Dave Macon became the first real star of the *Grand Ole Opry* and like many of his contemporaries was an amateur. He was middle age when he finally had the opportunity to record the music he had been playing for decades.

Dr. Humphrey Bate was a real country doctor who was the leader of one of the first popular string bands. He unfortunately didn't live long enough to see how much of an impact he made on the genre.

Vernon Dalhart was country music's first superstar. He combined the genuine elements of Southern music with the qualities of professional northern studio musicians. He sold over seventy-five million records.

Gid Tanner was the first musician-comedian to truly make a breakthrough. He was also the leader of the revered Skillet Lickers, an outfit based in Atlanta. Tanner is the father of the Georgia branch of country music.

A.P. Carter was the leader of the famed Carter family that remains popular to this day. Although criticized for poaching popular songs that had been floating around the southern hills for generations, he preserved many of the traditional tunes that would have otherwise been lost.

Charlie Poole epitomized the hard drinking musician but he was also very talented. As leader of the North Carolina Ramblers, he put the Tar Heel state on the country music map.

E.V. Stoneman was the patriarch of the Stoneman family from Virginia that included at one time as many as half a dozen members or more. He enjoyed a career in two phases.

Riley Puckett was a blind guitarist who spent his best years as part of the Skillet Lickers, but also had a successful solo career. Besides being a talented string player, he was a great singer who helped define the sound of Tanner's popular band.

Jimmie Rodgers is the Father of Country Music and along with Hank Williams, Sr., the most influential of the country artists. Unfortunately, both of them would die young, but not before making crucial contributions.

at the same time sparked a new era that saw the pure strain incorporated with other styles, including the emerging sound of rock and roll.

Rockabilly became all the rage. The combination of country music and rock and roll had its champions in Carl Perkins, Ronnie Hawkins, Johnny Cash, Jerry Lee Lewis and Wanda Jackson, among others. Early rock and rollers like Bill Haley and the Comets, and Elvis had strong roots in the country genre. To this day artists like Ronnie Hawkins continue to carry the rockabilly torch with pride.

The reign of rockabilly was short lived and gave way to the Nashville sound. This marked the beginning of the first period of modern country music as it is known today and many of the stars that emerged in the late 1950s and 1960s enjoyed great success for the next two decades. Although the genre had experienced both times of high popularity and periods of low public interest, it continued to forge on.

Despite the success of the Nashville Sound, there were those that felt it too constricting and a resistance movement began to swell, spreading far and wide. In Austin, Texas, Willie Nelson became the leader of the rebel group of country artists who turned their back on Music City U.S.A. In Bakersfield, California, Buck Owens developed his own style that included loud, amplified instruments and drums, in direct opposition to the more pop oriented product flowing out of Nashville.

The first era of country music faded away in the 1980s as a new breed of artists emerged with a new sound that was based on past exploits. The radio stations began to play the upstart artists, ignoring the older, more established stars.

This book is divided into five sections based on the significant branches of the music. The first section, The Pioneers, honors those who overcame many obstacles in order to present mountain music to a mass audience. The second section, Cowboys and Radio Stars, portrays those individuals who made radio the greatest means of communication of country music, as well as those who starred on the big screen. The third section, Western Swing, Bluegrass and Honky Tonk, focuses on how country music branched out in the 1940s and features the founders of each style as well as its main practitioners. The fourth section, Women of Country Music, reflects the major contributions that female artists have made since the genre's beginning. The fifth section, Outlaws, Rebels and Superstars, comprises a more modern country music sound that dominated the scene from the late 1950s to the mid–1980s.

This book champions the pioneers, the superstars, and the cult heroes born before 1940 and in some cases before the twentieth century. Although country music has endured many changes throughout its long history, it remains a dominant force. The flame continues to burn brightly.

# PART ONE

## *The Pioneers*

In the beginning were the pioneers, the individuals who established the parameters of the potential commercialism of the folk sounds of the Southern hill people. Many were poorly educated but extremely talented semi-professional musicians who played their brand of music that their ancestors had brought over from Europe with a special touch. The possibility of making money with these songs sparked a billion-dollar industry.

Although they sold millions of records, many of the pioneers never made much money at their craft. The first generation of country performers struggled as musicians, with only a handful attaining national recognition. However, their importance to the overall development of the genre can never be overstated.

Some of the most noted early performers included the Brinkley Brothers, the Dixie Clodhoppers, the Morrison Family, the Delmore Brothers, the McGhee Brothers, Clarence "Tom" Ashley, the Taylor Brothers, Burnett and Rutherford, Uncle Am Stuart, Frank Wilson, Charlie Bowman, and Clayton McMichen. Among the more colorful band names included Bird's Kentucky Corn Crackers, Dr. Smith's Champion Hoss Hair Pullers, Wilmer Watts and the Lonely Eagles, the West Virginia Snake Hunters, Fisher Headley and His Aristocratic Pigs, Bumboat Billy and the Sparrow, Seven Foot Dilly and His Hot Pickles, Joe Foss and His Hungry Sand-Lappers, Mumford Bean and His Itawambians and Ephriam Woodie and the Henpecked Husbands.

There were other important names, such as Carson J. Robison, Ralph Peer, and Frank Walker, in the early days of the new industry. Robison was an important songwriter who provided Vernon Dalhart with much of his stellar material. Ralph Peer was the roving industry man who recorded some of the first country stars, including Dalhart, Fiddlin' John Carson, the Carter Family, the Stoneman Family, and Jimmie Rodgers, to name a few. Frank Walker, the chief scout for the Columbia label, recorded Gid Tanner and His Skillet Lickers, among others.

Hundreds of semi-professional hill musicians had been playing some form of country music for years before the technology of records came along enabling them to supplement their meager incomes. However, for every star like Vernon Dalhart, there were dozens that never made it.

This section champions the most influential of the early country music pioneers.

Fiddlin' John Carson was the first authentic country musician to be recorded. A champion fiddler, he was a veteran of the marathon cutting contests that were a staple throughout the Southern hill region.

Uncle Dave Macon became the first real star of the *Grand Ole Opry* and like many of his contemporaries was an amateur. He was middle age when he finally had the opportunity to record the music he had been playing for decades.

Dr. Humphrey Bate was a real country doctor who was the leader of one of the first popular string bands. He unfortunately didn't live long enough to see how much of an impact he made on the genre.

Vernon Dalhart was country music's first superstar. He combined the genuine elements of Southern music with the qualities of professional northern studio musicians. He sold over seventy-five million records.

Gid Tanner was the first musician-comedian to truly make a breakthrough. He was also the leader of the revered Skillet Lickers, an outfit based in Atlanta. Tanner is the father of the Georgia branch of country music.

A.P. Carter was the leader of the famed Carter family that remains popular to this day. Although criticized for poaching popular songs that had been floating around the southern hills for generations, he preserved many of the traditional tunes that would have otherwise been lost.

Charlie Poole epitomized the hard drinking musician but he was also very talented. As leader of the North Carolina Ramblers, he put the Tar Heel state on the country music map.

E.V. Stoneman was the patriarch of the Stoneman family from Virginia that included at one time as many as half a dozen members or more. He enjoyed a career in two phases.

Riley Puckett was a blind guitarist who spent his best years as part of the Skillet Lickers, but also had a successful solo career. Besides being a talented string player, he was a great singer who helped define the sound of Tanner's popular band.

Jimmie Rodgers is the Father of Country Music and along with Hank Williams, Sr., the most influential of the country artists. Unfortunately, both of them would die young, but not before making crucial contributions.

# FIDDLIN' JOHN CARSON (1868–1949)

## *The Virginia Reeler*

Today, country music is a billion-dollar industry. But because of its humble beginnings, no one could have envisioned the tremendous growth of the genre. In the 1920s, although the first recordings of blues and jazz had been issued, the Appalachian Mountain music of the white working class had yet to be made available to the masses despite the large market that existed. The traditional folk sound needed a pioneer, someone to bring the modified English songs of the past four hundred years to life. That honor belonged to the Virginia Reeler. His name was Fiddlin' John Carson.

John Carson was born on March 23, 1868, in the Blue Ridge Mountains of Fannin County, Georgia. Carson learned to play the fiddle, the cherished instrument of the mountain folk of the South, because it was the only one available to him. Long before he became the first person to record authentic country music, Carson lived the life of a typical mountain man. He was married at a young age and populated the planet with his numerous offspring.

Although he was acclaimed the fiddling champion of Georgia on seven different occasions, the contests were more of a hobby than a way to make a living. In order to keep his family fed, he worked in a cotton mill, as a house painter and a moonshiner. While he scratched out an existence, he developed a style that contained a definite knack for producing danceable music.

Carson increased his popularity as a musician by joining a traveling minstrel show, as well as participating in the aforementioned fiddling contests. He was revered in his community because the popular square dance could not occur without his skills on the instrument. Like all old time players, he performed for the passion of the music rather than the money, simply because there were no substantial funds to be made.

But in the fall of 1922, he took a giant step towards earning a living as a real musician when he sang on radio for the first time. By this period in his career, he had assembled a group he called the Virginia Reelers that included his daughter, Moonshine Kate. Although a regular radio job was a positive move, bigger things were waiting for Carson.

In 1923, a roving field recording agent for the Okeh label came to Georgia searching for acceptable talent to sign to the company. Ralph Peer, a transplanted Missourian who would later launch the careers of the Carter family and the Father of Country Music, Jimmie Rodgers, was the first to uncover the rich abilities of the Virginia Reelers. At the time of this discovery Fiddlin' John was 55 years old.

On June 14, in Atlanta, Georgia, Fiddlin' John Carson became the first authentic country artist to lay down tracks. "Little Old Log Cabin in the Lane" and "The Old Hen Cackled and the Rooster's Going to Crow" were the first songs he recorded and just two of many that would make him famous. Although there were only 500 discs pressed of his first record, they sold out immediately in the furniture store where they were available. The country music industry was born.

That same year, Carson, who had never been out of his native state, traveled to the Big Apple to record for the Okeh label with the Virginia Reelers in tow. In all, he would cut over 150 sides for the company, assuring his place in history. Many of his songs were recordings of English tunes that had existed among the mountain people for generations.

After the recording session, Carson returned to his family and rural life in Georgia. Although the songs never made him an overnight star or a vast fortune, they did help establish country music as a viable force that could compete with blues and jazz. Like the "race records" made at the time, the old-timey tunes had their own market niche.

Throughout the rest of the 1920s, Carson continued to record for Okeh, building on his regional fame. Despite the numerous songs he cut, the old fiddler never changed his style and often recycled the same material over and over again. His writing skills were adequate, but not strong enough to sustain a diversified career.

The Great Depression hit both the industry and Carson's career hard. In 1934, he cut his last songs and finished his working life as an elevator operator. One can only wonder how many of the numerous elevator passengers recognized the man who started the country music boom.

On December 11, 1949, Fiddlin' John Carson died. He was eighty-one years old and had lived a rich, full life.

Fiddlin' John Carson was a genuine pioneer. He was the first legitimate country musician to record a country song. He was also one of the best of the early fiddlers and a man who proved his mettle winning several of the marathon contests that were part of the Appalachian culture of the mountain people during the nineteenth century.

It is interesting to note that he didn't achieve any commercial viability until his 55th birthday. Some of country music's best known artists, including Patsy Cline, Hank Williams, Sr., and Jimmie Rodgers had become legends long before that age. Carson's perseverance and dedication to the music make him a special individual. Most importantly, although he never made millions of dollars from his work, he continued to record as long as possible.

Carson was first to bring to light the deep, rich vein of American folk music that had existed since the arrival of the pioneers to the Appalachian region. The ability to deliver this product in a very commercial medium underlined his savvy as a musician. He proved that the hillbilly style had a very large built-in audience that would definitely support its artists.

His legacy lived on through the efforts of his daughter, Moonshine Kate. While she never enjoyed a stellar career, she continued the work initiated by her father. In a field where progeny is commonplace, she made sure that no one would forget her dad for his pioneering efforts.

Although he was the first, he did eventually have some contemporaries, including Charlie Poole and Gid Tanner, who like Carson were old time players that had been performing for years before being able to record their songs. Fiddlin' John influenced all who walked the path he blazed, but made his most serious impact on the immediate follower Tanner. Although the latter surpassed his idol, he would have never enjoyed the career he did without the pioneering efforts of the Virginia Reeler.

Carson often performed with his mountain band. These outfits consisted of a loose collection of skilled practitioners who lived within close proximity to one another because transportation in the Old South was limited. Carson's Virginia Reelers were no exception. At various times the group included Johnny Parth, Earl Johnson, Land Norris, and John Kong Carson.

To listen to today's eclectic country sound seems far removed from the music that Carson recorded more than eighty years ago. However, there remains an element in his style that still rings true in contemporary times. To forget men like Fiddlin' John Carson is to turn one's back on the entire tradition of country music that the Virginia Reeler began.

## The Virginia Reelers
Circa 1920s

| *Fiddle* | *Guitar* | *Banjo* |
|---|---|---|
| Fiddlin' John Carson | Moonshine Kate | Earl Johnson |
| Lund Norris | | Moonshine Kate |
| Earl Johnson | | |
| Jay Ungar | | |

## Discography

*The Old Hen Cackled*, Rounder 1003.
*Fiddlin' John Carson*, Rounder 1003.
*Complete Recorded Works*, Vol. 1 (1923–1924), Document 8014.
*Complete Recorded Works*, Vol. 2 (1924–1925), Document 7015.
*Complete Recorded Works*, Vol. 3 (1925–1926), Document 8016.
*Complete Recorded Works*, Vol. 4, Document 8017.

*Complete Recorded Works*, Vol. 5, Document 8018.
*Complete Recorded Works*, Vol. 6, Document 8019.
*Complete Recorded Works*, Vol. 7, Document 8020.

# UNCLE DAVE MACON (1870–1952)

## *King of the Hillbillies*

Although the term "hillbilly music" was first used to describe the mountain folk sound that was recorded in the 1920s, it was a derogatory one. It seemed to deride the seriousness and professionalism that so many strived to create. However, there was one performer who was quite comfortable to be known as the King of the Hillbillies. His name was Uncle Dave Macon.

Uncle Dave Macon was born Dave Harrison Macon on October 7, 1870, in Smart Station, Tennessee, into a theatrical environment. His parents owned and operated a Nashville boarding house that catered to traveling show biz folk. It was from this array of individuals in the entertainment field that Macon caught the fever of performing that would run throughout his entire life. He learned how to play the five-string banjo, but a career in country music seemed light years away.

After his marriage, he moved to a rural part of Tennessee, where he earned a living as the operator of a mule and wagon transport company. He was also a farmer and played his banjo at local functions for no money. In his era, an aspiring artist had to forge his own breaks and that is precisely what Macon did when he demanded a high fee for a wedding performance. It was at this event that he was spotted by a talent scout who offered him a job at an Alabama theatre. Macon was soon earning a living as a bona fide musician.

His career took a positive turn when he teamed up with Fiddlin' Sid Harkreader. The pair met in a local barbershop and after an impromptu cutting contest they quickly became partners. The duo performed at local theatres, then toured the South as part of a vaudeville show. During this period in his life as a traveling musician Macon was able to complete the education that had begun at his parents' boarding house.

In 1924, Macon and Harkreader were spotted at a furniture convention in a turn of fate that resulted in their huge break. A southern gentleman named C.C. Rutherford expressed interest in recording the pair and sent them to New York, where they cut fourteen sides for Vocalion. For the session, Macon formed His Fruit Jar Drinkers, a band that consisted of Harkreader, banjoist Sam McGee and his guitarist-fiddler brother Kirk McGee.

At the age of fifty-four, Uncle Dave Macon had finally achieved his goal of being a recorded country artist. He returned with Harkreader the following year and cut twenty-eight more singles for the label. The fact that they had waxed a few songs drove up their performance fee and enabled them to make a better living in an infant industry where the participants earned very little.

In 1928, Macon returned to record more songs with His Fruit Jar Drinkers in tow. They cut such numbers as "The Death of John Henry" and "Whoop 'Em Up, Cindy." The personnel in the band would change; the McGee Brothers moved on, but not before appearing on the *Grand Ole Opry*. Macon, who possessed a keen eye for talent, managed to recruit the Delmore Brothers, Roy Acuff and a young, unknown Bill Monroe into his group.

When he didn't record with His Fruit Jar Drinkers, he was cast as a soloist or as part of the Dixie Sacred Singers that included fiddler Mary Todd and Macon's old friends, the McGee Brothers. No matter the lineup, they created magic in the studio.

Macon was one of the first major stars at the *Grand Ole Opry* and remained there for twenty-five years. There he expanded on his popularity and eventually earned the familial nickname "Uncle." With his waistcoat, his winged collar and plug hat, he cut one of the most memorable figures on the show that was struggling to gain a foothold in the entertainment business. He was one of the reasons why the institution managed to endure during its early, lean years.

As the star, he was expected to entertain and he rarely disappointed the audience. He appeared on stage with a variety of artists, including his Fruit Jar Drinkers, as well as his son, Dorris. In 1940 the film *Grand Ole Opry* was made to bolster the radio show's appeal. It also featured Roy Acuff, but Macon stole the show.

On March 22, 1952, in Readyville, Tennessee, Uncle Dave Macon, one of the most beloved entertainers of the early country music years, died. His burial, a large affair, occurred in Coleman County, Mufreesboro, Tennessee, where hundreds of fans paid their last respects to one of the originators of the genre.

Uncle Dave Macon was a genuine country pioneer and a superstar. He enjoyed an incredible amount of success for someone with minimal education. But he was an entertainer and it was this gift that enabled him to dominate the industry for so long. His incredible sense of humor and his strong ability on the banjo won over a generation of country music fans and admirers.

Although best remembered for his warm and gentle touch, he was a fierce instrumentalist who could hold his own against any other performer. He played with the intensity and agility of a sure veteran. He added this excellent musical dimension to blend with the rest of his multi-faceted skills as an entertainer.

Uncle Dave Macon was also a very funny performer. He honed his comic skills until they seemed second nature to him. This ability to infuse his act with a good dose of old fashioned humor separated him from the rest of the country set. His comedic talents would influence an entire dimension of country artists.

Another of the qualities that made Macon famous was the truly astonishing range of his material. He injected his songs with a tinge of reality that dealt with a variety of subjects including current events, political corruption, historical figures, and everyday occurrences. The wealth, depth and breadth of his catalog is apparent even today as his records remain popular.

The legend of Uncle Dave Macon influenced a number of individuals, including the Chicken Chokers, Grandpa Jones, the New Lost City Ramblers, Marvin Gaster, DeFord Bailey, John Lair, the Dickel Brothers, Seven Foot Dilly and His Hot Pickles, the Four Virginians, Stringbean, and Cousin Jody. In truth, no country music artist of the past eighty years has been unable to escape the wide shadow he cast.

Not only was he the first legitimate country artist on the *Grand Ole Opry*, but he was an institution on the show for over three decades. The rise of the *Opry*'s popularity can be traced to Macon's meteoric ascent. He was instrumental in the acceptance of country music as a style with force.

In 1966, he was elected to the Country Music Hall of Fame. Throughout his long and distinguished career he was known by a number of nicknames, including the Dixie Dewdrop, the King of the Hillbillies, and the King of the Banjo Players. No matter the moniker, he will always hold a special place in the history of the style he helped flourish.

## The Fruit Jar Drinkers
### 1924–1930

| *Banjo* | *Fiddle* | *Guitar* | *Bass* |
|---|---|---|---|
| Uncle Dave Macon | John Harkreader | Kirk McGee | Golden Stewart |
| Sam McGee | Kirk McGee | Hubert Gregory | |
| Bill Monroe | | | |

## Discography

*Uncle Dave Macon*, Decca D-73760.
*Go Long Mule*, County 545.
*The Gayest Old Dude in Town*, Folk Variety 12503.
*At Home*, Bear Family BFX 15214.
*Keep My Skillet Good and Greasy*, Bear Family 15987.
*Laugh Your Blues Away*, Rounder 1028.
*Travelin' Down the Road*, County 115.
*Early Recordings*, County 521.
*Uncle Dave Macon, 1926–1939*, Historical 8006.
*Country Music Hall of Fame Series*, MCA MCAD 10546.
*Classic Sides (1924–1938)*, JSP 7729.
*Classic Cut, Vol. 2 (1924–1938)*, JSP 7769.

# DR. HUMPHREY BATE (1875–1936)

## *The Possum Hunter*

The tradition of the country music band has undergone many changes in the genre's one hundred and twenty-five years. Today's groups are usually electric with a minimal amount of instrumentation. But, before there were amplified instruments, the wall of sound had to emote from the individuals themselves and a larger ensemble was needed. One of the first and most popular original string bands featured the leadership of the Possum Hunter. His name was Dr. Humphrey Bate.

Dr. Humphrey Bate was born in Summer County, Tennessee, in 1875. He learned how to play the harmonica as a young boy from an ex-slave and continued to hone his skills on the instrument. He incorporated a number of traditional work songs, favorite tunes of the day, pop numbers, ragtime and even Sousa marches into his repertoire. Like other early artists, he earned a living outside of the music industry. An educated individual— a rarity in the early days of the genre—he was a real doctor, having graduated from Vanderbilt Medical School.

At the turn of the century, Bate, in his free time, fronted a number of string bands that played in the local area without much hope of ever breaking out on a national level; the opportunities just weren't available. But, being a doctor, he didn't need to survive on the meager earnings of a musician. This unique position enabled him to play solely as a side activity.

He and his various outfits played at picnics, riverboat excursions, and for silent movies. They all lived within close proximity of one another in a small hamlet northeast of Nashville. Although the members would come and go, Bate's aggregation was known as one of the finest string ensembles around. It was this popularity that led to his being discovered.

In 1925, after 25 years of leading various string bands, he caught his first break. By this time his group had settled on a set membership that included Bate on harmonica, Burt Hutcherson on guitar, Oscar Stone on fiddle, Walter Leggett on banjo, Stanley Walton on guitar, Oscar Albright on the bowed string bass, Buster Bate on guitar, tipple, harmonica and jew's harp, and Alcyone Bate on vocals, ukulele, and piano. Some of the instruments were strange for a country string band, including the tipple, jew's harp, and the bowed string bass. The group's shifting personnel worked around the stable lineup of Hutcherson, Leggett, Walton, Albright and Stone.

The group was able to broadcast on Nashville radio, which truly enhanced their reputation beyond the confines of Tennessee, as they were heard throughout the South. The exposure enabled them to join the forerunner of the *Opry* and it was essentially the lineup above that first played on the show. The Possum Hunters became so popular that they opened the show with the usual number "They'll Be a Hot Time in the Old Town Tonight." Bate and his band became the darlings of those early *Opry* years. They ensured that the fledging venue survived.

The group managed to secure a recording contract with Brunswick and cut a few singles that only increased their appeal. Their breakthrough helped launch several other musical outfits, including the Crook Brothers. Bate and his band continued to wax the songs that he had learned as a boy. The range of their material varied and sometimes reached outside the normal country lines.

Although a country doctor with a fine taste for the good life, including an ear for classical music, Bate was portrayed as a good ol' boy on the *Opry* show by its founder, George D. Hay. A publicity picture of the band in a cornfield was used to solidify their hayseed reputation. Although he was a proud man, Bate was no fool and went along with the posturing because he knew that it helped the audience accept him on a larger scale.

He continued to perform on Nashville radio while still holding down his top spot as the Dean of the Opry, a term coined by Hay. In the winter, when not appearing on the show, Bate would venture down to Florida and perform in the Sunshine State. The Possum Hunters, also an invention of Hay, backed the good doctor on the road.

The group recorded for a number of labels, including Victor in 1928. Although their records sold in good quantities, the Depression put a stop to the momentum they had built up. They continued to star on the *Opry*, but economic conditions forced Bate to reduce the size of his outfit. His two children, son Buster and daughter Alcyone, remained part of the band.

In the depths of the Depression, in 1936, Dr. Humphrey Bate passed away. The leadership of the group fell on the shoulders of fiddler Oscar Stone. Thirteen years later, Stanley Walton and Alcyone Bate took over command of the group. Alcyone would eventually hook up with the Crook Brothers Band and the Possum Hunters eventually dissolved as the members drifted away and joined other outfits.

Dr. Humphrey Bate was a country music pioneer. He was one of the most important cogs in the history of country music as a leader, recording artist and musician. He was an essential figure who guided the *Opry* throughout the first few tumultuous years.

Bate, a harmonica player, was never on par with blues legends such as Little Walter or Sonny Boy Williamson I or Sonny Boy Williamson II. But he was an adequate musician who managed to create excitement not solely on his own, but as part of his various string groups. He knew when to hit the right note in order to blend in with the other band members.

It was this talent as a bandleader that truly made him an early star of country music. His skill, determination, and ability to recruit the best players was his strong suit. He had the knack for acquiring those that completed the players that were already present in his band. His savvy in pitting and uniting the various personalities enabled him to stay on top as leader for over thirty years.

Perhaps it was his love of classical music or his early musical education that enabled him to instruct his aggregation to play in any style. Although a solid country band, his group injected bits and pieces of blues, pop, and traditional folk melodies into their repertoire that wasn't heard in the songs of other string bands. This gave Bate's outfit an edge and guaranteed that they remained popular.

Bate wasn't afraid to experiment, bringing in a strange array of instruments into the group that weren't normally part of a country string band. The bowed string bass was a rarity, but the good doctor included it in his overall sound to maximum effect. The ability to mesh these different instruments into one cohesive sound made Bate and His Possum Hunters stars.

Although their recorded output was not large, the group did cut a number of songs that were popular in their day. Everyone in the band contributed songs and with their natural ability could turn any tune from any available source into something special. They were always willing and able to give a variety of material a country twang.

Dr. Humphrey Bate was a seminal figure. His contributions are many and there was always an edge of professionalism in his playing and manner. He is remembered as the possum hunter, one of the true noble spirits in the early history of country music.

### The Possum Hunters
(Circa 1925–1936)

| *Harmonica and Vocals* | *Additional Vocals* | |
|---|---|---|
| Dr. Humphrey Bate | Alcyone Bate (Beasley) | |
| Buster Bate | | |

| *Fiddle* | *Guitars* | *Banjo* |
|---|---|---|
| Oscar Stone | Stanley Walton | Walter Leggett |
| Bill Barret | James Hart | |
| Buster Bate | | |

| *Bowed String Bass* | *Ukelele* | *Tipple* |
|---|---|---|
| Oscar Albright | Alcyon Bate (Beasley) | Buster Bate |

| *Jew's Harp* | *Piano* |
|---|---|
| Buster Bate | Alcyone Bate (Beasley) |

# VERNON DALHART (1883–1948)
## *A Country Star*

In the 1920s, at the dawn of the country music industry, there were countless semi-professional and amateur musicians hoping to make some money. Talent scouts were quick to sign up new acts for recording purposes. With the explosion of artists cutting hundreds of songs, it was only a matter of time before one of them emerged as the first star of the genre. His name was Vernon Dalhart.

Vernon Dalhart was born Marion Try Slaughter on April 6, 1883, in Jefferson, Texas, with a questionable family background. His grandfather had fought in the Civil War, had worked one side of the law as a sheriff and the other as a renegade member of the Ku Klux Klan. His father, a ranch owner, met a violent death when Vernon was just a young boy. Dalhart was determined to follow a different, calmer path than his paternal ancestry and turned to music as his career choice.

After his father's death, Vernon and his mother moved to Dallas, where he found work in a local mercantile and later sold pianos. His interest in music also included studying at the Conservatory of Music in his new hometown. He learned how to play the harmonica and jew's harp, honing his skills until he was proficient enough to play at local dances and other events.

Although Dallas offered good opportunities for an aspiring musician, he decided that New York could serve him better and relocated there around 1910. In the Big Apple, his career blossomed to include work in vaudeville, churches, and light opera. He landed a part in *Girl of the Golden West*, a Puccini work, and several others, including *HMS Pinafore*, as well as *Madame Butterfly*. This experience taught him valuable performance lessons and expanded his repertoire.

He first recorded song, made on an Edison cylinder, "Can't Yo' Hear Me Callin' Caroline," was released in 1917, seven years before the first country song was ever produced. The song was a blues dirge that Dalhart sang in African-American dialect. A deluge of recordings followed that included popular songs, World War I patriotic tunes and operatic arias; he waxed anything that could make him some quick up front money. Since many of the songs were cover versions he had no right to their origin, and therefore didn't receive any royalties.

Although probably the most recorded singer in America between 1917 and early 1924, he remained a virtual unknown. However, that all changed when he cut "The Wreck of the Old '97," cited in some circles as the first country song ever recorded. It made Dalhart the first true country music superstar. He achieved that status for his ability to combine the authentic elements of southern folk music with the professionalism of the northern studio musicians.

The massive hit "The Wreck of the Old 97," backed with "The Prisoner's Song," marked the beginning of Dalhart's shift from a pop singer to a more countrified sound. He was the first of what would be many crooners to undergo the Nashville treatment. The country trappings that highlighted his songs catapulted him to fame and gave the new style a tremendous boost.

Over the next few years Dalhart recorded a string of hits that opened the doors for other singers to follow. He touched everyone with his sentimental treatment of "The Letter Edged in Black," "Little Rosewood Casket," "Golden Slippers," "Barbara Allen," "My Blue Ridge Mountain Home," and "The Convict and the Rose," among others. Many of his songs reflected current events of the day, including the Scopes trial, the sinking of the *Titanic*, Lindbergh's record flight over the Atlantic, natural disasters, the activities of famous criminals, and local happenings with which rural people could identify. His songs contained a moral theme and their folksy style drenched with Dalhart's warm, soothing, and appealing voice equalled sure-fire hits.

One of the most important figures in Dalhart's rise to fame was Carson J. Robison, who wrote a number of the songs that the country crooner made famous. The relationship between the two proved a winning combination, since Vernon was always able to interpret and bring to life all of Robison's compositions. They were a one-two punch combo that was the best among the early country music production teams.

The good times and money flowed until 1930, when the Great Depression nearly wiped out the recording industry. Rural people, many of them dirt poor to begin with, could not support the recording business and Dalhart's fame declined. Although he did continue to record songs in the early 1930s, he had passed the zenith of his career.

From 1933 to 1938, Dalhart was out of music as the industry struggled to regain its financial footing. At the end of the decade he recorded a few sides for Bluebird, the blues label, that did not return him to his previous level of popularity. His attempt at a comeback failed and he was forced completely out of the music business.

Dalhart ended up in Connecticut, where he worked a series of menial jobs as a desk clerk and night watchman far removed from the glamour of his popular singing days. In 1948, he suffered the first of two heart attacks. On September 14 that same year, the first true country superstar died in a Bridgeport hospital.

Vernon Dalhart was a seminal figure in the early days of country music. He was instrumental in joining the simple, yet evocative, folk music of the rural South with a polished edge that turned him into the best known singer of his generation. He became one of the most prolific recording artists of the early pioneer period.

Dalhart had an interesting voice. He possessed a wide range that enabled him to sing opera, folk music, pop tunes and authentic country ditties. There was also a tinge of the blues in his vocal work, but more than anything else there was a folksy element that many people found comforting. He boasted that special timbre that touched people.

During his career he sang under 100 pseudonyms, released thousands of discs and sold in excess of one hundred million records. This is an astonishing number considering the population of the country during the 1920s and the number that were interested in his brand of music. The magnitude of his stardom is difficult to appreciate when some of the more popular modern country artists sell a few million copies of their latest CD release. To put Dalhart's efforts into modern perspective, he was in many ways the Garth Brooks of his time.

Vernon paved the way for many others to follow, including Carl T. Sprague, John White, Jimmie Rodgers, Charlie Poole, Riley Puckett, Hank Williams, Jr., Eddy Arnold, Jim Reeves, Marty Robbins, and, for that matter, anyone who ever sang a country tune. His achievements cast a shadow over country music for the rest of the century.

Although he learned to play the harmonica and piano in his youth, Dalhart never established himself as a skilled musician. His voice was his main instrument and it was certainly a powerful one. If he were compared to any pure country singer, then he would definitely hold his own even against the most popular of today's current stable of stars.

Although it took some time, he was eventually elected to the Country Music Hall of Fame, in 1981. His songs, although time pieces, have withstood the test of innovative technology and remain relevant to this day. If there was ever one person that could be singled out as having brought the right approach to the business, that man would be Vernon Dalhart, the country star.

## Discography

*Ballads and Railroad Songs*, Mark 56, Old Homestead OH 129.
*Inducted into the Hall of Fame*, 1981, King 3820.
*On the Lighter Side*, Old Homestead OH 166.
*That Good Old Country Town*, Vol. 4, Old Homestead OH 198.
*Wreck of the Old 97*, Old Homestead OH 167.
*Vernon Dalhart (The First Singing Cowboy on Record)*, Mark 56.
*Vernon Dalhart (First Recorded Railroad Songs)*, Mark 56.

# GID TANNER (1885–1960)

## *The Skillet Licker*

The early history of country music consists of important individuals as well as essential groups that helped shape the style. Many of the early old time country bands featured the triple driving threat of fiddle, guitar, and banjo. The leaders of these outfits were able to combine the various personalities to create some legitimate music. One of the best country musical commanders was the man known as the Skillet Licker. His name was Gid Tanner.

Gid Tanner was born on June 6, 1885, in Thomas Bridge, Georgia. Like other hill dwellers, Tanner picked up the fiddle at a young age so he could play at square dances and local events in order to earn a little extra money. He continued to perform into his teens but the thought of a musical career seemed very unlikely since no recording industry existed. He earned a living as a chicken farmer and played amateur shows first as a solo artist, then later as the leader of an authentic country string band.

In 1913, the Georgia Old Time Fiddler's Association was organized and sponsored an annual fiddling contest. Two years later, Tanner appeared and started to win with regularity the marathon sessions that often lasted several days. He combined his immense skills on the fiddle with the natural guitar talent of blind partner Riley Puckett. The two won first place in 1916 with a ripping version of "It's a Long Way to Tipperary." The interplay between the two adept musicians was absolutely dynamic.

Although he was a first rate musician and could bury anyone under with his potent abilities, Tanner was first and foremost a chicken farmer and treated music more as a hobby than an occupation. This is understandable since in his day a musician could not make a living simply playing his instrument around the South, something that he did on a semi-regular basis. By the end of the decade, after appearing at many annual fiddling contests, mostly in his native Georgia, Tanner was a very popular individual.

Aside from being a very able musician, he was also a top notch comedian and was easily able to hold a crowd's interest with a combination of his playing and his variety show patter. He was equal parts musician and funny man, an important element in those early days when the average semi-professional player was trying to establish a career despite having to overcome several obstacles.

Because of the rush to record authentic rural music, Tanner was invited down to New York to put down some tracks. He brought with him his best friend Puckett, and banjo-harmonica player Fate Norris. The trio were quite capable of creating magic, but those first sessions didn't spark anything that made the executives at Columbia stand up and take notice. He returned to his life back in Georgia as a chicken farmer and part-time fiddler.

Two years later, Tanner, and his group that still consisted of Puckett and Norris, recorded again. This time they also boasted the services of Clayton McMichen, an important first generation fiddler born in Georgia who proved to be the missing piece to the puzzle. McMichen and His Atlanta string band had recorded in 1925 without much success. The combination of Tanner's authentic folk music, Puckett's deep vocal skills, Norris' banjo-harmonica double attack, and the virtuoso McMichen proved to be an explosive one. Fiddlers Lowe Stokes, Gordon Tanner, and Bert Layne, mandolin and fiddle player Ted Hawkins, banjoist and guitarist Arthur Tanner, as well as second guitarists Mike Whitten and Hoke Rice rounded out the band.

They covered the traditional songs "Watermelon on the Vine,"

"Alabama Jubilee," "Turkey in the Straw," as well as self-penned tunes like "Bully of the Town" and "Pass Around the Bottle." The dynamics of the big four—Tanner, McMichen, Puckett and Norris—was augmented by the others aforementioned. There was no set lineup for each successive session and that proved somewhat confusing, since they often utilized three fiddlers and other multiple string instruments on the same song, creating a triple and double effect that would later be picked up by Bob Wills in his effort to nail down his western swing style.

From 1926 to 1931, the group recorded with frequency and became the most beloved string band on the touring circuit. The Skillet Lickers had achieved considerable fame, but truly rose to superstar status when they interlaced their serious playing with high skilled comedy. A perfect example of this was the song "A Corn Licker Still in Georgia." The tune was a huge hit and sold impressively well considering its release was restricted to a regional audience. There were several versions of the song and the final one, entitled "The Corn Licker Still in Georgia—Part 14" proved to be the last.

The band continued to tour and record during the depths of the depression, but they were losing interest in working with each other. Like every group, egos were prominent and eventually the old standard musical differences created incompatible divisions within the band. Tanner was criticized for being too old time, McMichen too pop-oriented and Puckett too innovative with his guitar work. They were all major talents that needed to pursue their own creative paths.

In 1931, the Skillet Lickers broke up and each member went his separate way. Tanner went back to his chicken farm, while Puckett and McMichen were keen on maintaining their careers. McMichen would form the Georgia Wildcats and enjoy mild success, while Puckett would completely step out of Tanner's shadow to become one of the important early country music pioneers.

In 1934, Tanner reformed the Skillet Lickers with a new lineup that consisted of Ted Hawkins, Mike Whitten, Rice Layne, guitarist Hugh Cross and Gid's two sons, Arthur and Gordon. They recorded a number of sides that produced the smash hit "Down Yonder," the band's last big hit. Eventually he retired and with him the name the Skillet Lickers.

McMichen's group and Puckett continued to make music, but were best remembered for their days as Skillet Lickers. They were much more powerful as a part of the whole than as individuals. Tanner needed McMichen's adventurous fiddle playing to give his own style a multi layered sound to create that special spark. He needed Puckett's timely guitar licks and powerful voice and Fate Norris' stability on banjo and harmonica to create a unified magic.

On May 13, 1960, Gid Tanner, the nimble fiddler with the hot licks known forever as the revered leader of the Skillet Lickers, passed away in Dacula, Georgia. Although he had been out of the music business for over twenty-five years, his name had remained prominent due to the impact he made in the late 1920s and the continued career of his sons.

Gid Tanner was a man of many talents. He was an expert fiddler, one of the best that country music ever produced, and perhaps the best of all time. As well, he was the leader of a band that spawned numerous followers. His importance in the early development of country music cannot be overstated.

Tanner was an all-star fiddler whose ability was the mark that many were measured against. He was a proud champion of the legendary cutting contests that took place in Georgia every year, where he outlasted and outplayed hundreds of others all over the state and the Southern region. He merits a place in the country music hall of fame solely on his contributions as an instrumentalist.

However, there were many dimensions to his career. His Skillet Lickers broke new ground for every group that was to follow and those that already existed, including Dr. Humphrey Bate's Possum Hunters. Only after Tanner's group had blazed the trail did Bate's band begin to make its way and gain notice.

The Skillet Lickers were simply one of the greatest country music groups of all time. The interplay between Tanner, McMichen, Puckett and Norris established the foundation that would later be explored by Bob Wills, the father of modern western swing, and Bill Monroe the father of bluegrass. Tanner understood the need for different personalities within a group and the juxtaposition of the many ideas to create exciting musical tension.

He was able to mesh the abundant talent of the various individuals into a strong synthesis of sound that earned the group many accolades. Tanner not only challenged his bandmates but he led by example and his legend spilled over to other styles of music. Undoubtedly, although they were all excellent individuals in their own right, they were much more formidable as a group.

There was also a comedic element in Tanner's delivery that spawned a side of country music that lives on today. He took his cue from Uncle Dave Macon. Stringbean, Cousin Jody, and the cast of characters on the popular syndicated television show *Hee Haw* can all trace their roots back to Tanner's clowning ability. He added a layer to the genre that was often missing in pop, blues and jazz.

Tanner and His Skillet Lickers influenced a number of country acts, including the Blue Sky Boys, J.P. Fraley, Nonnie Presson, Hugh Cross, Bert

Layne, Seven Foot Dilly and His Hot Pickles, Weems String Band, and Harry Kiker, among others. But in reality every country music outfit that has taken the stage in the past 85 years owes a debt to Gid and his group.

Gid Tanner continues to exert an influence on today's country music. A deserved Country Hall of Fame member, his name continues to fuel the world of authentic old time music. He was a trailblazer, and the Skillet Lickers' legend is solidly built on this fact.

## The Skillet Lickers
Circa 1927–1931

| *Fiddle* | *Banjo* | *Harmonica* |
|---|---|---|
| Gid Tanner | Fate Norris | Fate Norris |
| Clayton McMichen | Arthur Tanner | |
| Lowe Stokes | | |
| Gordon Tanner | | |
| Bert Layne | | |
| Ted Hawkins | | |

| *Vocals* | *Mandolin* | *Guitar* |
|---|---|---|
| Riley Puckett | Ted Hawkins | Riley Puckett |
| | | Mike Whitten |
| | | Hoke Rice |

## The Skillet Lickers 2
1934

| *Fiddle* | *Banjo* | *Mandolin* | *Guitar* |
|---|---|---|---|
| Gid Tanner | Arthur Tanner | Ted Hawkins | Mike Whitten |
| Gordon Tanner | | | Hugh Cross |
| Rice Layne | | | |
| Ted Hawkins | | | |

## Discography

*Old Time Fiddle Tunes and Songs from North Georgia*, Country 3509.
*Old Time Fiddle Tunes and Songs from North Georgia*, Country 526.
*Skillet Lickers, Vol. 2: 1927–1928*, Document 8057.
*The Skillet Lickers, Vol. 3: 1925–1929*, Document 8058.
*Hear These New Southern Fiddle (and Guitar) Sounds*, Rounder 1005.
*Kickapoo Medicine Show* [live], Rounder 1023.
*Skillet Lickers, Vol. 1*, Document 8056.
*The Skillet Lickers, Vol. 6: 1934*, Document 8061.
*The Skillet Lickers, Vol. 5: 1930–1934*, Document 8060.
*The Skillet Lickers, Vol. 4: 1929–1930*, Document 8059.

# A.P. CARTER (1891–1960)
## *Family Patriarch*

Country music has often been a family affair. Throughout the genre's long and colorful history, relatives have gathered together to create magic, particularly in the earliest days when it was common practice to include as many local able bodied musicians into the group as possible to cut down on traveling costs. The groups headed by Stoneman, Tanner, Bate and Carson all featured various kin folk in their respective outfits. But in the beginning, the name Carter reigned supreme as the first family of country music. The patriarch of that glorious Carter clan was A.P. Carter.

Alvin Pleasant Delaney Carter was born April 15, 1891, in Maces Spring, Virginia. He was one of nine children, and as with most mountain folk, music was a part of his life. His father was a banjo player and sang old ballads and spirituals after going religious. His mother hummed on standards such as "The Wife of Usher's Well," "Sailor Boy," and "Brown Girl" that A.P. learned, storing the songs away for future use.

The young Carter also sang in church alongside his two uncles and a sister, as well as at family gatherings. A.P. never did learn how to play any instrument proficiently enough to perform in front of a crowd; however, he was a fine vocalist. Although he possessed some talent, a career in music was an unforeseeable path since no industry existed.

Through his travels he met Sara Dougherty, a singer, guitarist, autoharp, and banjo player. A.P. and Sara married in 1915. In 1926, another talented musician was brought into the fold when Alvin's brother Ezra married Maybelle Addington. She was an adept guitar, autoharp and banjo player.

The trio, A.P., Sara and Maybelle, played at family and church events. In 1927, Ralph Peer, the roving talent scout for Victor, arrived in Bristol and immediately put out word that he was looking for local talent to record. Many of the hill residents were dirt poor farmers and the thought of making money for something they did for pleasure intrigued them. One of the groups to answer Peer's call were the three Carters, A.P., his wife Sara and sister-in-law Maybelle.

Although Sara and A.P. had been singing together for ten years, the inclusion of Maybelle added a new dimension to the group that created a three part harmony. When they arrived to record for Peer they had a polished act that was ready to set the country music industry—still in its infancy—on its ear. They did it on the first audition.

A.P., Sara and Maybelle arrived with their brood in tow. Their individual abilities meshed together in a seamless delivery and their large, diverse repertoire of material impressed Peer that day. They cut six sides, including "Bury Me Under the Weeping Willow," "Little Old Log Cabin by the Sea," "Storms Are on the Ocean," and "Single Girl, Married Girl," among others.

The songs sold well throughout the South, so it was with great excitement and self-confidence that the family entered the recording studio a second time in Camden, New Jersey, at the request of Peer. They cut some of their greatest standards that day, including "Keep on the Sunny Side," "Anchored in Love," "Little Darling Pal of Mine," and "Wildwood Flower." A.P. had collected the wide range of material that consisted of pop tunes, gospel hymns, and pre-bluegrass standards.

It was on the song "Wildwood Flower" that Maybelle's influential style emerged so brightly. She had the ability to pick the melody on the bass strings and keep rhythm on the treble strings. Her musical talent—combined with the seamless harmonies that they produced—was essential to their early success. They were able to bring the two worlds of church (gospel) and secular (folk) together as one in a way never heard before.

Despite their trailblazing ways, the Carters remained poor for years. They had to maintain non-musical jobs that often interrupted their ability to record and perform. The group was not properly promoted like Jimmie Rodgers was, and therefore missed out on the promising money of playing in big theaters. Instead, A.P. did his own promotion by advertising mostly through word of mouth. This backward attempt enabled the band to play many concerts but for very little money.

Although their musical life was a hardscrabble, the group continued to cut sides for a variety of labels and their songs gained popularity around the world. Sara and A.P. eventually split up, with the latter appearing with some of their children. In 1943, the group broke up for good but by then their legend was established. Mother Maybelle would continue singing with her three daughters into the 1960s and June would later marry country star Johnny Cash.

On November 7, 1960, A.P. Carter, the patriarch of country music's first family, died in his place of birth, Maces Spring, Virginia.

The importance of the Carter family cannot be overstated. They were true pioneers who helped shape the course of country music for the century as much as, or perhaps more than, anyone else before them. There was a unique chemistry between the three that no group could imitate. The seamless harmonies and musicianship would influence folk groups for the rest of the century.

They understood harmony and dynamics, creating a sound that contained many layers, including Sara's singing, Maybelle's playing and A.P.'s vocal interjections. The smoothness of the voices and instruments that combined to give them their sound put them years ahead of other musicians. They overshadowed other groups, such as Dr. Humphrey Bate and His Possum Hunters as well as Gid Tanner and His Skillet Lickers.

The Carter Family's repertoire came from a variety of sources. The most obvious was the rich mountain folk music that surrounded their Virginia home. As well, they traveled far and wide collecting a number of pop tunes that had their roots among the first families that settled in the area. Other songs came from the clan's lands of origin, the countryside of England and Scotland.

In some circles, A.P. was called a pirate for his practice of pillaging songs that he had never written and putting his own name to them. Although this might have been true, he managed to preserve the beauty of many of these classics that would have otherwise disappeared. Some of the their greatest hits included "Wabash Cannonball," "Lonesome Valley," "I'm Thinking Tonight of My Blue Eyes," "Foggy Mountain Top," "East Virginia Blues," "Jimmy Brown the Newsboy," "Will the Circle Be Unbroken," and "Gospel Ship."

They were able to put their own undeniable stamp on these songs and in essence helped preserve the traditional rich vein of American white folk music. Without the efforts of A.P. many of the tunes would have been lost treasures. The scramble in the early days of country music to put one's name on a piece that had been part of mountain culture for four hundred years created serious rivalries.

The trio delivered these songs to an audience that had heard them many times over and had probably even sung the tunes. But they were able to deliver them in a different manner. The Carters' concert was an all-around affair. The family often arrived at their destination hours before and mingled with the crowd before taking the stage. While the women sat down, A.P. roamed about and also acted as an emcee. The various members of the family that were available at the time rounded out the group. They took requests from the audience and knew how to put on a show, but curiously they presented only music. There was a serious, professional edge to their performance compared to other acts on the circuit at the time that included comedy, most notably Uncle Dave Macon and Gid Tanner.

The Carters' influence on country and other forms of music includes a long list of names: E.C. and Orna Ball, the Delmore Brothers, the Red Clay Ramblers, Joan Baez, Bryan Bowers, Hazel Dickens, Woody Guthrie, Uncle Tupelo, Skeeter Davis, Jay Farrar, Jimmy Martin, Gillian Welch, Last Forever, Jim and Jennie and the Pinetops, Roy Acuff, Earl Scruggs, Lester Flatt, Nitty Gritty Dirt Band, the Kingston Trio, Doc Watson, Bob Dylan and Emmylou Harris.

The story of the Carter family is one of endurance. They struggled during the Depression years to remain together and even recorded after Sara and A.P.'s marriage had failed. In fact, years after their divorce they even reformed the Carter family group with their children and cut some hundred sides for different labels. The Carter clan had dominated country music since its birth.

It is almost impossible to calculate the impact they made on the genre. Suffice it to say that they are as important to the genre's early development as Jimmie Rodgers. In 1970, the Carter clan was the first group to be inducted into the Country Music Hall of Fame, ten years after A.P.'s death. It was a fitting testimony and honor to the first family of country music history.

## Discography

*All Time Favorites*, Acme P-1.
*In Memory of A.P. Carter*, Acme P-2.
*Together Again*, RCA Victor 2580.
*The Carter Family*, Decca 4404.
*Anita Carter Sings Folk Songs Old and New*, Mercury 27770.
*Keep on the Sunnyside*, CBS CS-8952.
*More Favorites by the Carter Family*, Decca D-4557.
*The Country Album*, CBS CS-9417.
*Country's First Family*, Columbia 34266.
*Diamonds in the Rough*, Copper Creek 107.
*Clinch Mountain Treasures*, Country 112.
*Best of the Carter Family*, Prism Leisure 548.
*Family Album*, Longhorn 3103.
*Sunshine in the Shadows*, Recall 474.
*In the Shadow of Clinch Mountain*, Bear Family 15865.
*The Decca Sessions, Vol. 1 (1936)*, Catfish 188.
*The Decca Sessions, Vol. 2*, Catfish 218.
*The Carter Family, Vol. 2 (1935–1941)*, JSP 7708.
*Greatest Hits 1927–1934*, Fabulous 146.
*Country and Folk Roots*, Castle 651.
*RCA Country Legends*, RCA 59266.
*Gospel Gold*, Brentwood 40840.
*A Proper Introduction to the Carter Family: Keep on the Sunnyside*, Proper 2060.
*Will You Remember Me*, Fruit Tree 842.
*Best of the Carter Family [2005]*, Prism Platinum 548.
*20th Century Master: The Millennium Collection: The Best of the Carter Family*, Mercury 4544.
*Early Country Radio*, JSP 7757.
*Early Classics*, ACM 015.
*The Collection*, EMI 576324.
*The Carter Family, 1927–1934*, JSP 7701.
*The Carter Family* [ACM], ACM 022.
*Wildwood Flower*, PolyGram 834491.

*The Original and Great Carter Family*, Camden 586.
*'Mid the Green Fields of Virginia*, RCA 1107.
*The Collection of Favorites*, Decca 3022.
*Last Recordings, Vol. 1.*
*Country Music Hall of Fame*, MCA 10088.
*Country Music Hall of Fame*, King 3811.
*The Best of the Carter Family, Vol. 1*, Country Stars 55464.
*The Best of the Carter Family, Vol. 2*, Country Stars 55465.
*Wildwood Flowers*, ASL/Living 5323.
*Last Sessions: Their Complete Victor Recordings (1924–1842)*, Rounder 1072.
*Longing for Old Virginia: Their Complete Victor Recordings (1934)*, Rounder 1071.
*My Clinch Mountain Home: Their Complete Recordings*, Rounder 611065.
*Anchored in Love: Their Complete Victor Recordings*, Victor 611064.
*When the Roses Bloom in Dixieland*, Rounder 1066.
*Worried Man Blues: Their Complete Victor Sides*, Rounder 1067.
*On Border Radio, Vol. 1*, Arhoolie 411.
*Greatest Hits*, KRB 5155.
*Sunshine in the Shadows: Their Complete Recordings*, Rounder 1068.
*Give Me the Roses While I Live*, Rounder 1069.
*Country by the Carter Family*, Vanguard 79502.
*On Border Radio, Vol. 2: 1939*, Arhoolie 412.
*Best of the Best of the Original Carter Family*, Koch 1478.
*Gold Watch and Chain: Their Compete Victor Recordings*, Victor 1070.
*On Border Radio, Vol. 3; 1939*, Arhoolie 413.
*Can the Circle Be Unbroken? Country Music's First Family*, Columbia 65707.

# CHARLIE POOLE (1892–1931)
## *North Carolina Rambler*

There are many facets to country music. It is a diverse genre that has branched out in different directions in its long, colorful history, and all styles have something to offer. String bands that were very popular among the rural folk of the South originally performed a predecessor to the bluegrass style. One performer to initiate that sound was the North Carolina Rambler. His name was Charlie Poole.

Charlie Poole was born on March 22, 1892, in Alamance County, North Carolina. He learned how to play the banjo from an early age and despite an injury playing baseball, continued to hone his abilities until he was one of the best pickers in the South. Legend claims that it was the baseball injury to his thumb that forced him to redevelop his style and therefore was responsible for his unique technique. Whether this is true or not, by his early 20s, Poole was recognized as a very highly skilled player.

Although he would make a powerful impact on the country music world, for most of his life he worked in a textile mill to make ends meet. Poole played at local events but didn't really advance his musical career until he met Posey Rorer, a crippled miner who played fiddle as well as Charlie played banjo. Together they were dynamite and performed as a duo.

They toured the West Virginia/North Carolina area delivering to audiences their unique double threat instrumental act, which included Poole's distinct voice that earned him the nickname "the human bird," and a repertoire of rural songs, pop tunes and gospel-flecked songs. They were hard drinkers and carved wild legends for themselves between 1917 and the mid 1920s.

Along the way they picked up guitarist Norman Woodlieff, who was quick to add another musical dimension with his intense playing. He was cut in the same mold as his two singing partners, a hard drinking, hard working man with a precise touch on a string instrument that blended nicely with Poole's banjo and Rorer's fiddle. They became the North Carolina Ramblers, one of the finest string bands in the land.

In July of 1925, they made their first recordings, including "Don't Let Your Deal Go Down," for Columbia Records. The release of the four sides enhanced their popularity and they toured throughout the South as the Carolina Ramblers, although Poole was acknowledged as the official leader. Sometimes they were billed as Charlie Poole and the Carolina Ramblers.

Despite their popularity, lineup changes were frequent throughout the band's tenure in the late 1920s. For their second recording session guitarist Roy Harvey replaced Woodlieff. Rorer himself would leave in 1928 to be replaced by Lonnie Austin. Some time later Odell Smith took over Austin's position in the group. The one constant member was Poole, who managed to keep it all going despite his heavy drinking and his job at the textile mill.

No matter the lineup, the Ramblers delivered a mixture of country songs that were powered by quality instrumental workings. Poole had an uncanny ability to recruit top notch musicians that were sometimes better than the ones they had replaced. He also was able to bring in players that complemented his own style. Their repertoire consisted of minstrel tunes, Victorian ballads and comical pieces that he delivered with British dry humor.

After almost seventy-five sides for Columbia, the Great Depression wiped out Poole's musical ambitions. His drinking increased and he appeared to be headed back to the textile mill for good, but received another opportunity to extend his career. However, before he could begin working in the movies, Poole died of heart failure in May 1931 in Eden, North Carolina.

Poole was a genuine country music pioneer. He was an excellent banjo player and his five string exploits had a lasting impact on future stylists.

He was also the leader of the Carolina Ramblers, one of the most important of the early string bands. He brought to life many songs that had been part of rural repertoires for centuries.

Poole was the first important banjo player in country music. He defined the parameters of the instrument during the 1920s and for the next few years. His agility, speed, and sheer power made him one of the greats among early instrumentalists. But more than anything else, he was able to blend his tremendous skills with those of Rorer, Woodlieff and anyone else that played in his group.

He was a natural leader, able to take command of any situation, but always allowed those in his group to share the spotlight. His ability to challenge them only tightened the group's sound and gave their music a harder, more exciting edge. The personnel of the band were figures cut in the same mold as their leader—they were all hard drinking brawlers.

Poole would influence a number of country stars, including the great Hank Williams, Sr. Poole also made an impact on the New Lost City Ramblers, Hollow Rock String Band, Nonnie Presson, the Dickel Brothers, Roy Clark, Buck Owens, Chet Atkins, Bob Wills, Lester Flat, Earl Scruggs, and dozens of others.

Poole planted the seeds of bluegrass, a mantle that would later be taken up by the Monroe Brothers. Although they would surpass his initial efforts, there would not have been the Monroe Brothers bluegrass sound without the early efforts of the Carolina Rambler. If Poole had lived into the 1940s he would have fit right in with the Blue Grass Boys.

The North Carolina Ramblers continued after Poole's death; Rorer returned to the fold and shared the leadership with guitarist Roy Harvey. They recorded and performed under the name North Carolina Ramblers. Ironically, Poole would enjoy a major comeback (posthumously) during the explosion of folk music in the 1960s. Even today his recordings continue to sell.

Charlie Poole's contributions to country music were many. He was a superb instrumentalist, he was the leader of a popular string band, he helped preserve rural songs, and he ushered in the bluegrass sound. He was about tradition and took the core simple sound of folk music and created magic as the Carolina Rambler.

## The Carolina Ramblers
### 1925–1930

| *Banjo* | *Fiddle* | *Guitar* |
|---|---|---|
| Charlie Poole | Posey Rorer | Norman Woodlieff |
| | Lonnie Austin | Roy Harvey |
| | Odell Smith | |

## Discography

*You Ain't Talkin' to Me: Charlie Poole and the Roots of Country Music*, Columbia 92870.
*Charlie Poole and the North Carolina Ramblers 1926–1930*, Historical 8005.
*Old Time Songs Recorded from 1925 to 1930*, Country 3501.
*Charlie Poole and the North Carolina Ramblers, Vol. 2: Old Time Songs Recorded from 1926*, Country 3508
*With the North Carolina Ramblers and the Highlanders*, JSP 7734
*Legend of Charlie Poole, Vol. 3*, Country 3516.
*Legend of Charlie Poole, Vol. 4*, Country 540.

# E.V. "POP" STONEMAN (1893–1968)
## *Country Patriarch*

The early days of country featured many determined individuals who, although they possessed a very limited formal education, were well schooled in the subject of mountain music. Many of these songsters spent years learning the folk music of their people and honing their skills on a variety of instruments before searching for a recording contract. One of these musicians, after establishing his own career, included his family in the act and became a country patriarch, passing down the tradition to the next generation. His name was Pop Stoneman.

Ernest V. Stoneman was born on May 25, 1893, in Monorat, Virginia. Like other children growing up in the Appalachian Mountain region, he was exposed to the folk music of his people. He developed an ear for the style and learned how to play the harmonica, jew's harp, autoharp, and banjo by his early teens. However, any dreams of becoming a successful musician were put aside because the opportunities were not available. Also, he married early and started a family that would eventually number thirteen.

He was a carpenter by trade and for years played music on the side at barn dances and on holidays. He had a knack for turning the old English folk songs into something that the mountain folk could dance to, a talent that would eventually serve him well later in life. However, like Fiddlin' John Carson and Uncle Dave Macon, Stoneman had to be content with being a local legend and semiprofessional southern musician.

In 1924, a fellow mill worker, Henry Whitter, recorded "The Wreck of the Old 97," a popular folk song that had bounced around for years and was in every mountain musician's repertoire. Upon hearing Whitter's version, Pop was determined he could record a much better one and was able to convince Ralph Peer. After a test session, Stoneman cut some proper songs for Okeh, including "The Sinking of the Titanic," which became one of the best selling songs of the decade.

Like other songs of that period cut by country musicians, the tune had a moral message to it. Stoneman sang of the great ship and warned all that it was foolish to think that someone could build a ship that would never sink. It was this morality theme in country music songs that was a strong selling point to those that bought the records during this period.

The music business became a family affair. Everyone in the Stoneman clan learned how to play an instrument, from guitar to banjo to harmonica to anything that could make noise or keep a steady rhythm. With a large talent pool to choose from, Pop Stoneman was never lacking musicians to fill out the ranks of his band in the recording studio.

After the success of "The Sinking of the Titanic," Stoneman and his family group cut over two hundred sides for Okeh. Some of them were originals, but most were derived from the folk songs that the mountain people had been playing for centuries and that had been passed down from one generation to another. However, each song was "cleaned" up to give it a more current and country commercial feel. The result was a lot of money for Stoneman and his family.

Because he was also a quick learner with a faculty for remembering lyrics and adding new touches to an old song, Stoneman was popular in recording studios. A large wealth of the material he recorded was cover versions. Despite the fact that they had already been issued, he was able to make them sound different enough so he could get some extra mileage out of them.

Stoneman, who had been a hard working, uneducated man his entire life, made a lot of money as an interpreter of American folk songs. The new wealth was overwhelming and the family thought the good times would never end since the pot of gold at the end of the rainbow seemed infinite. For the rest of the 1920s they lived beyond their means.

The Great Depression hit the Stonemans extremely hard. The well had dried up and they had spent most of their money on material possessions that they had been unable to afford before becoming successful recording artists. With the crash of the recording industry the records were no longer selling well and many of the early acts fell on hard times.

With the good times over, Stoneman returned to his low paying job as a carpenter. He moved to the Washington, D.C., area in hopes of a better future, leaving his family to struggle without him back in the mountains. For much of the decade, he continued to work as a carpenter or at other menial jobs he could find.

It wasn't until the 1940s that Stoneman returned to the music scene with a number of his grown up children. Together they recorded *Old Tunes from the South* on the Folkways label, an effort that rejuvenated their careers. Suddenly they became very popular on the folk circuit with their unabashed brand of country tinged music that appealed to the white college crowd. They toured the coffeehouses and college campuses, but never did fully recapture their past glory.

In 1962, they made their debut on the *Grand Ole Opry* and continued to record. Although their albums still contained a commercial element, the band never sold as many discs as they had during their prime in the late 1920s. That they were able to forge a second phase to their career was remarkable.

But Pop Stoneman was a savvy individual in many ways and realized that television as an exciting new medium they had not yet conquered. They appeared on the *Jimmy Dean Show* and because of their rural appeal, musical abilities, and popularity, they had a show themselves called *Those Stonemans* in the mid–1960s. By this time they had joined the great migration to Nashville.

In 1967, the Stonemans won for best vocal group at the Country Music Awards. At this point the group consisted of Pop on guitar and autoharp, Scotty on fiddle, Jim on bass, Van on guitar, Donna on mandolin, and Roni on banjo. Their longevity as one of the premier family attractions was truly remarkable. They had conquered the recording industry, the touring circuit and television, one of the few country acts to triumph in all three mediums.

However, the family band was dealt a severe blow when Pop died of a stomach ailment on June 14, 1968, shortly after recording a new batch of songs. It was the end of an era.

Pop Stoneman was a country music success story. He enjoyed two distinct phases to his long career and if it had not been for the Great Depression there is no telling how many albums he would have sold. He was a multi-instrumentalist and recorded some of the gems of American folk music. For someone with a poor education, he made the most of his talents.

Stoneman was a solid musician, a factor that was partly responsible for his appeal during different decades. He was one of the first musicians of any style to record with an autoharp. There was something in his playing that was catchy and made people want to listen to his music repeatedly. He was a force on at least four instruments and probably could have been proficient on all of them.

But the story of Pop Stoneman and his brood is more than just one about gifted musicians. Pop was also very capable of transforming even the most obscure song with the strangest lyrics into a modern piece of marketable music. It was this ability that allowed him to record as much as and more than many of the early artists. He was quick on the note, learned songs easily, and was always able to back up his original or cover tunes with excellent musicianship.

In addition, he was the patriarch of one of the most important family groups in music history. His children began as the Blue Grass Champs and developed a fan base in the Washington, D.C., area. Eventually they rallied around their father and the strength of the group was doubled. They toured on a regular basis and even scored a hit with "Tupelo County Jail." They followed this up with "The Five Little Johnson Girls." After the death of Pop Stoneman, the rest of the group carried on some time before retiring.

The story of Pop Stoneman is an enchanting tale of an uneducated, semi-talented mountain man who created his own breaks in the music business. He was a colorful character who also had a hand in the successful careers of Jimmie Rodgers and the Carter Family as a leader of some of the sessions they cut. He was the patriarch of a family band that helped shape the early sound of country music.

## The Stoneman Family
### Circa 1967

| *Guitar* | *Auto Harp* | *Fiddle* |
|---|---|---|
| Pop Stoneman | Pop Stoneman | Scotty Stoneman |
| Van Stoneman | | |
| | | |
| *Bass* | *Mandolin* | *Banjo* |
| Jim Stoneman | Donna Stoneman | Roni Stoneman |

## Discography

*Family and Friends,* Old Homestead OH 173.
*Bluegrass Champs,* Nashville 2063.
*Great Stonemans,* MGM 4578.
*Pop Stoneman Memorial Album,* MGM 4588.
*Stoneman Christmas,* MGM 4613.
*The Stoneman Family Live,* Sunset 5203.
*Down on the Stonemans' Age,* RCA Victor 4264.
*California Blues,* RCA Victor 4431.
*In All Honesty,* RCA 4343.
*The Stonemans,* MGM 124.
*Stoneman Family,* Historical 8004.
*Cuttin' the Grass,* CMH 6210.
*On the Road,* CMH 6219.

*First Family in Country Music*, CMH 9029.
*Family Bible*, Rutabaga 3012.
*Stone B R Corns*, Rounder 1008.
*For God and Country*, Old Homestead 90200.
*Preachin', Prayin', Singin'*, Starday 303.
*Ernest V. Stoneman and the Dixie Mountaineers*, Diamond Cut 400.
*Ernest V. Stoneman and the Dixie Mountaineers, 1927–1928*, Historical 8004.
*Family Tradition: The Stoneman Legacy*, CMH 8626.
*Cool Cowboy*, Capitol 1230.
*Ernest. V. Stoneman and the Blue Ridge Corn Shuckers*, Rounder 1008.
*Ernest V. Stoneman*, Country 3510.
*Old Time Tunes of the South*, Folkways 2315.
*Ernest. V. Stoneman and the Stoneman Family*, Starday 200.
*Big Ball in Monterey*, World Pacific 1828.
*Great Old Timer at the Capitol*, Starday 275.
*Singin', Swingin', Stompin'*, MGM 4363.
*White Lightnin'*, Starday 393.
*All in the Family*, MGM 4511.
*28 Big Ones*, King 4119.
*Country*, MGM 4453.

# RILEY PUCKETT (1894–1946)
## Blind Ambition

The drive that characterizes musicians has often helped them overcome difficult obstacles in order to achieve their goals. The musical universe is filled with blind performers. The blues featured Blind Lemon Jefferson, Blind Willie McTell, Blind Willie Johnson, Sonny Terry, and Blind Boy Fuller among others. In modern times, Ray Charles and Stevie Wonder overcame their loss of vision to become superstars. In the early recording days of country, one sightless individual driven by his passion became one of the most important artists. His name was Riley Puckett.

Riley Puckett was born George Riley Puckett on May 7, 1894, in Alpharetta, Georgia. When he was three months old incorrect treatment of an eye ailment left him without his vision for the remainder of his life. It was while attending the Macon School for the Blind that he discovered the banjo and then later the guitar. His proficiency on both instruments made him a favorite at local cutting contests. Despite his physical disadvantage, he made quick work of anybody who challenged his musical prowess.

Although he was a talented singer and player, he might have remained in total obscurity if he hadn't caught a break when he joined forces with guitarist Clayton McMichen in the early 1920s. Puckett made his radio debut with McMichen on an Atlanta station. With his virtuoso skills and impressive yodeling-singing style, he became a favorite among listeners.

He began to do solo work as well as play in the Hometown Boys, a group that included fiddler Lowe Stokes and mandolin player Ted Hawkins. Both of them would later turn up in Gid Tanner's Skillet Lickers. The three struck out together for some time and developed a decent sized following, before Puckett became the first to move on to join Tanner.

The Skillet Lickers were one of the most popular regional outfits on the circuit and would gain greater fame when they began to record. They ventured to New York to cut a few sides for Columbia where in the studio, Puckett was a major asset because of his skills, his impeccable timing and ability to blend with the other musicians in the group.

But before they entered the studio Tanner, McMichen, Puckett and Fate Norris woodsheded (practiced) for hours perfecting a four-part attack that often sounded seamless. Puckett fit in perfectly with the other three and for the next ten years he would be an integral part in the Skillet Lickers' rise to fame.

In that recording session in 1924, they cut versions of "The Little Old Log Cabin" and "Steamboat Bill." Another, "Rock All Our Babies to Sleep," was the first yodeling song to appear on record three years ahead of the famed Mississippi yodeler Jimmie Rodgers. Undoubtedly, Puckett's distinctive vocals were instantly recognizable and catapulted the Skillet Lickers to greater prominence.

On another session, Puckett enhanced his rising reputation with the recording of "Oh Susannah" and "You'll Never Miss Your Mother Till She's Gone." When Columbia released a Hillbilly Series that included Puckett, it increased his star power. In the late 1920s with the recording industry at its peak, he made numerous recordings as a member of the Skillet Lickers, a solo artist and in a number of different groups.

In 1927, he recorded with Hugh Cross, a notable tenor, and together they put down the first version of "Red River Valley." On later sessions they would cut "Gonna Raise a Ruckus Tonight," "Call Me Back Pal o' Mine," and "My Wild Irish Rose," among others. The fact that he could be paired with a variety of singers indicated Puckett's great versatility.

When the Great Depression hit, Puckett continued to record but not at the pace he had previously enjoyed. Somehow he managed to continue his career in an era when many of his contemporaries had faded from the scene. In 1934, he left the Skillet Lickers after a ten-year stint with the band to pursue his solo ambitions.

He managed to keep busy cutting songs, including "My Carolina

Home," as part of McMichen's outfit, as well as "I Only Want a Buddy, Not a Sweetheart," and "St. Louis Blues" with Red Jones. During 1934–1941, Puckett recorded mostly for RCA Victor, but waxed a few sides for Decca in the latter part of the decade.

Puckett also managed to keep the performance side of his career intact. He joined McMichen's Georgia Wildcats and Bert Layne's Mountaineers for brief stints. He also played with John Love. Later, he led his own successful tent show that toured around the South. He recorded more sides with Red Jones, including "Altoona Train Wreck," "Take Me Back to My Carolina Home," and "The Broken Engagement." His 1940 session saw him record more pop oriented material with such songs as "Oh, Johnny, Oh," "Little Sir Echo" and "South of the Border." In 1941, he waxed his last batch of songs that included "How Come You Do Me Like You Do," "Railroad Blues" and "Peach Picking Time in Georgia." He also performed with the Mountain Boys off and on, until 1946.

Puckett was suspicious of the ways of city doctors and considering what had happened to him as an infant, his prejudices were understandable. It was this mistrust that led to his death on July 14, 1946, when an untreated boil on his neck caused blood poisoning.

Riley Puckett was one of the true pioneers of old time country music. He was a radio, recording and performing star whose magnitude was matched by very few of his contemporaries. He possessed one of the most distinct singing voices of the early 1920s and made numerous recordings that remain an archetype of the genre.

He established his legend as a singer who could handle any material, including country, folk, pop and even blues. There was a definite timbre in his voice that defined old timey music. He was the most famous vocalist of his generation and sold more records than anyone except Vernon Dalhart.

Riley was also a yodeler long before the style became famous in country music. He preceded the great Jimmie Rodgers by a few years and is recognized as the first singer to record a genuine yodeling song. Although his vocal powers certainly were an important part of his legend, they weren't his only asset as a country musician.

Puckett was a formidable force on the guitar. His wild bass-run style influenced a number of country artists and continues to do so indirectly today. Although not a superstar picker in the same mold as Chet Atkins, Riley set the table for such virtuosos. His style also influenced the bluegrass players Bill Monroe, Lester Flatt and Earl Scruggs. Others that took a page out of his book include Nonnie Presson, Hugh Cross, John Lair, Hoke Rice, the Four Virginians, Fred Pike, as well as more modern artists such as Buck Owens, Roy Clark, Glen Campbell, Willie Nelson and Waylon Jennings.

But perhaps he had the greatest influence on Jimmie Rodgers, the singing brakeman. The Father of Country Music was famous for his yodeling style. Arguably, Puckett was not the first mountain singer to yodel, but his recordings made a lasting impression on Rodgers.

Throughout his career he played on hundreds of sessions and recorded numerous songs. A short list includes "The Little Old Log Cabin," "Steamboat Bill," "Rock All Our Babies to Sleep," "Oh Susannah," "You'll Never Miss Your Mother Till She's Gone," "Red River Valley," "Gonna Raise a Ruckus Tonight," "Call Me Back Pal o' Mine," "My Wild Irish Rose," "I Only Want a Buddy, Not a Sweetheart," "St. Louis Blues," "Altoona Freight Wreck," "Take Me Back to My Carolina Home," "The Broken Engagement," "Oh, Johnny, Oh," "Little Sir Echo," "South of the Border," "How Come You Do Me Like You Do," "Railroad Blues" and "Peach Picking Time in Georgia." He was responsible for the preservation of the rich vein of rural music as much as anyone else.

He was a radio star and remained popular on that medium until the time of his death. He worked on stations all over the South, including Georgia, West Virginia, Kentucky, and Tennessee. He also remained a favorite in concert and on record. It was evident from the start that despite the obstacles in his way, Puckett was determined to succeed with his blind ambition.

## Discography

*Old Time Greats, Vol. 2*, Old Homestead OH 179
*Old Time Greats, Vol. 1*, Old Homestead OH 114
*Waitin' for the Evening Mail*, Country 411
*Red Sails in the Sunset*, Bear Family BFZ 15280

# JIMMIE RODGERS (1897–1933)

### *The Singing Brakeman*

Although country music had been regionally popular for centuries, and the first early recordings proved to be commercially successful, in order to survive the genre needed an individual who could take it into mainstream America. It required someone of star magnitude like jazz's Louis Armstrong or the blues' Bessie Smith. In the late 1920s a country yodeler emerged and became known as the Singing Brakeman. His name was Jimmie Rodgers.

James Charles Rodgers was born on September 8, 1897, in Meridian, Mississippi, the son of a section foreman on the famed Mobile and Ohio Railroad. When he was four his mother died of tuberculosis, a disease that would cast a shadow over much of his short life. He had little use for an education and quit school at age fourteen to join his father on the railroad, where he started out as a water carrier. He would later perform a number of duties, including callboy, baggagemaster, flagman and finally a brakeman. By the time he had moved up to his last position he had already been moonlighting as an amateur musician for several years.

He had carried a little banjo and guitar with him while at work and learned basic chords from the black laborers. More importantly he picked up elements of rhythm, a feeling for words, and harmony. He obtained the name "Singing Brakeman" because he was always whistling or humming a tune while driving the train. He also collected the basic material for the cycle of songs tinged with blues, folk and country strains that would make him famous. Somewhere down the line he heard yodeling and assimilated it into his own developing style.

In 1921, after a decade of working on the railroad, he developed pulmonary hemorrhage that forced him to seek less strenuous work. Since he had been an amateur musician for years, he decided to pursue that field and began to concentrate his efforts towards a successful career as a recording artist. His first semi-professional gig was as a black face artist traveling in a medicine show throughout the South. However, a year, later in 1926, he was working as a yodeler with Ernest Helton.

Later on, he and his second wife moved to Asheville, North Carolina, where he formed the Jimmie Rodgers Entertainers, a string band that consisted of guitarist Jack Pierce, mandolin and banjo player Jack Grant and banjoist Claude Grant. They appeared on a local radio station for a few weeks then toured the Southeast.

When they heard of a recording opportunity with Ralph Peer, they headed to Bristol, Tennessee. However, before they were set to record, there was an argument between Rodgers and the rest of the group, so he was forced to make do on his first session as a solo artist. Not to be deterred, he recorded "The Soldier's Sweetheart," and "Sleep, Baby, Sleep." After this, Rodgers moved his family to Washington, D.C., because of better opportunities and bided his time until he could record for Peer again.

At first, his records didn't sell all that well and he received a modest fee for his services. But, he would not be denied. Upon his persistence, Peer let him cut four more sides that included "T for Texas," or "Blue Yodel" as it was known. The song became a million seller and Rodgers' fame was sealed. Although he had struggled for years, it seemed overnight he was catapulted from obscure musician to country music star.

He had managed to combine the repetitive patterns of African-American blues songs with the white tradition of yodeling. From this point on he would cut numerous sessions that included "In the Jailhouse Now," "Treasures Untold," and "Brakeman Blues," among others. More songs would follow, including "Tuck Away My Lonesome Blues," his third million seller. By this time he had achieved national acclaim and was the most popular country artist of the era.

In 1929, at the zenith of his popularity, he made a short film titled *The Singing Brakeman* that was a solid success. By this time he had recorded numerous sides for different labels and often used a variety of musicians on these sessions. He even recorded with jazz trappings and on one session appeared with the great trumpeter Louis Armstrong. The depth of his popularity could be measured by the number of records he sold even during the Depression, when the bottom had fallen out of the industry.

Despite his grand success, his ill condition hung over him like a black cloud. As far back as 1924, he had been diagnosed with tuberculosis, yet he stubbornly refused to yield to doctor's orders to slow down. There was no stopping his drive and he continued to perform as well as record. In 1930 and 1931, he was forced to cancel a few concert dates because of his rapidly failing health, but continued to record, attempting in futility to win the race against time.

He pushed himself hard and recorded the song "TB Blues," an acknowledgement of the disease that was robbing him of his vitality and his ability to do the one thing he loved. He performed with comedian Will Rogers in order to help the drought sufferers of the southeastern region. He also sang on the radio, enhancing his legendary status. In his limited time frame, he wanted to accomplish as much as possible.

On May 24, 1933, he began what would be his last recording session. Later that day, he began to hemorrhage and fell into a coma from which he never recovered. Two days later he died.

Jimmie Rodgers was the father of country music. He was the first genuine superstar and eclipsed the efforts of all those that came before him and set the table for all to follow. Along with Hank Williams, Sr., he is the most influential country artist of the twentieth century. Rodgers possessed all of the elements anyone needed to achieve incredible fame.

Rodgers had a distinct singing and playing style that borrowed heavily from African-American music: the blues and labor songs he heard while working on the railroad. He was the first singer to whiten the blues, the folk song of the poor, hard working blacks, into a package that appealed to the hill dwellers and everyone else across the nation.

He was a yodeler, perhaps the greatest in the history of music; certainly the best in the annals of country. Rodgers' highly personalized singing style and his playing enabled him to mesh with other genres. Although he recorded initially as a solo performer, he would later commercialize his music to include jazz, dance and jug bands, as well as Hawaiian music, trumpets and clarinets. This strategy allowed him to attain crossover appeal and was a major reason for his national status.

Ralph Peer had an important hand in building and shaping the Jimmie Rodgers image. The music executive was savvy enough to be able to package anything his singer produced into an appealing parcel that provided a little something for everyone. The universal elements of his songs also went a long way in helping achieve the stardom that others never attained.

Many of Rodgers' songs were co-written by his sister-in-law, Elsie McWilliams. Together they gave the world a number of gems, including "My Old Pal," "Daddy and Home," "The Sailor's Plea," "I'm Lonely and Blue," "Mississippi Moon," "T for Texas," "Blue Yodel No. 4," "Muleskinner Blues," "Standin' on the Corner," "Pistol Packin' Papa," "Waiting for a Train," "In the Jailhouse Now," "Way Out on the Mountain," "Mother Was a Lady," "Ben Dewberry's Run," and "Fifteen Years Ago Today." Many of his songs became the starting point for countless country artists, and were recorded by many rock, blues and jazz musicians. For example, "T for Texas" was included in the southern-rock band Lynyrd Skynyrd's live album *One More for the Road*.

Rodgers was a major influence on a number of artists. A partial list includes Mississippi John Hurt, Big Jack Johnson, Gene Autry, Jimmie Davis, the Delmore Brothers, Lefty Frizzell, Merle Haggard, Patsy Montana, Woody Guthrie, Johnny Bond, Clifford Gibson, Webb Pierce, Joy Lynn White, Bob Wills, Rex Griffin, Kenny Roberts, Moe Bandy and Joe Stampley, Kasey Chambers, Jesse Rodgers, Bill Cox, Cliff Carlisle, Ernest Tubb and Hank Snow. In truth, any country artist to emerge after the mid–1920s followed the path Rodgers blazed and his music continues to fuel today's country strains.

It was Rodgers who ushered in the cowboy and radio star era with his ability to commercialize country music. His appearance in a movie touched off an industry where Ken Maynard, Wilf Carter, Tex Ritter, Gene Autry, Roy Rogers and many others would gain fame. He is also responsible for enabling Hank Williams to come along twenty some years later and make such a big splash with his blues flecked material.

Rodgers' fame transcended all borders that had previously existed. He did it with a very unique singing style and minor instrumental talent. He was not a handsome man cut in the mold of Elvis Presley, for instance. He didn't have large monetary backing and throughout his career he struggled financially despite writing and performing a handful of million sellers. He made more money than any other country artist before him, but he never amassed an amazing fortune.

It is hard to understand Rodgers' appeal in today's terms. He was a part of everyday life in the late 1920s and early 1930s. When people went to the corner store they often insisted the clerk slip in the latest recording by Jimmie Rodgers. Upon his death, his body was returned to Meridian and thousands of mourners awaited his arrival. He lay in state for several days so all could pay their last respects.

The Jimmie Rodgers story is a tale of a railroad man who made history by following his own path in music. He was an innovator and never afraid to try something new if he thought it would enable him to reach a wider audience. He is the father of country music and the first artist inducted in the Country Music Hall of Fame. Later, he would be elected to the Rock and Roll Hall of Fame, an honor that emphasizes his diversity. Undoubtedly, the lone railroad worker with the magic voice and clever rhythms will forever be known as "The Singing Brakeman."

## Jimmie Rodgers' Group

| *Guitar* | *Mandolin* | *Banjo* |
| --- | --- | --- |
| Jimmie Rodgers | Jack Grant | Claude Grant |
| Jack Pierce | | Jack Grant |

## Discography

*Jimmie the Kid*, RCA 2213.
*Country Music Hall of Fame*, RCA Victor 2531.
*Country Legacy*, Fair 1248.
*Never No Mo' Blues: Memorial Album*, RCA Victor 1232.
*Train Whistle Blues*, Koch International 7989.
*My Rough and Rowdy Ways*, RCA Victor 2112.
*The Short But Brilliant Life [M]*, RCA Victor 2634.
*My Time Ain't Long*, RCA Victor 2865.
*Twelve Immortal Hits*, Hamilton Hip-148.
*The Legendary Jimmie Rodgers, Vol. 1*, RCA Victor 0075.
*Memorial Album, Vol. 3*, RCA Victor PT-3039.
*My Rowdy and Rough Ways*, RCA Victor 1209.
*Memorial Album, Vol. 2*, RCA Victor PT-3038.
*This Is Jimmie Rodgers*, RCA Victor 6091.
*Unissued, Vol. 1*, ACM 011.
*My Old Pal*, ASV/Living Era 5058.
*First Sessions*, Rounder 1056.
*Vol. 5, American's Blue Yodeller, 1930–31*, Rounder 1060.
*The Early Years 1928–1929*, Rounder 1057.
*On the Way Up 1929*, Rounder 1058.
*Riding High 1929–1930*, Rounder 1059.

*Vol. 6: Down the Old Road 1931–32*, Rounder 1061.
*No Hard Times, 1932*, Rounder 1062.
*Last Sessions, 1933*, Rounder 1063.
*The Singing Brakeman*, Bear Family 15540.
*American Legends No. 16: Jimmie Rodgers*, Laserlight 12746.
*Memorial Album*, Collectables 2700.
*The Blues*, Fremeaux FA 254.
*The Essential Jimmie Rodgers*, RCA 67500.
*Father of Country Music*, Pearl 7814.
*The Yodelling Ranger*, Empress 806.
*Ultimate Collection*, Press Leisure 532.
*The Singing Brakeman*, Country Stars 55459.
*Country Music Hall of Fame: 1961*, King 3824.
*Jimmie Rodgers*, St. Claire 326.
*Brakeman's Blues*, Catfish 187.
*Yodelin' Cowboy*, Roots of Country 211008.
*Blue Yodel: The Recorded Legacy*, Arpeggio 28810.
*Classic Sides 1927–1933*, JSP 7704.
*Standing in the Corner*, Recall 396.
*RCA Country Legends*, RCA 65129.
*Recordings 1927–1933*, JSP 7704.
*Country and Folk Roots*, Castle 650.
*Blue Yodels*, Fabulous 153.
*Singing Brakeman*, Prism Platinum 532.
*A Legendary Performer*, RCA Victor 2504.
*Country Music 1966*, Dot 3710.
*Memorial Album, Vol. 1*, RCA Victor PT-3007.
*Travelin' Blues*, RCA Victor 3073.
*Troubled Times*, ASM 4242.
*Unheard, Vol. 2*, ACM 012.

# PART TWO

## *Cowboys and Radio Stars*

The late 1920s and 1930s marked a significant change in country music as it branched out further into radio, as well as the movie industry, to gain national recognition. Once the recording industry collapsed because of the Great Depression, the genre proved so popular that it filtered to the different mediums. By the end of the decade, country musicians appeared in dozens of movies and ruled a large portion of the radio airwaves.

In the mid–1920s, two major barn-dance programs were established, the *National Barn Dance* on WLS transmitting from Chicago to a very large part of the country and the *Grand Ole Opry* out of Nashville. Although the show from the Windy City would cease operations in 1960 after a thirty-six year run, the *Opry* continues strong to this day.

The founder of the *Grand Ole Opry* was George D. Hay, a no-nonsense individual nicknamed the Solemn Ol' Judge for his reserved ways. However, he was a skilled broadcaster who understood the basic principles of marketing. For twenty-five years, he guided the *Opry* through the Depression, World War II, a musician's union strike and stiff competition from WLS, but managed to increase the popularity of the institution tenfold. He was a master at featuring the best country music talent on his show, as well as bringing up new artists to keep everything fresh. He was elected to the Country Music Hall of Fame for his pioneering efforts.

Some of the early stars of the *Opry* included pioneers Uncle Dave Macon and Dr. Humphrey Bate and His Possum Hunters. As well, DeFord Bailey, Sam and Kirk McGee, Roy Acuff and His Smoky Mountain Boys, the Vagabonds, Arthur Smith, Jimmy Wakely, the Chuck Wagon Gang, Ernest Tubb, Red Foley, Merle Travis, and others starred on the program. Of note, the *Opry* was a wide open affair and although it did have the best country music had to offer, there was an equal side devoted to comedy routines and early elements of vaudeville.

The movies were a visual extension of what radio could do. Hollywood, in its infancy, was always keen on making any picture that could make the studios money. One of the staples from the 1930s through the mid–1950s was the B western movies that made stars out of Gene Autry, Roy Rogers and Dale Evans, among others. Many of the Saturday matinee idols were country musicians.

The movie industry forced a change in how the country entertainer was perceived by the public. Country musicians began appearing on stage in full cowboy regalia, spurs, and ten-gallon hats. The movie cowboy figures also expanded the parameters of the traditional hillbilly song to increase its popularity. There was a show tune, pop element in the material that the actors sang in the western movies. It presented a much different style than what had existed in the hills for three hundred years.

The Cowboy and Radio years were a golden era that emphasized a much simpler time. It is an era that is fondly remembered and still draws attention in the modern society. For every big star there were hundreds who performed stunts, had minor roles and never cracked the lead roles.

Those featured in this section were the stars of the cowboy radio and movie era.

Ken Maynard was the first cowboy movie star and had his start in the silent era. Although others that came after him would eclipse his efforts, he set the stage for others to follow.

Roy Acuff was a big radio star and, with his Smoky Mountain Boys, was one of the most influential artists of the 1930s. A talented musician, he was considered one of the best fiddlers in the business.

Wilf Carter was one of the first Canadians to make an impact in country music. He was a big radio star known as Montana Slim and his later role in the movies sealed his place in country music history.

Tex Ritter was one of the most popular motion picture cowboys. He would later move on to record a string of top ten hits. He also had his start in radio.

Gene Autry was the King of the Singing Cowboys and defined the role. He was a talented individual who would later fade from the scene to look after his burgeoning business empire.

Red Foley would be one of the hosts of the *Grand Ole Opry* and that would open doors for him. He would go on to record a string of unforgettable hits.

Roy Rogers broke into radio and the movies as a single figure, but would later marry Dale Evans after meeting her on a set. Their on-screen chemistry proved a winning formula. Later, they had a hit TV show in the infancy of that medium.

Hank Snow was another Canadian who was a huge hit in his native country before striking it big in the United States. He appeared on radio and in the movies and eventually became a fixture on the *Grand Ole Opry*.

Merle Travis was one of the most important guitar stylists of country music. His playing over the radio waves influenced generations of aspiring six stringers and spilled into other styles.

Eddy Arnold was one of the most treasured performers at the *Grand Ole Opry* with a commercial voice that helped him sell more records than anyone else before the arrival of Garth Brooks.

# KEN MAYNARD (1895–1973)
## *Wagon Master*

The mythical West was a magical place that held and continues to hold a fascination in American folklore. There remains a universal appeal in the wide open skies, the fresh air, and the tales that emerged from the frontier conquered by the hardy pioneers that helped build the nation. The romanticism of the West was something Hollywood cashed in on in the 1930s that tied in neatly with country music as the industry branched out after the stock market crash. The singing cowboy was a new breed of hero to worship and the first one was known as the Wagon Master, Ken Maynard.

Ken Maynard was born July 21, 1895, in Vevay, Indiana. In his youth, he was more interested in riding horses and practicing his various roping tricks so he could work on the rodeo circuit than concentrating on developing his musical abilities. He had a good voice and sang in the church choir, but his ambitions were pointed to a different career.

As a young man he made his way out West, where he became a genuine rodeo champion and trick rider. He also worked for Buffalo Bill and the Ringling Brothers Wild West shows. These varied experiences would serve him well for his later career in films. Although he had a promising future in working on the circuit, he had greater ambitions: he wanted to be a movie star.

He made it to California just when the movie industry was in its infancy. With his dashing good looks, riding skills and cowboy mannerisms, he found work immediately. By the end of the decade he had worked in almost twenty movies of both the silent and talking picture variety. However, the best was yet to come.

In 1929, he appeared in *The Wagon Master* and became the first cowboy actor to sing on the big screen. The idea became a sensation and his stardom was assured for the rest of the next decade. On the side he recorded eight authentic country songs for Columbia studios, the only time he ever cut any material. But those eight tunes went a long way in ensuring his place among singing cowboys.

But his real work was in films and he returned to that medium with a vengeance beginning in the 1930s. He won back-to-back titles as the highest money maker of Westerns in 1936 and 1937, the initial years that the poll existed. These would be the highlights of his years on film, because by the end of the decade, Gene Autry, Roy Rogers, Tex Ritter and a host of others had begun to overshadow him.

Although he made a couple of films in the 1940s, by this time Maynard's reign as a singing cowboy was over. He retired and on March 23, 1973, in Woodland Hills, California, Ken Maynard, the first singing cowboy died.

Ken Maynard was the first of a breed of country singers that would tie the genre with the movies. Although he might not have been the best of the singing cowboys, he opened the doors for others. He was a pioneer and set down the initial parameters of the role. All others that followed him were patterned after his initial efforts.

He was popular in the movies because he could do his own stunts that truly amazed the Saturday matinee crowd. He rode his sturdy and trusty horse, Tarzan, in the face of danger and emerged triumphantly. For a decade he starred on the big screen and then returned to the rodeo circuit. He would later appear in other films, but not as the lead role. He also performed at rodeos and state fairs long after his era in films was over.

He appeared in nearly a hundred movies as a lead actor and in smaller roles. He even produced and directed a number of the films he was in, but he is remembered mostly for his acting. Later, his brother Kermit would also go to Hollywood and become a singing cowboy to some acclaim.

A partial list of the movies he starred in includes *Man Who Won* (his first), *The Demon Rider, North Star* (his first starring role), *The Haunted Range, Gun Gospel, The Land Beyond the Law, Upland Rider, Glorious Trail, The Wagon Master* (his first as producer), *Tombstone Canyon, False Faces, Texas Gunfighter, King of the Arena, Six Shootin' Sheriff,* and *Flaming Lead* (his last in the 1930s). Later, in the 1940s, he would star in *Westward Bound, Blazing Guns, Arizona Whirlwind* and his last of the decade, *White Stallion*.

Twenty-five years after his last picture, he returned in 1972 in *Buck and the Preacher*. He would also star in *Big Foot* in a minor role a year later. In 1992, he made an archival appearance in the documentary *Western Trailers*. He is credited as a screenwriter for the movie *Heir to Trouble* released in 1936. Throughout all of the aforementioned movies, he sang and performed his rope tricks with sheer skill.

Maynard was never a great singer, nor was he particularly a talented instrumentalist. However, in many of the over 300 films that he starred in, he played the fiddle, strummed the banjo and guitar, and sang, providing musical interludes between the action sequences. Of course, he could throw a punch with the best of them, and his earlier training on the rodeo circuit served him well since he could ride and do rope tricks. In many ways, he was destined to star in the movies as a singing cowboy.

Although his formal recording career was brief, he sang hundreds of tunes that were scattered throughout the numerous films he appeared in. If this is taken into account then his catalog is quite extensive. Many of these songs were later collected and put on disc, but it was after his career as a singing cowboy was long over and he was unable to capitalize on it.

However, Maynard's place in country music is assured for four different reasons. One, he was the first cowboy to sing on film in *The Wagon Master* in 1929 (although accounts of this first feat is debated). Two, he was the first to use a western song as a film title in *The Strawberry Roan*, in 1933. Three, he was the first to introduce Gene Autry in films as a singer in the production *In Old Sante Fe* in 1934; and fourth, his 1930 recording session included eight traditional country songs.

He taught the legendary cowboy-actor John Wayne how to perform various feats. But more importantly, Maynard's action films set a precedent that still exists in Hollywood today. The action man remains popular and recent heroes such as Jean-Claude Van Damme, Sylvester Stallone, and Arnold Schwarzenegger can all trace their roots back to Maynard.

Maynard also made an impact on Clint Eastwood. Long before he made his tough guy, Dirty Harry, a household name, Clint earned a living making his famed spaghetti westerns, a series of low budget action flicks. On some of these, including *Paint Your Wagon*, Eastwood sang a few songs.

Ken Maynard was also a Hollywood legend. He made and lost several fortunes, courted many pretty ladies, and became one of the first matinee idols. He would ride big and tall in the saddle in thousands of theatres across the country, endearing himself in the hearts of millions of young boys and girls. Although he wasn't the best, during his reign (1922–1945), he was one of the most popular.

Ken Maynard was the original singing cowboy and opened the floodgates for all to follow. Although he never achieved the fame of John Wayne, Gene Autry or Roy Rogers, in his day he was something special. He managed to tie a different brand of country music to the movies as the Wagon Master.

## Discography

*The American Boy's Favorite Cowboy*, Columbia.
*Anthology of American Folk Music.*
*Singing Cowboys in the Movies.*
*Western Cowboy Ballads and Songs.*

# ROY ACUFF (1903–1992)
## *Wabash Cannonball*

Like other musical styles, country music has had its fair share of one hit wonders. Those unable to follow up on their initial breakthrough quickly faded from the scene, unlike those that were able to place songs constantly on the charts. One individual thrived on the pressure of producing top tunes and built a very successful career after breaking through with his unique version of "Wabash Cannonball." His name was Roy Acuff.

Roy Claxton Acuff was born on September 15, 1903, in Maynardsville, Tennessee, the son of a Baptist minister. Although he did learn how to play the harmonica and jew's harp when a boy, his teenage years were devoted to his athletic pursuits, for which he earned a number of letters while in high school. He was a formidable ball player, a star in the minor leagues, and almost made it to the majors with the New York Yankees. But fate stepped in and Acuff fell ill with severe sunstroke that put an end to his dreams of a major league baseball career.

After he recuperated from his illness, he decided that a career in baseball would be too stressful and turned to music for solace. He learned how to play the fiddle and became proficient enough to be hired by Dr. Haver's traveling show that toured small towns in Virginia and Tennessee. It was during this stint that he picked up invaluable performing tips that would serve him well for the rest of his career.

In 1933, he joined the Tennessee Crackerjacks, which featured Dobro player Clell Summey. Acuff was enthralled with the unique sound of the Dobro and included one in his band for the rest of his career. The Crackerjacks performed on a local radio station in Knoxville and gained widespread popularity. They later moved on to do other radio work and eventually landed on the *Merry-Go-Round*, a show that that would be a starting point for country music stars Kitty Wells and Bill Carlisle, among others.

The band toured throughout the state of Tennessee and enjoyed a loyal following for their brilliant instrumentation and their ability to entertain the crowd. In 1936, Acuff moved a step closer to achieving star status when he made his first of two sessions for Columbia Records. He recorded "The Great Speckled Bird" and "Wabash Cannonball." Both songs would make him a star overnight.

Acuff, a straight ahead entertainer with no pretenses about him, delivered each song in a simple manner that would influence hundreds of country musicians for the next sixty years. The clearness of his style was catchy and uncluttered and that made it easy for listeners to enjoy his music. The basic rhythmic sound became the essential trademark of country music.

The success of "The Great Speckled Bird" and "Wabash Cannonball" enabled Acuff to form his own band that debuted on the *Grand Ole Opry*, an essential venue for anyone that wanted to make it big in country music. His group, the Smoky Mountain Boys, were an instant hit and for the next fifty years plus, Acuff would be a standard performer on the most popular country music show in the nation.

There was something folksy in their sound that endeared them to the *Grand Ole Opry* audience and assured they would record on a consistent basis. He was able to connect with listeners with his sparse vocals and fine musicianship in a way others were not able to do. In a short time, Roy Acuff and His Smoky Mountain Boys climbed the heap of the country bands to assume the number one position.

The lineup of the Smoky Mountain Boys remained intact for the most part, although there were some changes. One of the most important additions was Pete (Bashful Brother Oswald) Kirby, an excellent Dobro player as well possessor of a high pitched voice that proved a perfect counterpart to Acuff's dry delivery. The partnership would go a long way in helping the group maintain their star status.

Acuff enjoyed a great decade in the 1940s as a true country superstar. He toured on a regular basis and recorded hundreds of sides, including the major hits "The Wreck on the Highway," "The Precious Jewel," "Beneath That Lonely Mound of Clay," "Fireball Mail," "Night Train to Memphis," "Pins and Needles," and "Low and Lonely." He became the most popular entertainer at the *Grand Ole Opry*, replacing Uncle Dave Macon, who had held the title of undisputed king for over two decades.

It was also in the 1940s that Acuff realized that the money to be made in music was in the title rights to a song, publishing and the royalties. He formed a company with Fred Rose entitled Acuff-Rose that became one of the most important music publishing companies in country music history. At one time they owned the rights to the songs of Hank Williams, the Louvin Brothers, Don Gibson, Roy Orbison, the Everly Brothers, John D. Loudermilk, Felice Bryant, Redd Stewart and Pee Wee King, including his number one hit "Tennessee Waltz."

Fred Rose, who was an integral part of the Acuff story, was born in Evansville, Indiana, on August 24, 1897. He learned how to play piano and eventually made his way to Chicago, where he recorded for Brunswick and other labels. He even recorded with Fats Waller, the mischievous jazz pianist. Rose played in Paul Whiteman's Orchestra during his heyday, then quickly formed a duo with singer Elmo Tanner.

Rose then moved into radio and had his own show in the Windy City in the 1930s for the CBS label. All along he had been writing songs and provided Sophie Tucker with "Red Hot Mama" and "Deed I Do." He then traveled throughout the country and penned songs for films, including a good number of them sung by Gene Autry. He met Acuff around this time and they established their company. In the late 1940s, he turned over his duties to his son Wesley, in order to manage the career of Hank Williams, Sr.

Fred Rose died in Nashville on December 1, 1954, after making enormous contributions to country music as a songwriter, publisher, producer and executive. His role in the emergence of the genre as a major force was recognized in 1961 when he became one of the first three members (Hank Williams and Jimmy Rodgers were the other two) to be elected to the Country Music Hall of Fame. In his day, Rose was responsible for writing such hits as "Be Honest with Me," "Blues Eyes Crying in the Rain," "Tears on My Pillow, " "Kaw-Liga," "I'll Never Get Out of This World Alive," "Crazy Heart," "Take These Chains from My Heart," "Texarkana Baby," and "Settin' the Woods on Fire," among others.

There were triumphs and failures in the 1940s for Acuff. In 1944 and again in 1946 he ran for governor of Tennessee but failed to get past the primaries. Finally, in 1948, he won the Republican primary but didn't win the election. This attempt at branching out into politics only added to his popularity, since he was one of the few artists able to successfully combine careers in two very distinct fields. In 1948, he established his Dunbar Cave Resort, a folk music park that proved to be a very successful business venture.

Acuff kept rolling on throughout the 1950s and 1960s although his records didn't sell as well as they had in the past. But he was able to expand his publishing empire during this time and his tours continued to draw people. As well, he remained the king of the *Grand Ole Opry*, performing there when his other duties allowed him to.

In 1965, a terrible car accident sidelined him for a few months, but he returned to touring. He concentrated on the performance side of his career and as a result his recording output suffered. Acuff even made a round to the Vietnam war front in the late 1960s. But by the end of the decade he gave up life on the road and decided to perform solely on the *Grand Ole Opry*.

Ill health and the deaths of his wife, as well as pianist Jimmie Riddle and fiddler Howdy Forrester, both longtime mainstays in his band, slowed him down. He recorded "The Precious Jewel" with Charlie Louvin, the last charting record of his long, illustrious career.

On November 23, 1992, Roy Acuff, the great country artist with the distinct voice and particular touch on the fiddle, died.

Roy Acuff was a country music institution. His contributions to the genre are enormous and almost immeasurable. His influence, his legacy, his business savvy all proved that he was an invaluable contributor and musical force in the entertainment industry.

Acuff was a talented musician, although he never gained widespread acclaim for his abilities. He was such a solid practitioner of the fiddle that he could play any country tune or take any other song and make it sound country. There was a beauty to his playing, a simplified approach that echoed all the way back to the roots of the genre to where it had all begun with the rural people. Because he played the instrument so simply, he made it look too easy and therefore was never really appreciated.

Acuff was a capable singer with a particular element in his voice that allowed him to reach a large audience. As with his fiddling, it is a credit to the man that he never tried to sing or play something he couldn't handle and remained within his personal boundaries. This honesty and straightforward approach sealed his legend.

He was also a savvy business man and with the help of Fred Rose wrestled the rights of much country music away from the big publishers in New York and left them to the Southern folk where they belonged. He preserved the authenticity of the style by making sure the Acuff-Rose company held the rights to as many songs as possible. In an industry with such humble beginnings, it is a tribute to both men that they possessed the vision and savvy to help build country music into the multi-billion dollar enterprise it is today.

With a career that spanned seven decades, it is not surprising that he had a large influence over a number of artists. A partial list includes Frankie Lee, Bill Anderson, Eddy Arnold, Little Jimmy Dickens, Lefty Frizzell, Clinton Gregory, George Jones, Melba Montgomery, Ray Price, Johnny Russell, Carl Butler, Stoney Cooper, Ira Louvin, Larry McNeely, Hank Williams, Ty England, the Dixon Brothers, Moe Bandy and Joe Stampley. In reality, just about anyone that arrived on the country music scene beginning in the 1940s was touched by the Acuff magic.

He also worked with a number of artists, including the Nitty Gritty Dirt Band, Joe Zinkan, Jimmy Riddle, Curly Rhodes, Richard Weize, Howdy Forrester, Pete "Oswald" Kirby, Randy Scruggs, Roy M. "Junior" Husky, Benny Martin, Earl Scruggs, Ray Crisp, and Louis Innis. As a member of the *Grand Ole Opry* for fifty-two years, he also performed with hundreds more country artists and there is scarcely one figure in the genre that he didn't share the stage with.

He gave the world a number of treasures, including "The Great Speckled Bird," "Wabash Cannonball," "Wreck on the Highway," "Fireball Mail," "Night Train to Memphis," "Pins and Needles," "Low and Lonely," "So Many Times," "Come and Knock," "Freight Train Blues," "The Precious Jewel," and "Beneath That Lonely Mound of Clay." Every song that he recorded was special because of his immense talent, but of his many hits it was "Wabash Cannonball" that truly established his style and launched his career.

Acuff also appeared in a number of films, including *Grande Ole Opry, Hi Neighbor, My Darling Clementine, Sing, Neighbor, Sing, Cowboy Canteen,* and *Night Train to Memphis.* Although he never made as big a splash in the movies as Gene Autry or Roy Rogers, Acuff could hold his own. He utilized his appearances in the movies and on the radio to expand his fan base.

In 1962, Ray Acuff became the first living country music artist to be elected to the Country Music Hall of Fame and fourth member overall. It is impossible to think that the genre would be such a powerful industry if it not had been for his contributions. Without a doubt, Roy Acuff, the Wabash Cannonball, was a true country icon.

## Discography

*Fly Birdie Fly '39–'41*, Rounder 5524.
*Songs of the Saddle*, CBS 9013.
*Songs of the Smoky Mountains*, Capitol 617.
*Favorite Hymns*, MGM 3707.
*Great Speckled Bird*, Harmony 7082.
*Old Time Barn Music*, CBS 9010.
*That Glory Bound Train*, Harmony 7294.
*Once More It's Roy Acuff*, Hickory 109.
*Hymn Time*, MGM 4044.
*Songs of the Smoky Mountains*, Capitol 1870.
*Country Music Hall of Fame*, Capitol 1870.
*Star of the Grand Ole Opry*, Hickory 113.
*The World Is His Stage*, Hickory 114.
*Roy Acuff Sings American Folk Songs*, Hickory 115.
*Hand-Clapping Songs*, Hickory 117.
*The Voice of Country Music*, Capitol 2276.

*The Great Roy Acuff*, Harmony 7342.
*Great Train Songs*, Hickory 125.
*Roy Acuff*, Metro 508.
*Waiting for My Call to Glory*, Harmony 7376.
*Roy Acuff Sings Hank Williams*, Hickory 134.
*Roy Acuff Time*, Hickory 156.
*I Saw the Light*, Hickory 158.
*Sunshine Special*, Hilltop 6090.
*Time*, Hickory 156.
*Back in the Country*, Hickory 4507.
*Smokey Mountain Memories*, Hickory 4517.
*That's Country*, Hickory 4521.
*Steamboat Whistle Blues*, Rounder 5523.
*So Many Times*, MCA 20466.
*Fireball Mail*, Proper 1379.
*Wabash Cannonball*, Intersound 5008.
*The Great Roy Acuff*, Capitol 2103.
*Famous Opry Favorites*, Hickory 139.
*Living Legend*, Hickory 145.
*Treasure of Country Hits*, Hickory 147.
*The Best of Roy Acuff*, Capitol 91621.
*Why Is*, Hickory 162.
*Greatest Hits*, Columbia 1034.
*Night Train*, Harmony 11043.
*King of Country Music, All Time Greatest Hits*, Hickory 109.
*King of Country Music*, TeeVee 6001.
*Columbia Historic Edition*, Columbia 39998.
*The Best of Roy Acuff*, Curb 77454.
*The Essential Roy Acuff (1936–1949)*, Columbia 48956.
*King of Country Music*, Bear Family 15652.
*Greatest Hits*, Cema Special Markets 56694.
*King of Country Music (1936–1947)*, ASV/Living Era 5244.
*R.C. Cola Radio Shows, Vol. 3* [live], RME 300.
*R.C. Cola Radio Shows, Vol. 1*, RME 199.
*R.C. Cola Radio Shows, Vol. 2*, RME 299.
*R.C. Cola Radio Shows, Vol. 4*, RME 400.
*Country Music Hall of Fame: 1962*, King 3816.
*20 Greatest Songs*, Varese 066224.
*The Crazy Tennessean*, Catfish 200.
*Hear the Mighty Rush of the Engine*, Jasmine 3532.
*The Good News According to Mr. Roy Acuff*, Audium 8128.
*Oh Boy Classics Presents Roy Acuff*, Oh Boy 409.
*Beautiful Brown Eyes*, Proper 1378.
*Great Speckled Bird*, Proper 1377.
*Wabash Cannonball*, Proper 1380.
*Once More It's Roy Acuff/King of Country Music*, Ace 988.
*Very Best of Roy Acuff: Wabash Cannonball*, Collectables 9406.
*Gospel Favorites*, Music Mill 70041.
*King of Country Music*, Proper Box 70.
*Sings American Folk Songs/Hand Clapping Gospel Songs*, Hickory/Ace 999.
*The Essential Roy Acuff*, Columbia 90906.
*The Best of Roy Acuff*, Music Hill 70044.

*Greatest Gospel Songs*, Curb 78926.
*Country Hit Parade*, Direct Source 52752.
*Country Music Legends*, RCR 650.

# WILF CARTER (1904–1996)

## Montana Slim

Although Canada is a large territory, it has produced only a small number of important country artists. However, despite the relatively few authentic musicians who have emerged from the Great White North, there is definite quality. One of the earliest and best earned the nickname Montana Slim. His name was Wilf Carter.

Wilf Carter was born Wilfred Arthur Charles Carter on December 18, 1904, in Port Hilford, Nova Scotia, into a poor, rural family. His father was a Baptist minister who preached a steady life of God, hard work, and strict rules. But young Wilf dreamed of adventures in the wild west and riding horses on the open range. His reveries often took place in the fields and orchards where he toiled long hours in all kinds of weather in order to help support the family.

Before his teens, he joined a traveling show that introduced him to country music and the yodeling singing style. However, his ambition of becoming a famous entertainer seemed like an impossible dream. At sixteen, he decided to strike out on his own, against the wishes of his austere father. But, it was essential that he find his own way in the world and he ended up running away from home.

He drifted to the East Coast of the United States with few marketable skills and some big dreams. He struggled for some time before returning to Nova Scotia. He soon realized that his ambitions would not be fulfilled in his native town. So he ventured out to the Canadian West with its infinite blue skies, appreciation for rural traditions, and overwhelming sense of freedom. Carter knew that he had found his home.

It was in the province of Alberta that he first learned how to ride a horse, a skill that would one day serve him well. It was also around this time that the shy young man started to sing at social events such as square dances. Much of his style was based on the yodeling he had learned while traveling in the medicine shows as a young boy. He often sang solo, but sometimes played the autoharp, despite his limited skills on the instrument.

He made a life for himself out West that included work on the rodeo circuit. He supplemented his income by singing on the streets for spare change. His fortunes improved when he finally landed a job on a radio station in Calgary, Alberta, that broke open for him a number of opportunities. He was signed to CBC, the leading radio station in Canada. He supplied songs to a Central publishing house and conducted tours for the CPR line, entertaining passing easterners with a desire for a taste of the western lifestyle. In an attempt to shore up his weak instrumental abilities, he taught himself how to play guitar and became proficient.

He criss-crossed the country, going from West to East and back again, singing and playing his guitar. He became a notable star and eventually was allowed to record some of his songs for the RCA label. His first record, "My Swiss Moonlight Lullaby," with "The Capture of Albert Johnson" on the other side, became a hit from coast to coast. But true stardom was still some time away and he continued to earn a meager living as a traveling and singing cowboy.

In the depths of the Depression, Carter was eking out an existence until he began to broadcast on CBS radio from New York. He was nicknamed Montana Slim and his show became very popular, but three years later after starring on the station he was dismissed. A severe automobile accident coupled with the outbreak of war destroyed any momentum that he had built up. He didn't record and performed very little until after the Second World War.

By 1947, he had recovered enough to pick up the threads of his once promising career. He landed a contract with RCA Victor stateside, and relocated to New Jersey. He also made his first and only appearance on the *Grand Ole Opry*. The fact that he didn't become a regular on the most popular country music show that was essential to anyone trying to make a living in the industry certainly hurt his career ambitions. However, Carter persevered.

He continued to work both sides of the border, as he had done for the past decade, and managed to earn a sufficient living. Eventually, his touring would include his two daughters as back up singers in the early 1950s. When his contract with RCA expired, he signed to Decca Records. The change in labels didn't do anything to pump up his slumping sales and eventually Decca dropped him. But Carter could always record in Canada and this became his base where he did much of the promotion work himself, and even financed the sessions.

For the next decade and a half, Carter split his time between Canada and the United States. He was able to forge enough interest on both sides of the border in order to keep his career rolling on. Most of his writing and recording was for RCA, but he moonlighted with other companies. By the late 1960s he toured and recorded sporadically; he continued to slow down in the following decades.

By the early 1990s, Carter entered his eighth and last decade as a performer. On Dec. 5, 1996, in Scottsdale, Arizona, he passed away at the age of 92 after being diagnosed with stomach cancer.

Wilf Carter was one of the first singing cowboys. He was a legitimate radio star although he never appeared in films. While he did achieve a generous degree of fame, he never reached his full potential. There always seemed to be something holding him back, a piece of bad luck, or a foul-up of his own doing. He could have become much more popular, but one cannot dismiss the fact that he sang country songs for over eight decades.

Although he wasn't the first to be influenced by Jimmie Rodgers, Wilf was one of the Singing Brakeman's genuine disciples with his traditional yodeling style. While many who fell under the spell of the great Mississippi yodeler eventually emerged from his shadow, arguably, Carter, never did. He remained in the same mold throughout his career and that is another of the reasons he never achieved greater acknowledgement.

However, he is one of the few country music stars of the early generation to lead two successful careers. He cleverly maintained two personas; in Canada, he was Wilf Carter, and in the United States, he was Montana Slim. Very few artists have ever been able to boast of solid success in different countries using a pseudonym.

Carter was also a noted songwriter and penned over five hundred cowboy tunes, creating a healthy catalog. He sang most of them himself but countless musicians, including Gene Autry, Roy Rogers and Hank Snow, among others, covered many of his songs. Although he never broke through with his numerous recordings under a variety of labels, including RCA, Bluebird, Decca, and Starday, he sold enough records to achieve a respectable web of popularity.

Carter added his own chapter to country music with his friendly, straightforward manner of singing and playing. There was an honesty in his music that was refreshing and enjoyable. He inspired a number of later Canadian artists, including Hank Snow and Anne Murray, among others.

The man known as Montana Slim was eventually elected to the Nashville Songwriters Hall of Fame in 1971. For twenty years he was a prominent network radio star with his dual personalities. In retrospect, the Wilf Carter story is one of a boy with a great imagination who dreamed of life as a cowboy in the wild, open American West and achieved these goals.

## Discography

*Wilf Carter/Montana Slim*, Camden Ca 527.
*I'm Ragged, But I'm Right*, Decca 8917.
*Reminiscin'*, Camden CA-668.

*Wilf Carter as Montana Slim*, Starday 300.
*Wilf Carter*, Starday 389.
*No Letter Today*, Camden 2171.
*Have a Nice Day*, RCA Victor 2313.
*Collector's*, RCA 7129.
*My Oklahoma Rose*, Cowgirlboy 5058.
*The Dynamite Trail: The Decca Years*, 4092.
*32 Wonderful Years*, Camden CA-846.
*Montana Slim*, Camden 0694.
*A Prairie Legend*, Bear Family 15754.
*The Golden Years*, Collector's 00812.
*Cowboy Songs*, Bear Family 5197.
*I'm Hittin' the Trail*, ASV/Living 5593.

# TEX RITTER (1907–1974)

## Lone Star Cowboy

When Hollywood discovered that it could generate a tremendous amount of money making films that starred singing cowboys for relatively little cost, it created a rush among aspiring actors and singers. They arrived from all over the country as far east as New York, as well as Cincinnati, Oklahoma, Virginia, and Texas. One of those who answered the call of the studios was known as the Lone Star Cowboy, Tex Ritter.

Tex Ritter was born Woodward Maurice Ritter on January 12, 1907, in Murval, Texas. He developed a love for authentic cowboy songs and ballads at an early age, but a career in music seemed an afterthought. A very brilliant student, Ritter had ambitions to be a lawyer and attended the University of Texas as well as Northwestern before abandoning his studies for an acting career.

He moved to New York and found work in a number of stage productions, including *Green Grow the Lilacs* in 1930. He found further roles as an actor on the popular radio series *Cowboy Tom's Round-Up*, as well, he co-hosted the WHN *Barn Dance* with fellow aspiring country music star Ray Whitley. In 1934, Ritter began his recording career with ARC.

But it was the glamorous life of Gene Autry that lured Ritter to Hollywood and because of his acting experience on Broadway he was an instant hit on the big screen. From 1936 to 1945, he appeared in over sixty cowboy films and became a bona fide star. He sang and acted in *Western Song of the Gringo, Trouble in Texas, Take Me Back to Oklahoma*, and in one of his last films, *The Texas Rangers*. He was a matinee idol.

With the reign of the singing cowboy in the movies starting to wane, he moved on to a successful recording career. Although his first attempts as far back as 1934—when he recorded "Good Bye Old Paint," "A-riding Old Paint," "Every Day in the Saddle," and "Rye Whiskey"—had failed, he had kept chipping away. His later efforts for Decca in 1935–1939 also proved to be unsuccessful. But in 1942, three years before he would quit his acting career, he signed to the new Capitol label.

It was finally magic time because for the next few years he would score a number of hits with material that ranged from cowboy tunes to country love songs and everything in between. His first song, "Jingle, Jangle, Jingle," released in 1942, was a huge hit. He followed that up with "Jealous Heart," "There's a New Moon Over My Shoulder," "I'm Wasting My Tears on You," "You Two Time Me One Time Too Often," "Rye Whiskey" (a re-recording), "Green Grow the Lilacs," "You Will Have to Pay," "Rock and Rye," "Daddy's Last Letter," "High Noon," "The Wayward Wind," and "I Dreamed of a Hillbilly Heaven."

He became one of the best selling country artists of the 1940s and with his band, the Texans, traveled all over the country. After years of singing on stage and in the movies, Ritter had sharpened his accessible, pleasant voice into a fine commercial weapon. There were few who could match the number of hits he poured out during the decade.

By 1950, Ritter was clearly established as a giant of country music, but didn't rest on his laurels. He co-hosted, with Johnny Bond, the much beloved *Town Hall Party* from 1953 to 1960. The series proved incredibly popular and only added to Ritter's already glowing reputation. During this decade, he also sang the theme song of the movie *High Noon* that won an Academy Award in 1953.

He continued to roll on in the 1960s, touring extensively with his band. He also served as president of the Country Music Association, which fueled further political ambitions to run for higher office. In 1970, he lost a bid for the U.S. Senate. By this time he had moved to Nashville, where he became a fixture on the *Grand Ole Opry*, and also pushed diligently to create a Country Music Hall of Fame that eventually became a reality.

On January 2, 1974, while bailing one of his band members out of jail Ritter suffered a heart attack and was later pronounced dead at the local Nashville hospital.

Tex Ritter was one of the most important of the singing cowboys and because of his diversity enjoyed an unbroken reign of popularity from the 1930s until his death in the 1970s. He was an actor, politician, singer, bandleader, composer, lover of authentic country songs, and inspiration to millions of singers. In many ways his popularity was as large as the state of Texas itself.

Although he didn't possess a powerful, clear voice, Ritter had his own special style. He was able to inject an emotional touch into the songs that he recorded with his unique accent, odd slurs and unique phrasing. There was also a healthy dose of honesty in his voice as well as a dual edge. He could produce a plaintive moan, as well as a gruff bark that gave the material a definite edge. There was enough distinctive quality in his voice to make him a legend.

Fans that loved him in the movies bought millions of his records and this was one of the secrets to his star appeal as a singer of country music. He already had a built-in audience when in 1942 he began to belt out those lonesome cowboy tunes that touched a particular nerve in listeners. As well, his behind the scenes insistence that a country music hall of fame be established made him a favorite with his fellow artists. More than anything else Ritter demonstrated a simple, but very emotional, love for authentic country music.

Tex Ritter was an influence on generations of country music singers and continues to exert a presence more than thirty years after his death. A number of Texans, including Bob Wills, Milton Brown, Bill Boyd, Hank Thompson and the Brazos Valley Boys, Commander Cody and His Lost Planet Airman, Ted Daffan, Floyd Tillman, Al Dexter, Ernest Tubb, Ray Price, George Jones, Johnny Horton, Lefty Frizzell, and Jim Reeves, all copied Ritter in some form.

However, of all the country artists that he touched, he made the largest impact on a young Johnny Cash. The man in black—who would eventually star in movies but never enjoyed the same film success as Ritter—stole a page or two from his idol. They shared the same stubborn streak, the same gruff vocal delivery, and the same affection for country music. In many ways, Cash picked up where Ritter left off.

Ritter's name has also survived through his namesake, John, who followed in his father's footsteps and became an actor. He starred in the highly successful television shows *Three's Company* and *Hooperman*, among others. Although he never recorded any country songs, John continued the tradition of the Ritter family as a popular actor until his untimely death.

Along with Gene Autry, Roy Rogers, Ken Maynard, and a handful of others, Tex Ritter established the cowboy as one of the favorites of the Saturday matinee idols. During his time in films he made as much impact with his singing as anyone else and more than others. In many ways, he was born to be a singing cowboy from his earliest days growing up.

Ritter worked with a number of important country artists, including Merle Travis, Andy Parker, Wesley Tuttle, Ken Nelson, Ernest Tubb, Roy Acuff, Johnny Cash, Gene Autry, Roy Rogers, Don Law, George Jones, Chet Atkins, Frank Jones, Glen Campbell, Buck Owens, Roy Clark, Jim

Reeves, Bob Wills, Eddy Arnold and Johnny Gimble, among others. Because of his extensive travel schedule there is scarcely a country music artist that Ritter didn't perform with on the same stage. As well, he always maintained his band, called the Texans, a consistently fine outfit.

In 1964, Tex Ritter was named to the Country Music Hall of Fame, a deserved honor since he was one of the initiators of the institute. His work in the many capacities he undertook enabled him to carve out a very special niche for himself in the universe of country music. Undoubtedly, the popularity of the Lone Star Cowboy will never fade.

## Discography

*Songs from the Western Screen*, Capitol 971.
*Psalms*, Capitol 1100.
*The Lincoln Hymns*, Capitol 1562.
*Hillbilly Heaven*, Capitol 1623.
*Stan Kenton and Tex Ritter*, Capitol 1757.
*Border Affair*, Capitol 1910.
*The Friendly Voice of Tex Ritter*, Capitol 2402.
*Sweet Land of Liberty*, Capitol 2743.
*Just Beyond the Moon*, Capitol 2786.
*Sings His Hits*, Hilltop 6043.
*Tex Ritter's Wild West*, Capitol 2974.
*Bump Tiddle Dee Bum Bum!*, Capitol 2890.
*Tennessee Blues*, Hilltop 6059.
*Chuck Wagon Days*, Capitol 213.
*Love You As Big As Texas*, Hilltop 6075.
*Jamboree, Nashville Style*, La Brea 8036.
*Green, Green Valley*, Capitol 467.
*Fall Away*, Capitol 11351.
*Comin' After Jinny*, Alive 0052.
*Cowboy Favorites*, Capitol 4004.
*What Am I Bid?* [original soundtrack], MGM 4506.
*Out of the Past*, Quicksilver 5059.
*Singin' in the Saddle*, Bear Family 15231.
*God Bless America*, Cema 57223.
*Arizona Days*, MCA 20410.
*Super Country Legendary Tex Ritter*, Capitol 11037.
*An American Legend*, Capitol 11241.
*The Best of Tex Ritter*, Capitol 2595.
*The Best of the Cowboys*, Hollywood 2148.
*Conservation with a Gun*, Richmond 2148.
*Greatest Hits*, Curb 77397.
*Country Music Hall of Fame*, MCA 10188.
*Capitol Collectors Series*, Capitol 95036.
*High Noon*, Bear Family 15634.
*High Noon and Other Hits*, Bear Family 9296.
*The Ritter Vintage Collections*, Capitol 36903.
*Blood on the Saddle*, Bear Family 16260.

*Country Hits and Cowboy Classics*, Country Stars 55462.
*The Very Best of Tex Ritter*, Varese 066135.
*Sing, Cowboy, Sing*, ASV/Living Era 55400.
*Old Time Country: Portrait of Tex Ritter*, Columbia River 110077.
*Have I Stayed Away Too Long*, Bear Family 16239.
*The Best of Tex Ritter*, Capitol Special Markets 36319.
*High Noon: 1942–1952*, ASV/Living Era 5479.
*A Proper Introduction to Tex Ritter*, Proper 2049.
*The Singing Cowboy*, Legacy 205.
*Western Heritage: America's Most Loved Cowboy*, BCI 41240.

# GENE AUTRY (1907–1998)
## *The Singing Cowboy*

When it became apparent that country music was a marketable product it was only a matter of time before Hollywood cashed in. The idea of action-packed stories with musical interludes was a brainstorm that swept the country. Although a number of individuals tried to fill the role, it wasn't until the arrival of the genuine Singing Cowboy that the movie industry had found its man. His name was Gene Autry.

Orvin Gene Autry was born on September 29, 1907, in Tioga Springs, Texas. Although his mother taught him to play guitar at an early age, the young boy was much more interested in pursuing a career in baseball. Later, in his early teens, he turned to music and earned some pocket change singing in various Tioga Springs night spots. Later he would spend one entire summer with the Field Brothers' Medicine Show.

The family moved to a cattle ranch in Oklahoma some time latter and Autry was charged with walking the cattle to the railroad yard, a chore he didn't enjoy much. But after hanging around the station long enough, he learned how to work the telegraph machine and landed a job filling in for the regular telegrapher. In his spare time, he would pick up his guitar and strum a few tunes.

It was about this point in time that he first heard the records of yodeler Jimmie Rodgers and like hundreds of other aspiring vocalists he fell under the spell of the Singing Brakeman. Although he never became a great yodeler, Autry did incorporate some of his hero's stylings into his own sound. Once he had mastered the ability to sing traditional and popular songs nearly as well as his idol, Gene headed to the Big Apple.

In New York, he went directly to the offices of Victor Records (the company Rodgers recorded for) and waited for an audition. However, when he was finally able to play and sing, he was declined for lack of experience behind a microphone. Autry, an enterprising young man, was determined to shore up this weakness in his armor and went off in search of a radio job to improve his ability.

He headed to Tulsa and found work on a local radio station. He didn't remain there long because he landed a spot on the WLS *National Barn Dance*, one of the most popular country programs in the country in 1930. There he sang pop tunes, sentimental old favorites and basic hillbilly music to enthusiastic audiences. This enabled him to round out his musical education and learn a number of new songs to add to his burgeoning repertoire.

Upon his return to New York, Autry made his first records for the American Record Company. He cut mostly old favorites of a rural tradition as well as some of his own selections (he had begun to write his own material), including "That Silver-Haired Daddy of Mine," which would eventually be a million seller. Another composition, "Oklahoma's Yodelling Cowboy," sealed his fame. In the depths of the Great Depression, Autry had become one of the most popular singers in America. Songbooks, guitar instructional manuals and an authentic Gene Autry Roundup guitar became available in the Sears catalog that was delivered to millions of homes.

In many ways Autry was a cowboy and became associated with that image in the public's psyche. Although he was a folk hero in every small center in America, he was unknown in the larger, metropolitan cities. Since Hollywood hadn't invited him for a big audition, the brash young Texan took it upon himself to go to them. He was signed to a contract along with his sidekick Smiley Burnette. Because of his popularity in the hinterlands, Autry was a natural to star in the B westerns, since the target audience was the small town folk across the nation.

He debuted in *Old Santa Fe*, alongside Ken Maynard, the reigning singing cowboy at the time. Despite the fact that Autry's role in the film was only ten minutes long, he made quite an impact with his singing and playing in between the fist fights. His second film, *Mystery Mountain,* once again starring Maynard, only featured a small glimpse of Autry. It was the twelve chapter series *Phantom Empire* that ensured his stardom. In a strange science fiction flick before the genre ever caught on, Autry sang "That Silver-Haired Daddy of Mine" in eight of the twelve installments.

His fourth film, his first starring role, was *Tumbling Tumbleweeds,* accompanied by a song of the same name. It was a huge hit and within two years, Autry was the king of the B westerns. He was a hit of stellar magnitude and helped shape the industry. The movies that he starred in always portrayed him as a singing hero, the good guy always victorious over the bad guys.

No matter the depth of evil in his way, Autry always saved the day with a song on his lips. By the end of the 1930s he was the greatest hero in American pop culture and with the advent of the Second World War, he only added to his status by fighting the hated Nazis. "Autry for President" was a common slogan during the times despite the popularity of FDR. Since none of the other singing cowboys, including Dick Foran, Fred Scott, Jack Randell, and Bob Baker, could project the larger than life image that the singing cowboy could, he remained seated on his high perch. By this time Tex Ritter (Autry's only serious rival) was out of the movie game and doing quite well as a country singer.

For five years, Autry ruled the business of making westerns, but his insistence that he wasn't sharing in the wealth that the movies were making ignited his eventual fall from grace. In 1938 he walked away from the Republican studios but returned soon after. His brief absence cost him dearly because Roy Rogers had in a very short time become as big a star as Autry.

In 1942, Autry enlisted in the Army Air Corps and flew missions over the Far East and North Africa. Upon his release, Rogers had definitely replaced him as the most popular singing cowboy, but Autry still appeared in movies for Columbia, including *Sioux City Sue, Guns and Saddles, and Last of the Pony Riders*. He also was a familiar voice on radio, starring in the Melody Brand programs for years.

The decline of the B-movies began with the advent of television, but Autry was not one to be caught in such a downturn. In one of the most remarkable metamorphoses in American popular culture, Gene Autry, the greatest singing cowboy, went from film star and musician to business entrepreneur. He had begun to buy up radio stations before the war and truly built up his empire after his return from the army. He operated a series of radio and television companies, his own recording studio, a hotel chain, a music publishing firm, and in 1961 his very own baseball team, the Los Angeles Angels.

Although he continued to record songs, most of his hits in the 1950s were holiday songs, including "Rudolph the Red Nose Reindeer," "Here Comes Santa Claus," "Frosty the Snowman," and "Peter Cottontail." He also recorded some country influenced songs mixed with pop tunes and old standards. As well, he starred on Saturday morning television, endearing himself to a whole new generation of American youth.

However, as the 1950s unfolded, Autry faded from the scene to concentrate on his various business ventures. He would cut the occasional record, but his best singing and acting days were past him. He remained a cultural icon to those that had grown up watching him on the big screen and television. As well, his name appeared in the news as the owner of a major league baseball team. However, the Angels never won a World Series under his ownership.

On October 2, 1998, Gene Autry, the Singing Cowboy, died in his California home. Although his best country songs had been recorded fifty years before, the Country Music Association fondly remembered him, as did much of the world. He was an institution, a legend in many circles.

Gene Autry was a cultural icon. He is the man most responsible for bringing country music to Hollywood, thus enlarging the fan base of the country sound. He changed the image of the country singer by throwing away the stereotypical overalls and straw hat in favor of cowboy attire. He sold millions of records that comprised a variety of musical styles.

Autry accomplished so much during his lifetime that it is impossible to point out one era as dominant. He was a gifted musician and singer, a sturdy actor, and a solid businessman. As a country music artist he is remembered for his many movie roles where he sang his way in between action scenes. As well, the many hits that he recorded were mostly million sellers, including "Ghost Riders in the Sky," a song numerous artists have covered.

More than any other singing cowboy, Autry purposely projected the myth, dressing and living the part. Although John Wayne, Roy Rogers, Ken Maynard, Tex Ritter and others would also star as well as sing their way through hundreds of films, no one had Autry's touch. He was the king of the B westerns and remained so long after the genre faded away.

He was the first genuine multi-media star. After his best acting and singing days were over, he became a successful business man promoting singers. He recorded over three hundred songs, earned nine gold records, starred in close to a hundred movies, and started where Jimmie Rodgers left off.

Autry had a profound influence on Ernest Tubb, Hank Williams, Eddy Arnold, Patsy Montana, Roy Acuff, Red Foley, Hank Snow, Roy Rogers, Rex Allen, Big Jack Johnson, Marty Robbins, Johnny Tillotson, Jack Guthrie, Johnny Bond, Wilf Carter, Jimmy C. Newman, Johnny Cash, Willie Nelson and dozens of others. In truth, Autry was an influence on anyone who picked up an instrument and tried to sing a country song from the 1930s to the present day.

In 1969, he was elected to the Country Music Hall of Fame. From 1929 to 1964, there were many stars to emerge in country music, but none were able to play as many roles so successfully as Autry. But no matter his achievements, even in the business world, he was and always will be known as the singing cowboy.

# Discography

*Little Johnny Pilgrim*, CBS 83.
*Rusty, the Rocking Horse*, CBS 94.
*Stampede*, CBS 3-8009.
*The Story of Nativity*, CBS 82.
*Champion Western Adventures*, CBS 677.
*Gene Autry Sings Peter Cottontail*, CBS 2568.
*Merry Christmas*, CBS 2547.
*Rudolph the Red-Nosed Reindeer*, Grand Prix 11.
*Gene Autry at the Rodeo*, Columbia 3-8001.
*Christmas with Gene Autry*, Challenge 600.
*Melody Ranch*, Melody Ranch 101.
*Christmas Album*, Bescol 40.
*Gene Autry Sings*, Harmony 7399.
*Rudolph the Red-Nosed Reindeer*, Pitz 449.
*Back in the Saddle Again*, Sony 14380.
*Melody Ranch: A Radio Adventure*, Radiola 1048.
*Live from Madison Square Gardens*, Republic 6014.
*Everyone's a Child at Christmas*, Columbia 15767.
*Columbia Historic Edition*, Columbia 37645.
*Sounds Like Jimmie Rodgers*, ACM 019.
*Christmas Favorites*, CBS Special 15766.
*South of the Border*, Castle 219.
*Christmas Album*, Legacy 03.
*The Essential Gene Autry*, Sony 63779.
*Sings Gene Autry and Other Favorites*, Bescol 6/2.
*Portrait of an Artist*, Sound Exchange 24553.
*Christmas Classics*, Staryday 103.
*Back in the Saddle Again*, ASV/Living Era 5188.
*Blues Singer 1929–1931: Booger Rooger Saturday*, Columbia 64987.
*Gene Autry Sings Gene Autry*, Tradition.
*Western Classics, Vol. 1*, CBS 9001.
*Western Classics, Vol. 2*, CBS 9002.
*Gene Autry's Greatest Hits*, Columbia 1575.
*Greatest Hits*, Evergreen 9077.
*Gene Autry's Golden Hits* [RCA] 2623.
*Original Rudolph the Red Nosed Reindeer and Other Children's Christmas Favorites*, Harmony 9550.
*Cowboy Hall of Fame*, Republic 6012.
*Gene Autry's Great Western Hits*, Harmony 7332.
*Country Music Hall of Fame*, Columbia 01035.
*South of the Border, All American Cowboy*, Republic 6011.
*Gene Autry Back in the Saddle Again*, Encore 14380.
*Greatest Hits*, Sony 18874.
*Gene Autry Sings Santa Claus Is Coming to Town*, Laserlight 15460.
*The Essential Gene Autry*, Columbia 48957.
*A Gene Autry Christmas*, Sony 57904.
*Christmas Cowboy*, Laserlight 15460.
*Sing Cowboy Sing: The Gene Autry Collection*, Rhino 73620.
*Gene Autry: Members Edition*, United Audio 3558.
*Gene Autry with the Legendary Singing Groups of the West*, Varese 5841.

*The Singing Cowboy, Chapter One*, 5840.
*Always Your Pal, Gene Autry*, Sony 63423.
*The Singing Cowboy, Chapter Two*, Varese 5909.
*With His Little Darlin' Mary Lou*, Varese 5910.
*Last Round-Up: 25 Cowboy Classics*, ASV/Living Era 5264.
*The Ultimate Collection*, Prism 244.
*20 Greatest Movie Hits*, Varese 5990.
*Love Songs*, Varese 5991.
*Country Music Hall of Fame 1969*, King 3819.
*Gene Autry Show, Vol. 1*, Varese 066166.
*Gene Autry Show, Vol. 2*, Varese 066167.
*Gene Autry Show, Vol. 3*, Varese 066168.
*20 Golden Cowboy Hits*, TeeVee 6028.
*The Gene Autry Show: The Complete 1950s Television Recordings*, Varese 66190.
*Gene Autry at the Melody Ranch*, Collector's 1029.
*South of the Border: The Best of Gene Autry*, St. Clair 219.
*Way Out West*, Roots of Country 211230.
*That's How I Got My Start: Jimmie and the Cowboys*, Jasmine 3527.
*Favorites*, Ember 145.
*Gene Autry's Back in Texas*, Varese 066272.
*The Western Collection*, Varese 066271.
*Paradise in the Moonlight*, Arpeggio Country 4.
*Classic Sung By Two Legendary Country Singers*, Direct Source 19172.
*Old Time Country: Portrait of Gene Autry*, Columbia 110076.
*The Cowboy Is a Patriot*, Varese 066408.
*San Antonio Rose*, Legacy 165.
*The Singing Cowboy*, Allegro 100105.
*Gene Autry Sings Gene Autry*, Tradition 2210/2.
*Original Radio Broadcast: Gene Autry's Melody Ranch*, Golden Age of Radio GA-5012.
*Yellow Rose of Texas*, Bear Family BFX 15204.

# RED FOLEY (1910–1968)
## *The Mainstream Voice*

The pages of country music history are filled with artists who made enormous contributions to the genre mostly by following their own paths. Although influenced by previous performers, these figures cast aside the present ideas of the genre to inject it with their individualism. One of those figures was known as the mainstream voice for his ability to smooth out the edges of hillbilly music and increase its popularity. His name was Red Foley.

Clyde Julian Foley was born on June 17, 1910, in Blue Lick, Kentucky. As a youngster, he divided his time between music and sports. He learned how to play the guitar and harmonica before his teens, and was a star athlete in high school and in college. But more importantly to the world of country music, he won a statewide contest when he was seventeen that pointed him towards his future direction.

After graduation, he spent the next three years honing his skills as well as pursuing his favorite sports. It was in college that he drew the attention of a talent scout that recruited him to be on the *National Barn Dance* on Chicago's WLS ratio station that broadcasted to most of the country. It was a huge break for Foley and he dutifully moved to the Windy City.

On the program he joined John Lair's Cumberland Ridge Runners. For the next seven years, Foley would increase his star magnitude as part of the radio show and as a member of the Runners. He helped popularize the show, giving it much stability in the market with his mainstream voice. However, all good things must come to an end and in 1937, Foley left the *Barn Dance* to become instrumental in yet another radio show.

Along with Lair, the two launched the *Renfro Valley Barn Dance* that showcased Foley's extensive talents. Two years later he broke new barriers as the first country artist to have his own radio program. It was called *Avalon Time* and his co-host was Red Skelton, the slapstick comedian who would go on to host his own television show. Foley also hosted *Boone County Jamboree* on Cincinnati's WLW radio station and also toured the country performing at small events and venues.

The *Barn Dance* welcomed him back and he stayed for another seven-year stint. He also stretched out into the movies, where he starred with Tex Ritter in *The Pioneers*. Foley would participate in other movies as a solo act as well as with his touring band, the Hoosier Hotshots. The exposure he received as a film star only increased his popularity.

Despite being acknowledged as a genuine radio star, Foley's few recordings had not sold well up to this point with the exception of "Old Shep." But in 1945, he was hired by the *Grand Ole Opry* to host the *Prince Albert Show*, replacing a disgruntled Roy Acuff. It was exactly the recipe for success he needed because from this point on Foley would sell millions of records and just about every song he recorded became a bona fide hit.

On the Decca label, "Tennessee Saturday Night," "Candy Kisses," "Tennessee Polka," "Sunday Down in Tennessee," "Chattanoogie Shoe Shine Boy," Steal Away," "Just a Closer Walk with Thee," "Peace in the Valley," "Birmingham Bounce," "Mississippi," "Cincinnati Dancing Pig," "Hot Rod Race," "Alabama Jubilee," "Midnight," "Don't Let the Stars Get in Your Eyes," "Hot Toddy," "Shake a Hand," "Jilted," "Hearts of Stone," and "A Satisfied Mind" all became million sellers. In the 1950s he was one of the most popular singers on the circuit with material that ranged from true country hits to rockabilly and gospel. Among his other songs that he recorded was the first of many duets with Kitty Wells, "One by One."

In 1951, after his wife committed suicide, Foley cut back on his touring. Three years later he left the *Opry* and moved to Missouri, where he hosted the *Ozark Jubilee*, one of the first successful country television series. When that show was over, he teamed up with Fess Parker (of Davey Crockett fame) to star in *Mr. Smith Goes to Washington*. He continued his radio, touring, and recording career. He also appeared as a guest on a host of television series.

By the mid-sixties his recording career had dried up, although he remained popular in country music circles. After a concert in Fort Wayne, Indiana, on September 19, 1968, Red Foley, the great voice who had helped the genre achieve widespread popularity, died.

Red Foley was a country jewel. His work on radio, television, on tour, and through records enabled the genre to gain footholds in mainstream America. He was a leading light in the establishment of country music as a solid form of entertainment. There were many elements to his career.

The basic foundation of his popularity was his smooth voice that soothed the listener. His vocal gifts enabled him to take the rough hillbilly songs and polish the harsh edges in order to appeal to a larger audience. He extended the parameters of original country roots to include various other styles and this enabled him to effectively sing blues, popular songs, and gospel. Although certainly not the first to sing religious songs, he helped bring the two genres closer together, giving country music more appeal among the religious sects.

His work as a radio star cannot be overstated. He helped stabilize the *National Barn Dance* and the *Renfro Valley Barn Dance*, making the genre a viable, commercial force. In the 1930s, before television, radio was the sole medium that could reach a large audience in one bold strike. Later, his hosting of the *Ozark Jubilee* helped country music to be accepted by the television viewing audience.

He also sold millions of records and his string of top ten hits can match up to anyone else during the era. His ability to deliver songs that proved popular to the masses only enhanced his career as well as the state of country music. There was a refined quality in his talent that allowed him to satisfy different people with the same song.

Later on, two of Foley's daughters enjoyed success. Betty became a country star and Shirley married Pat Boone, who was a pop star with country trappings. They carried on the Foley name long after their father had passed away.

Foley influenced countless country artists. A short list includes Pat Boone, Bill Haley, Wanda Jackson, Dave "Pappy" Hamel, Hank Williams, Sr., Ray Price, Charlie Rich, Charlie Pride, Ernest Tubb, Bob Wills, Eddy Arnold, Marty Robbins, Jim Reeves, George Jones, Patsy Cline, Mel Tillis, and Johnny Cash, among others. His popularity spilled over into rockabilly and he had an impact on Elvis, Jerry Lee Lewis, Carl Perkins, and many more. Even the outlaw, Willie Nelson, owes a debt to Red Foley.

During his reign of churning out top hits, 1945–1965, he often used Nashville session players such as Chet Atkins and in doing so helped establish the city as the Mecca of country music. His ability to make the *Grand Ole Opry* show a hit only enhanced the Tennessee center's reputation. He is as responsible as anyone else for making country music the respected industry it is today.

In 1967, Foley was elected to the Country Music Hall of Fame. It was a deserved honor for a man who did so much for the music he loved and sang with such painful brilliance. His multi-talented career proved that there was no stopping the mainstream voice.

## Discography

*Lift Up Your Voice*, Decca 5336.
*Red and Ernie*, Decca 3000.
*Souvenir Album*, Decca 5303.
*He Walks with Thee*, Decca 8767.
*My Keepsake Album*, Decca 8006.
*Beyond the Sunset*, Decca 147.
*Let's All Sing to Him*, Decca 8903.
*Let's All Sing with Red Foley*, Decca 8847.
*Company's Comin'*, Decca 4140.
*Songs of Devotion*, RCA 20759.
*Dear Hearts and Gentle People*, Decca 4290.
*The Red Foley Show*, Decca 4341.
*Songs Everybody Knows*, Decca 4603.
*Red Foley*, Vocalion 3751.
*Songs for the Soul*, Decca 4849.
*Old Master*, Decca 75154.
*Memories*, Vocallion 73920.
*Country Music Hall of Fame*, MCA 10084.
*Tennessee Saturday Night*, Charly.
*Blues in My Heart*, MCA 20266.
*Together*, MCA 20514.
*Red Foley's Golden Favorites*, Decca 4107.
*The Red Foley Story*, Decca 177.
*Red Foley's Greatest Hits*, Decca.
*Stay a Little Longer*, Decca 3523.
*Chattanoogie Shoe Shine Boy*, Import 51638.
*Tennessee Saturday Night*, Proper 105.
*Tennessee Saturday Night: 25 Greatest Hits*, Country Stars 55489.
*Hillbilly Fever: 24 Greatest Hits*, Blaricum 55519.
*1937–1939, Vol. 1*, Document 6024.

# ROY ROGERS (1911–1998)
## *Happy Trails Forever*

Although Gene Autry became known as the Singing Cowboy and helped popularize country music on a national and international scale, he wasn't the only one to play that role successfully. There were others who were quite musically gifted and capable of continuing the tradition of the cowboy songster. One individual followed in the footsteps of Autry and may have surpassed him on the happy trails forever. His name was Roy Rogers.

Roy Rogers was born Leonard Slye in November 5, 1911, in Cincinnati, Ohio, into a musical family. His father played mandolin and guitar when not working at the shoe factory. They lived on a small farm raising vegetables and farmyard animals, but not all their time was taken up with chores because by his teens Leonard was one of the best square dance callers in the county. He taught himself how to play guitar and added an element of yodeling to his singing after hearing the records of Jimmie Rodgers.

Leonard worked in a shoe factory for a while after graduation, but when the Depression hit he was whisked off to California. Slye adored the warm, breezy, clear weather of the West Coast and was disappointed when his father returned the family back to Ohio. Two months later, Leonard returned to the Los Angeles area and stayed with his sister until he could get on his own feet. He became a general laborer, picking fruit and working for a construction company, while honing his skills on the guitar.

He eventually joined the Rocky Mountaineers and recruited Bob Nolan and Bill Nichols into the group. After disbanding, Slye reformed the group with Tim Spencer and the loyal Nichols. After this group also broke up, Leonard joined Jack and His Texas Outlaws that sang on a local Los Angeles radio station. A new band eventually evolved into the Sons of the Pioneers and gained much publicity in a very short time.

The Sons of the Pioneers appeared in the movies alongside Dick Foran, Charles Starrett, and Gene Autry. They were featured on the *Hollywood Barn Dance* and recorded for Decca. The outfit grew to six men and by 1937 was acknowledged as the number one western group in the entire country.

But Rogers had greater ambitions. He wanted to be a singing cowboy in the movies and after hearing of an audition, showed up the next day and made a formidable impression. He was signed within a couple of weeks and some time later he stared in *Under Western Skies*. Almost overnight he became as popular as Gene Autry.

Although he started under the name Dick Weston, he eventually changed it to Roy Rogers. Over the next dozen years he would star in hundreds of movies, including *Carson City Kid, Robin Hood of the Pecos, The Man from Music Mountain, Along the Navajo Trail, Night Time in Nevada,* and *Son of Paleface.* Although he was the star, the Sons of the Pioneers, Spade Cooley and a host of others appeared in his films, providing adequate support. There was another frequent figure in his movies, a pretty gal that co-starred in a number of his flicks. Her name was Dale Evans.

When Rogers (who by this time was the most popular singing cowboy because Autry was in the Army) and Dale Evans were teamed together, there was magic in the air. The studio kept the pair together because their on-screen chemistry was pure dynamite. Although their relationship was strictly professional at first, love blossomed and, in 1947, they were married.

They continued to star in movies together and she was dubbed the queen of the cowgirls opposite his king of the cowboys. They dressed alike and became one of the most visible celebrity couples in the country. When the popularity of the B western movies began to fade, they had no problem making the move to television.

For seven years—1951–1958, Roy Rogers and Dale Evans entered American living rooms every week with their folksy, homespun show *Happy Trails.* It was a huge hit and one of the most genuine TV shows ever to appear on the air. It emphasized sound family values, God, and America. Their wholesome image only helped perpetuate their popularity until it was written in stone. With his horse Trigger, Rogers was easily the most popular cowboy on television and Evans was his trusted mate.

For the next forty years Roy Rogers and Dale Evans would expand their popularity with guest appearances on tours, television, radio and in person. They also enjoyed a prolific recording career with numerous hits that consisted of country material, as well as gospel pieces. Their marketability was assured and they rode every new fad without ever losing any of their popularity. If anything at all they only increased their appeal with a host of merchandise, new recorded output and their high visibility at country events. Not even when Rogers had his beloved horse Trigger stuffed did their reputation wane.

On July 6, 1998, Roy Rogers, the movie and TV star who had kept the image of the cowboy viable, passed away on his ranch in Apple Valley, California. His beloved soul mate of fifty years followed three years later.

Roy Rogers was a country institution. He made enormous contributions to the genre and long after the image of the cowboy had faded towards the setting sun he still championed the cause. Rogers was determined to keep the tradition alive and with the help of his faithful partner, he did just that.

Many of his cowboy movies filled the theatres across the country years after their release. With the new technology of VCRs, many of their movies were introduced to a new generation, ensuring his continued popularity. As well, they could be seen on television on different stations that featured cowboy flicks.

Although his contribution to country music as a whole didn't compare to the icon like image he projected in other outlets, it is not to be ignored. Because of his extensive popularity many of his albums that were packaged and repackaged sold well. There was an entire generation that would not allow his memory to fade away, and succeeding groups took up the cause.

As well, like Gene Autry, he went into business and founded a chain of successful restaurants. His business adventures were always well calculated and he avoided scandals. He also possessed a humanitarian side that only enhanced the respect he commanded throughout the entertainment industry. Along with his wife, they were glamorized with their own stars on the Hollywood Walk of Fame, placed side by side.

In 1988, he and Evans were elected to the Country Music Hall of Fame. It was the second time for Rogers, who had been inducted earlier as a member of the Sons of the Pioneers. There is a sincerity and honesty in the story of Rogers, reflecting a more innocent time. He, along with his wife, will always be remembered for their kindness, talent, versatility, and honesty. Together they rode happy trails into the sunset.

## The Sons of the Pioneers

| *Rhythm Guitar* | *String Bass* | *Fiddle* |
|---|---|---|
| Roy Rogers | Bob Nolan | Karl Farr |
| Pat Brady | | |

| *Guitar* | *Vocals* |
|---|---|
| Hugh Farr | Bob Nolan |
| | Roy Rogers |
| | Tim Spencer |
| | Lloyd Perryman |
| | Pat Brady |

## Discography

*Sweet Hour of Prayer*, RCA 3088.
*Jesus Loves Me*, RCA 1022.
*Jesus Loves Me*, Camden 1022.
*The Bible Tells Me So*, Capitol 9285.
*Peter Cottontail*, Golden 81.
*16 Great Songs of the Old West [1963]*, Golden 1987.
*16 Great Songs of the Old West [1964]*, Golden 8.
*Pecos Bill*, RCA 1054.

*Lore of the West*, Camden 1074.
*Christmas Is Always*, Capitol 2818.
*Peter Cottontail and His Friends*, Camden 1097.
*A Man from Duck Run*, Capitol 785.
*Take a Little Love*, Capitol 11020.
*In the Sweet By and By*, Word 8589.
*Good Life*, Word 8761.
*Roll on Texas Moon*, Bear Family 15203.
*Tribute*, RCA 3024.
*Songs of the Old West*, RCA 21110.
*Western Heritage: Home on the Range*, BCI 41239.
*Roy Rogers and the Sons of the Pioneers*, Varese 81212.
*Happy Trails to You*, 20th Century 467.
*Columbia Historic Edition*, Columbia 38907.
*The Best of the Roy Rogers*, Curb 77392.
*Country Music Hall of Fame*, MCA 10548.
*Say Yes to Tomorrow*, Homeland 9514.
*Melody of the Plains*, MCA 20361.
*Peace in the Valley*, Fair 1352.
*Double Barrel Country: The Legends of Roy Rogers and Dale Evans*, Madacy 5335.
*16 Great Songs of the Old West*, Drive 47007.
*A&E Biography*, Capitol 97851.
*King of the Cowboys*, ASV/Living Era 5297.
*Happy Trails: The Roy Rogers Collection 1937–1990*, Rhino 75722.
*Roy Rogers and Dale Evans*, Camden 6094.
*A Man From Duck Run/The Country Side of Roy Rogers*, EMI 499026.
*Home on the Range*, Prime Classics 571.
*Roy Rogers*, St. Clair 332.
*Ride Ranger*, Ride Audio Book and Music 1276.
*Along the Navajo Trail*, Naxos 8120542.
*Old Time Country: Portrait of Roy Rogers*, Columbia River 110078.
*King of the Singing Cowboys*, Collectors 1069.
*Happy, Gene and Me*, Madacy 51494.
*The Best of Roy Rogers*, Camden 0953.

# HANK SNOW (1914–1999)
## *The Travelin' Canadian*

Although country music has its roots firmly planted in the southern United States, the appeal of the music spread throughout the world, including America's northern neighbor, Canada. A generation of youngsters heard the early stars on the radio and that helped shape their future singing ambitions. One of the most celebrated country entertainers from the Great White North was the Travelin' Canadian. His name was Hank Snow.

Clarence Eugene Snow was born on May 9, 1914, in Liverpool, Nova Scotia. His parents' divorce, his mother's remarriage, and a yearning to travel around the country disrupted his childhood from the age of eight until he was twelve. Finally, he left home to work on ships and fulfil his desire to travel after suffering physical abuse at the hands of his stepfather, who believed a musical career was a waste of time.

For four years he sailed the seas and often entertained the sailors with his singing. Eventually, he returned to Nova Scotia when he was sixteen to a hard life of working low paying jobs and trying to pursue his dream of being an authentic country music singer. Like so many aspiring artists, Jimmie Rodgers had a major influence on Snow, as he began to imitate his idol by adding an element of yodeling to his blossoming style.

He picked up a guitar and learned some basic chords but never became proficient on the instrument. It was his voice that was his strong point and the tool he would utilize to build his career. However, it wasn't easy, since the obstacles for a singer from the Canadian hinterland to break into the American market proved almost insurmountable.

In the early part of the Depression he sang around dives in rural Nova Scotia before he moved to the big city of Halifax to improve his almost non-existent career. He found unpaid work on a local radio station billed as the Cowboy Blue Yodeler and did odd jobs to survive. In 1936, he caught a break when he found a paying radio gig on the network Canadian Farm Hour. His handle was Hank the Yodeling Ranger, linking him in the minds of listeners with the Royal Canadian Mounted Police, a strong symbol of Canadian pride.

His career blossomed when he signed with RCA-Victor. Two songs, "The Prisoned Cowboy" and "Lonesome Blue Yodel," helped establish him in his native country, but were not released in the United States, a much larger market and the true home of country music. For the next ten years, Snow would expand his popularity in Canada and become the main voice of country music in the nation.

His radio career with the CBC, the country's number one station, only enhanced his standing. Throughout his tenure he would change his handle to Hank the Singing Ranger, a name that possessed a true country ring. The fact that he was based in Montreal, the largest city in Canada at the time, certainly didn't hurt his career. However, he longed to be recognized in America.

He often ventured across the border trying to break in the American market, playing festivals all over the South, and he even spent time in Hollywood to no avail. Because RCA refused to release his records in the U.S., Hank remained well known in his native country, but relatively unknown across the border. It was only after he connected with Ernest Tubb that he finally caught the big break he was looking for and appeared at the *Grand Ole Opry*. Although he didn't make an immediate impact, his single "I'm Moving On," one of the greatest traveling songs ever written, became a number one hit and stayed on the charts for four months in the summer of 1950. He followed this up with "The Golden Rocket" and "The Rhumba Boogie."

From 1951 through 1955, Snow became one of the biggest country music stars, racking up over twenty top ten hits, and was a staple on the *Grand Ole Opry*. He had broken into the U.S. market and his power was undeniable. He was one of the few country artists who was a star on both sides of the border. His fame would spread throughout the entire globe and he would boast a loyal following in Great Britain.

A partnership with Colonel Tom Parker only helped Snow extend his status and also allowed him to connect with Elvis. Although he tried to sell Presley to country audiences without success, the rockabilly element found its way in Snow's work in such songs as "Hula Rock," and "Rockin' Rollin' Ocean." In the latter part of the 1950s and 1960s, Hank continued to place songs on the charts.

In the late 1960s, Snow's brand of music gave way to a more pop oriented sound and by the end of the decade he was considered passé. However, his live appearances on the *Grand Ole Opry* and his tours assured his name remained current in country circles. In 1974, Snow recorded his last hit, "Hello Love." Although he would have a couple of minor songs in the latter part of the 1970s, his best days were behind him.

After a 45-year association, RCA dropped him, ending one of the longest lasting recording relationships in music history. Snow continued to tour on a regular basis. He never cut another song, but continued to be a force at the *Grand Ole Opry*. The release of all of his material on the Bear Family label introduced him to another generation of country music fans.

On December 20, 1999, Hank Snow, the great Canadian country music traveler, died of a respiratory illness.

Hank Snow was an international country star. He overcame many obstacles to achieve his grand fame, and added his own element to the history of the genre. He scored many hits and probably more than any artist emphasized the longing for travel songs. There was a lonesome feeling to his tunes that made the listener yearn for a change of life, a new direction, a better path.

Hank Snow's voice evolved from a high pitch yodel to a rich baritone that enabled him to have one hit after another for a twenty year period. Although there were many important voices in country music, his was instantly recognizable. There was smoothness, originality, and sincerity in his voice, three qualities that easily explain why he became such a big star.

He is one of the few artists who broke through the Canadian and American markets. Although many of the singers from the United States became popular north of the border, none started from his point with the exception of Wilf Carter. Later, Anne Murray and k. d. lang would enjoy success in the American market, but not at the same level as Snow.

His outspoken stance against the commercialization of country music eventually fueled the fire for the stances of such rebels as Willie Nelson, Waylon Jennings and the entire outlaw movement. Snow was never afraid to speak his mind and his love for the style shone brilliantly through his tough words of criticism. He enjoyed the pure element of the genre and wished that it remained free of pop and rock and roll influences. It was a battle he lost.

He was a great ambassador and traveled the world spreading the gospel of country music. He was always proud to be a country artist and held his head up high. He even performed in Vietnam during the unpopular war, sometimes very close to the actual fighting. To Snow, it didn't matter if he sang in front of thousands or just a handful of people; he always gave it everything he had.

The biggest influence on Snow was Jimmie Rodgers. The many traveling and railroad songs were a direct tribute to his idol. There was the same general qualities of appeal in the Singing Brakeman's music that existed in the Canadian's songs. In many ways, Hank was an extension of his idol and helped keep the name of the blue yodeler fresh in the minds of country music fans.

In 1978, Snow was elected to the Nashville Songwriters International Hall of Fame, and in 1979, to the Country Music Hall of Fame. He was the most revered of all Canadian country performers and put the nation on the country music map. From his earliest days singing in the small clubs in Nova Scotia, to his radio gigs and his appearance at the *Grand Ole Opry*, Snow proved that he was the ultimate Travelin' Canadian Cowboy.

## Discography

*Hank Snow Sings*, RCA 3070.
*Just Keep A-Movin'*, RCA 1113.
*Old Doc Brown and Other Narrations*, RCA 1156.
*Hank Snow's Country Guitar*, RCA 1435.
*Country and Western Jamboree*, RCA 1419.
*Guitar*, RCA 1149.
*Hank Snow Sings Sacred Songs*, RCA 1638.
*When Tragedy Struck*, RCA 1861.
*Hank Snow Sings Jimmie Rodgers' Songs*, RCA 2043.
*Souvenirs*, RCA 2285.
*The Southern Cannonball*, Camden 680.
*Together Again*, RCA 2580.
*The One and Only Hank Snow*, Camden 722.
*I've Been Everywhere*, RCA 2675.

*Railroad Man*, RCA 2705.
*The Last Ride*, Camden 782.
*More Souvenirs*, RCA 2812.
*Songs of Tragedy*, RCA 2901.
*More Hank Snow Souvenirs*, RCA.
*Old and Great Songs by Hank Snow*, Camden 836.
*Reminiscing*, RCA 2952.
*Gloryland March*, RCA 3378.
*Heartbreak Trail*, RCA 3471.
*Your Favorite Country Hits*, RCA.
*The Highest Bidder and Other Favorites*, Camden 910.
*Gospel Train*, RCA 3595.
*The Guitar Stylings of Hank Snow*, RCA 3548.
*This Is My Story*, RCA 6014.
*Travelin' Blues*, Camden 964.
*Christmas with Hank Snow*, RCA 3826.
*Snow in Hawaii*, RCA 3737.
*Spanish Fireball*, RCA 3857.
*Lonely and Heartsick*, Camden 2251.
*My Nova Scotia Home*, Camden 2257.
*Somewhere Along Life's Highway*, Camden 2235.
*Hits, Hits and More Hits*, RCA.
*Tales of the Yukon*, RCA 4032.
*Hits Covered by Snow*, RCA 4166.
*I Went to Your Wedding*, Camden 2348.
*Snow in All Seasons*, RCA 4122.
*Cure for the Blues*, RCA 4379.
*In Memory of Jimmie Rodgers*, RCA 4306.
*By Special Interest*, RCA 4254.
*Hank Snow Sings*, RCA 4307.
*Lonesome Whistle*, Camden 2516.
*Tracks and Trains*, RCA 4501.
*Legend of Old Doc Brown*, Camden 2560.
*The Jimmie Rodgers Story*, RCA 4708.
*The Wreck of the Old 97*, Camden 9009.
*Grand Old Opry Favorites*, RCA Victor 0162.
*Snowbird*, Camden 0124.
*When My Blue Moon Turns to Gold*, Camden 0337.
*Hello Love*, RCA 0441.
*I'm Moving On*, RCA 216.
*That's You and Me*, RCA Victor 0608.
*To His Friends in New Zealand*, RCA 0010.
*All About Trains*, RCA 1052.
*You're Easy to Love*, RCA 0908.
*Live from Evangle Temple*, RCA 1361.
*Still Movin' On*, RCA 2400.
*Instrumentally Yours*, RCA 3511.
*Mysterious Lady*, RCA 3208.
*Living Legend*, RCA.
*Lovingly Yours*, RCA 3496.
*By Request*, RCA 0482.
*Win Some Lose Some Lonesome*, RCA 3987.

*Three Country Gentlemen*, RCA 2723.
*Snow Country*, Fair 1314.
*Hank Snow Salutes Jimmie Rodgers*, RCA 3131.
*Country Classics*, RCA 3226.
*Country Classics [1955]*, RCA 1233.
*Big Country Hits*, RCA 2458.
*Sings Your Favorite Country Hits*, RCA 3317.
*Your Favorite Country Hits*, RCA 3317.
*Hits, Hits and More Hits*, RCA 3965.
*Memories Are Made of This*, Camden 2443.
*The Best of Hank Snow*, RCA.
*Award Winners*, RCA 4601.
*The Best of Hank Snow, Vol. 1*, RCA 3478.
*The Best of Hank Snow, Vol. 2*, RCA 4798.
*Living Legend*, RCA 0134.
*The Singing Ranger: 1949–1953*, Bear Family 15426.
*I'm Movin' On and Other Country Hits*, RCA 9968-2-R.
*The Singing Ranger, Vol. 2*, Bear Family 15476.
*The Thesaurus Transcriptions*, Bear Family 15488.
*Collector's Series*, RCA 52279.
*The Singing Ranger, Vol. 3*, Bear Family 15502.
*Yodelling Ranger (1936–1947)*, Bear Family 15587.
*The Singing Ranger, Vol. 4*, Bear Family 15787.
*My Early Country Favorites*, Camden 2160.
*Singing Ranger* [Special Music Camden], 514.
*The Essential Hank Snow*, RCA 66931.
*Best of the Best*, King 1475.
*I've Been Everywhere: Encore Collection*, EMG Special 44693.
*Hall of Fame: 1979*, King 3825.
*Blues for My Blue Eyes*, Jasmine 3552.
*RCA Country Legends*, Buddha 99789.
*Down at the Rainbow's End*, Jasmine 3531.
*A Fool Such as I*, Arpeggio Country 3.
*The Best of Hank Snow*, Paradiso 789.
*Plays Guitar*, Jasmine 3556.
*Legendary*, BMG 97697.
*Wanderin' On, the Best of the Yodelling Ranger*, Bear Family 16661.
*We'll Never Say Goodbye: The Montreal Sessions 1937–1943*, Fab 126.
*All American Country*, BMG 68654.

# MERLE TRAVIS (1917–1983)
## *The Individualist*

Although country music artists have often been accused of sounding too much alike, nothing can be further from the truth. If there is a generalized sound, each artist is nonetheless an individual and has developed his or her unique approach. One performer, through his very personalized playing and songwriting, became known as the individualist. His name is Merle Travis.

Merle Travis was born on November 29, 1917, in Rosewood, Kentucky. Like every other country artist there were childhood forces that would go a long way in shaping his adult life. Travis's father was a hard working, low paid coal miner and the desire to escape that existence was fuel enough for the young Kentucky boy to turn to music. Although the five-string banjo was his first instrument of choice, he eventually elected to play the guitar. An essential element in Merle's development as a musician was the guiding friendships of Ike Everly, father of the famous rock and roll brothers, Don and Phil, as well as Mose Rager, who was perhaps the foremost exponent of the three finger picking technique, which he passed down to Travis.

Merle practiced hard and perfected the unique guitar style with the ability to apply it to a variety of genres including blues, ragtime, country, and folk. However, despite his abundant musical talent, it was a tough struggle and he scraped along by working a series of menial jobs. It seemed that he would fall into the same rut his father did until he finally caught a break.

Upon a trip to Evansville, Indiana, to pay his brother a visit, he was given the chance to entertain at a local dance. He impressed those around enough to earn him a spot on the radio and in a couple of local groups. Two years later, after playing in different outfits, he became a member of Clayton McMichen's Georgia Wildcats. He would later be a member of the Drifting Pioneers, who had a permanent radio gig in Cincinnati on the *Boone Country Jamboree.*

Although the war forced the group to go their separate ways, by this time Travis had acquired a sensational following. His reputation was enhanced when he joined Brown's Ferry Four that included the famed Delmore Brothers and Grandpa Jones. Later he and Jones would form the Shepherd Brothers and record for the King label.

A brief stint in the Marines interrupted Travis's musical progress, but he was soon back on track, plying his trade in Cincinnati until he moved to the West Coast. In Los Angeles, he appeared in a few cowboy flicks and became a member of Ray Whitley's band that played authentic western swing. Travis, who had been writing songs for years, emerged with "No Vacancy" and "Cincinnati Lou," providing him with two instant hits.

His momentum was partially halted with the release of *Folk Songs of the Hills*. Although the concept album would include several classics, including "Sixteen Tons," "Dark as a Dungeon," "Over by Number Nine," and "Nine Pound Hammer," it didn't sell very well. However, his distinct guitar style that would influence a generation of players was clearly evident on the album.

It was from this point on that Travis truly emerged as a leading figure in country music. He wrote the major hit "Smoke! Smoke! Smoke!" that Tex

Williams turned into gold. Travis recorded "Divorce Me C.O.D.," "So Round, So Firm, So Fully Packed," and "Three Times Seven," that greatly added to his burgeoning reputation. Travis, a fair country picker, was intrigued with the electric guitar and designed a model that would be improved on by builder Leo Fender. A few years down the road Jimi Hendrix, Eric Clapton, Jeff Beck and other rock stars would make the name Stratocaster famous.

Travis continued to tour, make records and even appear on television a few times. But his biggest splash of the year was a role in *From Here to Eternity*, where he rolled out "Re-Enlistment Blues," which exposed him to a totally new audience. He kept his foot solidly in country music by adding his expertise to the albums of friend Hank Thompson, one of the biggest stars at that time.

Although his influence had been clearly evident for a few years, in 1955, it truly sparkled. First, there was Tennessee Ernie Ford's recording of "Sixteen Tons," which was a massive hit, the song penned by Travis. As well, Scotty Moore, the guitar man behind the rise of Elvis Presley from truck driver to rock and roll icon, cited Travis as his main six-string inspiration. If this wasn't enough of a boost, Chet Atkins, perhaps the greatest picker in country music history and one of the all time great guitarists, emerged on the scene as a strict Travis disciple. At the same time the Everly Brothers were climbing the charts, making yet another Travis connection in the musical universe.

Although he was acknowledged as a gifted artist, Travis was also fingered as one who lived his life on the edge. His wild, hard drinking ways provided the gossip rags with plenty of fodder, since he often fell off the edge. He was arrested in public on several occasions for his out of control behavior. His skirmishes with the law tarnished his achievements and for much of the late 1950s and early 1960s, he teetered on losing everything he had worked so hard to accomplish.

It wasn't until the middle of the decade that he managed to regain control of his life by refocusing on his music. He released a number of highly influential records, including instrumental efforts such as *Walkin' the Strings, I'm a Natural Born Gambling Man,* and *Strictly Guitar*, among others.

In the era of the guitar hero, Travis was one of the acknowledged masters. He enhanced this reputation by teaming up with the other country superstar picker, Chet Atkins. They became popular touring together as the Atkins-and-Travis traveling show. He further returned to his former status by appearing with Grandpa Jones and dedicating a tribute album to the Georgia Wildcats, one of his early groups.

Since the 1970s had been a period of resurgence for him, he looked fondly into the next decade for continued success. However, on October 20, 1983, the great Merle Travis died in Tahlequah, Oklahoma.

Merle Travis was an instrumental whiz on the guitar. Although this is his lasting legacy in country music, he made a much greater impact. He was an effective singer, a songwriter of some note, and an influence on hundreds of aspiring musicians trying to break into the country field, as well as rock, blues, and even jazz.

The mere mention of his name triggers an immediate response to generations of guitarists as someone with multiple abilities. The Travis style—the complex finger picking method that proved impossible to duplicate—influenced a number of six-string warriors, including Jimi Hendrix, Chet Atkins, Jerry Reed, Roy Clark, Buck Owens, Willie Nelson, Hank Williams, Sr., Lester Flatt, Earl Scruggs, Scotty Moore, the Everly Brothers, Buddy Guy, Otis Rush, Joe Maphis, Link Wray, Bob Wills, Bill Monroe, Glen Campbell and Johnny Cash. In fact, he made an impact on everyone that he worked with, including Lee Gillette, Tennessee Ernie Ford, Roy Lanham, Roy Harte, Tex Ritter, Billy Liebert, Eddie Kirk, Johnny Bond, Jack Rivers, Wesley Tuttle, Jimmie Widener, Wesley Webb West, Billy Linneman, Don Law, Ray Edenton, and Billy Gray.

He was able to interpret any style of song and shape it into an exceptional hit with his inimitable guitar skills and unique vocals. Although he is best known for such songs as "So Round, So Firm, So Fully Packed," "Dark as a Dungeon," "Sixteen Tons," "No Vacancy," and "Smoke! Smoke! Smoke!," he also turned regular folk tunes such as "John Henry," "I Am a Pilgrim," and "Nine Pound Hammer" into something special. His ability to take simple passages of instrumental lines and create a masterpiece was a skill that perhaps only Chet Atkins surpassed him on.

He also made an impact outside the music scene as an actor, author and cartoonist. The multi-faceted talented man achieved success with any project that he attempted and made it look easy. As well, he was integral in shaping the sound of early rock and roll with his unique style as well as his invention of the first solid body electric guitar. Travis placed his interest in a variety of areas and always managed to improve on things.

A member of the Country Music Hall of Fame, Travis will forever be remembered as an outstanding guitarist, singer, songwriter and innovator. His influence continues to fuel contemporary country music twenty years after his death. But the most interesting aspect of his career was the fact that he accomplished his feats as "The Individualist."

## Discography

*The Merle Travis Guitar*, Capitol 650.
*Back Home*, Capitol 891.
*Walkin' the Strings*, Capitol 35089.

*Travis*, Capitol 1664.
*Songs of the Coal Mines*, Capitol 1956.
*Merle Travis and Joe Maphis*, Capitol 2102.
*I'm a Natural Born Gambling Man*, Spin-O-Rama 176.
*Great Songs of the Delmore Brothers*, Capitol 249.
*Strictly Guitar*, Capitol 2938.
*Country Guitar Giants*, Capitol 9017.
*Guitar Standards*, CMH 9024.
*Light Singin' and Pickin'*, CMH 6245.
*Travis Pickin'*, CMH 6255.
*Merle and Grandpa's Farm and Home Hour*, CMH 9032.
*Rough Rowdy and Blue*, CMH 6262.
*Merle Travis in Boston 1959*, Rounder 451.
*Country Hoedown Shows and Films*, Country 14.
*Unissued Radio Shows, 1944–1948*, Country 12.
*Folk Songs of the Hills*, Capitol 35810.
*Merle Travis*, Country 9001.
*Guitar Rags and a Too Far Past*, Bear Family 15637.
*Clayton McMichen Story*, CMH 9028.
*Country Guitar Thunder (1977–1981)*, 4901.
*Merle Travis Story: 24 Greatest Hits*, CMH 9018.
*The Best of Merle Travis*, Rhino 70993.
*The Radio Shows, 1945–1946* [live], Country Routes.
*Merle Travis 1944–49*, Country Routes 09.
*Unreleased Radio Transcriptions 1944–1949*, Rounder 09.
*Folk Songs of the Hills (Back Home/Songs of)*, Bear Family 15636.
*Guitar Retrospective*, CMH 8009.
*Turn Your Radio On (1944–1965)*, Country Routes 20.
*The Best of Merle Travis: Sweet Temptation*, Razor 82214.
*Sixteen Tons*, ASV/Living Era 5428.
*The Very Best of Merle Travis*, Varese 066370.
*Hot Pickin'*, Proper Pairs 123.
*Boogie Woogie Cowboy*, Country Routes 29.
*Live at Town Hall Party 1958/1959*, Sundazed Music 5209.

# EDDY ARNOLD (1918–)

## *The Tennessee Plowboy*

Every country singer can boast his or her own individual style. Throughout the history of the genre countless stars have made an impact on the music because of their distinct singing powers. One of these singers because of his smoothness managed to sell more records than almost anyone else. He was known as the Tennessee Plowboy, Eddy Arnold.

Richard Edward Arnold was born on May 15, 1918, in Madisonville,

Tennessee. He grew up on a farm and learned to follow the natural rhythms of rural life as well as its distinct sounds. He acquired his first guitar when he was ten, but tragedy struck the family a year later when Arnold's father died, forcing Eddy to quit school and go to work to support his mother and siblings.

However, when he wasn't busy working hard for minimal wages, he played dances, gaining valuable performing experience all the while honing his skills. He dreamed of a musical career despite the commitment to the security of his family. When he finally made it big, Arnold could look back at the many dues he paid, especially during his teen years when he traveled to various gigs on the back of a mule crawling down dark, lonely country roads.

After a stint in St. Louis as part of fiddler Speedy McNatt's outfit, Arnold returned to Nashville. He caught his first break when he appeared on radio in Jackson, in 1936, and although he wasn't offered a regular spot, he made a very good impression. It was a full six years later that he finally gained a steady gig on the station. He played in a number of groups, including Pee Wee King's Golden West Cowboys in 1942 that showcased his talents on the *Grand Ole Opry*.

He made enough of an impact to score a contract with RCA in 1944. In 1945, he recorded "Each Minute Seems a Million Years," and as a solo act, he recorded "It's a Sin" and "I'll Hold You in My Heart" in 1947 that quickly became huge hits. This was followed by "That's How Much I Love You" and "Chained to a Memory." But it was the song "I'll Hold You in My Heart (Till I Can Hold You in My Arms)" that truly established him. The single became one of the most successful of the entire decade.

In 1948, all of his nine singles reached the number one position, an unheard of feat that turned him into a superstar. The songs "Anytime," "What a Fool I Was," "Texarkana Baby," "Just a Little Lovin' (Will Go a Long, Long Way)," "My Daddy Is Only a Picture," and "Bouquet of Roses" had crossover charm. He could lay claim to being the number one recorded country star in the nation.

In 1949, he added several classics to his loaded cannon, including "Don't Rob Another Man's Castle," "One Kiss Too Many," "I'm Throwing Rice (at the Girl I Love)," and "Take Me in Your Arms and Hold Me." He was at the zenith of his power and he entered the next decade with much promise. He would not disappoint.

He continued his run in the 1950s and because of his pop appeal appeared on the TV shows of Perry Como, Milton Berle, Arthur Godfrey, Dinah Shore, Bob Hope and Spike Jones. He was also a regular on *Grand Ole Opry*, where he became a genuine star. His tours were broadcasted as true events, as he did shows all over the world performing his many number one hits.

He was so much in demand that it was only natural that he was awarded his own country music TV show called *Eddy Arnold Time*. Some of his best known releases in this era included "There's Been a Change in Me," "Kentucky Waltz," "I Wanna Play House with You," "Easy on the Eyes," "A Full Time Job," "Eddy's Song," "How's the World Treating You?," "I Really Don't Want to Know," "My Everything," "The Cattle Call," "That Do Make It Nice," "Just Call Me Lonesome," and "The Richest Man (in the World)." He sang these songs on his program, creating even more interest in them and in turn helping him sell more records.

His stranglehold on the charts slowed down in the late 1950s and 1960s due to his change in style. He was forgoing his sound that had proved so popular for a more slickly produced pop shine. Despite the bold, calculating move of messing with a formula that had proven so successful, he rebounded in the mid 1960s with his more urban style and continued to pile up the hits. Like Como, Andy Williams, Dean Martin, Bing Crosby and others, Arnold became a crooner. He reaped commercial rewards with songs such as "What's He Doing in My World." He not only scored big on the country charts but was a regular on the pop list with such hits as "Make the World Go Away," "I Want to Go with You," "The Last Word in Lonesome," "Somebody Like Me," "Lonely Again," "Turn the World Around," "Then You Can Tell Me Goodbye," "They Don't Make Love Like They Used To," and "Please Don't Go."

In the 1970s, he continued to roll right along although he reached more of a country audience than the pop section. In 1972, he switched labels, ending nearly a thirty year association with RCA. But the move was a bust since he only had one top hit with his new company, "I Wish That I Had Loved You Better." He later resigned with RCA, and enjoyed two hits at the end of the decade: "Cowboy" and "If Everyone Had Someone Like You."

As the 1980s beckoned, Arnold could look back at a very successful career; however, he wasn't finished charting top ten songs. He scored with "Let's Get It While the Gettin's Good," and "That's What I Get for Loving You." Despite the fact that he continued to record, he would never enjoy another top hit. He continued to perform and record into the 1990s. He also appeared on television.

Eddy Arnold is a country music cornerstone. He has been a rock solid performer for over six decades and is one of the few artists to chart in five consecutive decades. He has made enormous contributions to country music.

Eddy Arnold was chiefly responsible for moving the rural tradition of country music to a more urban audience. He was able to inject his singing style with a strong dose of pop that brought listeners into the genre who never liked country music before. He was a force and his ability to transform and spread the appeal of the style to the masses sealed his lofty position.

Although Arnold was first influenced by Gene Autry and Jimmie Rodgers, he moved to a smoother commercial style that served him well. There was a recognizable element in his vocal style that enabled him to sell more records than any other country artist in history. He spent more time on the charts than anyone else and his songs created a whole new breed of singer.

Arnold was an influence on George Morgan, Jim Reeves, Carl Smith, Gibson/Miller Band, Greasy Medlin, Luke Thompson and Cecil Thompson, and a host of pop singers such as Pat Boone. As well, the Beatles, Buddy Holly, Elvis, and even rocker Mick Jagger owe a debt to Arnold. The big band singers such as Frank Sinatra, Perry Como, Dean Martin, Andy Williams and Bob Crosby were in the same league as Arnold, but he had a broader country music fan base. His ability to appeal to different markets simultaneously was his strongest calling card that set him apart from other singers.

He has been well recognized for his achievements. He was the initial "Entertainer of the Year" named by the Country Music Association. In 1984, he won the Pioneer Award, and three years later was presented with the President's Award by the songwriters' guild. In 1966, he was named to the Country Music Hall of Fame.

Eddy Arnold is a country music institution who ruled in different eras to become one of the most important performers in the history of the genre. He was a true force that became a household named during the 1940s and to this day remains extremely popular with many fans. The Tennessee Plowboy will always hold a special place in all music circles.

## Discography

*Anytime/Eddy Arnold and His Guitar*, RCA 3027.
*An American Institution*, RCA Victor 3230.
*All-Time Favorites*, RCA Victor 3117.
*The Chapel on the Hill*, RCA Victor 3218.
*Wanderin'*, RCA Victor 1111.
*A Little on the Lonely Side*, RCA Victor 1377.
*My Darling, My Darling*, RCA Victor 1575.
*When They Were Young*, RCA Victor 1484.
*Praise Him, Praise Him*, RCA Victor 1733.
*Have Guitar, Will Travel*, RCA 1928.
*Thereby Hangs a Tale*, RCA Victor 2036.
*More Eddy Arnold*, Camden 563.
*That's How Much I Love You*, Camden 471.

*Eddy Arnold Sings Them Again*, RCA Victor 2185.
*You Gotta Have Love*, RCA Victor 2268.
*Let's Make Memories Tonight*, RCA Victor 2337.
*One More Time*, RCA Victor 2471.
*Christmas with Eddy Arnold*, RCA Victor 52554.
*Our Man Down South*, RCA Victor 2596.
*Cattle Call* [RCA], RCA Victor 2578.
*Faithfully Yours*, RCA Victor 2629.
*Folk Song Book*, RCA Victor 2811.
*Sometimes I'm Happy, Sometimes I'm Blue*, RCA Victor 2909.
*Eddy's Songs*, RCA Camden 798.
*Songs I Love to Sing*, Capitol 741.
*The Easy Way*, RCA Victor 3361.
*My World*, RCA Victor 2466.
*I Want to Go with You*, RCA Victor 3507.
*The Last Word in Lonesome*, RCA Victor 3622.
*Somebody Like Me*, RCA Victor 3715.
*Lonely Again*, RCA Victor 3753.
*Turn the World Around*, RCA Victor 3869.
*The Ever Lovin' World of Eddy Arnold*, RCA Victor 3931.
*The Romantic World of Eddy Arnold*, RCA Victor 4009.
*Walkin' in Love Land*, RCA 4089.
*Songs of the Young World*, RCA 4110.
*The Glory of Love*, RCA 4179.
*The Warmth of Eddy*, RCA 4231.
*Love and Guitars*, RCA 4304.
*Standing Alone*, RCA 4390.
*Loving Her Was Easier*, RCA 4625.
*Portrait of My Woman*, RCA 4471.
*Welcome to My World*, RCA 4570.
*Eddy Arnold Sings for Housewives and Other Lovers*, RCA 4738.
*Lonely People*, RCA 4718.
*The World of Eddy Arnold*, RCA 0239.
*Wished That I Loved You Better*, RCA 4961.
*She's Got Everything I Need*, MGM 4912.
*The Wonderful World of Eddy*, Arnold MGM 4992.
*Eddy*, RCA 1817.
*Many Tears Ago*, Capitol 979.
*Hand Holdin' Songs*, RCA 9963.
*You Don't Miss a Thing*, RCA 3020.
*TBD*, Atlantic 77908.
*Cattle Call*, Collector's Choice 5902.
*I Need You All the Time*, RCA 2277.
*This Is Eddy Arnold*, RCA 6032.
*Echoes*, RCA 7025.
*So Many Ways/If the Whole World Stopped Lovin'*, MGM 4878.
*Living Legend*, K-Tel 307.
*A Legend and His Lady*, RCA 3606.
*All-Time Hits from the Hills*, RCA Victor 3031.
*Country Classics*, MCA 3027.
*When It's Round Up Time in Heaven*, MCA 3219.
*A Dozen Hits*, RCA Victor 1293.

*Eddy Arnold*, Camden 471.
*Cattle Call/Thereby Hangs a Tale*, Bear Family 15441.
*Pop Hits from the Country Side*, RCA Victor 2951.
*I'm Throwing Rice*, Camden 897.
*The Best of Eddy Arnold* [RCA], RCA 3675.
*The Best of Eddy Arnold, Vol. 2*, DCC 157.
*Best of Eddy Arnold* [Curb], Curb 77416.
*Collector's Series*, RCA 6315.
*The Mellow Side of Eddy Arnold*, Fair 1000.
*Pure Gold*, RCA 58398.
*Last of the Love Song Singers: Then and Now*, RCA 66046.
*Greatest Songs*, Curb 77767.
*Memories Are Made of This*, Mercury 526879.
*The Essential Eddy Arnold*, RCA 66854.
*Standards by Eddy Arnold*, Ranwood 8269.
*Christmas Time*, Curb 77908.
*Legendary Eddy Arnold*, BMG Special 44524.
*Best of the Best*, King 1477.
*The Hits*, Mercury 558083.
*The Tennessee Plowboy and His Guitar*, Bear Family 15726.
*In the Chapel*, BMG Special 44892.
*Super Hits*, RCA 67757.
*Bouquet of Roses*, Country Stars 55457.
*Cattle Call* [Country Stars], Country Stars 55458.
*Early Hits of "The Tennessee Plowboy,"* ASV/Living Era 5321.
*Country Music Hall of Fame*, King 3826.
*Seven Decades of Hits*, Curb 78702.
*Then You Can Tell Me Goodbye*, CAK 2501.
*RCA Country Legends*, Buddha 99759.
*Hold You in My Heart*, Arpeggio Country 5.
*Looking Back*, RCA 67042.
*Great Early Recordings*, BMG 7430.
*Bouquet of Roses*, Proper 1365.
*Cattle Call*, Proper 1367.
*Full Time Job*, Proper 1368.
*Prison Without Walls*, Proper 1366.
*Ultimate Eddy Arnold*, BMG 56329.
*Eddy's Song*, Proper Box 37.
*All American Country*, BMG 48368.
*Country Songs I Love to Sing*, BMG 7308.
*That's How Much I Love You*, Collectables 7313.
*Songs of the Saviour*, Music Hill 70049.
*After All These Years*, RCA 70710.
*Legendary Performer*, RCA 4885.
*Make the World Go Away*, RCA 1071.

# PART THREE

# *Western Swing/Bluegrass/ Honky Tonk*

In the 1940s, country music began to branch out and the later styles were built on the foundation first set in place by the pioneers and the medium stars. The practitioners took the simple themes and tradition of the genre to turn it into something special. It was a crucial turning point in the history of country music.

Western swing had country overtones with a swinging beat that gave the music a spark. More importantly, it was dance material and when a solo figure or band could make people move to the beat, they knew they were playing the right stuff. The western swing bands were large outfits, complete with full rhythm and horn sections, that also specialized in dreamy lyrics of love lost or found.

Although Bob Wills is the acknowledged master of the western swing style, there were others who made a large impact. Bill Boyd's Cowboy Ramblers, the Hi-Flyers, the Tune Wranglers, Roy Newman and His Boys, the Nite Owls, Bob Skyles' Skyrockets, Adolph Hofner, Doug Bine, Cliff Bruner, Ted Daffan, the Crystal Springs Ramblers, the Blue Ridge Playboys and West Texas Cowboys were solid practitioners of the style. Two other pioneers who bridged old-timey country with western swing were the great fiddler Prince Albert Hunt and the group the East Texas Serenaders.

Bluegrass was an outgrowth of complexity of traditional sounds coupled with innovative effects. It began in the late 1930s, but came into prominence in the 1940s and continues to be a force today. The fast paced tempos, unique rhythms, and lonesome sound all combined to give the style an instant foothold in country music circles. Bill Monroe was the acknowledged champion of the style.

Some of the more important bluegrass artists included Red Allen, Byron Berline, the Bluegrass Cardinals, the Country Gentlemen, Dixie Gentlemen, Jim and Jesse, Ralph Stanley, Eddie Adcock, Norman Blake, Alison Krauss, Jimmy Martin, Del McCoury, Old and In the Way,

Osborne Brothers and Mac Wiseman. Later in the century, new groups would take up the bluegrass cause and create a progressive form of the music that many of the old time traditionalists would despise.

Honky tonk, the third major strain to rise during the 1940s, was a harsher style performed by a small band with electric guitar, driving fiddles and steel lead in order to cut through the rabble of the noisy roadside taverns where the sound was born. The themes of honky tonk—hard drinking, cheating on a lover, frustration in life and love, and a definite cynicism—gave the music a hard edge; it was often sung in a lonesome voice. The rise of the jukebox and dancing in small taverns were essential in the rise of honky tonk.

Some of the earliest honky tonk greats were Ted Daffan, Floyd Tillman, Moon Mullican, Al Dexter and Ernest Tubb. But it was Hank Williams who really personified the style. Later on Ray Price and George Jones would take up the cause. The genre has been revived several times, most notably in the 1960s with the advent of the Bakersfield Sound. Some of the important honky tonk artists not featured in this book include Tommy Collins, Lefty Frizzell, Mickey Gilley, Johnny Horton, Roger Miller, Red Sovine, Wynn Stewart and Faron Young.

The artists featured in this book were seminal figures who made enormous contributions to a specific branch of country music.

Bob Wills was the crowned king of western swing and with his band the Playboys was the most popular exponent of the style. Sadly, he never lived to see the renaissance of what he started.

Bill Monroe is the father of bluegrass and the whole tradition rests on his shoulders. The impact of this talented musician on country music cannot be overstated and to this day his influence is still felt.

Lester Flatt was a flashy, high speed guitarist who earned his spurs with Bill Monroe. A bluegrass enthusiast, he would later team up with Earl Scruggs and achieve greater acclaim.

Ernest Tubb, the father of honky tonk, made many contributions to country music and blazed the path that so many followed, including Hank Williams, Sr.

Hank Williams, Sr., along with Jimmie Rodgers, is the most influential country music artist of the twentieth century. A serious honky tonk singer, he lives on in legend half a century after his untimely death.

Earl Scruggs was a bluegrass enthusiast who spent time in Bill Monroe's Blue Grass Boys. He later split from the group and teamed up with Lester Flatt. A dynamic banjo player, Scruggs could hold his own against anyone.

Hank Thompson was the second greatest practitioner of western swing. He picked up where Bob Wills left off.

Ray Price was a dedicated honky tonk practitioner who not only sang with conviction, but lived the life. A disciple of Hank Williams, Sr., he carried on where the latter left off.

George Jones was a serious honky tonk man who not only sang about the life but lived it in every way.

# BOB WILLS (1905–1975)
## The Western Swing King

The state of Texas has always been a hot musical center for a myriad of styles, including blues, Mexican, folk, traditional tunes, country, and later on, rockabilly and rock and roll. Many of the musicians that emerged from the Lone Star State created their own sound by melding various genres into a cohesive sound. One of these individuals fashioned a number of influences to become the Western Swing King. His name was Bob Wills.

James Robert Wills was born on March 6, 1905, in Kosse, Texas, into a musical family. His father and grandfather were longtime players who taught him the rudiments of music. Jim Bob, as he was popularly known, began on the mandolin before moving on to guitar and finally making the fiddle his instrument of choice. When he was eight the family moved to Memphis, Tennessee, exposing Wills to an entirely new musical environment. By his teens he was proficient enough to play the fiddle at local square dances and his future direction was assured.

He earned his traveling spurs working for a medicine show, where he showed off his best fiddle licks and did black face comedy. It was during this tour that he became known as Bob Wills because of the surplus of Jims he worked with. Later, he formed a duo with guitarist Norman Arnspiger; they called themselves the Wills Fiddle Band.

The pair settled in the Fort Worth area and became local favorites, playing many events as well as on the radio. A year later they added vocalist Milton Brown, and eventually evolved into the Light Crust Doughboys peddling Light Crust Flour. In 1932, they made their first recordings, but soon after vocalist Tommy Duncan replaced Brown. Guitarist Durwood Brown (Milton's brother), and Clifton "Sleepy" Johnson, a banjo player, rounded out the group. The band's burgeoning career enabled Wills to forge a name for himself until he was fired for his hard drinking ways and his constant feuding with the manager, W. Lee O'Daniel.

A Texan through and through, armed with that fierce, Lone Star independent streak, Bob simply formed his own outfit consisting of Duncan and brother Johnny Lee Wills on the banjo. He renamed his small group Bob Wills and the Playboys and they immediately scored a spot on Waco radio. He was determined to show O'Daniel that he had made one very costly mistake.

Although beset by legal problems from his last employer, they plowed on with their small group and they eventually carved out their niche in Tulsa. Wills, a musical genius, knew exactly what type of sound he wanted to create and it differed drastically from what O'Daniel had wanted him to play. He wanted to unite pure country strains with western swing to give the music a dimension that a few had attempted but none had perfected. All he needed was the right personnel and although it took some time to find all of the pieces of the puzzle, he finally achieved his goal.

His group underwent many changes before settling on a stable lineup that consisted of Wills on fiddle, Duncan on piano and vocals, June Whalen on rhythm guitar, Johnnie Lee Wills on tenor banjo, and Kermit Whalen on steel guitar and bass. Eventually, Leon McAuliffe, who played electric steel guitar, Al Stricklin, a barrelhouse pianist with a jazz touch, and drummer Smokey Dacus augmented the band. A horn section was also added to produce Wills' vision of a swing band with country overtones. It was obvious that he fashioned his group from the swinging big bands, but the Playboys didn't play jazz, they kicked out riveting country jams with the power of Duke Ellington, Jimmie Lunceford and Count Basie.

By the mid–1930s the outfit had grown to thirteen members and would reach eighteen in the 1940s. The interplay between the horns and fiddles created a tension, an excitement that had never been heard in country music. They band played country ballads, blues and riffy themes that swung as hard as anything else anybody was churning out. The group was able to capture a piece of the big band fan base with their hot, driving sound.

It all came together nicely on "San Antonio Rose," a swinging tune that Wills had penned himself. The song epitomized all of the great elements of the outfit including Duncan's powerful lyrics, the swing thing, and the fierce interplay between the fiddles and the horns. It was a million seller and the band's reputation received another positive mark when Bing Crosby recorded a version that became a big hit.

More songs followed, including "Steel Guitar Rag," which showed off the abundant talents of McAuliffe, and "Right or Wrong," a perfect vehicle for Duncan's strong vocal abilities. The band became a popular concert attraction, selling out venues across the nation with its hot brand of western swing. It was one of the few country big bands and Wills knew how to make it all work. The group also cut numerous sides for ARC and other labels.

The advent of World War II decimated the outfit as members drifted away to serve their country, including Duncan, Stricklin, and McAuliffe. Even Wills was drafted but the stubborn Texas bandleader with the wild-eyed fiddle licks was too much for the brass in Uncle Sam's institution to handle and he was discharged.

Wills, with his band in disarray, headed to California where he appeared on radio shows and in the movies. He reformed his band but scaled it down and excluded a horn section, concentrating more on string instrumentals. Despite the shakeup, his little outfit cooked and created a wall of sound playing that driving western swing with precision and unrestrained energy.

Since Wills had worked with producer Art Satherley so successfully for years, when the latter moved to the Okeh label, Bob and his new band followed. A different version of "New San Antonio Rose" became a top ten hit, and was followed by "Smoke on the Water" and "Stars and Stripes on Iwo Jima." In 1945, his single "Texas Playboy Rag," cut on the Columbia label, became a hit. A couple of years later "New Spanish Two Step" went to number one, spending four months on the charts.

Wills moved labels once again in 1947, signing with MGM, but the change didn't affect his Midas touch, as "Bubbles in My Beer" and "Keeper of My Heart" were sizeable hits. Although he still performed and recorded on a regular basis, the Playboys would begin to disintegrate due to a number of reasons.

A good ol' boy, Wills worked hard but also played hard throughout his career. His excessive drinking caused so much internal strife within the band that Duncan left in 1948. As well, the decline of western swing didn't help matters and the magic touch he possessed in the recording studio vanished; he produced no more hits.

Throughout the 1950s, he moved around often, trying to recapture the spirit of the 1930s and 1940s, but was unable to do so. Two songs—"Ida Red Likes the Boogie" and "Faded Love" were his last top ten hits of the decade. It wasn't until 1959 that Wills recaptured past glories with the song "Heart to Heart Talk" that featured the return of Tommy Duncan. The band was rejuvenated for a brief spell.

In 1962, Wills suffered the first of a series of heart attacks, but he recovered and resumed leadership of the Playboys. However, a second heart attack two years later ended his reign. He recorded some solo material backed by Nashville studio musicians, but the hard swinging western sound with the biting edge was gone.

Wills would enjoy one more moment in the sun when he teamed with

Merle Haggard in the early 1970s during the revival of western swing. But on December 1, 1973, after cutting some twenty-seven titles in two days for United Artists, he slipped into a coma and never recovered. Seventeen months later, on May 17, 1975, the acknowledged king of western swing died in a nursing home. He had never regained consciousness. After his death the band continued under the direction of Leon McAuliffe.

Bob Wills was a western swing pioneer and the man most responsible for popularizing the genre. He not only realized his vision of creating country music with jazz overtones, but spawned a host of imitators and even influenced a new style—honky tonk. The music he created would also form part of the basic foundation of rockabilly and rock and roll.

He was a masterful fiddle player who could grind out a run of notes that sounded like a march of stampeding horses. He was a master at placing the right notes against each other and did it with blinding speed. He would have reached fame simply as a competent musician, but he made many more contributions.

He was a formidable bandleader and during his prime was able to combine eighteen different musicians into one cohesive unit. He wrote songs that specifically showcased the talents of the individual members of his band like his brother Johnny Lee, Duncan and McAuliffe. It was a practice that Ellington was noted for, and something that Wills introduced into country music.

He influenced dozens of other artists from all styles of music. A short list includes Lowell Fulson, Asleep at the Wheel, Merle Haggard, Waylon Jennings, George Jones, Willie Nelson, Buck Owens, Lee Roy Parnell, Red Steagall, George Strait, Chuck Berry, Bill Haley, Big Sandy and His Fly-Rite Boys, J. P. Fraley, Adolph Hofner, Spade Cooley, H. M. Barnes' Blue Ridge Ramblers, Dave Ferguson and Scott Joss. He made a mark on the entire rock and roll generation, as well as the big bands from which he borrowed ideas.

Although he couldn't be credited with inventing the western swing style, he perfected it and was the number one proponent of the genre. Many of the individuals in his band would go on to form their own outfits. Although none enjoyed the success of Wills' famed group, they did carry on the tradition that he had initiated.

For example, in 1940, Johnnie Lee formed his own group, Johnnie Lee Wills and His Boys, that included as many as fifteen members. They played the same western swing with country overtones that the Playboys did. The group featured some of the finest musicians of the era, including Leon Huff, Joe Holley and Jesse Ashlock. They recorded for Bullett Records and had a couple of hits, "Rag Mop" and "Peter Cottontail."

In 1968, Bob Wills was inducted into the Country Music Hall of

Fame, and in 1969, he was honored by the Texas State Legislature for his enormous contributions to Texas and American music. The accolades, the million-selling albums, the crowd adulation were all part of his legend. Wills made the music he wanted to and became the King of Western Swing on his own terms.

## Bob Wills and His Texas Playboys*
The original lineup

*Fiddle*
Bob Wills

*Piano/Vocals*
Tommy Duncan

*Steel Guitar*
Kermit Whalen

*Tenor Banjo*
Johnnie Lee Wills

*Bass/Rhythm Guitar*
June Whalen

*There were over six hundred members in the Texas Playboys through the years. The following is a partial list.

Teddy Adams, Danny Alguier, Les Anderson, Joe Andrews, Norman Arnspiger, Jesse Ashlock, Junior Bernard, Bobby Boatright, Noel Boggs, Billy Bowman, Alex Brashear, Billy Briggs, Billy Carter, Keith Coleman, Gene Crownover, Johnny Cuviello, Smokey Dacus, Casey Dickens, Glenn Duncan, Tommy Duncan, Joe Ferguson, Benny Garcia, Gene Gasaway, Johnny Gimbel, Cameron Hill, Joe Holley, Leon Huff, Sleepy Johnson, Millard Kelso, Tag Lambert, Sonny Lansford, Doc Lewis, Jack Lloyd, Leon McAuliffe, Billy McBay, Bobby McBay, Laura Lee McBride, Rusty McDonald, Paul McGhee, Dean McKinney, Evelyn McKinney, Zeb McNally, Frankie McWhorter, Tommy Morrell, Tiny Moore, Tiny Mott, Monty Mountjoy, Tommy Perkins, Leon Rausch, Ramona Reed, Herb Remington, Glen Rhees, Lee Ross, Louses Rowe, Eldon Shamblin, Al Stickland, Louie Tierney, Mancel Tierney, Gene Tomlins, June Whalen, Kermit Whalen, Bob White (steel guitar), Bob White (fiddle), Jimmy Widener, Billy Jack Wills, Johnnie Lee Wills, Luke Wills, Woody Wood and Jimmy Wyble.

## Hall of Fame Inductee Lineup

*Fiddle/Mandolin/Vocals*
Bob Wills

*Vocals*
Tommy Duncan

*Steel Guitar*
Leon McAuliffe

*Fiddle/Electric Mandolin*
Johnny Gimble

*Fiddle*
Joe "Jody" Holley

*Fiddle/Electric Mandolin*
Tiny Moore

*Steel Guitar*
Herb Remington

*Guitar*
Eldon Shamblin

*Piano*
Al Stricklin

## Discography

*Bob Wills Roundup*, CBS 9003.
*Old Time Favorites*, Antone's 6000.

*Dance-O-Rama #2*, Decca 5562.
*Ranch House Favorites*, MGM 91.
*Bob Wills and His Texas Playboys* [Decca/MCA], Decca 8727.
*Texas Playboys*, Antone's 6000.
*Together Again*, Liberty 7173.
*Mr. Words and Mr. Music*, Liberty 7194.
*Bob Wills and Tommy Duncan*, Liberty 1912.
*Bob Wills Sings and Plays*, Liberty 7303.
*Keepsake Album #1*, Longhorn P-001.
*Western Swing Along*, Vocalion 73735.
*San Antonio Rose [1965]*, Starday 375.
*From the Heart of Texas*, Kapp 3506.
*King of Western Swing* [MCA], Kapp 3523.
*Bob Wills* [Metro], Metro 594.
*Here's That Man Again*, Kapp 3542.
*Time Changes Everything*, Kapp 3569.
*The Greatest String Band Hits*, Kapp 38020.
*Country Walk*, Sunset 5248.
*Bob Wills in Person*, Kapp 3639.
*Bob Wills Day*, Delta 1177.
*A Tribute to Bob Wills*, MGM 171.
*Fathers and Sons*, Epic 33782.
*For the Last Time*, United Artists A216.
*Live from Panther Hall: 1963*, Big A Dist. 5010.
*Bob Wills' Original Texas Playboys*, Bellaire CA-114.
*Nashville's Fiddlin' Man*, Coronet 281.
*Roly Poly*, Classic 76512.
*The Best of Bob Wills*, Harmony 7304.
*The Great Bob Wills*, Harmony 7345.
*The Best of Bob Wills, Vol. 1*, MCA 5917.
*The Greatest String Band Hits*, Kapp 3601.
*The Best of Bob Wills*, Kapp 3641.
*The Bob Wills Story*, Starday 469.
*Legendary Masters*, United Artists 9962.
*Remembering*, CBS 34108.
*Bob Wills: In Concert* [live], Capitol 11550.
*The Late Bob Wills Original Texas Playboys*, Capitol 11612.
*Tiffany Transcriptions*, Tishomingo 01.
*Live and Kickin'*, Capitol 11725.
*Lone Star Rag*, Encore 14390.
*Original Texas Playboys Live and Kickin'*, Capitol 11917.
*Rare Presto Transcriptions*, Outlaw 1.
*More Rare Presto Transcriptions*, Outlaw 2.
*Bob Wills* [Time Life], Time-Life 15836.
*31st Street Blues*, Longhorn 011.
*Okeh Western Swing*, Epic 37324.
*Rare Presto, Vol. 3*, Cattle 33.
*On Stage*, Delta 1149.
*Columbia Historic Edition*, Columbia 37468.
*Tiffany Transcriptions, Vol. 1*, Rhino 71469.
*Basin St. Blues*, Kaleidoscope 20.
*Rare Presto, Vol. 4*, Cattle 70.

*Rare Presto, Vol. 5*, Cattle 71.
*For Collectors, Vol. 1*, Delta 1005.
*1953 California Radio, Vol. 1*, Delta 1117.
*Take Me Back to Tulsa*, Delta 1110.
*1953 California Radio, Vol. 2*, Delta 1162.
*Right or Wrong*, Delta 1181.
*For Collectors, Vol. 2*, Delta 1102.
*Tiffany Transcriptions, Vol. 2*, Rhino 71470.
*Tiffany Transcriptions, Vol. 3*, Rhino 71471.
*Tiffany Transcriptions, Vol. 4*, Rhino 71472.
*Tiffany Transcriptions, Vol. 5*, Rhino 71473.
*King of Western Swing: Wills*, MCA 38019.
*Fiddle*, Country Music 10.
*Tiffany Transcriptions, Vol. 6: Sally Goodin'*, 71474.
*Tiffany Transcriptions, Vol. 7: Keep Knockin'*, Rhino 71475.
*24 Greatest Hits*, PolyGram 27573.
*Tiffany Transcriptions, Vol. 10: McKinney*, Kaleidoscope 71478.
*In the Mood*, Kaleidoscope 75.
*The McKinney Sisters*, Rhino 71478.
*Bob Wills 1953*, Country Rout 9004.
*Country Music Hall of Fame Series*, MCA 10547.
*Longhorn Recordings*, Bear Family 15869.
*Encore*, Liberty 30275.
*Swinging Around the Christmas Tree*, Eagle Video 1198.
*Strictly by Ear*, Collectables 5570.
*San Antonio Rose and Other Hits*, CEMA 9193.
*The Ultimate Collection*, Prism Leisure 409.
*Faded Love* [Catfish], Catfish 205.
*Cherokee Maiden*, Proper 1226.
*Get with It*, Proper 1225.
*Just a Plain Country Boy*, Proper 1227.
*The End of the Line*, Proper 1228.
*Back to Back*, Sony 30819.
*Bob Wills*, St. Clair 331.
*From the Heart of Texas: 1963 MCA Reissue*, Stetson 3058.
*A Living Legend*, Liberty 7182.
*The History of Bob Wills and His Texas Playboys*, MGM 4866.
*Bob Wills Anthology*, Columbia 32416.
*The Legendary Bob Wills*, Columbia 212922.
*The Best of Bob Wills, Vol. 2*, MCA 24092.
*The Best of Johnny Lee Wills*, Crown 565.
*Historic Edition*, CBS 37468.
*Columbia Historic Edition*, Columbia CB 37468.
*The Best of Bob Wills* [Special Music], Special Music 3023.
*1932–41*, Texas Rose 2709.
*The Best of the Tiffanys*, Kaleidoscope 19.
*The Very Best of Bob Wills*, Liberty 2600431.
*Papa's Jumpin' MGM Years*, Bear Family 15179.
*The Golden Era*, Columbia 40149.
*Tiffany Transcriptions, Vol. 8: More of the Bob Wills Band*, Rhino 71476.
*21 Golden Hits*, Highland 411.
*Greatest Hits*, Curb 77389.

*Tiffany Transcriptions, Vol. 9: 1946–1947*, Rhino 71477.
*Anthology 1935–1973*, Rhino 70744.
*The Essential Bob Wills and His Texas Playboys*, Columbia/Legacy 48598.
*Classic Western Swing*, Rhino 71670.
*Anthology*, Columbia 70755.
*Faded Love* [Richmond], Richmond 2140.
*American Legends Number 13: Bob Wills, Jimmie Rodgers and Hank Williams*, LaserLight 12735.
*Legacy*, Collector's 12.
*Hits*, PolyGram 534669.
*San Antonio Rose* [RHFL], Rhino 72810.
*The King of Western Swing: 25 Hits*, ASV/Living Era 5250.
*Harmony Airshots 1953*, Country Routes 21.
*20th Century Masters—The Millennium Collection: The Best of Bob Wills*, MCA 170117.
*Hall of Fame*, DCC 183.
*The King of Western Swing* [Country Stars], Country Stars 55463.
*San Antonio Rose* [Bear Family], Bear Family 15933.
*Bob Wills* [St. Clair], St. Clair 331.
*Take Me Back to Tulsa: The Original Columbia Recordings*, Rounder 11145.
*Boot Heel Drag: The MGM Years*, Uptown/Universe 170206.
*Rare California Airshots*, Country Routes 24.
*Stay a Little Longer: The Original Columbia Recordings, Vol. 2, Rounder*, 1146.
*Inducted into the Hall of Fame 1968*, 6562.
*Wills Junction*, Classic 2088.
*He's a Ding Dong Daddy*, Jasmine 3526.
*King of Lonestar Swing*, President 553.
*Milkcow Blues*, Blue Moon 3065.
*Radio Days*, Tomato Music 2120.
*A Tribute to Bob's Music*, Smith Music Group 5072.
*It's Fun Dancing T#5*, Kaleidoscope 25.

# BILL MONROE (1911–1996)
## *The Bluegrass Rambler*

Bluegrass—a type of string band music utilizing banjo, fiddle, resonator guitar, mandolin and bass or various combinations of these instruments—first came to prominence in the 1940s. Although the essential elements of the style had existed for many years as individual parts, it took a champion to assemble all of the pieces into one cohesive sound. The task fell on the sturdy and capable shoulders of the Bluegrass Rambler. His name was Bill Monroe.

William Smith Monroe was born on September 13, 1911, in Rosine, Kentucky, the youngest of eight children. Many factors contributed to his development as a country music star, including the fact that he spent much of his time growing up alone. His next closest sibling was Charlie, who was born in 1903, eight years before. The large gap in age between himself and his older brother, as well as poor eyesight, made Bill develop a severe shy streak that saw him find solace in music.

Musical talent ran in the family—Charlie was an accomplished player well before his teens and the third brother, Birch, was an adept fiddler. As well, Uncle Pendleton Vandiver was a talented musician who had a large influence on his nephews. Vandiver was a rated fiddler and encouraged his nephews to practice hard and by the time Bill was in his teens, he traveled with his uncle performing at local events.

There were two other factors that proved to be important in Monroe's development as a musician. Since he helped out on the large family farm, Bill was able to develop his powerful singing style without hindrance. As well, since he had such poor eyesight he was forced to learn the music played in the church choir by ear. The high harmonies would later turn up in his bluegrass band.

He also befriended local blues singer Arnold Shultz, a fine musician who provided inspiration. Young Bill would jam with Shultz and some of his friends on a regular basis. This practical experience was invaluable. The older musicians passed on the secrets to Monroe, who proved to be an eager student with an insatiable appetite for learning.

The final piece of Bill's education that armed him with a complete arsenal of weapons allowing him to make such a strong musical impact were the early records of Charlie Poole and His Carolina Ramblers. Poole was a major force in the early development of country music and the sound that his band created would have a huge influence on Monroe when he formed his own outfit.

In 1929, Monroe moved to Indiana to join his brothers Birch and Charlie. There they paid their dues working a series of low paying jobs. Their only recreation came at night and on the weekends when they played at local events. They extended their practical experience by joining the *National Barn Dance* tour on station WLS, in Chicago. In 1934, the station offered the trio full time employment.

However, Birch decided against a career in music so Charlie and Bill were left to form a duo, billed the Monroe Brothers. They did a tremendous amount of radio work and eventually drifted down to Carolina. It was here that Bill married and started a family. Later, his two children would carry on the fine family tradition; his son James eventually formed his own bluegrass outfit called the Midnight Ramblers.

In 1936, the Monroe Brothers were able to cut some records and of the ten sides laid down, "What Would You Give (in Exchange for Your Soul" became a major hit. They would do five more recording sessions over the next year and enjoy much success despite the fact that they were more comfortable with radio and live broadcasts than the studio. At the time they covered the songs of the Skillet Lickers, the Carter Family, Bradley Kincaid, and Jimmie Rodgers. The brothers hadn't yet begun to write their own material.

Despite performing as a successful duet for a number of years, they eventually went their separate ways because of different artistic opinions and internal squabbling from being together for so long. Bill formed the Kentuckians in Little Rock that would eventually evolve into the Blue Grass Boys. The fact that he was no longer in a band with his brother brought about a change in his style. He began to sing lead more often and played longer mandolin solos, distancing himself from the other members of the band.

In 1939, two important events occurred that would enable him to reach greater heights. The first, he performed for the first time on the *Grand Ole Opry* and became an immediate hit and a regular. Secondly, he played the song "Mule Skinner Blues" on his next appearance on the *Opry*; that sealed his spot on the popular show. The song became an early signature tune for him and served as an example of what he was capable of doing.

His style underwent more changes during this period. He added accordion player Sally Ann Forester and banjo player Stringbean to his group. Although the band had a dynamite sound, Monroe wasn't finished tinkering with it. He eventually dropped the accordion, and added the incredible talents of banjoist Earl Scruggs and guitarist Lester Flatt. By this time he had moved closer to the bluegrass sound that he would make famous.

For the next three years the Blue Grass Boys broke down barriers and created new parameters with their experimental bluegrass sound. They possessed a trio of excellent musicians in Monroe, Flatt and Scruggs. All three could solo with emotion and unrecognized power, as well as work within a group unit with interesting interplay. The songs "Blue Moon of Kentucky," "I Hear a Sweet Voice Calling," "I'm Going Back to Old Kentucky" and "Will You Be Loving Another Man" all featured the skill of Monroe, Flatt and Scruggs as well as other members Chubby Wise on fiddle and Howard Watts on bass.

The year 1948 brought about more changes. Flatt and Scruggs left the group, but Monroe was able to recruit Jimmy Martin, a singer with a powerful, unique voice that blended well with his own. As well, he switched labels, leaving Columbia over an argument when they signed the Stanley Brothers, a serious bluegrass rival. On Decca, Monroe entered his golden age of songwriter with self-penned tunes including "Uncle Pen," a heartfelt tribute to his uncle, "Roanoke," "Scotland," "My Little Georgia Rose,"

"Walking to Jerusalem," and "Working on a Building." The last two songs contained a religious message, part of the Monroe repertoire since his early days in Indiana when he was jamming with his brothers.

Like other country artists, Monroe suffered a decline in popularity during the 1950s due to the rise of rock and roll and rockabilly. But in some ways he benefited from the new music, especially when a young, rising star named Elvis Presley cut a version of "Blue Moon of Kentucky." But overall, the entire decade was a struggle until the folk revival.

The sweeping folk boom that began in the late 1950s mushroomed in the 1960s as white college students reached into the past of the long-standing American folk tradition. Suddenly blues singers that had been forgotten such as Sam Lightnin' Hopkins, Mississippi John Hurt, Mississippi Fred McDowell, Skip James, and Son House revived their sagging careers. As well, Bill Monroe was hailed a hero and suddenly bluegrass burned with a new intensity.

He began to tour college campuses and to his surprise was very well received. Monroe, still capable of churning out the hot solos and driving rhythms, didn't disappoint. He even appeared at the Newport Folk Festival, where he held his own against everyone else on the bil. The festival circuit became one of his most important live venues in the following years. Even after the interest in folk music gave way to psychedelic rock, Monroe retained his new fan base.

Throughout the 1970s and 1980s he continued to tour, never moving away from his bluegrass sound. He overcame a cancer scare and serious surgery to keep his career alive and well into the 1990s. By then his legendary Blue Grass Boys outfit had seen dozens of artists come through, all learning from the master and then heading out on their own to make their own name.

On September 9, 1996, Bill Monroe, the legendary bluegrass figure, was silenced, and with him a piece of country music history died.

Bill Monroe is the father of bluegrass. Although he didn't invent the style, he gave the genre its name, and was the leading exponent for some fifty years. He rode the bluegrass sound through good times and bad, but never wavered from it no matter how low his popularity sunk. His contributions to country music are numerous.

Bill Monroe was a first rate mandolin player. He had the ability to created a riveting, high powered sound that rivaled any other country music instrumentalist. He was able to play fast runs of notes and weld them with his powerful tenor vocal abilities. As a musician he was the complete package and inspired two generations of bluegrass players.

It was his inimitable bluegrass style that he built his legend on. His creation of the new form of country was based on uniting old-time string bands with the blues, and instrumental virtuosity. He laid down the format for the archetypal bluegrass band, a five piece acoustic ensemble of mandolin, guitar, fiddle, banjo and bass. The all-string sound with stinging, rapid, precise solos, switching leads, and dry, lonesome voices was his trademark. The members in the band challenged each other creating an exciting interplay of call and response.

He spawned a host of imitators that played in his Blue Grass Band and who struck out on their own. A partial list includes Stringbean, Earl Scruggs, Lester Flatt, Mac Wiseman, the Stanley Brothers, the Country Gentlemen, the Johnson Mountain Boys, Del McCroury, the Nashville Bluegrass Band, Old and In the Way, the Osborne Brothers, Peter Rowan, Desert Rose Band, Chris Hillman, Bill Keith, Benny Martin, Northern Lights, Byron Berline, Red Rector, Herschel Sizemore, Blueground Undergrass, Smokin' Grass, and Jim and Jennie and the Pinetops. But, Monroe's influence goes beyond all those names because in his wake there were thousands of aspiring musicians that picked up a string instrument in order to play bluegrass.

His achievements did not go unrewarded and there were many, many accolades. In the 1950s, Monroe established a country theme place called Bean Blossom Park in Indiana. A decade later he founded his own bluegrass festival entitled the Bill Monroe Bean Blossom Festival, which continued into the '90s. It was one of thousands of such events that occur around the world on an annual basis.

In 1970, Bill Monroe was inducted into the Country Music Hall of Fame and one year later into the Nashville Songwriters Association International Hall of Fame. In 1993, he received a Lifetime Achievement Award from the Grammy committee. But the greatest reward he received was the satisfaction of hearing some bluegrass band on the radio or in concert, knowing that he had originated the style that earned him the nickname the Bluegrass Rambler.

## Blue Grass Boys

*Banjo*
David "Stringbean" Akeman
  1942–1945
Earl Scruggs 1945–1948
Don Reno 1948–1949
Rudy Lyle 1949–1951
Larry Richardson 1950–1951
Joe Drumright
  1951, 1958, 1959, 1964
James Gar Bowers 1951
Roland "Sonny" Osborne 1952, 1953

*Bass*
Amos Garren 1939–1940
Bill "Cousin Wilbur" Westbrooks
  1940–1944, 1946–1948, 1951
Howard "Cedric Rainwater" Watts
  1944–1945
Andy "Bijou" Boyett 1945
Birch Monroe 1945–1947
Joe Forrester 1945–1946
Chuck Stripling 1947
Joel Price 1947–1948, 1949–1951

*Banjo*

Jim Smook 1952–1953, 1954
Rudy Lyle 1953–1954
Bobby Atkins 1954, 1958, 1961
Noah Crase 1954–1955, 1956
Joe Stuart 1955–1957
Roger Smith 1956–1957
Don Stover 1957
Bob Johnson 1958
Robert Lee "Buddy" Pennington
 1958, 1959
Earl Snead 1958, 1970–1971
Eddie Adcock 1958
Curtis McPeake 1960–1962
Tony Ellis 1960–1962
David Deese 1962
Lonnie Hoppers 1962–1963
Bill "Brad" Keith 1963
Steve Arkin 1964
Dan Lineberger 1964–1965
Sandy Rothman 1964
Lamar Grier 1965–1967
Butch Robins 1967, 1977–1981
Vic Jordan 1967–1969
Rual Yarbrough 1969–1970
R.C. Harris 1971, 1981
Jack Hicks 1971–1973
Bruce Nemerov 1973
Ben Pedigo 1973
Jim Moratto 1973–1974
Dwight Dillman 1974
Bob Black 1974–1976
Bill Holden 1976–1977
Larry Beasley 1977
Blake Williams 1981–1991
Dana Cupp 1991–1996

*Bass*

Jack Thompson 1948–1949
Oscar "Shorty" Sheehan 1951
Bessie Lee Mauldin 1953–1964
Leslie Sandy 1953–1954
Jimmy Elrod 1957
James Monroe 1964–1969
Doug Green 1969
Bill Yates 1969
Skip Payne 1970
Joe Stuart 1970–1971
Doug Hutchens 1971
Monroe Fields 1971–1973
Guy Stevenson 1973
Gregg Kennedy 1973–1974
Randy Davis 1974–1979
Raymond Huffmaster 1979
Mark Hembree 1970–1984
Clarence "Tater" Tate 1984–1986,
 1987–1989, 1990–1996
Johnny Montgomery 1986–1987
Billy Rose 1989–1990
Mark Kuykendall 1994–1995
Ernie Sykes 1996

*Fiddle*

Art Wooten 1939–1940,
 1941–1942
Tommy Magness 1940–1941,
 1942–1943
Howard "Howdy" Forrester
 1942, 1945–1946
Carl Story 1942–1943
Floyd Ethridge 1943, 1949
Chubby Wise 1943–1945,
 1946–1948, 1949–1950

*Guitar*

Cleo Davis 1938–1940
Clyde Moody 1940–1941, 1942–1944
Pete Pyle 1941–1942, 1953
Tex Willis 1945
Lester Flatt 1945–1948
Jackie Phelps 1948, 1954, 1963
Doyle Wright 1948
Jim Eanes 1948
Vern Young 1949
Mac Wiseman 1949

*Fiddle*

Jim Shumate 1945
Benny Martin 1948–1949, 1959
Gene Christian 1949–1950
Vassar Clements 1949–1950,
   1955, 1961–1962, 1967
Merle "Red" Taylor 1950–1951,
   1953–1954, 1958
Gordon Terry 1950–1951,
   1954, 1957
Charlie Cline 1952–1955
L.E. White 1953
Bobby Hicks 1954–1956,
   1958–1959
Jack Youngblood 1954
Clarence "Tater" Tate 1956–1957,
   1986–1987, 1988–1990
Kenny Baker 1957–1958, 1962–1963,
   1969–1977, 1977–1984
Joe Meadows 1957
Charlie Smith 1958–1960
Dale Potter 1959–1960
Billy Baker 1961, 1963, 1964
Bobby Joe Lester 1961
Buddy Spicher 1961, 1964–1965,
   1977, 1987–1988
Buddy Pendleton 1962
Harold "Red" Stanley 1962
Benny Williams 1962, 1964–1965,
   1967
Joe Stuart 1963, 1970, 1971
Gene Lowinger 1965–1966
Richard Greene 1966–1967
Byron Berline 1967
Art Stamper 1984
Randall "Randy" Franks 1984
Glen Duncan 1985–1986
Dale Morris 1985
Mark Squires 1986
Mike Feagan 1987–1988
Billy Joe Foster 1987–1988
Wayne Jerrolds 1988–1989
Jimmy Campbell 1990–1993
Robert Bowlin 1993–1996

*Guitar*

Jimmy Martin 1949–1951,
   1952–1954
Vic Daniels 1951
Johnny Vipperman 1951
South Salyers 1951
Carter Stanley 1951
Edd Mayfield 1951–1952,
   1954, 1958
Carlos Brock 1954–1955
Bill Price 1954, 1956
Arnold Terry 1955–1956
Bob Metzel 1956
Yates Green 1956
Bill Duncan 1957, 1960
Lucky Saylor 1956
Enos Johnson 1957
Leslie Sandy 1957
Carl Vanover 1957
Ernest Graves 1957
Jack Cooke 1958–1959
Connie Gately 1958–1959
Frank Buchanan 1960, 1962
Porter Church 1960
Bobby Smith 1960–1961
Jimmy Maynard 1961, 1962, 1964
Benny Williams 1961, 1963
Joe Stuart 1962–1963, 1971–1973
Jake Landers 1963
Del McCoury 1963–1964
Garry Thurmond 1964
Peter Rowan 1964–1967
Jimmy Elrod 1965
Curtis Blackwell 1967
Doug Green 1967
Roland White 1967–1969
James Monroe 1969–1972
Travis Stewart 1971
Don James 1971
Bob Fowler 1973
Bill Box 1973–1974
Ralph Lewis 1974–1976
Bob Jones 1976
Wayne Lewis 1976–1986
Tom Ewing 1986–1988,
   1989–1996
Scottie Baugus 1989

*Jug, Bones, Spoons*
Tommy Millard 1939

*Accordion*
Wilene "Sally Ann" Forrester 1943–1946

*Harmonica/Guitar*
Curley Bradshaw 1944–1945

*Tenor Banjo*
Jim Andrews 1945

# Discography

*Knee Deep in Bluegrass*, Decca 78731.
*I Saw the Light*, Decca 78769.
*Mr. Bluegrass*, Decca 74080.
*The Great Bill Monroe*, Harmony 7290.
*My All Time Country Favorites*, Decca 74327.
*Bluegrass Special* [Decca], Decca 4382.
*Bluegrass Ramble*, Decca 74266.
*I'll Meet You in Church Sunday Morning*, Decca 74537.
*Bill Monroe Sings Country Songs*, Vocalion 3702.
*Original Blue Grass Sound*, Harmony 74601.
*Lord, Build Me a Cabin*, Starday 361.
*The High Lonesome Sound of Bill Monroe*, Decca 74780.
*Charlie Monroe Sings Again*, Starday 372.
*Bluegrass Time*, Decca 74896.
*Voice from on High*, Decca 75135.
*Who's Calling You Sweetheart Tonight*, Camden 2310.
*Great Bill Monroe and the Bluegrass Boys*, Harmony 11335.
*Bluegrass Style*, Vocalion 3870.
*Kentucky Bluegrass*, Decca 75213.
*Uncle Pen*, Decca 75238.
*Bean Blossom*, MCA 8002.
*Bill Monroe Sings Bluegrass, Body and Soul*, MCA 2251.
*Bill Monroe and Friends*, MCA 5435.
*Bluegrass '87*, MCA 31310.
*Southern Flavor*, MCA 42133.
*Live at the Opry: Celebrating 50 Years at the Grand Ole Opry*, MCA 42286.
*Instrumental/Bluegrass Special*, MCA 8017.
*Mule Skinner Blues*, Roadracer 2494.
*Cryin' Holy Unto the Lord*, MCA 10017.
*Blue Moon of Kentucky* [Sony], MCA 20308.
*16 All Time Greatest Hits*, CGBSA 01065.
*The Best of Bill Monroe*, MCA 409.
*In the Pines*, County 114.
*Silver Eagle Cross Country Presents Live: Bill Monroe*, Silver Eagle 70007.
*Live from Mountain Stage*, Blue Plate 400.
*Live, Vol. 1*, Rural Rhythm 1015.
*Mansions for Me*, Music Mill 71007.
*Blue Moon of Kentucky 1936–1949*, Bear Family 16399.
*July 1963: Two Days at Newport, and More*, Bears 25001.
*And the Blue Grass Boys: Live at Mechanic's Hall*, Acoustic Disc 59.
*Father of Bluegrass Music*, Camden 7219.

*Live Duet Recordings 1963–1980*, Smithsonian/Folkways 40064.
*Bill Monroe's Best*, Harmony 7315.
*Bill Monroe's Greatest Hits*, Decca 75010.
*Bill Monroe and His Bluegrass Boys*, Columbia 1065.
*Feast Here Tonight*, Bluebird 5510.
*The Bill Monroe/Flatt and Scruggs*, Rounder SS-06.
*Master of Bluegrass*, MCA 818.
*The Best of Bill Monroe* [Special Music], Special Music 3021.
*Columbia Historic Edition*, Columbia 38904.
*Bill Monroe at His Best*, Highland 409.
*Bluegrass 1950–1958*, Bear Family 15423.
*Bluegrass 1959–1969*, Bear Family 15529.
*Country Music Hall of Fame*, MCA 10082.
*The Essential Bill Monroe (1945–1949)*, Columbia/Legacy 52478.
*Live Recordings 1956–1959*, Smithsonian/Folkways 40063.
*The Music of Bill Monroe*, MCA 11048.
*Bluegrass (1970–1979)*, Bear Family 15606.
*Orange Blossom Special* [live], KRB 5038.
*16 Gems*, Columbia/Legacy 53908.
*The Essential Bill Monroe and Monroe Brothers*, RCA 67450.
*The Early Years*, Vanguard 79518.
*The Father of Bluegrass: Early Years 1940–1947*, ASV/Living Era 5298.
*20th Century Masters—The Millennium Collection: The Best of Bill Monroe*, MCA 70109.
*American Traveler*, County 119.
*Blue Moon of Kentucky* [Country Stars], Country Stars 55461.
*Greatest Hits*, Classic World 2006.
*Bluegrass Special* [Catfish], Catfish 198.
*RCA Country Legends*, RCA 65120.
*The Very Best of Bill Monroe and the Bluegrass Boys*, RCA 112982.
*Introduction*, Universal International 882881.
*Essential Collection*, Spectrum Music 113068.
*Anthology*, MCA 113207.
*The Gospel Spirit*, MCA 000290702.
*Shady Grove*, Fruit Tree 843.
*The Definitive Collection*, MCA 000442402.
*Bluegrass Legends*, Direct Source 53222.
*Country Hit Parade: Live*, Direct Source 54112.
*Nine Pound Hammer*, Tomato Music 21.

# ERNEST TUBB (1914–1984)

## *The Texas Troubadour*

To properly play country music one must live the life. Jimmie Rodgers, the Singing Brakeman, as well as Hank Williams, Sr., personified this philosophy perhaps more than any other performers before or since. There was another individual who took to heart this musical perspective, whose hero was the late, great Rodgers. Ernest Tubb, the Texas Troubadour, lived and breathed country music.

Ernest Dale Tubb was born on February 9, 1914, in Crisp, Texas. The first twenty years of his life were spent on the farm where he became acquainted with hard work and dreams of a musical career seemed as far away as the moon. It wasn't until he heard Jimmie Rodgers yodeling through his repertoire that Tubb decided to pursue a path in the entertainment field. However, despite his strong ambitions, his progress moved at a snail's pace.

It was upon a meeting with Carrie Rodgers (Jimmie's widow) that Tubb began to turn his dreams into reality. He obtained Rodgers' famous Martin 000–45 guitar that proved to be a strange talisman for him. It filled him with a creative energy and confidence, which was exactly what he had needed all along.

From this point on, Tubb's career accelerated quickly. Although his singing style was a direct imitation of his idol Rodgers, he was not to be denied. He started playing on the radio as well as cutting his first two songs for the Victor label, both tributes to his hero, "The Passing of Jimmie Rodgers," and "The Last Thoughts of Jimmie Rodgers." His radio gig in Fort Worth eventually led to his sponsorship by Universal Mills makers of Gold Chain Flour. Tubb became the Gold Chain Troubadour.

Tubb, a solid performer who eventually emerged from the shadow of Rodgers by developing his own distinct style, knew a good hook when he saw one. He began to project himself as the Gold Chain Troubadour, greatly enhancing his popularity. It was an image that fans could identify with and as a result his career exploded in a multitude of directions.

Aside from his regular radio show, he appeared in his first film in 1941, *Fightin' Buckaroos*, and continued to cut songs as a solo artist as well as with his band. He finally hit the top of the charts with a self-penned 1943 hit "Walking the Floor Over You." The song opened many doors, including a regular spot on the *Grand Ole Opry*.

He continued to add to his famed Texas Troubadour image by waxing numerous hits and appearing in such movies as *Ridin' West, Jamboree* and *Hollywood Barn Dance*. In 1947, he opened up his recording shop in Nashville and began broadcasting his Midnight Jamboree radio program from there. He was able to advertise his commercial adventure as well as self-promote his next concert. It was a pure stroke of marketing genius.

For the next thirty years, Tubb went about the business of adding to his future hall of fame career. He worked with the Andrews Sisters and Red Foley, among others, toured extensively in an attempt to live up to his troubadour image, and scored a number of top ten hits, many self-penned.

He was also a staple at the *Grand Ole Opry*, churning out his honky tonk music with pure emotional power.

In the mid–1940s he started to tour exclusively with the Texas Troubadours, his band, and began a streak of hit singles that would last well into the 1960s. Throughout the 1950s he was Mr. Consistency, one of the hardest working artists in country music. His appearances on the *Grand Ole Opry* helped solidify the appeal of the genre and made Nashville the universal center of the style.

In the 1960s he began to show signs of slowing down; his records began to sell less because of the stiff competition from newer honky tonk artists. Although he was diagnosed with emphysema near the end of the decade, he refused to heed doctor's orders to slow down. In many ways he was repeating the self-destructive path his hero Jimmie Rodgers had taken.

The 1970s were a difficult decade for Tubb. He scored a couple of minor hits, but his health forced him to tour less often. Although he was still acknowledged as a country music icon in some circles, he was being overshadowed by many of the rising stars in the industry. By the end of the decade his once burning career had completely fizzled out.

In the early 1980s, his career had come to an end. On September 6, 1984, Ernest Tubb, one of the greatest country music stars, died.

Ernest Tubb was a country troubadour. During an illustrious career that spanned six decades, he did as much as any other figure to expand the appeal of the music to a national audience. There was always a Texas stubborn streak in his attitude that enabled him to do things that no one else would dare attempt. His courage opened the doors for others.

Ernest Tubb recorded as many hits as anyone else, and more than most. A partial list includes "Slippin' Around," "Blue Christmas," "Goodnight Irene," "I Love You Because," " Missing in Action," "Two Glasses Joe," "Half a Mind," "Thanks a Lot," "Mr. and Mrs. Used to Be," "Another Story, Another Time, Another Place," "Try Me One More Time," "Soldier's Last Letter," "It's Been So Long Darling," "Rainbow at Midnight," "Filipino Baby," "Drivin' Nails in My Coffin," "Have You Ever Been Lonely? (Have You Ever Been Blue?)," "Let's Say Goodbye Like We Said Hello," "I'm Biting My Fingernails and Thinking of You" "I Love You Because," "Throw Your Love My Way" and "Tennessee Border No. 2." Each song contained that Tubb magic—the distinct voice and instrumental touch.

Tubb was someone who could claim a lot of firsts. He was the first one to make the electric guitar a part of his act on the *Opry*. He became the first artist to record in Nashville. He was the first country music artist to appear at the prestigious Carnegie Hall, usually reserved for classical or jazz concerts. He became the first artist to chart 13 hit records in one year (1949).

He was also the initiator of honky tonk. He took the essential elements of the Jimmie Rodgers style and gave it a rougher edge. Throughout the years Roy Acuff, Hank Williams, Lefty Frizzell, and George Jones would all be cited as major contributors to the style; however, it was Tubb with his wailing electric guitar and his ability to give his songs a razor edge that truly symbolized the movement.

Although Jimmie Rodgers had the greatest impact on Tubb, the latter developed his own distinct style which, in turn, influenced a host of followers. A partial list includes Buddy Emmons, Asleep at the Wheel, Johnny Cash, Lefty Frizzell, Jack Greene, Loretta Lynn, Cal Smith, Johnny Russell, Justin Tubb, Ronnie Dove, Skeeter Davis, Hank Williams, and the Crook Brothers. In truth, the Texas Troubadour had a special force on anyone he came in contact with, especially Hank Williams.

The raw-boned, semi-literate Williams, with a facility for lyrics and harmonies, stole a page from the Tubb musical book. One of the hardest honky tonk performers and the biggest modern influence on other artists, Williams emerged from the shadow of his idol much in the same way that Tubb had done by distancing himself from the sphere of Rodgers.

It was Tubb who introduced Canadian Hank Snow to American country music and ensured that he became a regular at the *Opry*. Without Tubb's help, it is doubtful that Snow would have cracked the U.S. music market to the same extent that he did. Throughout his career the Texas Troubadour was always glad to help out an aspiring musician.

Tubb, a proud father who sired a large brood, was perhaps proudest of his eldest son, Justin, who followed his famous father into country music. The young Tubb began performing in high school and eventually received solid recognition when his father recorded one of his songs. He also had a hit radio show and recorded for Decca in the 1950s. In 1955, he became a regular on the *Opry*. Like his father, he toured the world, including Canada, Bermuda, Spain, Britain, West Germany, Panama and Vietnam.

Ernest Tubb worked with a great number of country artists and those outside the genre. A partial list includes Owen Bradley, Grady Martin, Harold Bradley, Jack Drake, Pete Drake, Billy Byrd, the Wilburn Brothers, Hargus "Pig" Robbins, Ray Edenton, Marty Robbins, Waylon Jennings, Floyd Cramer, Chet Atkins, Teddy Wilburn, Farris Coursey, and Jerry Shook. Some of the aforementioned were members of his Texas Troubadours and logged thousands of miles performing on the international stage. Two members of his band, Cal Smith and Jack Greene, went on to successful solo careers after earning their performance spurs with the Troubadours.

Ernest Tubb was also a prime architect of the Texas country sound. Although he was not the originator of the style, his individual voice had that special twang that clearly indicated the location of his birth. There was always a Lone Star State ingredient to his music that was one of the reasons why he was so successful. As well, many of those that passed through his band, the Troubadours, were from Texas.

He made his native state proud, but he wasn't the only one. Along with Vernon Dalhart, Bob Wills, Hank Thompson, Willie Nelson, Tex Ritter, Gene Autry, Ray Price, George Jones, Dale Evans, Buck Owens, Waylon Jennings and Kenny Rogers, he helped put the Lone Star State on the country music map. Dozens of other country musicians hailed from the state that added to that lowdown Tex sound, including members of the Lost Valley Brazos Boys, Willie Nelson's group and the Cherokee Cowboys, among others. Texas has always been a hotbed of music styles and the aforementioned group rivals any of the blues, jazz, folk and rock personalities that can claim an authentic Texas birth certificate.

It was Tubb, Nelson, Rogers, Owens and others who sparked a new generation of Texas country artists. A partial list includes Barbara Mandrell, Louise Mandrell, Ronnie Dunn, the Dixie Chicks, George Strait, Lee Ann Womack, and Tanya Tucker, among others. These new Lone State country singers carry on the tradition that the older set established in the first 50 years of the genre.

In 1965, Tubb was the sixth member to be inducted to the Country Music Hall of Fame. In 1970, he became one of the initial members of the Nashville Songwriters International Hall of Fame. In a career that spanned from 1932 to 1984, there is very little that Tubb did not accomplish. His legacy and legend he left behind as the Texas Troubadour is one that will live forever.

## Ernest Tubb and the Texas Troubadours*
Original Lineup

| Guitar | Bass | Fiddle |
|---|---|---|
| Ernest Tubb | Jack Drake | Johnny Sapp |
| Harold Bradley | | |
| Chester Studdard | | |

| Steel Guitar | Comedy/Vocals | |
|---|---|---|
| Ray "Kemo" Head | Vernon Toby Reese | |

*There were over a hundred versions of the Texas Troubadours. Some of the alumni that passed through include Buddy Emmons, Cal Smith, Billy Byrd, Jan Kurtis, Leon Rhodes, Johnny Johnson, Jimmy Short, Buddy Charleton and Tommy "Butterball" Paige.

## Discography

*Old Rugged Cross*, Decca 5334.
*Jimmie Rodgers Songs*, Decca 5336.
*Ernest Tubb's Favorites [1952]*, Decca 5301.

*The Daddy of 'Em All*, Decca 8553.
*The Importance of Being Ernest*, Decca 78834.
*Record Shop*, Decca 74042.
*Ernest Tubb and His Texas Troubadours*, Vocalion 3684.
*Midnight Jamboree*, Decca 4045.
*On Tour*, Decca 4321.
*Family Bible*, Decca 74397.
*The Texas Troubadours*, Decca 74459.
*Just Call Me Lonesome*, Decca 74385.
*Thanks a Lot*, Decca 74514.
*Blue Christmas*, Decca 74518.
*Country Dance Time*, Decca 74644.
*My Pick of the Hits*, Decca 74640.
*Hittin' the Road*, Decca 74681.
*Mr. and Mrs. Used to Be*, Decca 74639.
*Ernest Tubb and Loretta Lynn*, Decca 4639.
*Ernest Tubb Sings Country Hits, Old and New*, Decca 74772.
*Ernest Tubb's Fabulous Texas Troubadours*, Decca 74745.
*By Request*, Decca 74746.
*Another Story*, Decca 74867.
*Singin' Again*, Decca 74872.
*Stand by Me*, Vocalion 3765.
*The Terrific Texas Troubadours*, Decca 75017.
*Ernest Tubb Sings Hank Williams*, Decca 74957.
*Country Hit Time*, Decca 75072.
*Let's Turn Back the Years*, Decca 7514.
*Saturday Satan, Sunday Saint*, Decca 75122.
*If We Put Our Heads Together*, Decca 75115.
*Great Country*, Vocalion 3877.
*Good Year for the Wine*, Decca 75222.
*One Sweet Hello*, Decca 75301.
*Say Something Nice to Sarah*, Decca 75345.
*Baby, It's So Hard to Be Good*, Decca 75388.
*I've Got All the Heartaches I Can Handle*, MCA 341.
*Ernest Tubb*, ACM 014.
*Ernest Tubb*, MCA 496.
*Ernest Tubb with T. Texas Tyler*, Radiola MR 1141.
*Family Bible*, MCA 20469.
*Slippin' Around*, MCA 20381.
*Christmas*, MCA 15043.
*Walking the Floor Over You*, MCA 20496.
*Tribute to a Legend*, Excelsior 7135.
*Live from the Lonestar Café*, First 105.
*Classics*, Varese 066489.
*Radio Shows*, Radio 1141.
*Together*, MCA 20514.
*Ernest Tubb Favorites [1956]*, Decca 8291.
*The Ernest Tubb Story [with the Texas Troubadours]*, Decca 159.
*All Time Hits*, Decca 70046.
*Golden Favorites*, Decca 74118.
*Ernest Tubb's Greatest Hits*, Decca 75006.
*Ernest Tubb's Greatest Hits, Vol. 2*, Decca 75252.

*Greatest Hits,* MCA 16.
*Greatest Hits,* Vol. 2 MCA 24.
*The Living Legend,* First Generation 101.
*The Legend and the Legacy,* Edsel 517.
*Honky Tonk Classics,* Rounder 0014.
*Country Hall of Fame,* CDL 8078.
*Country Music Hall of Fame,* MCA 10086.
*Retrospective, Vol. 1,* MCA 20505.
*Retrospective, Vol. 2,* MCA 20506.
*Mr. Juke Box,* MCA 20470.
*Live 1965,* Rhino 70902.
*The Ernest Tubb Collection,* Step 0014.
*Let's Say Goodbye Like We Said Hello,* Bear Family 15498.
*Legendary: It's Been So Long Darling,* Laserlight 12117.
*Waltz Across Texas,* Laserlight 72115.
*Legendary,* Laserlight 15955.
*Legendary, Vol. 4: Rainbow at Midnight,* Laserlight 12118.
*Legendary: Soldiers Last Letter,* Laserlight 12119.
*Yellow Rose of Texas,* Bear Family 15688.
*Walking the Floor Over You* [box set], Bear Family 15853.
*Tribute to a Legend,* Intercontinent 1135.
*The Best of Ernest Tubb,* Curb 77870.
*The Very Best of Ernest Tubb,* Half Moon 024.
*Complete Live 1965 Show,* Lost Gold 5018.
*Live New Year's Eve 1979,* Lost Gold 1979.
*Just You and Me Daddy,* First Generation 109.
*Another Story,* Bear Family 15935.
*Last Sessions: All Time Greatest Hits,* First Generation 108.
*Country Hoedown,* Jasmine 3511.
*Early Hits of "The Texas Troubadour,"* ASV/Living Era 5322.
*There's a Little Bit of Everything in Texas,* Jasmine 3525.
*Early Country Radio, Vol. 2,* ACM 023.
*Legendary, Vol. 2,* Laserlight 12116.

# LESTER FLATT (1914–1979)
## *Flat Pickin'*

The bluegrass tradition established by Bill Monroe fueled the imagination of hundreds of other country performers who were determined to ensure the genre's continued success. They arrived from every corner of the United States and many of them became part of Monroe's band, the Blue Grass Boys. One of these individuals became famous because of the prowess of his flat pickin' style. His name was Lester Flatt.

Lester Raymond Flatt was born on June 19, 1914, in Overton County,

Tennessee, into a musical family. Both of his parents played the banjo in an older style called frailing. Lester picked up the guitar and banjo as a youngster, but was strictly an amateur performing at local events with his parents. He eventually found work in a textile mill, but listened to hillbilly music and continued to hone his skills.

Through the magic of radio, Flatt heard the distinct sound of Bill and Charlie Monroe on a Carolina station in the years before the Second World War. At the time, Flatt was living in Covington, Virginia, and he would jam with local bands. By 1939, one of these groups evolved into the Harmonizers that played on the Roanoke, Virginia, station. He moved on to the Happy-Go-Lucky Boys that included Clyde Moody, who had played and recorded with the revered Bill Monroe.

In 1943, Charlie Monroe, Bill's older brother, hired Flatt for the Kentucky Pardners. Flatt boosted the outfit with his tenor harmony and mandolin abilities. However, Lester soon tired of the constant traveling and retired from professional music to become a trucker. But he had the fever and a few months later became a DJ on a North Carolina radio station. He might have remained as a part-time radio jockey and trucker if it hadn't been for a telegram Bill Monroe sent to him to head to Nashville to be on the *Grand Ole Opry*.

During his tenure in Bill Monroe's Blue Grass Boys, Flatt put the finishing touches on his vocal style by switching from lead to background tenor. As well, he developed the fame Lester Flatt G Run, a dash through a series of notes done at breakneck speed in true bluegrass fashion. In doing so, he became a vital member of Monroe's rise to popularity. In concert, Flatt learned how to entertain the crowd with his musical skills as well as comedy and variety stage patter.

The teamwork between the five members of the Blue Grass Boys helped popularize bluegrass and also injected much needed life into the *Grand Ole Opry*. During his three-year tenure with Monroe, Flatt played on many records and was even given credit on some of the songs. However, despite the accolades, he grew tired of the nonstop touring and left the fold in 1948.

At about the same time Earl Scruggs, the brilliant banjo player who had developed a fluid style that was integral to the sound of the Blue Grass Boys, also left. It was natural for Flatt and Scruggs to team up together since were both were keen on continuing the bluegrass tradition. They enjoyed working together and the interplay between the guitarist with the wild-eyed licks and the banjoist with the hot notes was pure dynamite.

They augmented their duo with the addition of fiddler Jim Shumate (who had played with Monroe), as well as bassist Howard Watts, who worked under the stage name Cedric Rainwater. The four moved to Hickory, North Carolina, and made their first recordings on the Mercury label. Mandolin player Mac Wiseman later joined the group, but left and Curly Seckler replaced him. The group needed a name and decided on Foggy Mountain Boys, taken from a Carter Family song "Foggy Mountain Top."

The diversity of the group ensured them a consistent fan base across the country music spectrum. They possessed a versatility that was uncommon in musical circles because each member could play all string instruments with the ferocity of a freight train rambling down the tracks at breakneck speed. They gave the bluegrass style a harsher edged sound that distanced them from their mentor Monroe.

The Foggy Mountain Boys continued to broadcast on the radio, usually out of Bristol, Tennessee, but also from other Southern stations. They jammed with other bluegrass enthusiasts including the Stanley Brothers and Don Reno. Whether they performed with other musicians or took to the stage as a single act, the group rarely failed to live up to the crowd's expectations. They delivered swinging music that was exciting and thrilling.

In 1949, they released "Foggy Mountain Breakdown," their signature song that left all competition in their wake. More than just being a massive hit, the song perfectly captured the bluegrass feel that they were trying to convey. It remained a popular and often requested live number that never lost any of its shine. The song would one day serve as the soundtrack for the movie *Bonnie and Clyde* during the famous car chase scene. The group also recorded old classics such as "Roll in My Baby's Sweet Arms" and "Old Salty Dog Blues" done with a bluegrass feeling.

Although bluegrass might be considered an acquired taste, the Foggy Mountain Boys were never out of work. They were one of the most popular attractions on the country music circuit and continued to record on a regular basis. For example, the group was part of a show that Ernest Tubb and Lefty Frizzell headlined. However, Flatt and Scruggs stole the spotlight with their song "Earl's Breakdown." During the number, Scruggs switched his tuning with the innovative Scruggs Peg.

The folk revival of the late 1950s and early 1960s brought bluegrass back into prominence and the Foggy Mountain Boys benefited from it. They became favorites of the folk crowd since they represented a side of the style that was unique and rich. They criss-crossed the country in order to fulfill the demand for their music and continued to cut albums with growing sales.

Throughout the 1960s they performed on every medium. They played all of their hits on Nashville radio as well as introducing new songs, tempting the public to go out and buy their records. In 1965, they expanded their popularity with their own television show as well as a regular spot on the *Grand Ole Opry*. Although their popularity had reached a high plateau by this point in their career, it truly exploded when they sang the "The Ballad of Jed Clampett," the theme song for the TV hit *The Beverly Hillbillies*. Their long admired pickin' style was at its finest on the opening and closing songs. Scruggs and Flatt even appeared on the show as themselves and would play a song or two. When the corny program ended its run, the show went into syndication and a new generation heard the song, widening the duo's already large fan base.

Later in the decade, after the folk boom subsided, the two carried on. Despite the lull in popularity for bluegrass, Flatt and Scruggs continued to pick their way to the top, winning numerous awards and fan polls. Their music transcended country music tastes to include fans of the burgeoning rock and roll sound, as well as blues and pop.

While they remained true to the bluegrass tradition, the pair also experimented with the basic sound, adding drums and gospel style harmonies. It did nothing to deter their popularity and exposed them to a new crowd that picked up on their incredible talent. Many country musicians were attempting to add to the rich country sound with electric guitars, strings and other ideas.

In 1969, the duo of Flatt and Scruggs went their separate ways. It had been a long and very successful run, but the artistic differences made it impossible for them to continue working together. In many ways, it was the end of an era.

Flatt continued along a more traditional path and formed the Nashville Grass, a group dedicated to keeping the bluegrass flame alive. He also made some recordings with his old friend Mac Wiseman. By the end of the 1970s, Flatt and Scruggs were planning a reunion that was brutally ended with Lester's death on May 11, 1979.

Lester Flatt was a bluegrass institution. Along with his partner Earl Scruggs, he was one of the single most important exponents of the genre and even overshadowed Bill Monroe, his former boss and the inventor of the style. Flatt was a tremendously talented musician, singer and songwriter, who developed his own distinct guitar style that influenced a generation of country pickers.

There was an honesty to his music. Although he never tried to make his sound overly complicated, because of his ability to pick out clear, precise notes with lightning speed, Flatt was hard to imitate. If he would have only added his distinct guitar touch to the genre, he would have become famous; but, he had much more to offer.

Lester Flatt is one of three men in history responsible for making bluegrass an acceptable and popular style. The other two were Bill Monroe and Earl Scruggs. It is impossible to say which one was the most talented musician of the three, but, arguably Flatt possessed the greatest diversity.

He was not only a very gifted musician, but he also possessed a rich tenor voice that could be used as a mighty lead weapon or blended in the background to create intense harmonies. It was his voice that entered the millions of living rooms every week via *The Beverly Hillbillies* television show. Perhaps he didn't possess the most original style; however, he did have an affectionate timbre that was both soothing, yet exciting.

Flatt had a major influence on a number of individuals. A partial list includes the Dillards, Reno and Smiley, Ricky Skaggs, Mac Wiseman, Chris Hillman, Benny Martin, the Nitty Gritty Dirt Band, Paul Warren, the Blue Shadows, the Bluegrass Alliance, Tommy Jarrell, the Ghost Rockets, Richard Gilewitz, and many others. His impact goes beyond bluegrass and many of the blues, folk and rock artists stole a page from the Flatt style. Undoubtedly, he was one of the most important post-war musical figures.

Although he achieved great fame and made a fortune, there was always a good ol' country boy side to Flatt. He never boasted of his bountiful abilities and let the music do his talking. His prominence was rewarded when he was inducted into the Country Music Hall of Fame in 1985 along with his partner Earl Scruggs. Whether a part of the famed duo, leading another band or as a solo artist, the enormous contributions Lester Flatt made to country music with his flat pickin' cannot be overstated.

## Foggy Mountain Boys
### 1948–1969

| *Guitar* | *Banjo* | *Fiddle* |
|---|---|---|
| Lester Flatt | Earl Scruggs | Paul Warren |
| Frank "Hylo" Brown | | Robert "Chubby" Wise |
| Jim Eanes | | Jim Shumate |
| Mac Wiseman | | Benny Martin |
| Billy E. Powers | | Benny Sims |
| Johnny Johnson | | Howdy Forrester |
| | | Art Wooten |

| *Mandolin* | *Dobro* | *Bass* |
|---|---|---|
| John Ray "Curly" Seckler | Burkett "Uncle Josh" Graves | Burkett "Uncle Josh" Graves |
| Everette Lilly | | English P. "Cousin Jake" Tullock |
| Curly Lambert | | Howard Watts aka Cedric Rainwater |
| | | Charles Johnson aka "Little Jody Rainwater" |
| | | Frank "Hylo" Brown |
| | | Charles "Little Darlin'" Elza |
| | | Joe Stuart |

## Discography

*Flatt on Victor*, RCA 4495.
*Nashville Airplane*, CBS 63570.
*The One and Only Lester Flatt*, King 508.
*Lester 'n' Mac*, RCA 4745.
*Foggy Mountain Breakdown*, RCA 4789.
*On the South Bound*, RCA 4688.
*Before You Go*, RCA 0470.
*Over the Hills to the Poorhouse*, RCA 0309.
*Heaven's Bluegrass Band*, Checkmate 1020.
*Lester Flatt*, Sonet 717.
*Foggy Mountain Banjo*, Bluegrass 701.
*Nashville Grass: Fantastic Pickin'*, CMH 6232.
*Lester Flatt's Greatest Performance*, CMH 6238.
*Flatt and Scruggs*, CBS 25018.
*Live Broadcast*, Sandy Hook 2104.
*Live at the Bluegrass Festival*, CMH 9009.
*Lester Raymond Flatt*, Flying Fish 19.
*Pickin' Time*, CMH 6226.
*Live at Vanderbilt*, Bear Family 16614.
*Greatest Bluegrass Hits, Vol. 1*, CMH 4503.
*20 Greatest Hits*, Gusto 1031.
*Golden Hits*, Gusto 297.
*At His Best*, Hollywood 291.
*Living Legend*, CMH 9002.
*Flatt on Victor Plus More*, Bear Family 15975.
*Lester Flatt and the Nashville Grass*, CMH 8414.
*RCA Country Legends*, RCA 65142.
*Essential Bluegrass Gospel*, CMH 6298.
*Gospel*, Music Hall 70051.

# HANK WILLIAMS, SR. (1923–1953)
## *Life to Legend*

By the 1940s country music was an established art form. It had been recorded for twenty years; it had been blessed with many talented individuals who had had spread the genre from coast to coast and internationally. But the genre needed to return to its roots and reinvent itself after the end of World War II. Another superstar was needed—someone with the charisma and talent of a Jimmie Rodgers. The individual arrived on the scene like a shooting star and in a brief four years ensured that country music would last for another century. His story was a genuine life to legend tale. His name was Hank Williams, Sr.

Hiram King Williams was born on September 17, 1923, in Georgiana, Alabama. His first exposure to music was through the church where he sang in the choir. A year later he received a guitar from his mother. One of the most remarkable parts of the Hank Williams legend is that the semi-literate, raw boned individual who made such an impact on country music was mostly self-taught, which underlines his vast talent. Aside from a few lessons from local black blues performer Tee-Pot (Rufe Payne), Williams developed his own style. He also listened closely to the records of Jimmie Rodgers.

Once he was proficient enough to play in front of an audience he appeared at local events at the small outlets around Alabama. In 1937, he moved to Montgomery and it was here that he formed his first group, the Drifting Cowboys. When he was a teenager he won first place at an amateur contest singing "WPA Blues." This led to a spot on the local radio WSFA station, where he remained for the next decade.

By 1946, Williams was married to Audrey Mae Sheppard, who would have a major impact on his career. Although he was a local hero, his frustration was real since he was unable to break out of the Alabama bar scene. Like most other country musicians trying to make it big in the business after the Second World War, the road led to Nashville. So that year, he and his bride moved to the capital of country music in order to give his career a much needed boost.

They sought out Fred Rose, perhaps the most powerful man in Nashville at the time (with the possible exception of George Hay, who ran the *Grand Ole Opry*). Eventually Williams was able to record for Sterling Records and cut "Never Again" as well as "Honky Tonkin'." The success of the two singles enabled him to score a contract with MGM a year later. Rose would play a vital role in the rise of Hank's career; he become his business manager and strategically plotted every move.

Williams, one of the greatest songwriters in the annals of country music, scored with his self-penned "Move It on Over," a song that has been covered by a variety of acts, including slide guitar blues-rocker George Thorogood. The hit earned Hank a spot on *Louisiana Hayride* in 1948, and he continued to churn out hits, including "I'm a Long Gone Daddy" and "Lovesick Blues."

On June 11, 1949, Hank Williams became a superstar. It was on this night that he debuted on the *Grand Ole Opry*, singing "Lovesick Blues." Over 50 years later it is still considered one of the greatest single moments in country music history, if not the greatest. He was brought back for a half dozen encores by the audience and the modern era in country music was born.

After his unprecedented performance on the *Grand Ole Opry*, it seemed that he could do no wrong. He cranked out top ten singles with monotonous regularity. With Fred Rose masterminding all aspects of the songs he cut, including production, songwriting, arranging and playing, Williams rocketed to the top of the country music heap with breathtaking speed.

Williams reformed his long-standing band the Drifting Cowboys to include guitarist Bob McNett, bassist Hillous Butrum, fiddler Jerry Rivers, and steel guitarist Don Helms. They traveled throughout the nation playing sold-out venues and earning more money than any other previous country music act. His fame continued to rise as he topped the charts in 1949, 1950, and 1951.

His appeal spread beyond the borders of country music, as he appeared on Perry Como's television show for an even wider audience. Williams and the Drifting Cowboys were part of package show and shared the stage with a variety of acts, including Bob Hope, Jack Benny, and Minnie Pearl. As well, after Tony Bennett had recorded a cover version of "Cold, Cold Heart," there began a deluge of artists waxing versions of Williams' songs, including Jo Stafford, Guy Mitchell, Frankie Laine, and Teresa Brewer, among others.

But the Law of Negative Compensation, the theory that stars are eventually dealt a bad hand, reared its ugly head in Williams' personal life in 1951. He was always a fan of the bottle, and his increasing alcoholism ran parallel with the increased pressures imposed on him in his climb to stardom. His marriage to Audrey was falling apart and a hunting accident left him with a cranky back that was only placated with heavy doses of morphine and his favorite painkiller, alcohol. He eventually became hooked on morphine.

In 1952, his marriage was finally over as Audrey could not handle his reckless ways anymore. Their fractious relationship had been a valuable source of many of his best songs, and the breakup also provided adequate fuel. He went to live with his mother and continued his descent into self-destruction.

It was his belligerent attitude as well as his heavy drinking that resulted in his firing from the *Grand Ole Opry* in 1952. As quickly as his star had risen it had fallen. Soon the members of the Drifting Cowboys abandoned him one by one because of his unpredictable and wild behavior. He eventually moved back to Nashville and started to play with Ray Price.

In the fall of 1952, he married Billy Jean Jones, ten years his junior. The problems continued to pile up despite his new love, as he was forced to pay child care to one of his on the side lovers, Bobbie Jett. He continued to play concerts when he showed up for them, but was backed by a pickup band and his once mighty musical muscle had long faded; he was a shell of his former self. As well, the prescriptions provided by a quack doctor only accelerated the failing of his health.

On January 1, 1953, Williams was scheduled to perform in Canton, Ohio. Because of severe weather, he hired a teenage chauffeur to drive him all the way to his destination instead of flying. Along the way, Hank Williams, Sr., after years of abusing his body, died of a heart attack induced by alcoholism and drug dependence. The country music legend was 29 years old.

Hank Williams is the single most important figure in post-war country music, and along with Jimmie Rodgers is the most influential artist of the last century. His ability to write songs that rang true, his skill in delivering them with a bravado edge, and his charisma are all part of the legend of Hank Williams.

There was a raw emotional edge to his singing that contained a plaintive, sad timbre, as well as a rambunctious element that hinted at something greater. He was a honky tonk specialist before the genre became an everyday word. He was born to sing that low down style that was injected with blues power and cut to the very bone of the loneliness, desperation, and darkness of the human condition.

The blues element in his music cannot be overstated, but he was more than just a talented blues shouter with a country twinge. He had a knack for delivering songs with a country twang that spoke volumes to his listeners. His music burned with an undying passion that has rarely been equalled by anyone before him or since his untimely death.

When he was buried in Montgomery, Alabama, his funeral drew thousands of mourners. There was a strong feeling of frustration over the fact that he could have lived longer had he taken better care of himself, but his early death is part of what makes the legend of Hank Williams so amazing. His life was like a bad Hollywood script without a happy ending.

For years after his death his songs continued to hit charts and sell records, although many of the songs that were released failed to live up to the top level production of his halcyon days. It seemed that several shady figures wanted to cash in on his name and many did. There was always a negative atmosphere of some of the characters that were part of the Hank Williams story. He was an easily led figure; undesirables often took advantage of him. But that is also part of his legend.

In his brief recording career he had dozens of hit singles. A partial list includes "Your Cheatin' Heart," "Kaw-Liga," "Take These Chains from My Heart," "Lovesick Blues," "Wedding Bells," "Mind Your Own

Business," "You're Gonna Change (or I'm Gonna Leave)," "My Bucket's Got a Hole in It," "Long Gone Lonesome Blues," "Why Don't You Love Me," "Moanin' the Blues," "I Just Don't Like This Kind of Livin'," "My Son Calls Another Man Daddy," "They'll Never Take Her Love from Me," "Why Should We Try," "Nobody's Lonesome for Me," "Cold, Cold Heart," "Dear John," "Hey, Good Lookin'" "Howlin' at the Moon," "I Can't Help It (If I'm Still in Love with You)," "Crazy Heart," "Lonesome Whistle," "Baby, We're Really in Love," "Honky Tonk Blues," "Half As Much," "Jambalaya," "Settin' the Woods on Fire," "You Win Again," and his last song, the foreshadowing "I'll Never Get Out of This World Alive." According to legend, Williams wrote over seven hundred songs and once wrote one in a mere 20 minutes to impress a record executive.

His son, Hank Williams, Jr., also a successful recording artist, carried on the hard hitting honky tonk tradition established by Hank senior. Although it was difficult living in the shadow of his famous father, and for a while seemed to be following in the same path of self-destruction, he re-evaluated his life and cleaned up his act. Hank Williams, Jr. remains a well-known country figure.

The elder Williams's impact on country music can be measured by the number of artists he influenced. A partial list includes Bill Anderson, the Mavericks, Conway Twitty, Phil Alvin, the Sir Douglas Quintet, Sammy Kershaw, George Thorogood, Joe Stampley, Big Sandy and His Fly-Rite Boys, Gibson/Miller Band, Dion DiMucci, Ira Louvin, Mary Janes, Trick Pony, David Anderson, and Jesse Rodgers. But there are others, including Willie Nelson, Johnny Cash, Ray Price, George Jones, Charlie Rich, Mel Tillis, Merle Haggard, Waylon Jennings, Kris Kristofferson, Roy Clark, Buck Owens, Chet Atkins, Randy Travis, and Garth Brooks, to name a few. In truth, he made an impact on all of music and his influence is far reaching.

In 1961, Hank Williams, Sr., was elected to the Country Music Hall of Fame, one of the first three to be so honored. A movie of his life was made three years later with his son providing some of the soundtrack and George Hamilton portraying Hank. Numerous books appeared all trying to cash in on his name. The Hank Williams story is that of a musical genius who shot like a comet across the musical horizon, then fell in burning fragments as his career went out of control. He truly went from life to legend.

## The Drifting Cowboys
### 1938–1953

*Guitar*

Smith "Hezzy" Adair 1938
Paul Compton
 (dates unknown)
Clyde "Chris" Criswell 1946
Zeke Crittenden 1941
Richard Paul Dennis 1940s
Allen M. Dunkin 1941–1942
Clent Holmes 1948–1949
Dale Lohman 1940s
Mexican Charlie Mays 1939
Bob McNett 1948–1950
 1944, 1945–1949
Joe "Penny" Pennington
 1947–1948
Samuel K. Pruett
 1944, 1947, 1950–1952
Braxton Schuffert 1938
Bernice Hilburn Turner
 1945–1946

*Fiddle*

Freddy Beach 1938
Allen M. Dunkin
 1941–1942
Tony Francini
 1948–1949
Mexican Charlie
 Mays 1939
Jerry "Burrhead"
 Rivers 1949

*Bass*

Hillous Buel "Bew"
 Butrum 1949–1950
Shorty Seals 1941
William Elon Smith
 (dates unknown)
Rufus "Puddin'" Taylor
 1940–1942
Howard Staton "Cedric
 Rainwater" Watts
 1950–1951
Jimmy Wilkinson
 1939–1941
William Herbert
 "Lum" York

*Rhythm Guitar*

Daniel Jack "Beanpole"
 Boling 1939
Winston "Red" Todd

*Mandolin*

Allen M. Dunkin
 1941–1942

*Piano*

Eulon E.B. Fulmer
 1946

*Saxophone*

Lefty Clark 1946

*Dobro*

Charles Hill 1943

*Multi-instrumentalist*

Ernest Carl "Wimpy"
 Jones 1940s

*Accordion*

Cois "Pee Wee" Elmo Moultrie
 1939–1940

*Singers*

Carolyn "Little Caroline" Parker
 1930s
Sue Williams Taylor 1939

*Steel Guitar*

Clyde "Boots" Harris 1941–1942
Donald "Shag" Hugh Helms
 1944, 1947/1948, 1949–1952
Charles Hill 1943
Millard Jarett 1939–1945
R.D. Sonny Norred 1947–1948
Jimmy Porter 1941–1944
Felton Pruett 1948–1949

*Unofficial Drifting Cowboys*

Chester Burton Atkins, guitar
Clyde Baum, mandolin
Owen Bradley, piano
Howard Bradley, guitar
William Lewis Byrd, lead guitar
Jerry Byrd, steel guitar
Floyd Taylor "Lightnin'" Chance, bass
Farris Coursey, drums

*Steel Guitar*
Doyle Turner 1945–1946
Jimmy Webster 1946

*Unofficial Drifting Cowboys*
L.C. Cryel, fiddle
Don Davis, steel guitar
James Clayton "Jimmy" Day, steel guitar
Bill Drake, rhythm guitar
Ray Edenton, rhythm guitar
Herman Herron, steel guitar
Tommy Hill, guitar
Louis Innis, bass/rhythm guitar
Thomas Lee "Tommy" Jackson, fiddle
Dale "Smokey" Lohman, steel guitar
"Pappy" Neal McCormick, steel guitar
Thomas Grady Martin, guitar
Dale Potter, fiddle
Bronson "Brownie" Reynolds, bass
Billy Robinson, steel guitar
Fred Rose, piano
Loren Otis "Jack" Shook, rhythm guitar
Willie Thawl, bass fiddle
"Slim" Thomas, rhythm guitar
"Zeb Turner" Edward Grishaw, lead guitar
"Zeke Turner" James Cecil Grishaw
Velma Williams, bass
James U. "Guy" Willis, guitar
Charles Ray "Skeeter" Willis, fiddle
John Victor "Vic" Willis, accordion
Robert Russel "Chubby" Wise, fiddle
Charles "Indian" Wright, bass

# Discography

*Hank Williams Sings*, MGM E-107.
*Hank Williams as Luke the Drifter* [10"], MGM E-203.
*Live at the Grand Ole Opry*, MGM 5019.
*Ramblin' Man*, MGM E-291.
*I Saw the Light*, Mercury 5032.
*Sing Me a Blue Song*, MGM E-3560.
*Honky Tonkin'*, MGM 3412.
*Honky Tonkin'*, PolyGram 11091.
*The Lonesome Sound of Hank Williams*, MGM E-3803.
*Wait for the Light to Shine*, Polydor 833071.
*Wonderin' Around*, PolyGram 033072.
*On Stage! Hank Williams Recorded Live*, MGM E-3999.
*Hank Williams as Luke the Drifter* [12"], MGM 3267.
*Hank Williams on Stage, Vol. 2* [live], MGM 4109.
*Hank Williams* [Metro], Metro 509.
*More Hank Williams and Strings*, MGM SE-4429.

*The Immortal Hank Williams*, Metro 602.
*Again*, MGM SE-4378.
*Father and Son Again*, MGM E-4378.
*Luke the Drifter*, MGM 4380.
*I Won't Be Home No More*, MGM.
*Hank Williams and Strings, Vol. 3*, MGM SE-4529.
*Hank Williams in the Beginning*, MGM SE-4576.
*Mr. and Mrs. Hank Williams*, Metro MS-547.
*The Last Picture Show* [original soundtrack], MGM 15E-33ST.
*Moanin' the Blues*, PolyGram 11899.
*Reflections of Those Who Loved Him*, MGM 912.
*Hank Williams Memorial Album*, MGM E-202.
*36 of Hank Williams' Greatest Hits*, MGM 3E-2.
*36 More Greatest Hits*, MGM 3E-4.
*The Unforgettable Hank Williams*, MGM E-3733.
*Hank Williams' Greatest Hits*, MGM E-3918.
*Hank Williams Lives Again*, MGM E-3923.
*I'm Blue Inside*, MGM E-3926.
*First, Last and Always, Hank Williams*, MGM E-3928.
*The Spirit of Hank Williams*, MGM E-3955.
*14 More Greatest Hits, Vol. 2*, MGM E-4040.
*14 More Greatest Hits, Vol. 3*, MGM E-4140.
*The Very Best of Hank Williams*, PolyGram 23292.
*Beyond the Sunset*, MGM 4138.
*The Very Best of Hank Williams, Vol. 2*, MGM 4227.
*Insights into Hank Williams in Song and Story*, MGM 4975.
*Father and Son*, MGM 4276.
*Lost Highway (and Other Folk Ballads)*, MGM E-4254.
*The Hank Williams Story*, MGM E-4267.
*Kaw-Liga and Other Humorous Songs*, MGM 4300.
*Hank Williams, Sr. and Hank Williams, Jr.*, MGM.
*The Legend Lives Anew (Hank Williams with)*, MGM 4377.
*The Essential Hank Williams*, MGM SE-4651.
*Lonesome Blues*, PolyGram 843769.
*Health and Happiness Shows*, Mercury 517862.
*Life to Legend*, MGM SE-4680.
*24 of Hank Williams' Greatest Hits*, MGM SE-4755-2.
*The Legend of Hank Williams in Song and Story*, MGM 4865.
*24 Karat Hits*, MGM SE-240.
*24 Greatest Hits, Vol. 2*, PolyGram 823294.
*Hank Williams Treasury*, Columbia P45-5616.
*24 Greatest*, Mercury 823 293.
*40 Greatest Hits*, Mercury 821233-2.
*Greatest Hits [1961]*, PolyGram 23291.
*I Ain't Got Nothin' But Time (December 1946–April 1947): Vol. 1*, Mercury 825548.
*Memorial Album*, PolyGram 27568.
*Lovesick Blues (August 1947–December 1948)*, Mercury 825551.
*Just Me and My Guitar*, Country Music 006.
*On the Air*, Polydor 27531.
*Lost Highway (December 1948–March 1949): Vol. III*, Mercury 825554.
*I'm So Lonesome I Could Cry (March 1949–August 1949): Vol. IV*, Mercury 825557.
*The First Recordings*, Country Music 007.

*Let's Turn Back the Years (July 1951–June 1952): Vol. VII*, Mercury 833749.
*I Won't Be Home No More (June 1952–September 1952): Vol. VIII*, MGM 833752.
*Long Gone Lonesome Blues (August 1949–December 1950): Vol. V*, Mercury 831633.
*Hey, Good Lookin' (December 1950–July 1951): Vol. VI*, Mercury 831634.
*The Collectors' Edition*, Mercury 311527419.
*Grand Ole Country Classics*, Pair 1165.
*Rare Takes and Radio Cuts*, PolyGram 067.
*Greatest Hits [1990]*, PolyGram 536029.
*Rare Demos: First to Last*, Country Music 23695.
*24 Greatest Songs*, Huub 75622.
*Songbook*, CBS 47995.
*Back to Back: Like Father, Like Son*, K-Tel 30493 Health and Happiness Shows [live], Mercury.
*Best of the Early Years*, PolyGram 0601196.
*The Hits, Vol. 1*, PolyGram 522338.
*Hits, Vol. 1* [Expanded], PolyGram 528340.
*Alone and Forsaken*, Mercury 124057.
*American Legends: Best of the Early Years*, PSM 520286.
*Back to Back: Their Greatest Hit*, Rebound 520223.
*Hits, Vol. 2*, Mercury 528237.
*Legendary*, Special Music 5008.
*American Legends, No. 18: Hank Williams*, Laserlight 12478.
*Original Drifting Cowboys*, Eagle Video 1195.
*Low Down Blues*, PolyGram 532737.
*Commerative Collection*, Valley 1067.
*The Complete Hank Williams*, Mercury 536077.
*There's Nothing as Sweet as My Baby*, Mount Olive 1153.
*Move It on Over*, Country Stars 55453.
*Honky Tonkin'*, Charly 8356.
*Live at the Grand Ole Opry*, Mercury 546466.
*20th Century Masters—The Millennium Collection: The Best of Hank Williams*, Mercury 46660.
*Lovesick Blues*, Goldies 25351.
*Lovesick Blues* [Country Stars], 55456.
*The Legendary Hank Williams*, Prism 469.
*Move It on Over*, Golden Stars 5279.
*Honky Tonkin'*, Valley 15010.
*Alive with His Guitar*, Mercury 170164.
*Honky Tonkin'*, Pearl 7848.
*Best of Hank Williams*, Mastersound 50040.
*Original Singles Collection*, 847194.
*I Saw the Light*, Mercury 170183.
*Hank Williams*, St. Clair 328.
*Blues Come Around*, Catfish 194.
*Prodigal Son*, Arpeggio Country 1.
*Greatest Country Singer of All Time*, K-Tel 3580.
*Hey Good Lookin': Hank Williams, Hillbilly Hero*, Proper 1255.
*Long Gone Daddy*, Recall 381.
*Cheating Hearts*, 04 Music Group 8029.
*Best of Hank Williams, Vol. 1*, Columbia River 191005.
*The Ultimate Collection*, Mercury 170268.
*Legend* [Musicbank] 1162.

*Jambalaya*, ASV/Living Era 5461.
*Cold, Cold Heart*, Country Stars 55840.
*Lost Highway and Other Live Favorites*, Universal UK 9822561.
*Hank Williams*, Direct Source 4398.
*The Hillbilly Shakespeare*, American Legends 100122.
*No More Darkness*, Trikont 311.
*Gold*, Mercury 000439002.
*The Honky Tonk Man*, American Legends 192003.
*Hank Williams' Original Drifting Cowboys*, Bellaire CA-1113.

# EARL SCRUGGS (1924–)

## *Dueling Banjoist*

The speed, dexterity and skill level of the average bluegrass enthusiast raised the respect that country musicians received throughout music circles. A number of individuals were responsible for this, including Bill Monroe, the father of bluegrass, and the members of his band. One of these individuals was known as the dueling banjoist. His name was Earl Scruggs.

Earl Scruggs was born on January 6, 1924, in Cleveland County, North Carolina. He picked up the banjo at an early age and developed a three finger technique that had been flourishing through the area east of the Appalachians for decades. Uncle Dave Macon, Charlie Poole and Snuffy Jenkins, a local unknown, were all adept at the three finger method.

Scruggs started to perform with his brothers at the age of six and by his teens he was playing on North Carolina radio stations with the Carolina Wildcats. He also played with the Morris Brothers broadcasting from Spartanburg, South Carolina. He worked in a textile mill during the day and played at night. The war temporarily interrupted his musical progress, but after the conflict he joined Lost John Miller in Knoxville and was exposed to a large audience on Nashville radio.

When Miller stopped touring, Scruggs was out of work and his career seemed stalled until he received a call from Bill Monroe to join him on the *Opry*. Scruggs jumped at the chance. Although Monroe wasn't the most popular performer at the time, he played a style that not only showcased Scruggs' abilities, but the type of music that the young talented banjoist envisioned.

Scruggs was given carte blanche by Monroe to develop his ever evolving banjo style that was built on the old three-finger method. Earl had invented a higher level that possessed two distinctive advantages. It was a much more syncopated and rhythmic approach that blended with the other instruments, but could break out on its own with alarming speed. The fastest fingers in the South enabled him to rip out notes with a precise, delicate touch that ran like a super express train.

During his tenure in Bill Monroe's Blue Grass Boys, Scruggs sang very little and let Flatt take the limelight in that area. If he sang, it was as a background tenor, melding his voice with that of the others. It was his banjo playing, the hard driving bluegrass style, that proved his true value as a member of the band. In concert, Scruggs wowed the audience as well as his bandmates with his incomparable style, especially on numbers such as "Blue Grass Breakdown."

The teamwork between the five members of the Blue Grass Boys helped popularize the music and also injected much needed life into the *Grand Ole Opry*. During his three-year tenure with Monroe, Scruggs played on many records and was even given credit on some of the songs. However, despite the accolades, he grew tired of the nonstop touring and left in 1948.

At the same time, Flatt also left Monroe's band. In many ways, it was natural for Flatt and Scruggs to team up together since were both were keen on continuing the bluegrass tradition. They enjoyed working together and the interplay between the guitarist with the hot solos and the banjoist with the slick licks was pure dynamite. They set out to continue Monroe's groundbreaking work, as well as to expand on their own fame.

In time, they recruited fiddler Jim Shumate, who had played with Monroe and bassist Howard Watts, whose stage name was Cedric Rainwater. The four moved to Hickory, North Carolina, and made their first recordings on the Mercury label. Mac Wiseman joined the group sometime later, but mandolin player Curly Seckler eventually replaced him. They called themselves the Foggy Mountain Boys from a Carter Family tune, "Foggy Mountain Top."

The diversity of the group ensured them that they would always have a large following. They were versatile and could play most string instruments with the ferocity of a hurricane, pushing the parameters of the bluegrass style to the brink and beyond. They possessed a harsher edged sound and eventually Flatt and Scruggs surpassed Monroe's popularity.

The leaders of the Foggy Mountain Boys continued to broadcast on the radio out of Bristol, Tennessee, as well as other southern points. They also jammed with the Stanley Brothers, as well as Don Reno, who were also bluegrass enthusiasts. A Foggy Mountain Boys concert was an event in music; it was a good old-fashioned time that featured local performers and some of the best foot stompin' music in the country spectrum of performers.

The 1949 release of "Foggy Mountain Breakdown" sealed a measure of respect and acknowledgement for the band. It was a massive hit and if it didn't exactly usher in the new bluegrass sound, it certainly went a long way in popularizing the genre. The song would one day serve as the soundtrack for the movie *Bonnie and Clyde* during the famous car chase. As well, the boys were recording bluegrass treated versions of old classics such as "Roll in My Baby's Sweet Arms" and "Old Salty Dog Blues."

They continued to climb the ladder of success with more recordings, concerts, and radio appearances. They also were part of a show that Ernest Tubb and Lefty Frizzell headlined; however, Flatt and Scruggs stole the show with their song "Earl's Breakdown," a clever tune that included Scruggs tuning during the song with his innovative Scruggs Peg. Later they would broadcast on Nashville radio, further enhancing their country music prominence.

In 1955, they appeared on television with their syndicated show and became regulars at the *Grand Ole Opry*. Flatt and Scruggs continued to pick their way to the top, winning numerous awards and fan polls. Their sound transcended country music tastes to include early rock and roll, blues and pop. They were a household name and recognized by fans that didn't particularly like country.

The folk revival of the late 1950s and early 1960s only added to their legendary status. They were adopted by the folk crowd as the authentic thing and did more traveling during this period than they had while members of the Blue Grass Boys. They continued to cut albums, each one earning larger sales than the previous release.

Whatever popularity they had amassed at this time paled in comparison to the national recognition they received for their part in writing and playing the theme song "The Ballad of Jed Clampett," on the show *The Beverly Hillbillies*. Their pickin' style is in clear evidence on the title tune and the closing song. The duo would make a few cameo appearances on the show as themselves and often jammed on a number or two. With the show in syndication and with a new generation discovering the zany comedy of the show's cast, the music of Flatt and Scruggs reached new ears.

They became household names and sold millions of albums despite experimenting with new folk songs, drums, and gospel style harmonies. In 1969, the duo of Flatt and Scruggs broke up. It had been a long and very successful run, but the artistic differences made it impossible for them to continue playing together. It was a sad day in music history.

After the breakup, Scruggs formed the Earl Scruggs Revue. It included his two sons and moved to a more rocking sound that appealed to a younger, citified audience. Although he had not forsaken his country roots, he was a musical innovator who was constantly diversifying the original sound of not only old time music, but bluegrass as well. It was Scruggs who laid down the seeds that would allow bluegrass to keep developing and stay alive. Many of the style's new enthusiasts were young players from the East Coast, as the older fans who had championed Flatt and Scruggs throughout much of their career had moved on to a different style of country music.

Whatever style he played in, he left audiences stunned because he could play that banjo like a man possessed. He recorded many albums with his Earl Scruggs Revue that ushered in a more modern country song. Although he retired in 1985, the master banjoist can still be seen at certain reunions.

Earl Scruggs was a dynamite banjo player and arguably the greatest in the history of country music. No one possessed his gift of being able to play clear notes with super speed and dexterity. His three-finger method became the standard practice and influenced a large number of practitioners in every style of music.

Scruggs made an impact on a number of different musicians. A partial list includes Eddie Adcock, John Hartford, Bill Keith, Eric Weissberg, the Five Pennies, Wade Mainer, J. D. Crowe, Courtney Johnson, Rual Yarbrough, Noah Crase, Lynwood Lunsford, Dana Cupp, Jr., Smokin' Grass, Cumberland Highlanders, "Tater" Tate, Luke Thompson and Cecil Thompson, Garland Shuping, and Steve Arkin. However, like his long time partner Flatt and his former boss Monroe, Scruggs influenced everyone who decided to play bluegrass.

He was an architect of modern bluegrass along with Flatt and Monroe. It must be pointed out that in the latter part of his career, Scruggs did much to integrate the strains of bluegrass with rock and pop, while Flatt remained true to his country roots. The new bluegrass tradition owes a debt to Scruggs and his former band mates.

Earl Scruggs was to the country banjo what Jimi Hendrix was to the electric guitar in rock-blues. Both exhibited a controlled, rollicking style that changed the face of how each instrument was to be played forever. Scruggs developed the Scruggs peg that allowed him to quickly retune his banjo strings on certain numbers, especially the hard-driving "Earl's Breakdown."

In 1985, Earl Scruggs along with the late Lester Flatt was elected to the Country Music Hall of Fame. During his career he redefined how the instrument was to be played and brought bluegrass respectability. He will forever be known as the swift-playing, no-nonsense instrumentalist with the wild eyed licks on his dueling banjo.

## Foggy Mountain Boys
1948–1969

| Guitar | Banjo | Fiddle |
|---|---|---|
| Lester Flatt | Earl Scruggs | Paul Warren |
| Frank "Hylo" Brown | | Robert "Chubby" Wise |
| Jim Eanes | | Jim Shumate |
| Mac Wiseman | | Benny Martin |
| Billy E. Powers | | Benny Sims |
| Johnny Johnson | | Howdy Forrester |
| | | Art Wooten |

| Mandolin | Dobro | Bass |
|---|---|---|
| John Ray "Curly" Seckler | Burkett "Uncle Josh" Graves | Burkett "Uncle Josh" Graves |
| Everette Lilly | | English P. "Cousin Jake" Tullock |
| Curly Lambert | | Howard Watts aka Cedric Rainwater |
| | | Charles Johnson aka "Little Jody Rainwater" |
| | | Frank "Hylo" Brown |
| | | Charles "Little Darlin'" Elza |
| | | Joe Stuart |

## Discography

*Nashville Airplane*, CBS 63570.
*Earl Scruggs: His Family and Friends*, Columbia 30584.
*I Saw the Light with the Help of Friends*, Sony 92793.
*Live at Kansas State*, Columbia 31758.
*Dueling Banjos*, Columbia 32268.
*Rockin' Across the Country*, CBS 32943.
*The Earl Scruggs Revue*, CBS 32426.
*Family Portrait*, CBS 34346.
*The Earl Scruggs Revue 2*, CBS 34090.
*Live From Austin City Limits*, CBS 34464.
*Strike Anywhere*, CBS 34878.
*Bold and New*, CBS 35319.
*Today and Forever*, CBS 36084.
*Flatt and Scruggs*, CBS 25018.
*Storyteller and the Banjo Man*, CBS 37953.
*Top of the World*, CBS 25097.
*Superjammin'*, CBS 39370.
*Earl Scruggs and Friends*, MCA 170189.
*Three Pickers*, Rounder 610526.
*Anniversary Specials Vol. 1 and 2*, Gott Discs 21.
*Nashville Rock*, CBS 1007.
*Where Lilies Bloom*, CBS 32806.

*Foggy Mountain Jamboree*, Sony 77627.
*Anniversary Special*, CBS 33416.
*Artist's Choice: The Best Tracks (1970–1980)*, Edsel 552.
*Dueling Banjos/Live at Kansas State*, Collectables 6478.
*Classic Bluegrass Live: 1959–1966*, Vanguard 79706.
*The Essential Earl Scruggs*, Columbia 90858.

# HANK THOMPSON (1925–)
## Texas Swing

The state of Texas has provided country music with a number of important artists. Tex Ritter was a matinee idol who starred in many films and later enjoyed a successful recording career. Bob Wills was the founder of western swing. Ernest Tubb was the Texas Troubadour. In the 1950s and 1960s there was another musician from the Lone Star State renowned for his Texas Swing. His name was Hank Thompson.

Hank Thompson was born on September 3, 1925, in Waco, Texas. The music bug bit him early and he grew up with stars in his eyes for Western Swing King Bob Wills, the Father of Country Music, Jimmy Rodgers, and, the Singing Cowboy, Gene Autry. Thompson picked up the harmonica and guitar. He honed his skills quickly and was performing at talent shows in his early teens. He eventually landed his own radio show, where he was known as Hank the Hired Hand.

In 1943, he graduated from high school and went directly into the Navy, where he learned how to fix radios. It was in Uncle Sam's army that he began to write songs that he tested on his fellow crewmen. Upon his discharge, he went to Princeton where he studied electrical engineering, but never graduated from the prestigious school. Instead he gave in to his musical ambitions.

He returned to Waco and found work in a radio station. On the side he was putting together a band that he would later call the Brazos Valley Boys. Once the band was assembled they found plenty of work around the area and made a solid name for themselves. They recorded their initial song, "Whoa Sailor," a song that Thompson wrote while in the Navy. Later, the group recorded a few more singles for different labels. It was around this time that Hank and his group first garnered the attention of Texas legend Tex Ritter.

With Ritter's help, Thompson and His Brazos Valley Boys landed a major recording contract with Capitol in 1947. For the next decade the partnership would prove very fruitful. In 1949, Thompson and his outfit recorded "Humpty Dumpty Heart," a huge hit that was one of his six chart toppers that year.

But the best was yet to come. In 1951, Ken Nelson entered as producer and the machine really began to roll. A year later, Thompson and His Brazos Valley Boys would hit pay dirt with "The Wild Side of Life," a monster hit that stayed at number one for three months. Not only was the song good for the group, it enabled Kitty Wells to also enjoy a number one hit with "It Wasn't God Who Made Honky Tonk Angels" in response to Hank's signature tune.

The hits followed one after another throughout the decade. In 1954, he had over twenty songs reach the Top 20 on the country charts. But the music was only part of it. He dressed fancier than the other cowboys on tour and boasted a television show that was broadcasted in color in Oklahoma City. His tour was the first to utilize a sound and lighting system. He was also the first to enjoy corporate sponsorship and the first to record in hi-fi stereo.

Thompson and his group, the Brazos Valley Boys, were famous throughout Texas and the rest of the country. The band would feature many skilled musicians, including Merle Travis and country heartbreak singer Wanda Jackson. Billy Gray, a poor son from the Lone Star State, would eventually join the band and contribute some of their best songs. He would later lead his own outfit with limited success.

Thompson was never afraid to take chances with his band. They recorded the first true full-length albums in country music—*Dance Ranch* and *Songs for Rounders*. The records were more than just a few singles and fillers, they were a cohesive effort that predated concept albums. The group also became the first in country music to release a live effort: *Live at the Golden Nugget*.

Although he continued to record throughout the 1960s and 1970s, Thompson and his group were unable to maintain the torrid pace they had set in the 1950s. The public's taste changed and western swing and honky tonk fell out of favor. But they continued to tour all over North America and the world, bringing his brand of country music to every corner of the globe.

In later years, he and the various members of the Brazos Valley Boys managed to maintain a strong level of popularity. Although their heyday was past them, there was a powerful curiosity among country music fans to witness the semi-legends perform in concert. He continues to perform on occasion.

Hank Thompson is a western swing jewel. He was an early enthusiast who embraced the style and added his own dimension to it. He was an adept musician, excellent bandleader and country music innovator. He established his legend during the 1950s and early 1960s with a string of major hits and concerts that showed a true artistic flair.

Although never a great instrumentalist, Thompson knew how music should sound. He was able to mesh all of the various musicians in the Brazos Valley Boys into a cohesive unit. The band could swing with the best of them and their ability to deliver hard driving country music that people could dance to sealed their fortune. Along with producer Nelson, Hank always knew when to put an extra guitar line or drum beat in a song to give it that special ring.

He gave the world a number of memorable songs. A partial list includes "Humpty Dumpty Heart," "Wild Side of Life," "Yesterday's Girl," "Honky Tonk Girl," "Six Pack to Go," "Bubbles in My Beer," "Warm Red Wine," "Just an Old Flame," "It's Better to Have Loved a Little," "How Do You Hold a Memory?" "On Tap, in the Can, or in the Bottle," "Love Walked Out Before She Did," "Let the Four Winds Choose," "Oklahoma Hills," "Total Stranger," "Dry Bread," "Condo in Hondo," "Lobo the Hobo," and "Scotch and Soda." Countless country musicians have covered his songs, a genuine tribute to Thompson's fertile songwriting imagination.

The personnel in the Brazos Valley Boys changed but there was always an abundance of talent in the group. Merle Travis and Wanda Jackson were alumni. Billy Gray and Billy Raymond Carson were important contributors. Whatever the lineup, they guaranteed a sound that always played on the right side of honky tonk and had western swing at heart.

Hank Thompson had a strong influence on a number of country musicians. The list includes Willie Nelson, Johnny Cash, Carl Perkins, Roy Clark, Glen Campbell, Marty Robbins, Charlie Pride, Charlie Rich and a host of others. His shadow cast beyond normal boundaries to include rockabilly, rock and roll and jazz. The swing element in his music was an ingredient that every working band incorporated into their own style in order to survive the cutthroat music business.

He was a western swing torch carrier, taking up where Bob Wills left off. He took everything his idol had established and built on it, enabling him to reach a wider audience. Although the popularity of western swing faded in the 1960s as it gave way to the harder edged Bakersfield sound and the country pop flavor of Nashville, Thompson never switched styles.

Hank Thompson is a legend and was elected to the Country Music Hall of Fame in 1989. For a decade he had more number one hits than any other country artist. A clever individual, he was never afraid to experiment and try something new. He claimed many firsts in country music and gave the genre an incredible boost with his sensational Texas swing.

## Hank Thompson and the Brazos Valley Boys*
Circa 1950s

| Guitar and Vocals | Leader | Trumpet | |
|---|---|---|---|
| Hank Thompson | Billy Gray | Dubert Dobson | |
| *Bass* | *Drums* | *Fiddles* | *Lead Guitar* |
| Junior Nichols | Billy Stewart | Curley Lewis | Merle Travis |
| Bob White | | | |

*The Brazos Valley Boys had many incarnations, but the lineup above is the best known.

## Discography

*North of the Rio Grande*, Capitol 618.
*Songs of the Brazos Valley*, Capitol 418.
*Hank*, Capitol 826.
*Dance Ranch*, Capitol 975.
*Songs for Rounders*, Capitol 1246.
*Most of All*, Capitol 1360.
*The Broken Heart of Mine*, Capitol 1469.
*An Old Love Affair*, Capitol 1544.
*At the Golden Nugget*, Capitol 33601.
*Cheyenne Frontier Days*, Capitol 1775.
*Live at the State Fair of Texas*, Capitol 1955.
*It's Christmas Time*, Capitol 2154.
*Breakin' In Another Heart*, Capitol 2274.
*The Luckiest Heartache in Town*, Capitol 2342.
*A Six Pack to Go*, Capitol 2460.
*Breakin' the Rules*, Capitol 2575.
*Just an Old Flame*, Capitol 2826.
*The Countrypolitan Sound of Hank's Brazo Boys*, Warner Bros. 1679.
*Country Blues*, Tower 5120.
*On Tap, in the Can or in the Bottle*, Dot 25894.
*Hank Thompson Salutes Oklahoma*, Dot 25971.
*Smoky the Bar*, Dot 25932.
*Next Time I Fall in Love, I Won't*, Dot 25591.
*Cab Driver: A Salute to the Mills Brothers*, Dot 25996.
*Kindly Keep It Country*, Dot 26015.
*Moving On*, ABC 20023.
*Back in the Swings of Things*, Dot/ABC 2060.
*Brand New Hank*, ABC 1095.
*Here's to Country Music*, Step One 27.
*Real Thing*, Curb 77925.
*Seven Decades*, Hightone 8121.
*New Recordings of Hanks' Old Hits*, Capitol 729.
*The Best of Hank Thompson*, Capitol 1878.
*Golden Country Hits*, Capitol 2089.
*Where Is the Circus (and Other Heart Breakin' Hits)*, Warner Bros. 1664.
*A Gold Standard Collection of Hank Thompson*, Warner Bros. 1686.

*The Best of Hank Thompson, Vol. 2*, Capitol 2661.
*Gold Standards*, Dot 25864.
*25th Anniversary Album*, Dot 2000.
*Hank Thompson's Greatest Hits*, Dot 26004.
*The Best of the Best of Hank Thompson*, Hollywood 443.
*20 Greatest Hits*, Deluxe 7807.
*Greatest Hits, Vol. 1*, Step One 25.
*Greatest Hits, Vol. 2*, Step One 26.
*Capitol Collection Series*, Capitol 92124.
*All Time Greatest Hits*, Capitol CDP-7 92124 2.
*Greatest Hits*, Curb 77329.
*Country Music Hall of Fame Series*, MCA 10545.
*Greatest Hits*, CEMA 9402.
*Greatest Hits, Vol. 2*, Curb 77613.
*Stars, Vol. 3*, Hollywood 138.
*Greatest Songs, Vol. 1*, Curb 77734.
*Greatest Songs, Vol. 2*, Curb 77735.
*Hank Thompson and His Brazos Valley Boys*, Country Routes 9003.
*Hank Thompson and His Brazos Valley Boys (1946–1964)*, Bear Family 15904.
*Vintage*, Capitol 36901.
*The Wild Side of Life*, Richmond 2190.
*The Best of Hank Thompson 1966–1979*, Varese 5747.
*Radio Broadcast (1952)*, Flyright 948.
*Sound of the Brazos Valley*, Country Routes 19.
*Hank World: The Unissued World Transcriptions*, Bloodshot 803.
*Country Music Hall of Fame 1989*, King 3806.
*In the Mood for Hank*, Jasmine 3509.
*Hank Thompson*, St. Clair 330.
*A Proper Introduction to Hank Thompson: The Wild Side of Life*, Proper 2074.
*Swing Wide Your Gate of Love: Best of Hank Thompson, Vol. 1*, Acrobat 4032.
*Hank Thompson*, Dot 39089.

# RAY PRICE (1926–)

## Cherokee Cowboy

Like other genres, country music has always attracted a wide range of performers. Uncle Dave Macon, Roy Acuff and Ernest Tubb were some of the earliest genuine characters that graced the industry with their unique presence. Later, Hank Williams, Sr., Johnny Cash, Willie Nelson, Hank Thompson and Conway Twitty made their special mark. There was another modern figure who added his distinct touch known—the Cherokee Cowboy, Ray Price.

Ray Noble Price was born on January 12, 1926, in Perryville, East

Texas, of Cherokee ancestry. His family moved to Dallas when he was a young boy and it was there that the music bug bit. He learned how to play guitar, sing, and started to write songs while still in high school. Roy Acuff was his main hero. Since music at the time was only a hobby for him, Price set his sights on being a veterinarian and studied at the North Texas Agricultural College in Abilene.

His career ambition was put aside when he joined the Marines in 1942 and stayed in the military until 1946. He returned to college to fulfill his dreams but became sidetracked when he performed at school events and local clubs. Audiences liked his music and it encouraged him to follow a different path. He made his debut as a professional musician in 1948 when he appeared on radio for the first time on an Abilene station. Later he worked on the *Big D Jamboree*, a Dallas program that received network coverage. It was about this point in time that he was dubbed the Cherokee Cowboy.

He cut his first singles for Bullet Records, "Your Wedding Corsage" and "Jealous Lies." A year later, he relocated to Nashville and Columbia signed him to a contract. By this time, like so many other country artists, he was a devotee to Hank the Great. The two became fast friends and Williams gave "Weary Blues" to Price to record. As well, Ray became the substitute for Williams on the *Grand Ole Opry* when the latter couldn't make it because of his excessive drinking, which, in 1952, happened often. Upon the early demise of Williams, Price inherited the members of the Drifting Cowboys and renamed them the Cherokee Cowboys.

After a brief taste of success with "Talk to Your Heart" and "Don't Let the Stars Get in Your Eyes," he fell off the charts, but returned with a vengeance in 1954 to begin a twenty year run of top ten hits. Although the members of Hank Williams' old group provided Price with adequate support, he desired to move away from his idol's shadow, so he reformed the Cherokee Cowboys. An astute judge of talent throughout the years, he would choose for his band the diverse talents of Willie Nelson, Buddy Emmons, Johnny Bush, Roger Miller, Johnny Paycheck, and Jimmy Day.

A pure honky tonk artist, Price took Williams' driving sound and added certain touches like a drummer. Although the *Opry* banned the use of the instrument, he was adamant about its inclusion in his group. Eventually, the rhythmic instrument would become a regular part in several groups and find a permanent home in the Bakersfield style.

For the next decade his career continued to gain momentum. Although the lineup for the Cherokee Cowboys changed, the group was always able to rally around Price. He was a solid country entertainer, a staple on the *Opry*, and a regular chart topper. After the release of "Crazy Arms" in 1956, life was never the same. He became one of the top five artists on the circuit.

In the mid–1960s, Price reinvented his sound, drifting away from the hard honky tonk that had brought him much success. Instead, he shifted to a more country-pop style that angered hard core fans and as a result his popularity waned for the next few years. However, by the early 1970s he was back on top of the charts and remained there for a few years until the taste of country music fans changed once again.

Price had adopted a slicker produced sound that saw him use strings like a pop star rather than a hard drinking, quick fisted honky tonk bad boy. His lushly orchestrated country-pop fell out of favor and he was forced to reinvent himself. He left Columbia after a 20-year association and signed with ABC/Dot. He struggled until he reunited with a former member of the Cherokee Cowboys, Willie Nelson. The red headed bassist and the Cherokee Cowboy hit pay dirt with the album *San Antonio Rose* that spawned two top ten hits.

After this brief sweep of success, Price fell back on hard times and spent much of the 1980s switching labels without finding a winning combination. The neo-traditional country music sound that dominated the decade seemed to have left him behind. In order not to be forgotten, he bought his own theatre in Branson, Missouri, and performed there frequently. He also continued to record but none of his albums brought him back atop the charts. He continues to perform and record sporadically.

Ray Price was a mainstay of the country music scene for a long period of time. A diverse artist, he carried on the honky tonk tradition of Hank Williams, but also dabbled in the country-pop fad that was predominant in the late 1960s and early 1970s. Although not a great judge of changing musical tastes, he was always able to reinvent himself to please the current trend.

Ray Price has a versatile voice that has always allowed him to switch from one style to another with relative ease. Although he started out as a hard driving honky tonk in imitation of his hero Hank Williams, he later was able to transform into a pure country crooner that earned a different kind of audience. His rich, sentimental voice afforded him the luxury of diversity.

One of the best judges of talent, he has worked with a number of individuals that cut their musical teeth in his Cherokee Cowboys band only to go on to greater success. A partial list includes Willie Nelson, Harold Bradley, Don Law, Jimmy Day, Joe Zinkan, Hargus "Pig" Robbins, Pete Drake, Johnny Gimble, Floyd Cramer, Thomas Lee Jackson, Jr., William Whitney Pursell, Walter Haynes, Roger Miller, and Johnny Bush, to name a few. Miller would collect an unprecedented six Grammys in

1965. Of course, perhaps the most famous of all alumni is the redhead outlaw, Willie Nelson. The Austin Rebel learned invaluable lessons from Price that served him well later on in his stellar career.

Price has also given the world a number of classic songs. A partial list includes "Jealous Lies," "I Won't Mention It Again," "She's Got to Be a Saint," "You're the Best Thing That Ever Happened to Me," "Mansion on the Hill," "Faded Love," "It Don't Hurt Me Half as Bad," "Diamonds in the Stars, "Talk to Your Heart," "Don't Let the Stars Get in Your Eyes," "Crazy Arms," "I've Got a New Heartache," "My Shoes Keep Walking Back to You," "City Lights," "Heartaches by the Number," "Make the World Go Away," "Burning Memories," "The Other Woman," "Touch My Heart," "For the Good Times," "I'd Rather Be Sorry," "Lonesomest Lonesome," and "Roses and Love Songs."

In 1996, Ray Price was elected to the Country Music Hall of Fame, a deserved honor for someone who had made enormous contributions to the genre. Although he has flipped between serious honky tonk and country-pop there is no denying the Cherokee Cowboy's place in the history of the genre.

## Cherokee Cowboys
### Circa 1960s

| Guitar | Bass | Fiddle |
|---|---|---|
| Ray Price | Pete Burke | Keith Coleman |
| Pete Burke | | |

| Steel Guitar | Drums |
|---|---|
| Buddy Emmons | Johnny Bush |

## Discography

*Ray Price Sings Heart Songs*, Columbia C-1015.
*Talk to Your Heart*, Columbia C-1148.
*Faith*, Columbia 1494.
*San Antonio Rose* [Koch], Koch 7917.
*Night Life* [Columbia], Columbia 8771.
*The Same Old Me*, Special Music 3013.
*Love Life*, Columbia 8989.
*Western Strings*, Columbia 9139.
*Burning Memories*, Columbia 2289.
*The Other Woman*, Koch 7947.
*Another Bridge to Burn*, Columbia 9328.
*Touch My Heart*, Columbia 9406.
*Danny Boy*, Columbia 9477.
*Born to Lose*, Harmony 11240.
*Take Me as I Am*, Columbia 9606.

*She Wears My Ring*, Columbia 9733.
*Sweetheart of the Year*, Columbia 9022.
*Ray Price's Christmas Album*, CBS 9861.
*I Fall to Pieces*, Harmony 11373.
*For the Good Times*, Columbia 30106.
*You Wouldn't Know Love*, Columbia 9918.
*Make the World Go Away*, Harmony 30272.
*The World of Ray Price*, Columbia 28.
*I Won't Mention It Again*, CBS 30510.
*Welcome to My World*, CBS 30878-2.
*The Lonesomest Lonesome*, CBS 31546.
*She's Got to Be a Saint*, CBS 32033.
*This Time Lord*, Myrth 6532.
*Like Old Times Again*, ABC/Myrrh 6538.
*You're the Best Thing That Ever Happened to Me*, Columbia 32777.
*If You Ever Change Your Mind*, Columbia 33560.
*Hank (Williams) 'n' Me*, ABC 2062.
*Say I Do*, ABC/Dot 2037.
*Precious Memories*, Word 8723.
*Rainbows and Tears*, ABC/Dot 2053.
*Reunited*, ABC/Dot 2073.
*Help Me*, Columbia 34710.
*There's Always Me*, Monument 7633.
*Town and Country*, Dimension 5003.
*Tribute to Willie and Kris*, CBS 37061.
*Somewhere in Texas*, Dimension 5006.
*Master of the Art*, Viva 23782.
*Christmas Gift for You from Ray Price*, Step One 28.
*Heart of Country Music*, Step One 19.
*Revival of Old Time Singing*, Step One 16.
*By Request*, Step One 0050.
*Just Enough Love*, Step One 33.
*Welcome to Ray Price Country*, Step One 7.
*American Originals*, Columbia 45068.
*Sometimes a Rose*, Columbia/Legacy 48980.
*Christmas Gift for You*, Rock Bottom 28.
*The Old Rugged Cross*, Arrival 3182.
*Release Me*, Sony Special 13253.
*Prisoner of Love*, Buddha 99705.
*Priceless*, Pair 1096.
*Ray Price's Greatest Hits*, Columbia 08866.
*Night Life* [Koch], Koch 7928.
*Greatest Western Hits, Vol. 1*, Columbia 1976.
*Ray Price's Greatest Hits, Vol. 2*, Columbia 9470.
*Greatest Hits, Vol. 1*, Step One 13.
*Ray Price's All-Time Greatest Hits*, Step One 28.
*Greatest Hits, Vol. 3*, Step One 14.
*The Best of Ray Price*, Columbia 34160.
*Happens to Be the Best*, Pair 1044.
*Portrait of a Singer*, Step One 9.
*Greatest Hits, Vols. 1-3*, Step One 1234.
*Greatest Hits, Vol. 4 (By Request)*, Step One 0050.

*Greatest Hits* [Dominion], Dominion 3142-2.
*Greatest Hits*, Sony 8866.
*All-Time Greatest Hits*, Sony 31364.
*For the Good Times/I Won't Mention It Again*, 33633.
*Honky Tonk Years (1951–1953)*, Rounder SS22.
*Hall of Fame Series*, Step One 69.
*The Essential Ray Price (1951–1962)*, Columbia/Legacy 48532.
*Hits on Monument*, CBS 52961.
*Collectors' Choice*, Sony Special 13250.
*Gold*, King 489.
*20 Hits*, TeeVee 6022.
*The Honky Tonk Years (1950–1966)*, Bear Family 16843.
*Super Hits*, Sony 68198.
*Country Music Hall of Fame 1996*, King 3802.
*16 Biggest Hits*, Columbia 69972.
*All His Greatest Hits*, Platinum Disc 1497.
*In a Honky Tonk Mood*, Jasmine 3505.
*Good Old Country*, St. Clair 78142.
*All-Time Greatest Hits* [K-Tel], K-Tel 3022.
*Time*, Audium 8156.
*20 All Time Greatest Hits*, TeeVee 710.
*Best of the Best*, Federal 524.
*Burning Memory/Touch My Heart*, Audium 8180.
*Gospel*, K-Tel 3067.
*Greatest Hits*, Gusto 567.
*Country Legends*, St. Clair 6756.
*Crazy Arms*, Platinum Disc 3152.
*Country Hit Parade*, Direct Source 52732.
*K-Tel Country Gospel*, K-Tel 50025.
*Step One Records Hall of Fame*, Step One 0069.

# GEORGE JONES (1931–)
## *Honky Tonk Texan*

The origins of honky tonk began in the 1940s and the boundaries were clearly established after Hank Williams came through. There were many that followed in his footsteps and continued the faith, including Ray Price for at least a decade after the death of his idol. Another of the major practitioners of the style was the Honky Tonk Texan. His name is George Jones.

George Jones was born on September 12, 1931, in Saratoga, Texas. He was introduced to music through the normal channels of church, radio and family. His mother played organ in support of the local choir and his father was an amateur guitarist. Although he was enchanted with the sounds of country music, he burned with the desire to play it himself. He acquired his first guitar at an early age and practiced constantly. He honed his skills on street corners working for spare change and the thrill of actually being paid to perform only helped fuel his drive.

He pursued his musical dreams feverishly throughout his teens, which included running away from home. His travels took him to other parts of Texas where he found work at a radio station. He found love early but wasn't ready for the trials of marriage, and the pain he suffered when the marriage broke up would find its way into his later recordings.

A stint in the Marines during the Korean War didn't impede his musical progress; he remained stationed in California and played in local dives and clubs. After his release, he painted houses, but his ambition to be a force in country music wasn't forgotten. Finally, in 1954, he caught his first break when H. W. "Pappy" Daily spotted him. Daily owned a studio in Houston and was eager to record Jones.

Jones cut his first song, "No Money in This Deal," for Starday Records, although the song never became a hit. His next release, "Why Baby Why," garnered him more success. A spot on the *Louisiana Hayride* program where he shared the stage with Elvis Presley gained him a wider range of appeal. At this point, the hits started to roll in, including "What Am I Worth" and "Just One More." Later songs cut in rockabilly style didn't go very far.

The year 1957 was a turning point in his career. He switched to Mercury Records and also appeared on the *Grand Ole Opry* for the first time. His first album, recorded in Nashville, was a big hit, yielding "Don't Stop the Music." He had broken through and provided a great amount of promise.

In 1958, he enjoyed his greatest success up to that point with a song called "White Lightning," which included a novelty chorus. Three years later, he switched to United Artists and scored more hits with "Window Up Above," "She Thinks I Still Care," "We Must Have Been Out of Our Minds," and "The Race Is On." He specialized in songs about two-timing women and delivered them with heartfelt anguish. Perhaps they reminded him of his previous marriage and past stormy relationships.

Jones continued to churn out the hits, including "Aching, Breaking Heart," as well as duets with pretty country singer Melba Montgomery. The pair enjoyed great success—she provided a direct opposite voice of the woman who had done him wrong to his expression of the man who had been wronged. They possessed an exciting chemistry that sold thousands of records before their partnership ended in 1967.

In 1965, Daily offered Jones a spot on his new label, Musicor. During this period, "Take Me," "Things Have Gone to Pieces," "Love Bug," "I'm a People," and "You Can't Get There from Here" were further hits added to his already impressive list. Despite the hits, Jones was unhappy with the production of the songs and in order to be freed from his contract he had to give up his royalties. He sank into a funk and started to drink heavily, often having to be helped on stage. He also divorced his third wife. In all, it was one of the most depressing parts of his career.

His honky tonk angel and savior appeared in 1967; her name was Tammy Wynette. Together they were pure country dynamite and married in 1969. After some legal wrangling they were finally able to record as a duo for Epic and cut numerous hit singles to become the king and queen of country music. Wynette had been touted as the new female star of country music, and her teaming with Jones only intensified the promise.

His change from his drinking and wild ways to a more responsible way revived his career. Under the direction of producer Billy Sherrill, he and wife Tammy ruled the country music charts during the early 1970s. "We Can Make It," "The Ceremony," and "Loving You Could Never Be Better" were just some of the hits that they delivered to middle America. They were a much publicized couple and their fans (who numbers had mushroomed from their first song together) adored the duo.

However, the promise of love and living happily ever after seemed to be lost on them as they began to have serious relationship problems. Their soap opera marriage provided valuable fodder for the scandal magazines and it was just a matter of time before they divorced. Jones had sunk back into alcoholism and drug abuse, putting further strain on the fragile union.

In 1973, she filed for divorce, but like the lyrics in a genuine honky tonk song, they reconciled and scored a hit with "We're Gonna Hold On." They were also recording as solo artists and in 1974, Jones hit the charts with "The Grand Tour," a serious comment on the difficulties of marriage. As his own style of music began to gain in popularity, he enjoyed a number of top releases with "The Door" and "These Days (I Barely Get By)." Soon after the couple divorced for good.

Although they had split up, it didn't stop them from working together and he enjoyed more hits with his ex-wife than he did as a solo artist. But Jones continued his downward spiral with his erratic behavior, his dependency on cocaine, and his uncommunicative manners. He missed shows with regularity and that forced promoters to back off from booking him.

He attempted to pull himself out of his bad ways through his music. He covered "Maybelline," the old Chuck Berry chestnut, giving it the George Jones treatment. He further pushed his rock and roll image performing duets with hard driving Johnny Paycheck and James Taylor. An album of duets, entitled *My Very Special Guests*, provided hope, but he was still mired in the drugs and alcohol that threatened to end his career and life.

Just as it seemed that he was going to be another country music casualty, Jones pulled himself out of the ring of fire. A duet with Wynette, "Two Story House," began the process and the solo cut "He Stopped Loving Her Today" boldly announced his return. He enjoyed a run of top ten singles throughout much of the 1980s and seemed to have conquered his substance abuse problems. His arrest while driving drunk through the streets of Nashville signaled that he had not fully recovered. But with the help of his new honky tonk angel and savior, wife Nancy Sepulvada, he managed to finally clean up his act. A strong effort meant a new record label and in 1991 his initial release for MCA, *And Along Came Jones*, was a hit.

He continued to churn out songs for MCA but never found the success of his Epic days. A reunion with Tammy Wynette in 1995 produced a top ten hit. In 1998, he moved to Electra/Asylum but before he could finish recording his first album for the label he was involved in a serious car accident that was alcohol related. After being charged he went to a rehab center and his subsequent album, *Cold Hard Truth*, an eponym of his life, was released. He continues to record and perform.

George Jones is a country music survivor. He has had many phases to his career, which has enabled him to enjoy incredible success as well as miserable times. He has often been his own worst enemy, but he has also made enormous contributions to the genre. He has often been regarded as a prime vocal stylist.

Jones has been called the Rolls-Royce of country singers for his effective, smoothly rich textured vocal delivery. Although he started out as a hard honky tonk singer trying to emulate his hero Hank Williams, he polished the rough edges to attain a level that allowed him to deliver ballads with a plaintive but convincing style. He became a diversified artist without ever leaving his roots. He managed to combine the harsh honky tonk style that he liked with a stronger voice.

Despite his battle with the bottle and drugs—a battle that nearly cost him his life—Jones has constantly been in the top ten of the charts. It is a tribute to the man's immense talents and his penchant for delivering songs that speak directly to the listener. He knew about trouble since he lived the life, but there was always a splinter of hope in his songs that encouraged the individual to carry on. It was this element that helped certify his popularity.

Jones has worked with a number of artists, including Eddie Bayers, Vince Gill, Ernest Tubb, Ricky Skaggs, Lou Bradley, Waylon Jennings, Terry McMillan, Brent Mason, Randy Travis, Melba Montgomery, James Taylor, Conway Twitty, Buck Owens, Merle Haggard, Little Jimmy Dickens, Gene Watson, Ray Price, and a host of others. Of course, his most popular partner was Tammy Wynette. Together they were too good and perhaps that is why their union was doomed. Like most honky tonk songs, the marriage that was filled with so much promise eventually ventured down the slippery path.

Jones influenced many contemporaries and young stars. A short list includes the Bellamy Brothers, Garth Brooks, Jim Lauderdale, Johnny Paycheck, Jo-El Sonnier, Steve Wariner, Gene Watson, Dwight Yoakam, Joe Ely, Sammy Kershaw, Randy Travis, Keith Whitley and Tex Beaumont. Interestingly, he also made a strong impact on his former wife and singing partner Wynette.

Despite his despondency for a good part of his career, Jones was inducted into the Country Music Hall of Fame in 1992. Although he certainly had his fair share of problems and obstacles to overcome, he did so to become one of the most important country music figures of the modern area. There is no denying the honky tonk Texan his place in the annals of the genre.

## Discography

*The Grand Ole Opry's New Star*, Starday 101.
*Long Live King George*, Starday 344.
*Hillbilly Hit Parade*, Starday 102.
*Country Church Time*, Mercury 20462.
*White Lightning and Other Favorites*, Mercury 20477.
*The Crown Prince of Country Music*, Starday 125.
*George Jones Salutes Hank Williams*, Mercury 822464–1.
*Country and Western Hits*, Mercury 60624.
*From the Heart*, Mercury 20694.
*George Jones Sings Bob Wills*, Razor and Tie 2047.
*Sings Country and Western Hits*, Mercury 20624.
*The Sings the Hits of His Country Cousins*, Razor and Tie 2064.
*The New Favorites of George Jones*, Liberty 32463.
*The Fabulous Country Music Sound of George Jones*, Starday 151.
*Homecoming in Heaven*, Razor and Tie 2065.
*My Favorites of Hank Williams*, Razor and Tie 2048.
*Sings More New Favorites*, United Artists 6338.
*I Wish Tonight Would Never End*, United Artists 6270.
*What's in Our Hearts*, United Artists 6301.
*George Jones Sings Like the Dickens!*, Razor and Tie 82071.
*Bluegrass Hootenanny*, United Artists 6352.
*A King and Two Queens*, United Artists 6367.
*Heartaches and Tears*, Mercury 60990.
*I Get Lonely in a Hurry*, United Artists 3388.
*King of Broken Hearts*, United Artists 3442.
*Old Brush Arbors*, Musicor 3061.
*Mr. Country and Western Music*, Musicor 3046.
*New Country Hits*, Musicor 3060.
*Starday Presents*, Starday 335.

*The Great George Jones*, United Artists 657.
*The Race Is On*, Razor and Tie 2070.
*Trouble in Mind*, United Artists 6408.
*Famous Country Duets*, Musicor MS-3709.
*George Jones and Gene Pitney: For the First Time! Two Great Singers*, Musicor 3044.
*George Jones and Gene Pitney (Recorded in Nashville)*, Musicor 2223.
*Country Heart*, Musicor P25-5094.
*George Jones* [Starday], Starday 335.
*We Found Heaven Right Here on Earth at "4033,"* Musicor 3106.
*I'm a People*, Musicor M-2099.
*Love Bug*, Musicor 3088.
*Blue Moon of Kentucky*, United Artists 6420.
*It's Country Time Again!*, Musicor 3065.
*Cup of Loneliness*, Musicor 3124.
*Hits by George*, Musicor 3128.
*Walk through This World with Me*, Musicor 3119.
*Book of Memories*, United Artists 521002.
*Sings the Songs of Dallas Frazier*, Musicor 3149.
*The Musical Loves, Life and Sorrows of America's Great Country Star*, Musicor 3159.
*Song Book and Picture Album*, Starday 401.
*If My Heart Had Windows*, Musicor 3158.
*George Jones and Melba Montgomery*, Deluxe 111.
*I'll Share My World with You*, Musicor 3177.
*My Country*, Musicor 3169.
*Where Grass Won't Grow*, Musicor 3181.
*George Jones' Golden Hits Vol. 3*, United Artists 6696.
*Will You Visit Me on Sunday?*, Musicor 3188.
*George Jones with Love*, Musicor 3194.
*We Go Together*, Epic 30802.
*The Great Songs of Leon Payne*, Musicor 3204.
*A Picture of Me (Without You)*, Epic 31718.
*George Jones (We Can Make It)*, Epic 31321.
*Me and the First Lady*, Epic 31544.
*We Love to Sing About Jesus*, Razor and Tie 2118.
*Let's Build a World Together*, Epic 32113.
*Nothing Ever Hurt Me*, Epic 32412.
*We're Gonna Hold On*, Epic 32757.
*In a Gospel Way*, Razor and Tie 2138.
*George and Tammy and Tina*, Epic 33351.
*The Grand Tour*, Razor and Tie 2115.
*Memories of Us*, Epic 33547.
*Battle*, Epic 34034.
*Alone Again*, Epic 34290.
*Golden Ring*, Razor and Tie 2159.
*Bartender's Blues*, Razor and Tie 2101.
*My Very Special Guests*, Epic 35544.
*Double Trouble*, Razor and Tie 2100.
*I Am What I Am*, Epic/Legacy 63591.
*Encore: George Jones and Tammy Wynette* [live], Epic 37348.
*Still the Same Ole Me*, Epic 37106.
*A Taste of Yesterday's Wine*, Epic 38203.
*Shine On*, Epic 38406.

*By Request*, Epic 39546.
*You've Still Got a Place in My Heart*, Epic 39002.
*Ladies' Choice*, Epic 39272.
*Who's Gonna Fill Their Shoes*, Epic 39598.
*First Time Live*, Epic 39899.
*Wine Colored Roses*, Epic 40413.
*Too Wild Too Long*, Epic 40781.
*Live at Dancetown U.S.A.*, Ace 156.
*One Woman Man*, Epic 44078.
*You Oughta Be Here with Me*, Epic 46028.
*Friends in High Places*, Epic 45014.
*And Along Came Jones*, MCA 10398.
*Walls Can Fall*, MCA 10652.
*High-Tech Redneck*, MCA 10910.
*Bradley Barn Sessions*, MCA 11096.
*One*, MCA 11248.
*I Lived to Tell It All*, MCA 11478.
*It Don't Get Any Better Than This*, MCA 70005.
*The Cold Hard Truth*, Elektra 62368.
*Live with the Possum*, Elektra/Asylum 62480.
*The Rock Stone Cold Country 2001*, BNA 67029.
*Live in Concert*, Brentwood 40800.
*The Gospel Set*, BMG Special Products 48991.
*Hits I Missed ... and One I Didn't*, Brandt 79792.
*George Jones Sings from the Heart*, Wing 12323.
*Duets Country Style*, Mercury 60747.
*George Jones Sings His Greatest Hits*, Starday 150.
*Blue and Lonesome*, Mercury 60906.
*The Novelty Side of George Jones*, Mercury 60793.
*The Ballad Side of George Jones*, Mercury 20836.
*The Best of George Jones* [UA], United Artists 6291.
*Country and Western Number 1 Male Singer*, Mercury 60937.
*George Jones' Greatest Hits*, Vol. 2 61048.
*Singing the Blues*, Mercury 21029.
*George Jones' Golden Hits*, Vol. 1, United Artists 3532.
*Close Together as You and Me*, Musicor 3109.
*Four O Thirty Three*, Richmond 2180.
*The George Jones Story*, Starday 366.
*The Young George Jones*, United Artists 6558.
*George Jones' Golden Hits*, Vol. 2, United Artists 6566.
*Let's Get Together/Boy Meets Girl*, Musicor 3127.
*Greatest Hits* [Musicor], Musicor 3116.
*George Jones and Dolly Parton*, Starday 429.
*The Golden Country Hits of George Jones*, Starday 440.
*Party Pickin'*, Gusto 0134.
*The Best of George Jones* [Musicor], Musicor 3191.
*The Best of Sacred Music*, Musicor 3203.
*The Best of George Jones*, Vol. 1 [RCA], RCA 4716.
*I Made Leaving Easy for You*, RCA 4726.
*Poor Man's Riches*, RCA 4725.
*Tender Years*, RCA 4786.
*14 Country Favorites*, Mercury 20306.

*20 Golden Pieces of George Jones*, Bulldog 2009.
*I Can Still See Him in Your Eyes*, RCA 4847.
*Take Me to Your World*, RCA 4787.
*Greatest Hits* [PolyGram], PolyGram 826248.
*George Jones Sings His Songs*, RCA 0612.
*I Can Love Enough*, RCA 0815.
*You Gotta Be My Baby*, RCA 0486.
*The Best of George Jones*, Vol. 2 [RCA], RCA 0316.
*The Best of the Best*, RCA 1113.
*We Go Together/Me and the First Lady*, Epic 33752.
*Country George*, Pair 1080.
*16 Greatest Hits*, Deluxe 1012.
*All-Time Greatest Hits*, Vol. 1, Epic 34692.
*Greatest Hits*, Epic 34716.
*The Best of George Jones* [Epic], Epic 33352.
*Together Again*, BMG Special 46693.
*Anniversary: Ten Years of Hits*, Epic 38323.
*Jones Country*, Epic 38978.
*White Lightning* [Ace], Ace CH-13.
*The Lone Star Legend*, Ace 139.
*She Thinks I Still Care* [CEMA], CEMA 9032.
*Burn the Honky-Tonk Down*, Rounder SS15.
*20 Greatest Hits*, Deluxe 7778.
*Super Hits*, Epic 40776.
*Don't Stop the Music*, Ace 912.
*14 Greats*, Hollywood 389.
*He Stopped Loving Her Today*, King 380.
*My Mom and Santa*, Hollywood 401.
*24 Gospel Greats*, Deluxe 7791.
*Country Store Collection*, Country Store CST 45.
*Golden Hits*, Hollywood 103.
*Greatest Hits, Vol. 2* [Hollywood], 402.
*Lonely Christmas Call*, Hollywood 400.
*Cold Cold Heart*, Pickwick JS-4108.
*Mr. Country Music*, Classic 1139.
*Heartaches and Hangovers* [Rounder], Rounder S517.
*At His Best*, Hollywood 380.
*Hallelujah Weekend*, Epic 46078.
*The Greatest Country Hits*, Curb 77369.
*Hardcore Honky Tonk*, Mercury 848978.
*Jazz Hour*, Huub 73523.
*The Best of George Jones, Vol. 1: Hardcore Honky Tonk*, Mercury 848978.
*The Best of George Jones 1955–1967*, Rhino 70531.
*Greatest Hits, Vol. 2*, Epic 48839.
*Super Hits, Vol. 2*, CBS 53312.
*Frozen in Time*, Quicksilver 1011.
*Nothin' Like George Jones*, Sony Special 20589.
*Your Tender Years*, Classic Sound Inc., 7563.
*How I Love These Old Songs*, Intermedia 5061.
*I Can't Change Overnight*, Intermedia 5044.
*Stars 3*, Hollywood 140.
*Good Old Bible*, Hollywood 189.

*Life Turned Her That Way*, Rounder 351.
*I'm a One Woman Man [Collection]*, Hollywood 392.
*The Essential George Jones: The Spirit of Country*, Epic/Legacy 65718.
*All Time Greatest Hits* [UA], Liberty 30135.
*White Lightning* [Drive], Drive Archive 41030.
*Cup of Loneliness: The Mercury Years*, Mercury 522279.
*George and Tammy Super Hits*, Sony 67133.
*Songs I Wanta Sing*, Epic 34717.
*George Jones and Gene Pitney*, Bear Family 15790.
*Hank by George: George Jones Sings Hank Williams*, King 1426.
*Songs from the Heart*, King 1436.
*Fine Country Wine*, King 465.
*George Jones and Conway Twitty*, King 480.
*I'm the Only Hell Mama Ever Raised*, King 472.
*Lovin' Time*, King 488.
*Wishing and Dreaming with George Jones*, King 491.
*The Best of Country*, Richmond 2177.
*Color of the Blues*, Richmond 2297.
*Family Bible*, Richmond 2150.
*A Good Year for the Roses*, Richmond 2168.
*I Can't Get There from Here*, Richmond 2197.
*Image of Me*, Richmond 2266.
*Lily of the Valley*, Richmond 2254.
*Living on Easy Street*, Richmond 2313.
*One Has My Name*, Richmond 2239.
*Sometimes You Just Can't Win*, Richmond 2227.
*Things Have Gone to Pieces*, Richmond 2234.
*White Lightning* [Richmond], Richmond 2284.
*Why Baby Why*, Richmond 2203.
*Your Heart Turned Left*, Richmond 2258.
*Vintage Collections Series*, Capitol 33832.
*24 Greatest Hits*, TeeVee 6012.
*The Classic Years*, Mercury 532341.
*The Best of the Best of George Jones*, Federal 6503.
*Seasons of My Heart*, Richmond 2163.
*The President and the First Lady*, TeeVee 6005.
*She Thinks I Still Care: The George Jones Collection*, Razor and Tie 2136.
*Super Hits/Super Hits, Vol. 2/George and Tammy Super Hits*, Sony 65379.
*Hits*, PolyGram 536220.
*Pure Country: George Jones and Friends*, Coyote 4602.
*18 Country Classics*, Spectrum 552562.
*Country Classics*, EMI 724385603327.
*Honky Tonkin'*, PolyGram 836691.
*16 Biggest Hits*, Legacy/Epic 69319.
*1998 A Picture of Me (Without You)/Nothing Ever Hurt Me (Half as Bad as Losing You)*, Koch 8025.
*Grand Tour/Alone Again*, Epic 494895.
*The Best of the Best*, Federal 6528.
*Blue Side of Lonesome*, King 1472.
*Together Again: Jones and Wynette*, BMG Special 44899.
*The George Jones Collection*, MCA 70062.
*Memories of Us/Battle*, Koch 8046.

*Double Barrel Country*, Madacy 563.
*16 Biggest Hits [Duets]*, Sony 69699.
*Classic George*, Universal 21153.
*Country Music Hall of Fame 1992*, King 3801.
*20 Gospel Greats*, Tee Vee 6025.
*My Favorites of Hank Williams*, EMI 499027.
*White Lightnin'* [Classic Sound], Classic Sound 7563.
*20th Century Masters—The Millennium Collection: The Best of George Jones*, MCA 170110.
*Ways of the World*, Starburst 8.
*The Very Best of George Jones*, Lonestar 137.
*Country Music Hall of Famer*, Legacy 103.
*Greatest Hits* [CEMA], MCA Special 18239.
*Friends in High Places/Ladies Choice*, DCC 206.
*Heartaches and Hangovers* [Mastersound], Mastersound 50130.
*It Sure Was Good*, Sony Special Products 32379.
*Definite Country Collection*, Columbia 5013982.
*Country Stars and Stripes*, Direct Source 1291.
*George Jones* [St. Clair], St. Clair 321.
*Best of George Jones*, Columbia River 190047.
*Greatest Hits* [Madacy], Madacy 1746.
*Classic Country Collection*, Aim 3002.
*The Legend Lives On*, Music Deluxe 24.
*Love Songs*, Epic 87151.
*The Gospel Collection*, BNA 67063.
*Best of the Best: Hall of Fame 1992*, Gusto 519.
*The Very Best of Love*, Madacy 2523.
*Jones by George*, Proper Pairs 135.
*Some of the Best of Love*, Acrobat 105.
*All American Country*, Universal International 552562.
*Love Songs*, Epic/Legacy 90899.
*20 Original Greatest Hits*, TeeVee 717.
*Country Standards*, EMI 82647.
*Live Recordings from the Louisiana Hayride*, Scena 271900.
*The Definitive Collection 1955–1962*, Mercury 000250002.
*50 Years of Hits*, Brandt 220/23.
*The Rock*, Collectables 8438.
*Loving You Can Never Be Better*, Platinum Disc 3151.
*George Jones*, Direct Source 4340.
*How Beautiful Heaven Must Be*, Direct Source 4321.
*Dispatches: 1990–99*, Raven 199.
*The Complete '60s Duets*, Varese 066642.
*The Collection: Super Hits/Super Hits, Vol. 2*, Sony 93979.
*The Great George Jones*, Rajon 355.
*Greatest Collection*, Platinum Disc 3581.
*The Initial Music Collection*, Direct Source 4329.
*At His Best*, Gusto 581.
*The Essential George Jones*, Sony 92565.
*16 Country Hits*, Starday 3021.
*George Jones' Greatest Hits*, Mercury 826248-4.
*Honky Tonks and Heartaches*, Mercury 8342771
*Stop, Look, Listen*, Allegiance 72924.
*Rockin' the Country*, Mercury 826095-1.

*Greatest Hits, Vol. 1* [Country Stars], Satellite 7542.
*Greatest Hits, Vol. 2* [Country Stars], Satellite 7543.
*Real McCoy*, Epic 40787.
*Texas Tornado*, Crown 1001.
*Good Year for the Roses/20 Great Country Hits*, Woodford Music 5664.
*Maybe Little Baby*, Sears 125.
*Rock It*, Encore 193196.

# PART FOUR

# *Women of Country Music*

The history of country music is enriched with many interesting and colorful characters. Although the male singers have received more attention, women artists have made formidable contributions in every style from the genre's inception to the present day.

Some of the pioneers of country music were the people of the Appalachian mountains who had been playing their brand of folk songs for hundreds of years. When the recording industry realized that there was a large market for this rich vein of American music, there was a feverish call to anyone interested in recording a few songs. Two of the most important pioneers—Sara Carter and Maybelle Carter—answered that call.

Although they made enormous contributions, the Carter women weren't the only important female pioneers in the early days of country music. The Coon Creek Girls was one of the first all-female string bands. Lily May Ledford was the leader of the group and along with her sister Rose, Evelyn "Daisy" Lange and Ester "Violet" Koehler, they created history. Although they didn't receive the same attention as Dr. Humphrey Bate and His Possum Hunters or Gid Tanner and His Skillet Lickers, the Coon Creek Girls boasted their own legions of fans. Later, after the outfit broke up, Minnie Ledford joined her two sisters and the trio forged on. Other pioneers of the era include Wilma Lee Cooper, Aunt Molly Jackson, Patsy Montana, Cindy Walker and Lulu Jackson, among others.

The cowboy and radio era was predominantly a male oriented business. However, among the dozens of singing cowboys gallantly riding their horses, fighting the bad guys and performing rope tricks, one woman—Dale Evans—stood out and became a star. She was the queen of the cowgirl set and later teamed up with Roy Rogers to form a dynamic movie duo. Others who added a female dimension to this chapter of country music include Texas Rose Bascom, Bertha Blancett, Faye Blesing, Polly Burson, Gail Davis, Bernice Dean, Ruby Gobble, Bonnie Gray Harris, Alice Van-Springsteen, and Mabel Strickland Woodward.

The bluegrass and western swing styles were predominantly male oriented since the majority of female contributors in the first fifty years of the genre's existence were vocalists rather than instrumentalists. Although each singer began her career rooted in one particular style, she often welded different elements into one cohesive unit and carved their own niche.

Kitty Wells, Molly O'Day, June Carter Cash, Patsy Cline, Loretta Lynn and Wanda Jackson all delivered eclectic styles comprised of the Nashville sound, countrypolitan, honky tonk, rockabilly, pop-country, bluegrass, western swing, and a more traditional version of country music. Whatever angle they approached a song, there was no mistaking their sheer talent and spirit.

Other female artists that made important contributions to country music but are not included in this book include Judy Canova, Bonnie Brown, Wilma Burgess, Lorraine "Lee" Hammond, Martha Carson, Ann Nation, Alice Gerrard, Carla Sciaky, Goldie Hill, Minnie Pearl, Dorothy Good, Patsy Montana, Anita Kerr, Ella Brown, Skeeter Davis, Betty Davis, Connie Eatson, Barbara Fairchild, Melba Montgomery, Mildred Good, Judy Lynn, Rose Maddox, and Dottie West.

The following are featured in this book.

Sara Carter was married to A.P. Carter. Together with her cousin Maybelle, she established the presence of females in country music in the 1920s.

Mother Maybelle Carter was a noted guitar and autoharp player. She also brought her three daughters to the scene, including June, who would carve out her own niche.

Dale Evans was Roy Rogers' partner for many years. She was a definite movie and radio cowgirl star. Her songwriting abilities were never truly appreciated.

Kitty Wells paved the way for the many female country artists that followed including Loretta Lynn.

Molly O'Day had a brief but powerful career and her influence on later singers is crucial.

June Carter Cash was from the famous Carter family, but gained further exposure as the wife of superstar Johnny Cash.

Patsy Cline was a fiery singer whose incredible career was cut short in its prime. She has been rated the greatest singer—male or female—in country music history.

Loretta Lynn was one of the superstars of country music in the 1970s and 1980s. She remains a revered figure.

Wanda Jackson mixed country music with rockabilly before singing more gospel tinged material. She would make a comeback late in her career and regain her old fan base.

## SARA CARTER (1899–1979)
### *Wildwood Flower*

From the earliest days of country music women have made vital contributions. The pioneer era is filled with female influences who were essential in launching the music from its humble beginnings. One of these crucial first generation country artists that made a huge impact was the Wildwood Flower. Her name was Sara Carter.

Sara Carter was born Sara Dougherty on July 21, 1899, in Flat Woods, Virginia. She was steeped in mountain traditions and developed a keen interest in music at an early age. Her love of folk songs was fueled by her cousin Maybelle and the two would often gather together to hum a few of the old favorites that had been sung in the mountains for centuries. Sara's ability to remember the lyrics to hundreds of songs would eventually prove very beneficial.

It was custom in the area at the turn of the century to marry young and Sara was no exception. One day, she was sitting on the porch strumming her autoharp and singing in her rich voice when a young Virginian happened to be passing by. Alvin Pleasant Delaney Carter was also steeped in the mountain traditions and was a good musician. It was, according to legend, love at first sight. A year later the two were married.

Their marriage was more than a partnership between a man and a woman; it was the unification of a dynamic singing duo. They performed at social gatherings and carved a strong niche for themselves, even if it was only in a very regional market. But this small fan base would be a good anchor for their later exploits.

When cousin Maybelle married A.P.'s brother she joined Sara and her husband to form a trio. The three called themselves the Carter Family and were among the first to answer the call of Ralph Peer, a talent scout for Victor Records looking to record mountain music. They drove from their home in Virginia to Bristol, Tennessee, in July of 1927. Not only did they pass the audition, but they were selected to record a couple of days later. The songs they cut proved to be a commercial success and the saga of the Carter Family in country music had begun.

The three next recorded in New Jersey, where they cut the definitive version of "Wildwood Flower." There was magic among them: Sara played rhythm autoharp and guitar that proved a counterpoint to Maybelle's distinct guitar lines. Sara's voice was a rich contrast to A.P.'s and that created a cohesive sound. They would go on to wax almost three hundred songs together and many became treasured country classics.

The Great Depression proved to be a turning point for the fortunes of the Carter family. Like many other country musical acts, the trio suffered through tough times. In 1933, Sara and A.P. divorced, although they continued to work together. The Carter family continued to switch labels throughout the decade, first in 1935 when they moved to ARC and a year later to Decca. At the latter company they received a royalty that helped ease the financial strain of the harsh economic times.

They were also trying to broaden their appeal when they began appearing on as many radio stations that would feature them. They ventured throughout the South as far as the Texas/Mexican border. By this time they were known throughout the land as one of the important founders of country music.

Sara would travel the farthest of the trio. In 1939, she moved to California with her new husband, Coy Bayes, one of A.P.'s cousins. However, her recording duties with the Carter family were not finished. In 1941, they cut a dozen of new songs that earned Sara her first songwriting credit.

Unfortunately, by this time, the saga of the Carter family had in many ways come to an end. They had enjoyed a successful run, but by the 1940s Sara and A.P. had retired from the music business. Maybelle continued to perform with her three daughters.

In 1952, Sara and A.P. came out of retirement. They made it a family affair as two of the couple's children, Joe and Janette, joined them. During this period they recorded almost a hundred songs on the Acme label. However, their attempt to recapture past glory proved futile and they retired for good. Four years later, A.P. died.

Sara would enter the spotlight one more time in 1967 when she teamed up with Maybelle to record *An Historic Reunion*. It proved to be her last performance. On January 8, 1979, Sara Carter, one of the most important personalities of the early days of country music, passed away.

Sara Carter was an important pioneer in country music. She was a vital member of the Carter clan, as well as one of the greatest contributors to the early days of the genre. She was also an adept musician and possessed a good voice. Her contributions to the music of her ancestors were many.

Sara, along with A.P. and Maybelle, is credited with recording close to five hundred songs. Many were old standards that had existed in the region for years, while others were original compositions. The Carter trio could create magic with any material due to their incredible blend of individual talent into a unique single unit.

Sara was an excellent rhythm guitarist and autoharpist, she had the knack to provide cousin Maybelle with the right amount of scratch in order for the latter to launch another definitive melodic line. Although she would never rank among the greatest country music virtuosos, Sara could hold her own in a recording studio.

Sara's voice boasted a genuine appeal that enabled her to develop such a large following. There was a soothing reassurance in her delivery that enabled the listener to partake in a wonderful journey to unexplored worlds. Her vocal abilities were a good solo weapon, but were dynamite when combined with that of her two partners, A.P. and Maybelle.

Although her signature tune was "Wildwood Flower," she is responsible for putting down on vinyl a number of other songs. A short list includes "Little Houses," "Little Log Cabin by the Sea," "Room in Heaven for Me," "The Storms Are on the Ocean," "Your Mother Still Prays," "Engine 143," "Homestead on the Farm," "Diamonds in the Rough," "Broken-Hearted Lover," "My Heavenly Home Is Bright and Fair," "Cannon Ball Blues," "For Lovin' Me," "That'll Be the Day," "Bury Me Under the Weeping Willow," "The Ship That Never Returned," "A Song for Mama," and "Behind Those Stone Walls." It didn't matter what kind of material the trio recorded, they were sure to put their own stamp on it.

Since she was an important role model for the next three generations to follow, Sara had a large influence on a number of country artists. A partial list of those touched by her magic includes Anita, Helen, and June Carter, Molly O'Day, Wanda Jackson, Tammy Wynette, Loretta Lynn, Dolly Parton, Lynn Anderson, Patsy Cline, Skeeter Davis, Crystal Gayle, Trisha Yearwood, Barbara Mandrell, k. d. lang, and many more. She was a matriarch and had a strong presence on the course of the genre for 20 years.

In 1970, the Carter Family was inducted into the Country Music Hall of Fame. It was a fitting honor bestowed on the first family of country music. Sara, along with Maybelle, broke new ground for female performers. Undoubtedly, the Wildwood Flower has her special place in the history of the genre.

## Discography

*All Time Favorites*, Acme P-1.
*In Memory of A.P. Carter*, Acme P-2.

*Together Again*, RCA Victor 2580.
*The Carter Family*, Decca 4404.
*Anita Carter Sings Folk Songs Old and New*, Mercury 27770.
*Keep on the Sunnyside*, CBS CS-8952.
*More Favorites by the Carter Family*, Decca D-4557.
*The Country Album*, CBS CS-9417.
*Country's First Family*, Columbia 34266.
*Diamonds in the Rough*, Copper Creek 107.
*Clinch Mountain Treasures*, Country 112.
*Best of the Carter Family*, Prism Leisure 548.
*Family Album*, Longhorn 3103.
*Sunshine in the Shadows*, Recall 474.
*In the Shadow of Clinch Mountain*, Bear Family 15865.
*The Decca Sessions, Vol. 1 (1936)*, Catfish 188.
*The Decca Sessions, Vol. 2*, Catfish 218.
*The Carter Family, Vol. 2. (1935–1941)*, JSP 7708.
*Greatest Hits 1927–1934*, Fabulous 146.
*Country and Folk Roots*, Castle 651.
*RCA Country Legends*, RCA 59266.
*Gospel Gold*, Brentwood 40840.
*A Proper Introduction to the Carter Family: Keep on the Sunnyside*, Proper 2060.
*Will You Remember Me*, Fruit Tree 842.
*Best of the Carter Family [2005]*, Prism Platinum 548.
*20th Century Master—The Millennium Collection: The Best of the Carter Family*, Mercury 4544.
*Early Country Radio*, JSP 7757.
*Early Classics*, ACM 015.
*The Collection*, EMI 576324.
*The Carter Family: 1927–1934*, JSP 7701.
*The Carter Family [ACM]*, ACM 022.
*Wildwood Flower*, PolyGram 834491.
*The Original and Great Carter Family*, Camden 586.
*'Mid the Green Fields of Virginia*, RCA 1107.
*The Collection of Favorites*, Decca 3022.
*Last Recordings, Vol. 1.*
*Country Music Hall of Fame*, MCA 10088.
*Country Music Hall of Fame*, King 3811.
*The Best of the Carter Family, Vol. 1*, Country Stars 55464.
*The Best of the Carter Family, Vol. 2*, Country Stars 55465.
*Wildwood Flowers*, ASL/Living 5323.
*Last Sessions: Their Complete Victor Recordings (1924–1842)*, Rounder 1072.
*Longing for Old Virginia: Their Complete Victor Recordings (1934)*, Rounder 1071.
*My Clinch Mountain Home: Their Complete Recordings*, Rounder 611065.
*Anchored in Love: Their Complete Victor Recordings*, Victor 611064.
*When the Roses Bloom in Dixieland*, Rounder 1066.
*Worried Man Blues: Their Complete Victor Sides*, Rounder 1067.
*On Border Radio, Vol. 1*, Arhoolie 411.
*Greatest Hits*, KRB 5155.
*Sunshine in the Shadows: Their Complete Recordings*, Rounder 1068.
*Give Me the Roses While I Live*, Rounder 1069.
*Country by the Carter Family*, Vanguard 79502.
*On Border Radio, Vol. 2: 1939*, Arhoolie 412.

*Best of the Best of the Original Carter Family*, Koch 1478.
*Gold Watch and Chain: Their Complete Victor Recordings*, Victor 1070.
*On Border Radio, Vol. 3; 1939*, Arhoolie 413.
*Can the Circle Be Unbroken? Country Music's First Family*, Columbia 65707.

# MAYBELLE CARTER (1909–1978)
## Country Matriarch

In its infancy, country music was a style that was looking for direction. It needed sturdy individuals who were not making records to make large amounts of money, but artists who truly loved the music and wanted to spread the richness of the Appalachian folk songs throughout the world. One of these figures would later be known as the country matriarch because of her motherly presence in the business for over fifty years. Her name was Maybelle Carter.

Maybelle Carter was born Maybelle Addington on March 10, 1909, in Nickelsville, Virginia. She developed an interest in music from an early age and learned how to play the autoharp, guitar, and banjo. But she was more than just a folk music enthusiast; she was a dedicated learner who honed her skills until she was proficient on two instruments: the guitar and autoharp. She was able to coax beautiful music and developed a knack for creating sweet melodic lines.

She was steeped in mountain musical traditions that also represented a cultural education of the ways of her people. This knowledge and familiarity allowed her the confidence to perform the songs she held so dear to the very audience that would appreciate her talent the most. She played at social and church gatherings eliciting a smile from all those who heard her, since it was blatantly apparent from an early age that Maybelle had a song in her heart.

Sometimes, she teamed up with her cousin Sara Dougherty. The two spent hours honing their vocal skills together as they learned how to blend their voices to make it sound as one. They built up a huge repertoire since both had a facility to learn a tune once and have it stored in their memories forever. They traded songs back and forth and the bond developed between the two was magical. Later, Sara married A.P. Carter and went on to sing with her new husband many of the same tunes she had practiced as a girl at numerous local events.

It wasn't until 1926 that Maybelle joined the duo when she married

A.P.'s brother Ezra. The addition of her voice and instrumental skills to the seasoned pair was pure excitement. Although Sara and A.P. sounded good together, with Maybelle they were that much better. There was a definite chemistry between the trio that would enable them to launch a successful musical career.

It all began in 1927 when the three decided to answer the call for rural talent in Bristol, Tennessee. It was there that pioneer recording master Ralph Peer had set up shop, knowing full well that the mountain folk had a special musical knack. The trio proved that they possessed that unique quality at the audition and were asked to record the next couple of days. Their polished material contained a commercial appeal that assured them immense future success.

For the next sixteen years, the Carter family recorded consistently (despite the Great Depression) and delivered hundreds of songs to the public. On these sides the unmistakable sound of Maybelle's musical prowess was present. She added a dimension to the group that was essential to their sound. In 1943, the trio ceased operations, as A.P. and Sara retired from the music business.

Maybelle continued to press on and recruited her three daughters, Helen, Anita and June, into the music fold. The four of them astonished audiences with their sharp melodies and harmonies. The three girls provided different aspects to the group, billed as Mother Maybelle and the Carter Sisters. Helen was an excellent musician, Anita possessed a powerful lead voice, and June gave the family a warm stage presence with her entertaining sense of humor.

They became staples on Richmond radio, performing for two different stations until 1948 when they moved to a spot in Knoxville where a young guitar virtuoso trying to break into the business backed them. His name was Chet Atkins. In 1949, they were singing on Missouri radio and a year later moved to Nashville. In 1950, they joined the *Grand Ole Opry* and remained there for the next decade. In the late 1950s, Mother Maybelle and her three talented daughters toured with Elvis.

When A.P. died, Mother Maybelle and her three daughters assumed the name, the Carter Family. In 1963, they started to back Johnny Cash. When not touring with the man in black, they performed under their usual guise and released the album *Keep on the Sunny Side* in 1964. In 1968, June married Cash, but that was not the end of the career of the four Carter women. The group continued to record, including *Travelin' Minstrel Band* and *Three Generations* in 1972 and 1974 respectively.

But, the greatest musical accomplishment of Mother Maybelle's career during the 1960s was the reunion with Sara. The two performed at the Newport Folk Festival to a large, enthusiastic audience who were keen enough to realize that they were witnessing an exciting moment in history. The pair later released the album *An Historic Reunion*.

Throughout the 1970s, Maybelle performed and recorded sporadically. After many years in the country music spotlight she allowed the younger generation the time to find their own way in the music business. Any performance or recording she made was a genuine treat for all fans.

On October 23, 1978, Mother Maybelle Carter, the beloved matriarch of not only the Carter clan but two generations of country artists, passed away.

Mother Maybelle Carter was a true country music institution. Her career stretched fifty years and there were many major accomplishments and awards. She was part of the genre's first successful trio, then presided over her three very talented daughters. She made contributions to any project she participated in.

She was a legendary musician. Although not the greatest instrumentalist in the history of country music, she was able to deliver strong melodic lines on the guitar, autoharp and banjo. Many of the hundreds of pictures taken of her show Mother Maybelle strumming an autoharp and was arguably the foremost exponent of the instrument. She also played a solid guitar and banjo. On the hundreds of songs that she recorded with Sara and A.P., it was often Maybelle that provided the musical punch.

Maybelle Carter was also a female pioneer in country music and along with her cousin Sara established the female role in the genre. The two rose above their contemporaries because of their sheer talent and determination. As a leading voice in the genre's infancy, Maybelle was assured a special role in the history books.

She had a large influence on a number of female artists, including her cousin Sara and daughters Anita, Helen and June. She also had an impact on Molly O'Day, Patsy Cline, Kitty Wells, Loretta Lynn, Crystal Gayle, Barbara Mandrell, Wanda Jackson, the Dixie Chicks, Lynn Anderson, Tammy Wynette, Melba Montgomery and many others. But she was also a special counsel to dozens of country music acts, spinning out her solid wisdom to anyone who was clever enough to listen. In her later years, many performers sought out her advice on numerous subjects.

Mother Maybelle contributed as many songs as any one else in country music circles. A short list includes "Arkansas Traveler," "Black Mountain Rag," "Bully of the Town," "Coal Miner's Blues," "Farther On," "Happiest Days of All," "Little Brown Jug," "My Native Home," "Never on Sunday," "Rocky Top," "San Antonio Rose," "Sun of the Soul," "Higher Ground," "Gold Watch and Chain," "Tennessee Waltz," and countless others. Although she was not the creator of these songs, she was able to inject her warm voice and instrumental talents into each tune turning them into something special.

In 1970, she was inducted as a member of the Carter Family into the Country Music Hall of Fame. It was a fitting honor for someone who made so many contributions to the genre in a variety of roles. She oversaw the growth of the music from its infancy to its modern day position as a billion dollar industry. Undoubtedly, the country matriarch occupies a special place in the history of country music.

## Discography

*Mother Maybelle Carter*, Ambassador 98069.
*Queen of the Autoharp*, Kapp KS-3413.
*Wildwood Pickin'*, Vanguard 77021.
*Living Legend*, Columbia CS-9275.
With Sara Carter:
*A Historical Reunion: Sara and Maybelle, The Original Carters*, Koch 7925.
*Sara and Maybelle Carter*, Bear Family 15471.
With the Carter Family:
*All Time Favorites*, Acme P-1.
*In Memory of A.P. Carter*, Acme P-2.
*Together Again*, RCA Victor 2580.
*The Carter Family*, Decca 4404.
*Anita Carter Sings Folk Songs Old and New*, Mercury 27770.
*Keep on the Sunnyside*, CBS CS-8952.
*More Favorites by the Carter Family*, Decca D-4557.
*The Country Album*, CBS CS-9417.
*Country's First Family*, Columbia 34266.
*Diamonds in the Rough*, Copper Creek 107.
*Clinch Mountain Treasures*, Country 112.
*Best of the Carter Family*, Prism Leisure 548.
*Family Album*, Longhorn 3103.
*Sunshine in the Shadows*, Recall 474.
*In the Shadow of Clinch Mountain*, Bear Family 15865.
*The Decca Sessions, Vol. 1 (1936)*, Catfish 188.
*The Decca Sessions, Vol. 2*, Catfish 218.
*The Carter Family, Vol. 2. (1935–1941)*, JSP 7708.
*Greatest Hits 1927–1934*, Fabulous 146.
*Country and Folk Roots*, Castle 651.
*RCA Country Legends*, RCA 59266.
*Gospel Gold*, Brentwood 40840.
*A Proper Introduction to the Carter Family: Keep on the Sunnyside*, Proper 2060.
*Will You Remember Me*, Fruit Tree 842.
*Best of the Carter Family [2005]*, Prism Platinum 548.
*20th Century Master—The Millennium Collection: The Best of the Carter Family*, Mercury 4544.
*Early Country Radio*, JSP 7757.
*Early Classics*, ACM 015.
*The Collection*, EMI 576324.

*The Carter Family: 1927–1934*, JSP 7701.
*The Carter Family* [ACM], ACM 022.
*Wildwood Flower*, PolyGram 834491.
*The Original and Great Carter Family*, Camden 586.
*'Mid the Green Fields of Virginia*, RCA 1107.
*The Collection of Favorites*, Decca 3022.
*Last Recordings, Vol. 1.*
*Country Music Hall of Fame*, MCA 10088.
*Country Music Hall of Fame*, King 3811.
*The Best of the Carter Family, Vol. 1*, Country Stars 55464.
*The Best of the Carter Family, Vol. 2*, Country Stars 55465.
*Wildwood Flowers*, ASL/Living 5323.
*Last Sessions: Their Complete Victor Recordings (1924–1842)*, Rounder 1072.
*Longing for Old Virginia: Their Complete Victor Recordings (1934)*, Rounder 1071.
*My Clinch Mountain Home: Their Complete Recordings*, Rounder 611065.
*Anchored in Love: Their Complete Victor Recordings*, Victor 611064.
*When the Roses Bloom in Dixieland*, Rounder 1066.
*Worried Man Blues: Their Complete Victor Sides*, Rounder 1067.
*On Border Radio, Vol. 1*, Arhoolie 411.
*Greatest Hits*, KRB 5155.
*Sunshine in the Shadows: Their Complete Recordings*, Rounder 1068.
*Give Me the Roses While I Live*, Rounder 1069.
*Country by the Carter Family*, Vanguard 79502.
*On Border Radio, Vol. 2: 1939*, Arhoolie 412.
*Best of the Best of the Original Carter Family*, Koch 1478.
*Gold Watch and Chain: Their Complete Victor Recordings*, Victor 1070.
*On Border Radio, Vol. 3; 1939*, Arhoolie 413.
*Can the Circle Be Unbroken? Country Music's First Family*, Columbia 65707.

# DALE EVANS (1912–2001)
## Queen of the Cowgirls

The male stars—Ken Maynard, Gene Autry, Roy Rogers, Tex Ritter and many others—dominated the western movie industry. The singing cowboys were the action heroes of their era as they punched, sang, roped and rode their way into the psyche of audiences as dashing matinee idols. Although western flicks did include women they often played second fiddle to the star—all except one female who claimed the title Queen of the Cowgirls. Her name was Dale Evans.

Dale Evans was born Francis Smith on October 31, 1912, in Uvalde, Texas. She sang in the church choir, but had no real ambitions to be a singer until her late teens, when she was forced to support a child. She had eloped in order to escape the pressures of a very strict society and when her husband died a couple of years later, she was a single mom. She turned to music to earn a living for her and her infant.

She had an appealing voice and found work with the Anson Weeks Orchestra during the Depression. She also worked for the *CBS News and Rhythm* radio program and appeared on the Edgar Bergen–Eugene McCarthy show before making her debut in films. She starred in *Orchestra Wives, Swing Your Partner, Casanova in Burlesque, Utah, Bells of Rosarita, My Pal Trigger, Apache Pass, Slippy McGee, Susanna Pass, Twilight in the Sierras* and *Pals of the Golden West*. By the end of the 1930s she had endeared herself into the hearts of the B-movie enthusiasts.

The studios desperately wanted a female cowgirl who could add a new dimension to their established star, Roy Rogers. He was a national figure and a few actresses had been cast as his opposite. But when Rogers and Evans (she had changed her name by this time) teamed together there was a definite chemistry. The studio had found the right combination they had been seeking. Although their relationship was strictly professional at first, love blossomed and they were married in 1947.

She was eventually crowned Queen of the Cowgirls and became the single most important female film star of the genre. She dressed like Rogers in full western regalia and together they became the darlings of the Saturday movie circuit. When the popularity of the B-movies began to fade, they had no problem making the transition to television.

For seven years, 1951–1958, Roy Rogers and Dale Evans entered American living rooms every week with their folksy, homespun show *Happy Trails*. It was a huge hit and one of the most genuine TV shows ever to transmit over the air. Their wholesome image that emphasized sound family values, God, and America only propelled their popularity until it was written in stone. With his horse, Trigger, Rogers was easily the most popular cowboy on television and Evans was his trusted equal.

After their TV series was cancelled, Evans and Rogers continued their career in show business. They appeared on package tours, various television programs and radio, enabling them to remain a high profile couple. They were instantly recognizable and in a more innocent time the duo symbolized everything that was pure in America.

In 1962, they returned to television with their own variety show on ABC. Once again, their program featured solid moral values. Although it was eventually cancelled, their popularity did not wane, as they remained a publicly visible couple. In the early 1980s, Evans hosted a long-running syndicated religious talk show without Rogers.

They also enjoyed a prolific recording career with numerous hits that consisted of country material as well as gospel pieces. Their marketability was assured and they rode out every new fad without ever losing any of their popularity. They increased their appeal with a host of merchandise, new recorded output and high visibility at country events. Not even when Rogers had his beloved horse Trigger stuffed did their reputation wane in the public's eye.

The Roy Rogers and Dale Evans mystique never really faded despite the changing times. Their simple, wholesome image served as an anchor to an ever increasing demoralized society. Their star in the country music universe remained ablaze throughout the many changes to the genre. There was always an audience interested in their music and the image they projected.

The pair would eventually do very well in business, as they opened up a series of restaurants. But despite the variety, they never lost their country music audience and added new fans when each successive generation discovered what they had to offer. Their longevity in show business was a tribute to their simple and strong moral lifestyle.

On July 6, 1998, Roy Rogers, the movie and TV star, died. It was the end of an era in American entertainment. Three years later, on February 7, 2001, Dale Evans, his bride of 51 years, joined him to ride Happy Trails forever.

Evans' contributions to country music are far and wide. She was a star of the cowboy films and her rich voice helped sell millions of movie tickets as well as albums. But she was also a spokesman, a songwriter, and a symbol for everything that was American. She was one of the first high profile women to combine career and family.

She wrote hundreds of songs, including "Happy Trails," the theme song to their popular 1950s TV show. Many country artists covered the song and even the heavy metal rock group Van Halen recorded a version of the all-time hit. The song—a stone classic—displayed an inherent talent in Evans that was never fully recognized. She is also credited with writing "Hazy Mountain" and "The Bible Tells Me So," which became a Sunday school standard.

In all, she wrote and co-wrote over four hundred songs. She penned several books and was the co-founder of the Happy Trails Children's Foundation that stood up for severely abused and neglected children. Her charity work was as important as the numerous films she starred in as well as the many songs she recorded and wrote.

Many remember her for the numerous roles she played in the movies. In 1939, she made her debut in the *Arizona Kid*. After a few other appearances she starred in her first film in 1943, *Here Comes Elmer*. She would go on to star in almost thirty flicks, mostly westerns and often as Rogers' sidekick.

Some of her best known roles include *The West Side Kid, The Cowboy and the Senorita, The Yellow Rose of Texas, The Lights of Old Santa Fe, Along the Navajo Trail, Man from Oklahoma, Bells of San Angelo, Down Dakota Way* and *Trigger, Jr.* Later on, she would appear on TV in *M Stands for Murder*. Perhaps not the most gifted actress to appear on the silver screen, she always put a lot of energy and wholesomeness in whatever role she played.

Evans was inducted into the Cowgirls Hall of Fame in 1995. The institution is dedicated to those women who made important contributions to the spirit of the American West and contains nearly two hundred females, including deserved candidates Patsy Cline, Laura Ingalls Wilder and Willa Cather. But none had the diverse impact of Dale Evans.

Dale Evans had a strong impact on all country music women that followed her, including Melba Montgomery, Patsy Cline, Loretta Lynn, Dolly Parton, Tammy Wynette, Crystal Gayle, Trisha Yearwood, LeAnn Rimes, June Carter Cash, Barbara Mandrell, Wanda Jackson and many others. She would also influence a host of actresses on the big screen and television. Her fame includes three stars on the Hollywood Walk of Fame.

Dale Evans lived a rich, full life. She starred in many movies, including 27 with Roy Rogers. She did important charity work and was a successful business woman. She also became a vital symbol of country music and would forever ride the title Queen of the Cowgirls.

## Discography

*It's Real*, Capitol ST-2772.
*Sweetheart of the West*, Collector's Choice Music 1050.
*The Bible Tells Me So*, Capitol 9285.
*16 Great Songs of the Old West [1963]*, Golden 1987.
*Songs of the Old West*, Universal Special Products 21110.
*Double Barrel Country: The Legends of Roy Rogers and Dale Evans*, Madacy 5335.
*Roy Rogers and Dale Evans*, Camden 6094.

# KITTY WELLS (1918–)

## *Queen of Country Music*

In the long history of country music women have made enormous contributions, as singers, instrumentalists, and songwriters. Patsy Cline is still fondly remembered years after she died tragically in a plane crash. Mother Maybelle Carter was an important early guitar player with a distinct style all of her own. Dale Evans was the better half of Roy Rogers for over 50 years. Another female who made a strong impact on the genre was Kitty Wells, who earned the title Queen of Country Music.

Kitty Wells was born Muriel Deason on August 30, 1918, in Nashville, Tennessee. She began her musical career singing in church and learned how to play guitar in her teens. Later on, she would perform at local events with her sisters. Her experience also included radio work. When she was 18 she landed a spot on the *Dixie Early Birds Show*, where she met Johnny Wright. Two years later they married and she became part of the Jack and Johnny show that also included singer, songwriter Jack Anglin.

Johnny Wright was born Mt. Juliet, Tennessee, on May 13, 1914, into a musical family. His grandfather was a champion old time fiddler and his father played the five string banjo. He moved to Nashville in 1933, and did odd jobs while trying to break into the music business. He met Jack Anglin, who was born May 13, 1916, in Columbia, Tennessee, to form the duo Jack and Johnny.

The three—Jack, John and Muriel—went on the road together and Deason adopted the name Kitty Wells from the song "Sweet Kitty Wells." Other sources indicate that she adopted her stage name from the song "I'm A-Goin' to Marry Kitty Wells." Whatever the origin of her name, her talent shone through. The group also included Louise Wright, who eventually married Jack Anglin. After several name changes, they settled on the Tennessee Mountain Boys.

For the next few years they toured the country and appeared on radio in Greensboro, North Carolina, and then later in Knoxville on the *Merry-Go-Round* program. The group broke up when Anglin was drafted into Uncle Sam's outfit not long after Pearl Harbor and they continued as a trio. Eventually, Anglin returned from the war and rejoined the group.

In 1947, the foursome earned a spot on the *Grand Ole Opry* and were an instant hit. However, they moved to Shreveport, Louisiana, in order to become the stars of the *Louisiana Hayride*, the second most popular country music radio show in the nation. For five years they remained with the program and carved out a huge fan base.

In 1952, they were offered a regular spot on the *Grand Ole Opry*, as well as a recording contract from Decca. Wells had previously recorded for Victor-RCA with none of the singles becoming hits. That was about to change in a drastic way. Her first release on her new label, "It Wasn't God Who Made Honky Tonk Angels," became a number one hit, making her the first county female singer to have the top song on the charts.

From this point on the pace of her career accelerated and she became a true star. She cut a number of top ten hits with a variety of established country stars, including Red Foley, Roy Acuff, Webb Pierce, and Roy Drusky, among others. She also rolled out solo hits, including "Paying for that Back Street Affair," "Making Believe," "Searching," "Jealousy," "Mommy for a Day," "Amigo's Guitar," "Left to Right," "Heartbreak U.S.A.," "Unloved, Unwanted," "Password," and "You Don't Hear."

Despite the hits drying up in 1960s, she continued to record songs and perform on a regular basis. In the mid–1970s she left Decca and joined Capricorn, cutting the album *Forever Young*. Over the next two decades she would wax a few more complete efforts, but her power as a recording artist had faded. However, she was still regarded as the queen of country music and occasionally appeared on the *Grand Ole Opry*. She is now mostly retired.

Kitty Wells is more than just the queen of country music. She is a pioneer and although not the first female country singer, she opened doors for all that would follow her. She had the first million selling album and proved that women could make an impact on the genre as much as their male counterparts.

Wells has a voice that was built for country music. She has an earthy sound with multiple layers that allows her to emphasize certain lyrics that give her a bittersweet edge. She can belt out traditional songs as well as honky tonk numbers with the same power and determination as a roomful of singers. There is also an accessibility to her style that proved to be the selling point for listeners.

She broke down barriers and paved the way for the wave of female country singers that would invade the genre in the 1960s and after. A short list includes Patsy Cline, Jean Shephard, Loretta Lynn, Melba Montgomery, Linda Ronstadt, Jane Voss, Skeeter Davis, k.d. lang, Dolly Parton, Tammy Wynette, Tanya Tucker, Lynn Anderson, Dottie West, Donna Fargo, Trisha Yearwood, Shania Twain, Lee Ann Womack, Reba McEntire, LeAnn Rimes, Faith Hill, the Dixie Chicks, Crystal Gayle, and Barbara Mandrell. In fact, just about any female that has sung a country song in modern times owes a debt to Wells.

The elite of the country music scene have recognized her contributions during her career. She was *Billboard*'s number one country music female artist of the year from 1954 to 1965. In 1974, she won the Woman of the Year award from the Nashville Association of Business and Professional Women. In 1954, the governor of the state presented her with An Outstanding Tennessee Citizen citation.

Her children have gone on to solid country music careers, including son Bobby Wright, who often toured with Wells and her husband. At age eight he was a regular on the *Louisiana Hayride*, and three years later cut his first album. He spread his appeal by landing a role in the zany comedy *McHale's Navy*. He scored a couple of hits with "Lay Some Happiness on Me" and "Here I Go Again." He continues to record and perform.

In 1974, Kitty Wells was elected to the Country Music Hall of Fame, a befitting honor for such an influential and talented lady. Although she doesn't pack the same punch she did during her heyday, there is no denying the fact that she remains in many circles the Queen of Country Music.

## Discography

*Country Hit Parade*, Decca D-78293.
*Winner of Your Heart*, Decca D-78552.
*After Dark*, Decca D-78888.
*Dust on the Bible*, Decca D-78858.
*Kitty's Choice*, Decca D-78979.
*Seasons of My Heart*, Decca 74075.
*Heartbreak U.S.A.*, Decca 74141.
*Kitty Wells' Golden Favorites*, Decca 74108.
*Christmas with Kitty Wells*, Decca 74349.
*Singing on Sunday*, Decca 74720.
*The Queen of Country Music*, Decca 74197.
*Country Music Time*, Decca 74554.
*Especially for You*, Decca 74993.
*Burning Memories*, Decca 74612.
*The Kitty Wells Family Gospel Sing*, Decca 74679.
*Lonesome, Sad and Blue*, Decca 74658.
*Lonely Street*, Decca 8732.
*Country All the Way*, Decca 74776.
*Guilty Street*, Decca 75098.
*The Kitty Wells Show*, Decca 74831.
*Songs Made Famous by Jim Reeves*, Decca 74741.
*Kitty Wells* [Vocalion], Vocalion 3786.
*Kitty Wells*, MCA 20189.
*Love Makes the World Go Around*, Decca 74857.
*Queen of Honky Tonk Street*, Decca 74929.
*Together Again*, Decca 74906.
*Cream of Country Hits*, Decca 75067.
*Showcase*, Decca 74961.
*Bouquet of Country Hits*, Decca 75164.
*We'll Stick Together*, Decca 75026.
*Country Heart*, Vocalion 3875.
*Singin' 'Em Country*, Decca 75221.
*Your Love Is the Way*, Decca 75245.
*Pledging My Love*, Decca 75313.
*They're Stepping All Over My Heart*, Decca 75277.
*I've Got Yesterday*, Decca 75382.
*Sincerely*, Decca 75350.
*Heartwarming Gospel Songs*, Decca 75325.
*Country*, Rounder SS-13.
*Forever Young*, Capricorn 146.
*It Wasn't God Who Made Honky Tonk Angels*, MCA 20497.
*Jesus Is Coming Soon*, MCA 20599.
*Christmas Day*, MCA 15052.

*Country Spotlight*, K-Tel 3026.
*Country Music Hall of Fame Series*, MCA 10081.
*Queen of Country Music* [box set], Bear Family 15638.
*Kitty Wells Duets*, Pair 1342.
*Christmas with Kitty Wells* [Eclipse], Eclipse Music 64901.
*Christmas Legends*, Direct Source 9106.
*Release Me*, Prestige Elite 208.
*Kitty Wells and Red Foley's Greatest Hits*, Decca 4109.
*The Kitty Wells Story*, Decca 174.
*Kitty Wells' Greatest Hits*, Decca 75001.
*The Golden Years*, Rounder 613.
*Greatest Hits, Vol. 1*, Step One 46.
*Greatest Hits, Vol. 2*, Step One 47.
*Greatest Hits*, Hollywood 403.
*Greatest Songs*, Curb 77766.
*Twenty Greatest Hits*, TeeVee 6023.
*Kitty Wells Greatest Hits*, King 1414.
*The Best of Kitty Wells* [King], King 1432.
*One Day at a Time*, King 490.
*Kitty Wells* [Eclipse], Eclipse Music 64706.
*Together*, Playback 12335.
*Country Music Hall of Fame 1976*, King 3804.
*Good Old Country*, St. Clair 78202.
*God's Honky Tonk Angel: The First Queen of Country Music*, Edsel 640.
*Country Stars and Stripes*, Direct Source 1293.
*20th Century Masters—The Millennium Collection: The Best of Kitty Wells*, MCA 170282.
*Collection*, Spectrum Music 113211.
*Sings Her Gospel Hits: Duet on the Bible*, King 327.
*20 All Time Greatest Hits*, TeeVee 725.
*It Wasn't God Who Made Honky Tonk Angels*, Dynamic 2129.
*Greatest Hits*, K-Tel 3083.
*Greatest Hits*, MCA 121.
*The Best of Kitty Wells*, Exact 213.
*The Legendary Kitty Wells*, MCA Special Products 20771.

# MOLLY O'DAY (1923–1987)

## *A Defining Role*

Each important woman in country music possessed a special role in helping shape the genre. Maybelle Carter and her cousin Sara were true pioneers. Dale Evans was the queen of the cowgirls, while Kitty Wells holds down the honor of queen of country music. There was another country music female artist who not only established the boundaries, but helped define the role. Her name was Molly O'Day.

Molly O'Day was born Lois LaVerne Williamson on July 9, 1923, in Pike County, Kentucky, in a hard-working coal mining family that lived in a backwoods section of the Appalachian community. Because of the isolation and poverty, Lois grew up with big dreams. She wanted to sing like her heroines Patsy Montana, Lulu Belle Wiseman, Texas Ruby Owens and Lily May Ledford in order escape the economic struggles of her childhood.

She sang to whittle the hours away while doing chores. Later she would pick up the guitar and eventually joined a string band that included her brothers Cecil, a fiddler, and Joe, a banjoist. The group played at regional events throughout the 1930s. At the end of the decade, she hooked up with her brother Skeets on a Charleston, West Virginia, radio station performing under the name Mountain Fern and later Dixie Lee Williamson.

In 1940, she joined guitarist Lynn Davis' string band, the Forty-Niners. A year later she and Davis married and in a short time became one of the top performing couples on the country music tour. For the next five years they crossed the South playing numerous venues and building a solid reputation. They settled in Beckley, West Virginia, then moved on to Birmingham, Alabama. Later they moved to Louisville and then on to Dallas where they remained for a brief time before relocating to Knoxville.

In 1946, they settled in Louisville, Kentucky, for an extended stay. By this time, Lois had adopted the name Molly O'Day. The focal point of the group was the duets the couple sang, but more important were her solo performances. She belted out the songs with so much inspiration and emotion that it truly moved the audience.

It was these heartfelt solo numbers that eventually earned them a recording contract with Fred Rose of Columbia. In the studio, O'Day sang a variety of songs, including many that Hank Williams had written. The two were long lost friends, having performed on the radio circuit together years before. Of the many songs that he wrote for her, perhaps the best was "Tramp on the Street," which along with seven others made up her first recording sessions.

The studio musicians Davis, Skeets, bassist Mac Wiseman and George "Speedy" Krise on Dobro backed her. The subsequent release of the songs on that first session magnified her popularity tenfold. Overnight, her star in the country music universe shone brighter than ever before, but unfortunately she was unable to manage her growing success. The pressures of being in the public eye had begun to take their toll.

Although 1947 was a disappointing year, O'Day did manage to make a few recordings at the end of the year. The sessions included the favorite "Matthew Twenty-Four" that proved she still possessed her fiery spirit.

However, over the next few years, while she managed to regain her foothold in the country music tour circuit, they were uneven times.

She began to perform and record more religious material than in previous years and this began to turn her once devoted fans away. Some of the more interesting songs she recorded during this period include "Teardrops Falling in the Snow," "Poor Ellen Smith," and "On the Evening Train."

In 1949, O'Day suffered a nervous breakdown that led to a lengthy hospital stay. She would return to record a few songs in 1950, and again in 1951, but eventually turned her back on show business. Instead she turned her full attention to performing in churches. Her husband became an ordained minister and they toured the coal mining communities of West Virginia to preach the gospel of the Lord.

From this point on, her recording career was exclusively devoted to sacred material and her country fans had to cling to her past catalog. In 1973, O'Day and Davis hosted a daily gospel program around their home base. On December 5, 1987, Molly O'Day, the fierce country female singer who redefined the role, passed away from cancer.

Molly O'Day was an exceptional talent. She possessed a special voice that reached everyone in the audience in a different way. During her heyday she was on top of the female country circuit and established the boundaries for the role. It is difficult to speculate, but if she had not suffered a nervous breakdown and continued on with her country music career, she might have been the greatest female singer of all-time.

O'Day's performances sealed her legend. She gave everything she had to each song, creating an aura that elevated her to a different level. Although a country music artist, her solo outings contained a strong dose of soul. Her gut-wrenching approach also reminded one of Bessie Smith, the empress of the blues. When she was on, there was no one on the tour circuit that could match her fire and passion.

She gave the world a number of great treasures. A partial list includes "Tramp on the Street," "Don't Sell Daddy Anymore Whiskey," "I Heard My Mother Weeping," "Teardrops in the Snow," "When God Comes and Gathers His Jewels," "Black Sheep Returned to the Fold, "Put My Rubber Doll Away," "I Don't Care If Tomorrow Never Comes," "The Tear Stained Letter," "The Evening Train" and "Singing Waterfall." Whether she was cutting country tunes or religious material, her talent came through on every song.

Despite the fact that her time in the limelight wasn't long, O'Day did have a very strong influence on a number of artists. A short list includes Mac Wiseman, Patty Loveless, Dolly Parton, Wanda Jackson, Loretta Lynn, June Carter Cash, Patsy Cline, Tammy Wynette, Barbara Mandrell,

Louise Mandrell, Emmylou Harris, Trisha Yearwood, Crystal Gayle, LeAnn Rimes and others. Her power also spilled over into other styles of music. Aretha Franklin, Koko Taylor, Janis Joplin, and Lou Ann Barton are also a handful of the artists who owe a debt to O'Day.

In the grand scheme of female artists, O'Day holds a special position. She didn't have the longevity of a Maybelle Carter, and certainly didn't draw the same raves as Patsy Cline. She was not a superstar like Loretta Lynn and didn't have three phases to her career like Wanda Jackson. But, O'Day was in many ways a pioneer and helped define the role of the female artist in country music.

O'Day was the link between the early pioneers, Sara and Maybelle Carter, and the second generation, June Carter Cash, Loretta Lynn and Wanda Jackson. She built upon what the early stars had established and directed the latter arrivals as to what path to take. Most importantly, she accomplished her feat in much less time than many others.

Molly O'Day possessed an abundance of talent that could have made her the most important female country singer of all-time. But, the pressures of performance and the very popularity that she sought to attain were too much for her. Along with her immense talent she also exuded a strong, positive appeal. Despite her short time in the spotlight, she did make a powerful impact and defined the role of the country female solo artist.

## Discography

*Hymns for the Country Folks*, Audio Lab 1544.
*The Unforgettable Molly O'Day*, Harmony 7299.
*And the Cumberland Mountain Folks*, Bear Family 15565.
*Sacred Collection*, Old Homestead OH 101.
*With Lynn Davis, Vol. 1*, Old Homestead OH 312.
*In Memory*, Old Homestead OHS 196.
*Radio Favorites*, Old Homestead OH 140.
*The Living Legend of Country Music*, Starday 367.
*Molly O'Day and the Cumberland Mountain Folks*, Bear Family 155652.

# JUNE CARTER CASH (1929–2003)
## *A Song in Her Heart*

Perhaps the most famous family in country music history is the Carter clan. Their impact on the genre stretches from the earliest days with the trio of A.P., Sara, and Maybelle to the present day with a new generation to carry on the tradition. Among the finest country music personalities for 50 years was the woman with a song in her heart. Her name was June Carter Cash.

Valerie June Carter was born on January 23, 1929, in Maces Spring, Virginia, into a highly skilled musical family. Her uncle A.P. had made some of the first country music recordings along with June's mother Maybelle and aunt Sara. It was her mother who would teach her how to play the autoharp, launching June on a path to a musical career.

At the age of eight, June was on the road performing with her sisters Anita and Helen. They called themselves the Carter Sisters and assumed the family torch when A.P. passed away. Of the three sisters, June was the one with the most talent, which she demonstrated with her musical skills, her gifted sense of humor and ability to work a crowd.

Her quick wit enabled her to cut a single with the humorous country music duo Homer and Jethro. The song, "Baby, It's Cold Outside," reached number nine on the country charts in 1949. At age 20, June had already tasted success and it was only the beginning. The future held great promise for the rising star.

After marrying Carl Smith in 1952, Carter and her husband performed at the *Grand Ole Opry*. The couple divorced in the late 1950s. The union produced one daughter, Rebecca Carlene, who would grow up to follow in her mom's footsteps and record country songs. She also continued the tradition of the Carter family's involvement in the music industry.

By the early 1960s, June came under the managerial control of Col. Tom Parker, Elvis Presley's Svengali. Although his reign as the king of rock and roll was over, Elvis still performed in front of large audiences and that enabled Carter to gain further exposure. Despite having tasted success, she was still trying to find her niche in the music world.

After her second marriage (that produced another daughter) ended quickly, Carter returned to perform with her sisters. The trio joined Johnny Cash's traveling road show and the love spark between the two was instant magic. The Man in Black, one of country music's major rebels at the time, had long kept an eye on the beautiful June.

The relationship was sealed when Cash recorded the song "Ring of Fire" that June had written in collaboration with Merle Kilgore, taking it to number one. Five years later the couple married after she had managed to get him off amphetamines. The man in black—who was on a path of self-destruction for a decade and had nearly drowned in his own self-indulgence—had discovered his honky tonk angel.

They recorded the songs "Jackson" and "If I Were a Carpenter" that earned them Grammy Awards. With these hits and others ("A Boy Named Sue") they soon became the darlings of the country music set. His strong marriage to June, a string of colorful, entertaining songs as well as a collaboration with Bob Dylan propelled the man in black to the top of the country music heap.

The Cashes had their own television show that boasted the firm moral values of God, family and America. As one of the most visible couples on the circuit, they did much to keep the genre on a national level. Long after the cancellation of their TV variety hour, they remained part of pop culture because the coolest couple in country music were by now household names.

For the remainder of her career, June Carter Cash demanded respect throughout the music world despite the fact that she was out of the limelight throughout most of the 1970s and 1980s. As the wife of the Man in Black, she allowed him to continue his musical career while she was content with marriage and family. She lent her talents to other media outlets.

She wrote two autobiographies: *Among My Klediments* (1979) and *From My Heart* (1987). She also acted, appearing most notably on the TV show *Dr. Quinn Medicine Woman*, as well as a role in the movie *The Apostle* starring opposite Robert Duvall. But her first love was always music and she returned to the recording studio in the late 1990s to make the album *Press On*. It was a collection of both traditional folk songs and Carter-Cash originals. The CD would win a Grammy for best traditional folk album.

The biggest news concerning the couple in the 1990s was Johnny's failing health. She stood by his side and dealt with the press while caring for her man. The love, devotion and respect they shared was touching. Despite the fact that he appeared to be the weaker of the two physically, it was, sadly, June who died first on May 15, 2003, in Nashville, following complications from heart surgery. Her beloved husband followed her four months later.

June Carter Cash was a great woman of country music. She had a knack for delivering a song that appealed to every type of music fan. She had many phases to her career and each one displayed her special talent and heart. Her contributions as performer, writer, TV personality, movie actress and spokeswoman earned her much praise.

Although she will best be remembered for her long association with Johnny Cash, she also collaborated with Elvis and her two sisters, as well as her mother. It was as a member of the Carter Sisters that she first gained major exposure. All four Carter women were an important part of country music in the 1950s. They carried on the tradition of the famous family while adding a new chapter to it.

Carter also toured with Elvis. Although the two didn't record any albums together, the exposure of touring with the king enabled her to develop a different side of her career. The time she spent with Presley prepared her for the role as Johnny Cash's longtime partner.

June and Johnny Cash took the country music world by storm when they first started to work together. Although they had enjoyed considerable success as solo artists or part of other packages, the union of the two was something special. Their decision to join forces was pure magic in every medium. They remain one of the most successful country husband-wife teams in history. In 2005, the movie *Walk the Line* focused on their special relationship and was a box office hit.

Carter had a large influence on a number of artists. A partial list includes Tammy Wynette, Lynn Anderson, Wanda Jackson, Emmylou Harris, Trisha Yearwood, Crystal Gayle, Skeeter Davis, LeAnn Rimes, Dixie Chicks, Barbara Mandrell, k. d. lang, Dolly Parton, Faith Hill, Lee Ann Womack, Reba McIntire, Tanya Tucker, Shania Twain, and the Judds. Her tremendous power held others spellbound and many borrowed something from her style.

Perhaps her most important legacy is the children, Rebecca, Rosie, and Johnny junior. They followed in their mother's footsteps and provided the world with a third generation of Carter musical talent.

June Carter Cash was a country music institution. From the very beginning of her stage appearance at the tender age of eight she exuded a confidence, a positive attitude, a supreme talent. In every phase of her career she displayed her abilities that touched millions of people because she always carried a song in her heart.

## Discography

*Dress On*, Risk 4107.
*The Making of Wildwood Flower Radio Special*, DualTone 1142.
*Wildwood Flower*, Dualtone 1142.
*Louisiana Hayride*, Scana 270708.
*Keep on the Sunny Side: Her Life in Music*, Sony 90908.
*Church in the Wildwood*, Dualtone 1219.
*Ring of Fire: The Best of June Carter Cash*, Dualtone 1216.
With Johnny Cash:
*It's All in the Family*, Bear Family 16132.

# PATSY CLINE (1932–1963)
## *A Country Music Treasure*

As in all other styles, about every decade a superior talent arrives on the country music scene and takes everyone's breath away. The artist is a special individual who transcends normal boundaries to achieve a massive following. In the late 1950s, a female singer began to turn heads and a decade later had become a country music treasure. Her name was Patsy Cline.

Patsy Cline was born Virginia Patterson Hensley on September 8, 1932, in Gore, Virginia. She started her show business career early when at four she won a tap dancing contest. The talented little girl began to study the piano a couple of years later and by her early teens was singing at local clubs. Although she was a long way from cutting her first single or scoring a number one hit, already it was evident that she possessed a magical voice that could stun an audience.

She graduated from the bar scene very quickly when she won a singing contest with first prize being a trip to Nashville. Once in Music City USA, she didn't waste any time establishing the fact that she was determined to make it as a singer. She performed in a few clubs but the big break she was waiting for never materialized and despite her fierce intentions her dreams fell apart and she returned home.

Once back in her native Virginia she returned to the dives and honky tonk bars, waiting for another break. She honed her skills and was convinced more than ever to make better on a second chance if it came her way. In 1957, she entered the *Arthur Godfrey Talent Scouts* show and won it with a rousing version of "Walking After Midnight."

She was signed to Decca and waxed a version of the song that stayed on both the pop and country charts for an extended period. The song went a long way in establishing her name in Nashville circles. In three years she would record a wealth of material, with none really hitting the mark until "I Fall to Pieces," in 1961. It was a mega hit that solidified her position as one of the brightest female singers on the scene. The number became a regular part of her repertoire and was a genuine showstopper.

Although her early material had featured rockabilly as well as gospel-flecked songs, the latter songs she cut were more rooted in country. She wasn't really cut out to sing rockabilly and had too much talent to limit herself to weepy tunes. It was the crossover songs that appealed to the pop and country crowd that was her true calling card and when she began to record this type of material, there was no denying her rise to stardom.

The songs "Crazy," "Who Can I Count On?" "She's Got You," "Strange," and "When I Get Through with You" were all massive hits. WIth this run of success it was not surprising that she would become a regular star on the *Opry*, and soon challenged Kitty West for the crown of queen of country music. Her popularity overspilled the normal boundaries and she became a household name throughout America and abroad.

She continued to roll out the hits, including "Imagine That," "So Wrong," and "Leavin' on Your Mind." At this point she could do no wrong and her popularity scaled even greater heights. Many of her recordings were lavishly produced affairs with orchestral strings and back up singers (usually the Jordanaires). She also utilized the best Nashville country session players available, including guitarist Hank Garland, pianist Floyd Cramer and drummer Buddy Harmon.

In 1961, she was involved in a serious car accident that gave her a taste of her own mortality. Unfortunately, it was a foreshadowing of future events. She recovered from her injuries and continued to forge ahead. During this period she received material from a variety of sources, including Hank Cochran, Harlan Howard, and Willie Nelson. The latter had penned the hit "Crazy."

She was a regular member of the *Opry* and considered the most talented female country singer of the day. She was a crowd favorite and an easy choice for multiple awards. Cline, at 31 years old, had already accomplished much in her brief career and looked towards years of success.

However, on March 5, 1963, the great voice of country, returning from a benefit in Kansas City, died in a tragic plane crash in Camden, Tennessee. In the same stunning accident, Hawkshaw Hawkins and Cowboy Copas were also killed.

Patsy Cline was a country music superstar. Although she attained incredible popularity during her prime, she never quite displaced Kitty Wells as the queen of country music. But she did leave behind a lasting legacy that continues to this day. Even after her death her records continued to sell. "Sweet Dreams (of You)," "Faded Love," "When You Need a Laugh," "He Called Me Baby," and "Anytime" were just some of her posthumous hits.

Cline had a voice of a commercial angel that contained enough range and shades to appeal to a variety of tastes. She was as popular in pop music circles as she was on the country scene. That jewel of a voice that made listeners shiver but want still more continues to reverberate through music circles decades after her untimely death. There has never been another voice quite like hers since that fateful day in 1963.

Arguably, an integral part of the Patsy Cline story is her meteoric rise and her tragic ending. She was really in the public eye for six years, but in that time reached heights that it had taken other singers years to scale. Her mature sound and the direction it would have taken in the latter part of her career remains a question mark. It is generally agreed that she would have become the greatest country singer of all time if she had lived longer.

She gave the world a number of classics. A partial list includes "Walking After Midnight," "I Fall to Pieces," "Crazy," "Who Can I Count On?" "She's Got You," "Strange," "When I Get Through with You," "Imagine

That," "So Wrong," "Leavin' on Your Mind," "Sweet Dreams (of You)," "Faded Love," "When You Need a Laugh," "He Called Me Baby," and "Anytime." In fact, any song that she recorded was a treasure. She could take a classic like "Blue Moon of Kentucky" and make it sound fresh and exciting. There was no limit to what she could do to a song.

Despite her early departure from the planet, she still managed to create a body of work that influenced hundreds of singers. A partial list includes Crystal Gayle, Loretta Lynn, Shelby Lynne, the Mavericks, Tammy Wynette, Connie Smith, Lou Ann Barton, Linda Ronstadt, Jane Voss, Deborah Allen, Kelly Hogan, k.d. lang, Mandy Barnett, LeAnn Rimes, Skeeter Davis, the Mandrell Sisters, Faith Hill, Lynn Anderson, Lee Ann Womack, Reba McEntire, Shania Twain, Tanya Tucker, Trisha Yearwood, and Dolly Parton. Any female singer of the past 40 years that has crooned a pop or country hit can trace a lineage to Cline.

Although she has long passed away, she is not forgotten. Every generation discovers her magical musical gifts and with the reissuing of all her songs on CD, she has appealed to a modern audience, enlarging her fan base. Many of her radio appearances were kept for posterity and videos of her performances have been created in order to preserve her legacy.

Patsy Cline lived on the edge and often she clashed with those around her. She was a wild spirit who was very difficult to tame. But the intensity of her action and opinions are also part of the legend. Her life in the public consisted of two parts: one as the darling of singers, the other the perfect material for the gossip columnists.

The story of Patsy Cline is that of a young, very talented girl who won the hearts of millions of listeners with her accessible, bittersweet, poignant voice that remains entrenched in the public psyche. Despite the great number of very accomplished female country singers that has graced the genre since her departure, none are a Patsy Cline. In 1973, she was elected to the Country Music Hall of Fame, preserving the memory of the country music treasure.

## Discography

*Patsy Cline* [Black and Silver Label], Decca 8611.
*Patsy Cline* [MCA], MCA 25200.
*Patsy Cline Showcase*, MCA 74202.
*Sentimentally Yours*, MCA 74282.
*Today, Tomorrow and Forever* [MCA], MCA 1463.
*That's How a Heartache Begins*, Decca 74586.
*Gotta Lot of Rhythm in My Soul*, Metro MS540.
*I Can't Forget You*, Hilltop 6016.
*Stop the World and Let Me Off*, Hilltop 6039.
*Miss Country Music*, Hilltop 6054.

*Sweet Dreams*, MCA 6149.
*Heartaches* [MCA], MCA 20265.
*Live at the Opry*, MCA 42142.
*Live, Vol. 2*, MCA 42284.
*In Care of the Blues*, Rhino 71457.
*Today, Tomorrow and Forever* [Laserlight], Laserlight 15408.
*Try Again*, Quicksilver 1008.
*Sings Songs of Love*, Universal Special 20879.
*Dear God*, MCA Special 20848.
*Loved and Lost Again*, Sony Special 18282.
*The Birth of a Star*, Razor and Tie 2108.
*Remembering the Queen of Country*, Intercontinent 1116.
*Rhythm N Country*, Hallmark 300012.
*Live at the Cimarron Ballroom*, MCA 11579.
*With Love*, Dressed To Kill 309.
*Walkin' After Midnight*, Dualtone 1144.
*Collector's Edition*, Madacy 3438.
*Collector's Edition*, Madacy 3439.
*Blue Moon of Kentucky*, United Recordings 104.
*Patsy Cline* [Everest], Everest 5302.
*Patsy Cline's Golden Hits*, Everest 1200.
*Encores*, Everest 5204.
*In Memorium*, Everest 5217.
*Patsy Cline: A Legend*, Everest 5223.
*The Patsy Cline Story*, MCA 4038.
*Reflections*, Everest 5229.
*A Portrait of Patsy Cline*, MCA 224.
*Gone, But Not Forgotten*, Starday 346.
*Here's Patsy Cline*, MCA 738.
*Patsy Cline's Greatest Hits*, Decca 74854.
*Songwriter's Tribute*, MCA 25019.
*Country Great*, MCA Special 736.
*Remembering*, MCA 1467.
*Greatest Hits*, RCA 5152.
*Last Sessions*, MCA 25199.
*Commemorative Collection*, MCA 8925.
*12 Greatest Hits*, MCA 012.
*The Legendary*, Pair 1236.
*Faded Love*, MCA 20467.
*20 Golden Hits* [Deluxe], Deluxe 5050.
*Her First Recordings, Vol. 2: Hungry for Love*, Rhino 70049.
*Her First Recordings, Vol. 3: Rockin' Side*, Rhino 70050.
*Her First Recordings, Vol. 1: Walkin' Dreams*, Rhino 70048.
*Walkin' After Midnight* [Compose], 9109.
*Walkin' After Midnight*, Country Stars 55404.
*Patsy Cline Showcase: Sentimentally Yours*, MCA 38015.
*Portrait of Patsy Cline: Country Great*, MCA 38018.
*Stop, Look and Listen*, Allegiance 72924.
*20 Golden Pieces of Patsy Cline*, Bulldog 2003.
*Always*, MCA 27069.
*26 Greatest Hits*, Huub 75617.
*Let the Teardrops Fall* [Special Music], Special Music 4959.

*More of the Legendary*, Pair 1307.
*The Best of Patsy Cline* [Curb], Curb 77518.
*The Patsy Cline Collection*, MCA 10421.
*Patsy Cline*, Laserlight 55509.
*Walkin' After Midnight*, Laserlight 15407.
*At Her Best* [Hollywood], International 462.
*Forever and Always*, Epic 53018.
*Walkin After Midnight* [Rhino], Rhino 71458.
*Today, Tomorrow and Forever* [Madacy], Sony Special 18263.
*Don't Ever Leave, Vol. 3*, Laserlight 15409.
*Country Spotlight*, Dominion 3011.
*The Legendary Patsy Cline*, Fat Boy 115.
*The Legendary Patsy Cline, Vol. 2*, Fat Boy 150.
*20 Great Hits*, Deluxe 7880.
*Classics Collection: Patsy Cline*, Capitol/Curb 77871.
*Golden Classics*, Collectables 5059.
*Patsy Cline* [Timeless], Timeless 102.
*Loved and Lost*, Drive Archive 41028.
*Classics*, Sun 7017.
*Just a Closer Walk with Thee*, MCA 20492.
*Hungry for Love*, Chicago Music 116.
*Sings More Great Songs of Love*, MCA Special 20887.
*Back to Back* [K-Tel], K-Tel 3506.
*Discovery!*, Prism 5902.
*Crazy*, Sundown 501.
*Crazy Dreams: The Four Star Years*, Magnum 3001.
*3-CD Set*, Eclipse Music 64713.
*Patsy Cline, Vol. 1*, Eclipse Music 64710.
*Patsy Cline, Vol. 2*, Eclipse Music 64711.
*Patsy Cline, Vol. 3*, Eclipse Music 64712.
*Very Best of Patsy Cline* [Eclipse], Eclipse Music 64885.
*Sincerely Yours*, Prime Cuts 23232.
*Golden Hits*, Intercontinent 1004.
*Cry Not for Me*, Starburst 5.
*Great*, Goldies 63111.
*American Legends*, Delta 12806.
*Walking After Midnight* [Kingfisher], Kingfisher 8.
*Golden Classics: 23 Classic Tracks*, Masters 4003.
*Critique Country Classics Collection, Vol. 1*, Critique 15463.
*Forever*, Simitar 5502.
*Platinum Collection*, Start Entertainment 615.
*The Essential Patsy Cline*, RCA 66983.
*Lovesick Blues*, Kingfisher 15.
*Crazy Dreams: The Classic Early Years*, Music Club 50028.
*Back to Back* [MCA], MCA Special 21014.
*Best of Patsy Cline* [Madacy], Madacy 2134.
*Walkin After Midnight* [Rhino Flashback], Rhino 72809.
*Walk Through This World with Me*, Beacon 51583.
*Patsy Cline: Members Edition*, United Audio 3018.
*The Best of Patsy Cline* [Excelsior],Excelsior 2064.
*The Heart You Break May Be Your Own*, Retro Music 2371.
*Ultimate Collection* [Crimson], Crimson 88.

*Volume 2*, Castle 223.
*Through the Eyes of Patsy Cline*, Recall 156.
*Live Broadcasts*, Cema Special 19383.
*Walkin' After Midnight: The Best of Patsy Cline*, Delta 46134.
*Today Tomorrow and Forever: The Best of Patsy Cline*, Delta 46010.
*Heartaches* [Music Club], Music Club 317.
*Walkin' After Midnight: The Very Best of Patsy Cline*, Collectables *6034*.
*At Her Best* [box sets], Box sets 9888.
*Ultimate Collection* [MCA International], MCA 73115.
*Four Star Recordings, Vol. 2*, Country Stars 55452.
*Patsy Cline's 4 Star Recordings*, Country Stars 55451.
*The Best of Patsy Cline*, Delta 24735.
*The Best of Patsy Cline*, Master Sound 550272.
*Immortal Patsy Cline*, Unison 82892.
*The Masters*, Cleopatra 398.
*Today, Tomorrow and Forever* [Cleopatra], Cleopatra 439.
*Collection* [Madacy], Madacy 2389.
*Volume 1: Walking After Midnight*, Platinum Disc 6762.
*Volume 2: Legendary Patsy*, Platinum Disc 6772.
*Volume 3: Stranger in My Arms*, Platinum Disc 7312.
*Country Music Hall of Fame 1973*, King 3810.
*20th Century Masters—The Millennium Collection: The Best of Patsy Cline*, MCA 70095.
*Forever Gold*, St. Clair 5717.
*Double Barrel Country*, Madacy 565.
*Duets, Vol. 1*, Crash 417097.
*Universal Members Collection*, Universal International 112166.
*Come on In*, Legacy 049.
*Patsy Cline* [Platinum Disc], Platinum Disc 6782.
*True Love: A Standards Collection*, MCA 112249.
*Walkin' After Midnight: The Best of Patsy Cline*, 7-N 77007.
*The Best of Country*, Direct Source 6851.
*Country Gold: Today and Forever*, Direct Source 6003.
*The Best of Patsy Cline* [Delta], Delta 46009.
*Country Spotlight* [Direct Source], Direct Source 6170.
*Classic Country*, Direct Source 7523.
*Dueling Country*, Direct Source 9045.
*Platinum Series*, D-3 33329.
*Good Old Country*, St. Clair 78262.
*Patsy Cline*, Legend 64012.
*Forever Gold (Walking After Midnight) Sincerely Yours*, St. Clair 9281.
*25 All-Time Greatest Recordings: The 4 Star Patsy Cline*, Varèse 066165.
*The Ultimate Collection* [MCA Nashville], MCA Nashville 560214.
*Let the Teardrops Fall* [Planet Media], Planet Media 1009.
*That's How Much I Love You*, Mastersound 50127.
*The Best of Patsy Cline*, Delta 24708.
*Today, Tomorrow and Forever* [Sony], Sony Music 3489.
*20 Golden Hits* [TeeVee], TeeVee 6031.
*Patsy Cline* [St. Clair], St. Clair 173.
*The Best of Patsy Cline*, Columbia River 190041.
*Walkin' After Midnight*, Columbia River 190040.
*The Legends Collection*, Dressed to Kill 590.
*The Legends Collection, Vol. 1*, Dressed to Kill 556.

*Legends Collection, Vol. 1,* Dressed to Kill 555.
*Stop, Look and Listen* [Direct Source], Direct Source 3618.
*That Wonderful Someone,* Direct Source 3619.
*Signature Series,* Direct Source 1496.
*36 Classics Tracks,* Big Eye 4126.
*Very Best of Patsy Cline* [BMG International], BMG 30507.
*Too Many Secrets,* Magnum 7013.
*Essential Collection,* PolyGram 544535.
*Patsy Cline: 20 Great Hits,* Platinum Disc 2155.
*Lonely Street,* Prism 697.
*Love Songs,* Varese 066300.
*The Great Patsy Cline,* 404 Music Group 8037.
*The Legend,* Orpheus 90646.
*Patsy Cline: The Collection,* Madacy 6342.
*Walkin' After Midnight,* Matersong 191045.
*At Her Very Best,* King 302.
*That's How Much I Love You,* Columbia River 191044.
*Walking Dream,* Magnum 1375.
*Patsy Cline Forever,* Direct Source 1160.
*Country,* Music Mill 70033.
*Classic Masters,* Capitol 43478.
*Ultimate Collection,* United Multi License 40202.
*Classic American Voices,* Direct Source 2518.
*Country Sweetheart,* American Legends 100124.
*I'm Blue Again,* Fabulous 148.
*Remembering,* Direct Source 2939.
*The Heart of a Legend,* Madacy 6485.
*40th Anniversary,* King Special 537.
*The Essential First Recordings,* Varese 066569.
*Country Legends,* St. Clair 6750.
*Lovesick Blues,* Delta 32169.
*Timeless Classics,* St. Clair 41512.
*Golden Legends,* St. Clair 3752.
*Duets,* Brentwood 40893.
*Gold,* MCA Nashville 000411902.
*Pick Me Up on Your Way Down,* RCR 607.
*Walking and Dreaming,* Masked Weasel 304.
*Honky Tonk Angel,* American Legends 2015.
*Songs of Love,* Music Mill 40262.
*50 Golden Greats: The Complete Early Years,* Empire 508152.

# LORETTA LYNN (1934–)
## *Coal Miner Heartbreak*

The essence of country music is its simple harmonies, melodies and lyrics, but there are many layers to the genre. Those who sing about the troubles, hardship and poverty in their songs often have lived the life, as their plaintive voices and emotional outcry is very real. Such is the case of the female singer known as the Coal Miner Heartbreak. Her name is Loretta Lynn.

Loretta Webb was born on April 14, 1934, in Butcher Hollow, Kentucky. One of the elements that countless country music artists share is a first hand knowledge of poverty and Lynn was no exception. The daughter of a coal miner, she grew up in abject hardship, one of eight children that also included her younger sister Brenda Gayle Webb, who would later be known to the world as Crystal Gayle. Like her sibling, Loretta possessed a special gift that was her ticket to a better life.

Her climb to stardom was not an easy road. She was married before her fourteenth birthday to Oliver Moonshine Lynn, and in the mountain tradition immediately started a family. Although she had sung in the church choir and other local events, her budding musical career was interrupted by family duties. They moved to Custer, Washington, and for the next ten years she concentrated on being a wife and a mother.

She joined Jay Lee Webb's band (her brother) performing in a series of forgettable dives. A decade of paying her dues eventually paid off when she signed with Zero Records. Her first single, "I'm a Honky Tonk Girl," became a hit after Lynn and her husband "Moonie" did much of the promotion, touring around and selling copies of the song to DJs at various country music radio stations.

After a stint with the Wilburn Brothers, she relocated to Nashville and signed to Decca Records. Behind the skilled work of Owen Bradley, who had made Patsy Cline a star, Lynn quickly rose through the ranks of the country music set. Her first single for her new label, "Success," was a foreshadowing of future events. She began a run of top singles that would carry her for the next two decades.

A hard driving honky tonk angel, she made her mark with that style in her first few years on the charts, but evolved as an artist and singer. A talented individual able to work comfortably outside the confines of honky tonk, she took a much tougher, independent stand in the latter part of the 1960s. A woman who had seen her fair share of good and bad men, she began to write songs that popularized a feminine opinion. In the male dominated world of country music, this was an unprecedented move.

However, she only expanded her appeal with a more personal style that included songs of a rebellious, nature including "You Ain't Woman Enough," "Don't Come Home A-Drinkin' (with Lovin' on Your Mind)," "Your Squaw Is on the Warpath," "Woman of the World (Leave My World Alone)," and "The Pill." The last was a strictly feminist song dealing with the dilemma of birth control. Other hits included "Coal Miner's Daughter," "One's on the Way," "Here I Am Again," and "Hey Loretta."

In the early 1970s, she teamed up with country star Conway Twitty and the duo became best selling artists for much of the decade. A few of their hit singles included "After Me the Fire Is Gone," "Lead Me On," "Louisiana Woman, Mississippi Man," "As Soon as I Hang Up the Phone," "This Time I've Hurt Her More Than She Loves Me," "The Letter," and "Feelings." They won numerous awards that included a four year consecutive run (1972–1975) as Vocal Duo of the Year. They continued to have top ten hits from 1976 through to 1981.

But her biggest success occurred in 1980 with the release of the movie *Coal Miner's Daughter*. The title song reflected the poverty and struggle of her childhood. It starred Sissy Spacek, who would win an Academy Award for her performance. The critically acclaimed film propelled Lynn, already a popular singer, into the same stratosphere as Johnny Cash, Willie Nelson, Dolly Parton and Kenny Rogers. She even appeared on the *Dukes of Hazzard* television show, which exposed her to an even wider audience.

When country radio stations started to play the newer crop of country singers, Lynn's domination of the charts ceased. However, she continued to perform on a regular basis and her shows proved to be extremely popular. There was a desire to see, to hear, and to talk to the original coal miner's daughter.

Although her recorded catalog thinned out in the 1990s, she did cut one album, *Honky Tonk Angels*, with Tammy Wynette and Dolly Parton. Her fans regarded her own solo release, *Still Woman Enough*, as a genuine treat. She continues to record sporadically and perform frequently.

Loretta Lynn is a country music angel. For two decades she was the most successful female country artist, recording numerous hits as a solo artist and in partnership with Conway Twitty. She spread her fame through appearances on television plugging various products, as a live act touring the country and the world, and with her phenomenal best selling autobiography, *Coal Miner's Daughter*.

She has a voice that was tailor made to sing country music. There is an honesty in her delivery that convinces the listener she has known her fair share of hard times. The authenticity of her songs sung in a relaxed yet determined manner proved to be a winning combination. Lynn's style contains a solid country strain that is earthy, passionate and earnest.

Her distinct style influenced a large number of followers. A partial list includes Tammy Wynette, Lynn Anderson, Barbara Mandrell, Reba McEntire, Dolly Parton, Irene Kelley, k. d. lang, Chely Wright, Sherrie Austin, Florence Dore, Tammy Cochran, Crystal Gayle, Linda Ronstadt, Trisha Yearwood, Faith Hill, LeAnn Rimes, Shania Twain, and many others. Her feminist stance predated the rock-country tinged songs of Helen Reddy, a popular 1970s singer who roared that she was a woman and proud of it. In many ways, Lynn opened doors for female singers from all styles of music.

During the 1970s, despite competition from Tammy Wynette, Lynn was the most popular and dominant female country music artist. She not only ruled the charts, but her name was the first on any listing of women in the field. She enjoyed widespread popularity that culminated in her being forever identified with the genre.

She gave the world a number of great classics. A partial list includes "I'm a Honky Tonk Girl," "Success," "You Ain't Woman Enough," "Don't Come Home A-Drinkin' (with Lovin' on Your Mind)," "Your Squaw Is on the Warpath," "Woman of the World (Leave My World Alone)," "The Pill," "Coal Miner's Daughter," "One's on the Way," "Here I Am Again," "Hey Loretta," "After Me the Fire Is Gone," "Lead Me On," "Louisiana Woman, Mississippi Man," "As Soon as I Hang Up the Phone," "This Time I've Hurt Her More Than She Loves Me," "The Letter," and "Feelings." Any song she sang contained that special Loretta Lynn touch since she always possessed the knack of bringing any tune to life.

Loretta Lynn was the fifth female elected to the Country Music Hall of Fame in 1988. A deserved honor, she blazed a trail for future female singers of all styles. Her tale is an engaging one, a triumph of the human spirit. The poor little country girl who grew up to become one of the finest singers in the history of the genre shared with the world her coal miner heartbreak.

## Discography

*Loretta Lynn Sings*, Decca 4457.
*Before I'm Over You*, Decca 4541.
*Blue Kentucky Girl*, Decca 74665.
*Songs from My Heart*, Decca 4620.
*Ernest Tubb and Loretta Lynn*, Decca 4639.
*Hymns*, King 5200.
*I Like 'Em Country*, Decca 4744.
*A Country Christmas*, MCA 15022.
*You Ain't Woman Enough*, MCA 006.
*Singin' with Feelin'*, Decca 4930.
*Ernest Tubb and Loretta Lynn Singin' Again*, Decca 4872.
*Don't Come Home a Drinkin'*, MCA 113.
*Fist City*, Decca 4997.
*Here's Loretta Lynn*, Columbia 20056.
*Who Says God Is Dead!*, MCA 5103.
*Your Squaw Is on the Warpath*, Decca 5084.
*A Woman of the World*, Decca 75113.

*Loretta Lynn Writes 'Em and Sings 'Em*, Decca 75198.
*Wings Upon Your Horns*, Decca 5163.
*I Wanna Be Free*, Decca 5282.
*One's on the Way*, Decca 5334.
*You're Lookin' at Country*, Decca 5310.
*Coal Miner's Daughter*, MCA 936.
*God Bless America Again*, Decca 5351.
*Here I Am Again*, Decca 5381.
*Louisiana Woman/Mississippi Man*, MCA 335.
*Entertainer of the Year*, MCA 300.
*Love Is the Foundation*, MCA 355.
*Country Partners*, MCA 836.
*They Don't Make 'Em Like My Daddy*, MCA 444.
*Back to the Country*, MCA 471.
*Home*, MCA 2146.
*Somebody Somewhere*, MCA 2228.
*When the Tingle Becomes a Chill*, MCA 2179.
*Blue-Eyed Kentucky Girl*, Decca 20261.
*I Remember Patsy*, MCA 31235.
*In Concert: Recorded with the Edmonton Symphony Orchestra*, Dep Entertainment 3326.
*Out of My Head and Back in My Bed*, MCA 2330.
*We've Come a Long Way, Baby*, MCA 3073.
*Lookin' Good*, MCA 874.
*Loretta*, MCA 3217.
*I Lie*, MCA 5293.
*Making Love from Memory*, MCA Special 22005.
*Lyin' Cheatin' Woman Chasin' Honky Tonkin' Whiskey Drinkin' You*, MCA 877.
*Loretta Lynn [MCA]*, MCA 20163.
*Just a Woman*, MCA 27116.
*Who Was That Stranger*, MCA 42174.
*I'll Just Call You Darlin'*, MCA 20509.
*Peace in the Valley*, MCA 22024.
*The Old Rugged Cross*, MCA 20679.
*Sings Patsy Cline's Favorites*, MCA Special 20687.
*Hey Good Lookin'*, MCA Special 20735.
*An Evening with Loretta Lynn*, Musketeer 5069.
*Loretta Lynn and Patsy Cline on Tour, Vol. 1* [live], MCA Special 20915.
*Loretta Lynn and Patsy Cline on Tour, Vol. 2* [live], MCA Special 20916.
*Still Country*, Audium 8119.
*Van Lear Rose*, Interscope 000251302.
*Back to the Country/They Don't Make 'Em Like My Daddy*, MCA 38007.
*Don't Come Home a Drinkin' (with Lovin' on Your Mind)/You Ain't Woman Enough*, MCA 38001.
*Christmas Without Daddy*, MCA 22037.
*Greatest Hits*, MCA 31234.
*The Ernest Tubb/Loretta Lynn Story*, MCA 4000.
*Greatest Hits, Vol. 2*, MCA 932.
*The Best of Loretta Lynn [MCA]*, MCA 20709.
*Greatest Hits Live*, K-Tel 3075-2.
*20 Greatest Hits*, MCA 5943.
*The Very Best of Conway and Loretta*, MCA 3162.
*Country Music Hall of Fame*, MCA 10083.

*Country's Favorite Daughter*, Pair 1320.
*Honky Tonk Girl: Collection*, MCA 11070.
*From Seven Till Ten*, MCA 20680.
*Loretta Lynn* [Columbia River], Columbia River 1172.
*All Time Gospel Favorites*, Madacy 8117.
*The Very Best of Loretta Lynn* [Half Moon], Half Moon 013.
*20th Century Masters — The Millennium Collection: The Best of Loretta Lynn*, MCA 70106.
*Best of the Best of Loretta Lynn: Her Gospel Side*, Federal 6540.
*Sings*, Longhorn 3023.
*Best of Loretta Lynn*, Music Club 142.
*Somebody Somewhere*, Columbia River 110018.
*20th Century Masters — The Millennium Collection: The Best of Loretta Lynn, Vol. 2*, MCA 170215.
*All Time Greatest Hits*, MCA 170281.
*All Time Gospel Favorites*, Time Life 19009.
*Gospel Spirit*, MCA Nashville 000290802.
*Very Best of Loretta Lynn*, Universal International 111694.
*Coal Miner's Daughter*, Legacy 210.
*Coal Miner's Daughter*, Dynamic 2123.
*Concert Collection*, Prism Platinum 171.
*The Definitive Collection*, MCA Nashville 4537.
*20th Century Masters — The Christmas Collection*, MCA Nashville 5033.
*Gold*, MCA Nashville 0006084.
*Chronicles*, Mercury 471202.
*The Best of Loretta Lynn Number 2*, MCA Special Products 20709.
*Back to the Country/They Don't Make 'Em Like Daddy*, MCA 38010.
*Hymns/Who Says God Is Dead!*, MCA 38000.

# WANDA JACKSON (1937–)
## *Country Music Heart*

There have been many female country artists who carved out their own special place in the history of the genre with their talent, heart and determination. Because of the male dominated industry, women have had to fight harder in order to achieve the same kind of recognition. One of the artists who proved that she had a country music heart battled hard for every ounce of success she earned. Her name is Wanda Jackson.

Wanda Jackson was born on October 20, 1937, in Maud, Oklahoma. When she was four her country singing father moved the family to California. During her stay in the Golden State she received a musical education that her father greatly encouraged. He bought her a guitar and taught her how to play it. He also gave her piano lessons and took her to the concerts of such country music stars as Tex Ritter, Spade

Cooley, and Bob Wills. When she was twelve, the family moved back to Oklahoma.

When she was fifteen she took the first major step in achieving her dreams of becoming a famous singer when she won a local talent contest, with first prize being a fifteen minute radio spot. She also performed on the radio throughout her high school years. In her graduating year, Hank Thompson heard her and asked if she would sing with his band, the Brazos Valley Boys. She accepted the challenge and cut the song "You Can't Have My Love," which turned out to be a national hit.

She finished high school and set out on the road with the help of her parents. Her father came along to see to her business affairs and her mother designed her stage costumes. Aside from the strong encouragement from her parents, she also derived support from an unlikely source, the king of rock and roll, Elvis. The two toured together and it was Presley who influenced her source of song material. She began to sing more rockabilly material.

Perhaps it was the versatility of her material, or perhaps it was the fact that she was a dynamic singer, but from the mid–1950s and on, she continually placed songs in top of the North American charts as well as around the world. For example, her 1958 release "Fujiyama Mama" was a sensation in Japan. In 1965, she had a major hit with "Santa Domingo" in Germany (she recorded the song in German). In North America, she scored with "Let's Have a Party" (which inspired the name of her band, Party Timers), as well as "Right and Wrong" and "In the Middle of a Heartache" in 1961.

She was a staple on the country touring circuit that included a regular stint in Las Vegas beginning in the 1950s. Unlike other singers who quit their careers after marriage, when Jackson married Wendell Goodman, she continued to press on. Her new husband quit his executive job to manage her affairs. They later had two sons. A savvy businessman, Goodman made sure that Jackson's TV Show, *Music Village,* went into syndication.

The pressures of being on the road eventually took their toll on their marriage, but they managed to save it through religion. From this point on, Jackson's releases focused on gospel material. *Praise the Lord* appeared in 1972, and she recorded another three on the Myrth label before switching to Word Records, where she would record two more gospel albums.

In the 1980s, Jackson returned to a more country and rockabilly flavored sound. She toured Europe and played at the many musical festivals, which turned into an annual affair. She quickly won back her country music fans that she had alienated while recording gospel material for much of the 1970s.

Jackson, on the road for the better part of forty years, has inspired many female singers, including Rosie Flores. Together they did a major U.S. tour and Wanda helped Flores on her album *Rockabilly Filly*. The return of one of the most celebrated country music singers into the fold was a joyous occasion for many of her loyal fans. Jackson continues to record and perform.

Wanda Jackson is a country music sweetheart. Despite the fact that she has been derailed from her country and rockabilly flavored music on occasion, she has always returned to the genre. Her long, illustrious career has earned her a special place on the scene. Although she played the guitar and the piano at an early age, it is her voice that she built her career on.

Jackson has a very versatile voice. It is a multi-faceted vehicle that has allowed her to sing and dominate in every major genre she has attempted, including country, rockabilly, gospel, blues, show tunes and even jazz tinged material. Her sound is instantly recognizable from the first few notes.

Her ability to belt out a rockabilly tune with the force of a hurricane demonstrates only one part of her vocal style. She has also been able to wrap her delivery around a ballad with all of the tenderness of a soft blanket. Jackson could have also enjoyed a stellar career singing just blues, as she has always been able to dig deep down to emote a passion that few have been able to match.

Another truly remarkable quality of her voice is her ability to perform the songs of many different writers and put her own stamp on it. She has sung material penned from the imaginations of Sonny James, Jessie Mae Robinson, Harlan Howard, Willie Nelson, Mike Stoller, Jerry Leiber, Earl Burrows, Vicki Countryman, Curtis Wayne, Hank Cochran, Danny Barker, Pat Franzese, Yvonne DeVaney, Don Raye, Dale Davis, Laurie Christianson, Vic McAlpin, Billy Sherrill and Don Covay. Whatever the song or style, Jackson has always been able to make the tune her own.

Some of her best known songs are "I Gotta Know," "Riot in Cell Block Number 9," "Fujiyama Mama," "Hot Dog! That Made Him Mad," "Let's Have a Party," "It Doesn't Matter Anymore," "You Don't Know Baby," "(Let's Stop) Kickin' Our Hearts Around," "Silver Threads and Golden Needles," and "Tunnel of Love." The often dubbed queen of rockabilly has given the world a treasure trove of classics.

It is easy to understand why she has had such a large influence on a plethora of singers. A partial list includes Lou Ann Barton, Rosie Flores, Michelle Wright, Dawn Sears, Tanya Tucker, Chely Wright, Clarice Rose, Loretta Lynn, Dolly Parton, Susan Tedeschi, Janis Joplin, Sue Foley, Angela Strehli, LeAnn Rimes, Tammy Wynette, Lynn Anderson and many others. Any singer who's ever heard Jackson's tough, passionate voice cannot help but be greatly influenced.

She has shared the stage with Elvis, Rosie Flores, Ray Edenton, Jann Browne, Velvetone, Richard Weize, Hugh Gordon Stoker, Bill Walker, Jerry Shook, June Page, Ken Nelson, Weldon Myrick, Ralph Mooney, Neal Matthews, Jerry Carrigan, Larry Butler, Harold Bradley, Grady Martin, James Burton, Albert Lee and Hank Snow. But as a performer in various venues for the past forty years, she has shared the stage with hundreds of other country, blues, gospel, rockabilly, and pop artists.

In the annals of female country artists Jackson holds a special place. Her popularity soared in the 1950s and 1960s with her rockabilly screech and softer country tones that lit up the charts. Later, her career fizzled in some respects as she devoted her energies to God. But she rebounded when she returned to country and rockabilly material beginning in the 1980s. Although not a country icon in the same vein as June Carter Cash or Loretta Lynn, Wanda Jackson maintains a large fan base.

The Wanda Jackson story is that of a special singer with a burning passion and the ability to push across any type of material. She has achieved near legendary status around the globe years before major tours outside the United States were part of the regular itinerary. Despite sidetracks into other genres, she has always displayed her country music heart.

## Discography

*Wanda Jackson*, Capitol 1041.
*There's a Party Goin' On*, Capitol 1511.
*Rockin' with Wanda*, Capitol 1384.
*Right or Wrong*, Capitol 1596.
*Wonderful Wanda*, Capitol 1776.
*Lovin' Country Style*, Capitol 3021.
*Love Me Forever*, Capitol 1911.
*Blues in My Heart*, Capitol 2306.
*Sings Country Songs*, Capitol 2438.
*Wanda Jackson Salutes the Country Music Hall of Fame*, Capitol 2606.
*You'll Always Have My Love*, Capitol 2812.
*Closer to Jesus*, Word 9580.
*Reckless Love Affair*, Capitol 2704.
*Cream of the Crop*, Capitol 2976.
*Wanda Jackson in Person* [live], Capitol 345.
*The Many Moods of Wanda Jackson*, Capitol 129.
*The Happy Side of Wanda Jackson*, Capitol 238.
*A Woman Lives to Love*, Capitol 554.
*Country*, Capitol 434.
*I Got to Sing*, Capitol 669.
*Praise the Lord*, Capitol 11023.
*I Wouldn't Want You Any Other Way*, Capitol 11096.

*Country Keepsakes*, Capitol 11161.
*When It's Time to Fall in Love Again*, Capitol 6513.
*Country Gospel*, Word 9514.
*Now I Have Everything*, Myrrh 6533.
*Leave My Baby*, Hilltop 6074.
*Please Help Me I'm Falling*, Hilltop 6058.
*We'll Sing in Sunshine*, Hilltop 6116.
*By the Time I Get to Phoenix*, Hilltop 6123.
*Tears at Grand Ole Opry*, Hilltop 6184.
*My Testament*, Word 9617.
*Rock and Roll Away Your Blues*, Varrick 025.
*2 Sides of Wanda*, Capitol 2030.
*Ultimate Compilation: Live and Still Kickin'*, DCN 1013.
*Heart Trouble*, 8708.
*I Remember Elvis*, Cleopatra 1568.
*Santa Domingo-Deutsche ufnohemen*, 15582.
*Best of Wanda Jackson*, Capitol 2883.
*Nobody's Darlin'*, Vocalion 73861.
*A Portrait of Wanda Jackson*, Capitol 21530.
*Pioneers of Rock*, Starline 5120.
*I'll Still Love You*, DJM 20493.
*Rock'n'roll History*, Capitol 82098.
*Greatest Hits*, Curb 77398.
*Country Classics*, Capitol 1033.
*Her Greatest Country Hits*, EMI 53025.
*Early Wanda Jackson*, Bear Family 15109.
*Let's Have a Party*, Charly 1022.
*Greatest Hits*, Hollywood 442.
*Rockin' in the Country: The Best of Wanda Jackson*, Rhino 70990.
*Right or Wrong* [Box], Bear Family 15629.
*Vintage Collections Series*, Capitol 36185.
*Tears Will Be the Chaser for Your Wine*, Bear Family 16114.
*Queen of Rockabilly*, Ace 776.
*Wanda Rocks*, Bear Family 16631.
*Country Classics*, Emi Gold 527035.
*Heartache*, Varese 066540.
*The Best of Wanda Jackson*, K-Tel 3089.

# PART FIVE

# *Outlaws, Rebels and Superstars*

Throughout the illustrious history of country music there have been many pioneers, innovators, superstars and cult heroes. In order to achieve their proper status they stubbornly followed their own individual path. It is this strain of rebelliousness that has given the genre its strength and vitality.

In the 1950s, Nashville was just beginning to reap the rewards of thirty years as a country music center. Ten years later it was one of the hottest musical spots on earth and had carved out its own niche in the international music map. Throughout the 1960s pop, folk, blues and rock artists rushed to Music City USA to record. Despite its well founded reputation there began an underground movement to reject the slick, all-business atmosphere of the Nashville sound.

It began with the red headed Texas cowboy Willie Nelson, who became so frustrated of his treatment in Nashville that he returned to his roots and settled in Austin. It was here, a year later, that he would start the outlaw movement. He was joined by Waylon Jennings, another alumni of the Lone Star State who had also grown very tired of the stale concept of country music produced in Nashville.

Soon others would join in, including Tompall Glaser, Jessi Colter, Guy Clark, Kris Kristofferson, Billy Joe Shaver, Mickey Newbury, Johnny Paycheck, Jerry Jeff Walker, John Anderson, Ed Bruce, Lee Clayton, Joe Ely, Kinky Friedman, Sammi Smith, Johnny Rodriguez and David Allen Coe. At first they were shunned by the industry but when they began to win polls and awards, as well as sell hundreds of thousands of records, they were gradually accepted. Although the movement that produced a tougher, grittier, back-to-the-roots-of-honky-tonk sound faded out sometime in the late 1980s, it profoundly changed the face of country music forever.

Although country music had boasted a handful of special artists— including Vernon Dalhart, Jimmie Rodgers, Roy Rogers, Gene Autry and Hank Williams—who had put the genre on the map, the 1960s and 1970s ushered in the era of the superstar. Johnny Cash, Glen Campbell, Willie Nelson, Buck Owens, Roy Clark, Conway Twitty and Kenny Rogers transcended all boundaries that had been established. They became household names. This section features some of the outlaws, rebels and superstars of a golden period in country music.

Chet Atkins was arguably the greatest guitarist in country music history, an incredible feat considering the dozens of fine six string slingers that the genre has produced. His work behind the scenes in Nashville only enhanced his reputation.

Marty Robbins was a rebel and a solid western swing man who also delved into various other styles, including pop ballads. A popular performer, he enjoyed enormous crossover success throughout his career.

Buck Owens, another rebel of the period, turned his back on Nashville to create the Bakersfield Sound that boasted a hard rock edge. As the co-host of the corny TV show *Hee Haw*, he sealed his place in country music history.

Johnny Cash, the Man in Black, was a rebel from his very first appearance. Although he started out as a rockabilly artist, he eventually became one of the greatest country artists of the era. He championed the outlaw movement.

Charlie Rich, the Silver Fox, was another rebel. He toiled for years to achieve success before exploding on the scene, only to slowly withdraw from the pressures of stardom.

Glen Campbell became an important recording artist in the 1960s and continued to dominate the charts in the 1970s. The zenith of his popularity included his own TV show.

Roy Clark struggled for a long period before he was picked to co-host the TV comedy/country music show *Hee Haw*. His supreme instrumental skills invaded living rooms every week and that only added to his burgeoning reputation.

Willie Nelson, the red headed Texan with a penchant for barroom songs, turned Austin into one of the most important country music centers. Despite his battles with the IRS, he remains one of the most beloved artists of the period.

Conway Twitty was a great man of country music who rolled out top ten hits with such ease that it seemed like a rule. His pairing with Loretta Lynn was pure dynamite.

Waylon Jennings was a prime figure in the outlaw movement. With his strong voice and personality, he forced the industry to accept his style.

Merle Haggard was another rebel of the period. He never officially joined the outlaw movement, but he made music on his own terms that celebrated the roots of country.

Kenny Rogers enjoyed some success as part of various vocal groups until he became a superstar in the late 1970s and early 1980s.

## CHET ATKINS (1924–2001)
### *The Superpicker*

There have been a large number of excellent musicians in the history of country music that rival those of any other style. Certainly, the bluegrass trio of Bill Monroe, Lester Flatt and Earl Scruggs immediately come to mind. Merle Travis was also a member of the country super instrumentalists category. The early performers such as Fiddlin' John Carson, Gid Tanner, Riley Puckett and Clayton McMichen were highly skilled individuals. In the 1960s, the Nashville sound dominated the country music industry and one man played a huge role in its rise in popularity as the superpicker. His name was Chet Atkins.

Charles Burton Atkins was born on June 20, 1924, in Luttrell, Tennessee, into a musical family. His father was an accomplished musician and his brother Jim was a longtime member of Les Paul's band. Interestingly, the finest guitar player in country music history began on the fiddle. But later he switched to the guitar and proved that it was in him because he made quick progress. By the time he had graduated from high school, he was ready to embark on a musical career.

However, it wasn't overnight stardom. He played on a radio station in Knoxville and earned his traveling spurs by touring with Archie Campbell and Bill Carlisle. In 1944, after failing an audition for a spot in Roy Acuff's band, he headed to Cincinnati to work in radio. He later toured with Red Foley in 1946, including an appearance on the *Grand Ole Opry*. It was also at this time that he made his initial recordings with Foley, but none of the music said exactly what he was trying to do.

In 1950, he moved to Nashville. It was there he hoped to record his own material, but it would be a few years before he would be able to do so. Instead, he had more dues to pay. That same year, he backed Mother Maybelle and the Carter Sisters, taking a giant step in solidifying his name in country circles.

Atkins didn't stay in Nashville long—he moved around the country making stops in Richmond, Virginia, Springfield, Missouri, Colorado (where he played with Shorty Thompson and His Rangers), and, finally, Chicago, where he was signed to the RCA label. He then returned to

Nashville to begin a series of events that would eventually make him a superstar.

Atkins cut a number of songs on his first session, most of them containing vocals, but also some instrumentals. Although a fine singer, it was his guitar work that truly caught the imagination of executives so much that he was asked to become the session man on all songs cut at the Nashville Studios. It was a tremendous responsibility but Atkins accepted the challenge.

His multi-talented abilities as singer/songwriter/instrumentalist truly endeared him to the country music crowd. He became a top session man, adding his distinct guitar touch to the songs of dozens of artists. In an effort to broaden the appeal of country music, Atkins supplemented all the recordings he supervised with a fuller, more lush sound that included strings, background vocals and horns. This approach enabled the genre to compete with rock, jazz, and folk.

Although he worked on the countless songs of other musicians, he also found time to work on his own material. In 1953, he released *Gallopin' Guitar*, a landmark album that clearly demonstrated his superlative guitar skills. It was evident that Chet Atkins wasn't going to take a back seat to anyone in the instrumental department, including Merle Travis, the then reigning king of country guitar.

One of the most impressive sessions that Atkins worked on was the one that produced "Heartbreak Hotel," a top hit for Elvis. Chet's ability to rock and roll underlined his multi-faceted musical personality. In 1960, he was hired as the man in charge of the new RCA studio, becoming A and R manager and then vice-president a few years later.

He continued to build on his legend throughout the 1960s as the man who produced hit records for Hank Snow, Perry Como, Waylon Jennings, Al Hirt and so many more. He was the consummate chameleon in the studio, able to reproduce any style. When not overseeing another star recording another chart topper, he was taking care of his own career. He had his fair share of major top ten placements and displayed an uncommon diversity by performing at the Newport Jazz Festival and with the Atlanta Symphony Orchestra.

As the A and R man he was also chiefly responsible for discovering new talent. Don Gibson, Waylon Jennings, Floyd Cramer, Charley Pride, Bobby Bare, and Connie Smith are just a handful of the artists whose careers he launched. Thousands flocked to Nashville with a song in their heart and visions of stardom dancing in their head. The man responsible for making those dreams come true was Chet Atkins.

He kept on rolling through the 1970s and by that time he had produced the Nashville Sound, which brought many pop and rock acts scurrying to the center of country music to record. It was Atkins, more than anyone else, who was responsible for putting the studios on the map. However, despite the fact that he enjoyed tremendous success at the helm of RCA, he craved a change.

In 1982, after more than twenty years as the background man for RCA, Atkins left the label and signed with Columbia. The new lease on life (he had become disenchanted with the mechanical production atmosphere at RCA), enabled him to stretch out as an artist. He recorded jazz albums, as well as more pop oriented material that truly displayed his still dazzling guitar skills.

In 1997, he was diagnosed with cancer, and despite major surgery, eventually lost the battle. On June 30, 2001, Chet Atkins, the multi-talented guitar great with the slick licks and record making savvy, passed away.

Chet Atkins was a country music icon. He almost single handedly created the Nashville sound and played a major role in the direction that the genre has explored in the past 40 years. His methods and technique put the Southern city on the international music map. His work in the Nashville studios was so monumental that it almost overshadows the fact that he was the greatest guitarist in the annals of country music.

Chet Atkins was to country music what Jimi Hendrix was to rock-blues. Atkins' guitar work demonstrated a phenomenally talented individual who could play in any style. He was able to coax sounds out of his instrument that few before him or after have been able to emulate. He was a guitarist's guitarist, a man who played the instrument for the sheer joy of it and even designed models for the Gibson company that have since become collector's items.

He had a huge influence on a number of artists in country music circles and outside the genre. The list includes Jerry Reed, Steve Wariner, Eugene Chadbourne, Mark Knopfler, Eric Johnson, Albert Lee, the Notting Hillbillies, the Shadows, Lenny Breau, Larry Coryell, Jack Jezzro, Earl Klugh, Atlanta, Jim Glaser, Sam Neely, Junior Brown, Danny Davis, Terry McMillan, Johnny A. and Eric Dane. Atkins was such an superb stylist that he touched anyone who picked up a guitar in the past 50 years.

As an invaluable session man, he had his part in hundreds of recordings of every top country artist in the past 60 years. There is scarcely a period in time that has gone by where he didn't have a hand in a song or songs that dominated the charts. He worked with a number of individuals and a complete list would fill a book. A partial number includes Bob Ferguson, Bob L. Moore, Buddy Harman, Steve Sholes, Hargus "Pig" Robbins, Henry Strzelecki, Owen Bradley, Waylon Jennings, Bill Porter,

Murray Harman, Jr., Buddy Emmons, Roy Clark, Mark Knopfler, Jerry Reed, Johnny Cash, Loretta Lynn, Bob Dylan, and scores of others. With hundreds of country, rock, blues, jazz, pop and folk hits to his credit, he is arguably the most important session man in the history of music with the possible exception of blues great Willie Dixon, the genius behind the scenes at Chess Records in the 1950s that created stars of many Chicago blues performers. However, Atkins played a larger role than Dixon, and he also enjoyed a much more successful recording career than the old blues legend.

A few of Atkins' best songs include "Poor People of Paris," "Boo Boo Stick Beat Beat," "One Mint Julep," "Teensville," "Yakety Axe," "Mr. Sandman," "Silver Bell," and "Prissy." No matter the source of the material, whether it was a self-penned tune or a cover version, he was always able to give it a distinct treatment that made it something special. In his hands, a song became magic.

It is not surprising that he won numerous awards in his lifetime, including an unprecedented reign as the best instrumentalist in the Cash Box Poll. He dominated the prize as the best country guitarist. He won a dozen Grammy awards, a similar amount of CMA Instrumentalist of the Year honors, as well as a Lifetime Achievement Award. In 1973, he was inducted to the Country Music Hall of Fame, a fitting honor for the man known as the Superpicker.

## Discography

*Chet Atkins' Gallopin' Guitar*, RCA Victor 3379.
*A Session with Chet Atkins*, RCA Victor 1090.
*Stringin' Along with Chet Atkins*, RCA Victor 1236.
*Chet Atkins in Three Dimensions*, Longhorn 3083.
*Finger Style Guitar*, RCA Victor 1383.
*Chet Atkins at Home*, RCA Victor 1544.
*Hi Fi in Focus*, RCA Victor 1577.
*Guitar for All Seasons*, Pair 1959.
*Chet Atkins in Hollywood*, RCA 1993.
*Mister Guitar*, RCA Victor 2103.
*Hum and Strum Along with Chet Atkins*, RCA Victor 2025.
*The Other Chet Atkins*, RCA 2175.
*Teensville*, RCA 27168.
*Chet Atkins' Workshop*, RCA Victor 27214.
*The Most Popular Guitar*, RCA Victor 2346.
*Christmas with Chet Atkins*, RCA Victor 2423.
*Down Home Guitar*, RCA 2450.
*Caribbean Guitar*, RCA Victor 2549.
*Plays Back Home Hymns*, RCA 2007.
*Our Man in Nashville*, RCA 7529.
*Teen Scene*, RCA 7602.

*Travelin' Guitar*, RCA 2678.
*The Guitar Genius*, Camden 6071.
*Guitar Country*, RCA 2783.
*My Favorite Guitars*, RCA 3316.
*Progressive Pickin'*, RCA 2908.
*More of That Guitar Country*, RCA 3429.
*Chet Atkins Picks on the Beatles*, RCA 3531.
*Music from Nashville*, Camden 981.
*From Nashville with Love*, RCA 3647.
*The Pops Goes Country*, RCA Victor 2870.
*It's a Guitar World*, RCA 3728.
*Class Guitar*, RCA 3885.
*Chet*, Camden 1014.
*Solo Flights*, RCA 7934.
*Solid Gold 68*, RCA 4061.
*Hometown Guitar*, RCA 4017.
*Relaxin' with Chet*, Camden 6072.
*Lovers Guitar*, RCA 4035.
*Solid Gold 69*, RCA 4244.
*Chet Atkins and C.E. Snow*, RCA 4254.
*Chet Picks on the Pops*, RCA Victor 3104.
*A Man and His Other Guitar*, RCA 196.
*Pickin' My Way*, Mobile 2–787.
*Yestergroovin'*, RCA 4331.
*Me and Jerry*, RCA 4396.
*Chet Picks the Pops*, RCA 11567.
*By Special*, RCA Victor 5254.
*Solid Gold 70*, RCA 4244.
*This Is Chet Atkins*, RCA 1018.
*Guitar Picker*, Camden 2464.
*For the Good Times*, RCA 4464.
*Chet and Boots*, Camden 2523.
*Picks on the Hits*, Special Music 2712.
*Now and Then*, RCA 6091/2.
*Picks the Hits*, RCA 4754.
*Strum Along Guitar Method*, RCA 36932.
*Atkins: Travis Traveling Show*, RCA 0479.
*Chet Atkins Picks on Jerry Reed*, RCA 0545.
*The Night Atlanta Burned*, RCA 1233.
*Famous Country Music Makers*, RCA 2063.
*Chester and Lester*, RCA 11167.
*In Concert* [live], RCA 21014.
*Guitar Monsters*, RCA 3682.
*The Best of Chet Atkins and Friends*, RCA 61093.
*Love Letters*, Camden 17042.
*Goes to the Movies*, RCA 10845.
*Me and My Guitar*, RCA 2405.
*Chet Floyd and Danny*, RCA 12311.
*Legendary Performer*, RCA 12503.
*Best of Chet on the Road*, RCA 3515.
*Reflections*, Sugar Hill 3896.
*First Nashville Guitar Quartet*, RCA 13302.

*And Then Came Chet*, RCA 42939.
*Country After All These Years*, RCA 4044.
*The Best of Chet Atkins*, RCA 7664.
*Solid Gold Guitar*, RCA 9008.
*Guitar Pickin' Man*, Cambra 062.
*Work It Out with Chet Atkins C.G.P.*, CBS 38536.
*East Tennessee Christmas*, CBS 39003.
*Great Hits of the Past*, RCA 4724.
*Stay Tuned*, Columbia 39591.
*Street Dreams*, Columbia 40256.
*Sails*, CBS 40593.
*C.G.P.*, CBS 44323.
*Neck and Neck*, Columbia 45307.
*Sneakin' Around*, CBS 47873.
*Read My Licks*, Columbia 53756.
*Almost Alone*, Columbia 67497.
*The Day Finger Pickers Took Over the World*, Sony 67915.
*Discover Japan*, BMG 7398.
*And His Guitar/The Guitar Genius*, Collectables 7306.
*Guitar Picker/Finger Pickin' Good*, Collectables 7312.
*Music from Nashville: My Hometown/Chet*, Collectables 7324. American Salute, RCA 3277.
*The Best of Chet Atkins*, RCA 61091.
*And His Guitar*, RCA Camden 654.
*Best of Chet Atkins, Vol. 2*, RCA 3558.
*Picks the Best*, RCA 3818.
*Mr. Atkins Guitar Picker*, Camden 1090.
*The Early Years*, Camden 659.
*Finger Pickin' Good*, Camden 2600.
*Tennessee Guitar Man*, Pair 1047.
*20 of the Best*, RCA 89849.
*The Best of Chet Atkins and Friends, Vol. 2*, 61092.
*Pickin' on Country*, Pair 1211.
*Guitar for All Season*, Pair 1115.
*Picks on the Hits*, Pair 1225.
*Masters of the Guitar: Together Pair, 1230.*
*Country Gems*, Pair 1282.
*Picks on the Hits* [Special], Special Music 2712.
*The RCA Years*, RCA 61095-2.
*Collection*, RCA 214094.
*Galloping Guitar: The Early Years*, Bear Family 15714.
*Caribbean Guitar/Travelin'*, One Way 35124.
*My Favorite Guitar/It's a Guitar World*, One Way 35121.
*The Most Popular Guitar/Down Home*, One Way 35123.
*Me and My Guitar/The First Nashville Guitar Quartet*, One Way 35122.
*The Essential Chet Atkins*, RCA 66855.
*Essential Chet Atkins, Vol. 2*, RCA 266948.
*Pickin' the Hits* [Sony Special Products], Sony Special 70032.
*Super Hits*, RCA 67717.
*Mister Guitar/Chet Atkins in Three Dimensions*, One Way 35125.
*Picks on the Hits/Superpickers*, One Way 35126.
*Me and Chet/Me and Jerry*, One Way 35127.

*Finger Style Guitar/Stringin' Along with Chet Atkins*, One Way 35128.
*Hum and Strum Along with Chet Atkins/The Other Chet Atkins*, One Way 35129.
*Chester and Lester/Guitar Monsters*, One Way 35120.
*Chet Atkins*, Camden 6070.
*Nashville Gold*, RCA 2551.
*Chet Atkins/Doug Stone*, Platinum Disc 1774.
*Guitar Legend: The RCA Years*, Buddha 99673.
*Masters*, Import 44107.
*Heartbreak Hotel*, Legend 64021.
*Guitar Genius/Relaxin' with Chet/Nashville Gold*, 6070.
*Guitar Country/More of That Guitar Country*, Collectables 2819.
*A Master and His Music*, RCA 67019.
*RCA Country Legends*, Buddha 99836.
*Chet Picks on the Grammys*, Columbia 85375.
*Best Selections*, RCA B230-41053.
*Mister Guitar/Chet Atkin's Workshop*, Classic Compact Disc 2103.
*Back Home Hymns*, BMG Special Products 46675.
*Tribute to Bluegrass*, BMG Special Products 46902.
*Hall of Fame 1973*, King 3830.
*The Best of Chet Atkins*, Paradiso 788.
*Legendary*, BMG International 97696.
*Early Chet Atkins*, Country Routes 32.
*High Rockin' Swing*, Universe 123.
*The Essential Chet Atkins: The Columbia Years*, Sony 92796.
*Mr. Guitar: The Complete Recordings 1955–1960*, Bear Family 16539.
*The Great Chet Atkins*, Rajon 380.
*Country Gentleman*, BCI Eclipse Company 41140.
*In Three Dimensions*, Universe Italy 157.
*All American Country*, BMG 40471.
*Country Pickin'*, RCA 9006.

# MARTY ROBBINS (1925–1982)
## *The Country Chameleon*

The parameters of country music remained pure in the first years of its recorded history. But eventually, like other genres, it was forced to expand its borders to include different styles in order to survive in the competitive music business. One individual was an expert at blending different styles with his roots to create something new and fresh. Because of his multi-faceted abilities he was known as the Country Chameleon. His name is Marty Robbins.

Marty David Robbins was born on September 26, 1925, in Glendale, Arizona. The Robertson men (his official birth name in some files is Robertson), were true characters, including his harmonica playing father and his maternal grandfather, Texas Bob Heckle, who had been a traveling medicine man. As a youngster, Robbins was enthralled with his grandfather's tales that provided a rich source for his songwriter ideas.

Robbins took the romanticism of the freedom of the traveling cowboy on the lone prairie to heart and spent most of his time dreaming about living the lifestyle. Eventually he did just that and roamed the desert collecting material for his cycle of songs that would one day make him famous. A three-year term of service in the Navy interrupted his hobo days. It was a blessing since he had begun to sink into a life of petty crime.

It was during his stint in the Navy that he developed his musical abilities and was exposed to the beauty of the Hawaiian sound. Upon his release from his military duties, he returned to the Arizona desert and began to sing at local clubs. Later on, he would land a radio gig and his career blossomed to eventually include his own television show, *Western Caravan*. Although not a national hit, it did elevate his status in his native state. One of his guests was Little Jimmy Dickens, who was so impressed with Robbins (by this time he had adopted it as his stage name), that he put in a good word with the executives at Columbia Records.

But it wasn't overnight success for Robbins, as his first couple of singles flopped. However, his third release, "I'll Go Alone," hit the top ten and he was on his way. He appeared as a permanent member of the *Grand Ole Opry* in 1953 and started to hit the charts with regular ease, including his own stamp on "That's All Right, Mama," the blues original from Arthur "Big Boy" Crudup, with which Elvis Presley made his debut.

Although he would someday be known for his musical diversity, in the beginning of his recording career he was cutting cry-in-your-beer ballads that earned him the nickname Mr. Teardrop. However, with the release of "That's All Right, Mama," and "Singing the Blues," he proved that he could handle any style. He also recorded "Maybelline," which made him a favorite of rock fans, especially in Great Britain.

Despite his success recording a diverse amount of material, for a period of time other artists—namely Guy Mitchell—had greater placements than Robbins himself. It was a great point of frustration for Marty. After "Singing the Blues" raced to the top of the country parade, Mitchell cut a more pop oriented version that pushed ahead of Robbins' effort. The process would be repeated with the song "Knee Deep in Blues."

In order to end the frustration, Robbins changed gears and collaborated with Ray Conniff, a conductor of some note. The result was that he was no longer overshadowed by Mitchell, and gained a handful of top hits. He was also branching out in different directions by recording "She Was Only Seventeen," "Stairway of Love," and in 1959, "El Paso." With the latter, a rich tune embellished by western lyrics, Mexican rhythms and an easy pop feel, he assured all that no one would ever overshadow him again. His multi-faceted talent proved that he could rock, play beautiful Hawaiian music, sing tearjerker pop ballads, and be a genuine country boy. Each style found its own audience that greatly expanded his fan base.

He branched out even further, establishing a movie career. He played roles in *The Gun and the Gavel, The Badge of Marshal Brennan, The Western Raiders of Old California,* and *Buffalo Gun,* among others. He also became a businessman, forming his own booking agency and record label. During this western period, he recorded such theme songs such as "The Hanging Tree" that was used in the movie of the same name starring Gary Cooper.

The album *Gunfighter Ballads and Trail Songs* saw him delve into the Western Cowboy theme even deeper. It set the stage for the rebels and outlaws that would infiltrate country music beginning in the 1960s and that would carry on into the 1970s and 1980s. The image he cultivated provided him with his greatest success and it was one that he would revisit time and time again.

The hits poured forth. "Big Iron" was derived from the many tall tales his grandfather had told him. "Don't Worry," complete with fuzz-toned guitar, became another number one hit that featured his macho western feel coupled with his precise melodic sentiment in a full, powerful voice that hinted at a greater dimension. "Devil Woman" became another top hit that enabled him to occupy the pop charts on both sides of the Atlantic.

He became a fixture on American television and toured regularly to audiences that were divided between his rock and roll side, his pop-country persona, his Hawaiian sound, and his feeling for western themes. He picked up race car driving as a hobby to relieve some of the pressures he faced as a performer and eventually competed in NASCAR races. The racing theme would sneak into a few of his releases in the early 1960s.

He had not abandoned his movie career, and in 1963 appeared in *Ballad of a Gunfighter.* The irresistible theme of the Western folklore was the seemingly infinite well he tapped into. Because of his many side projects that included working on his television series *The Drifter,* Robbins slipped in the charts. He would eventually rebound with "Tonight Carmen," and assume his familiar perch atop the heap later in the decade.

But he devoted much more time to his acting career and appeared in *Country Music Caravan, The Nashville Story, Tennessee Jamboree,* and the stock-car drama *Hell on Wheels.* In 1969, the relatively young Robbins suffered a heart attack and needed delicate surgery to repair his ailment. Despite being out of action for over a year, upon his return to the *Opry* in 1970, he was given a standing ovation and played for some 45 minutes to the enthusiastic crowd that had not forgotten the desert rat.

He continued to perform at music venues as well as the movies, but after 1972, he enjoyed less commercial success. However, he was still a major force, since he was chosen to close the Ryman Auditorium and open the new *Grand Ole Opry* concert venue. His previous accomplishments still carried much weight in country circles; he was a firmly established name.

In the mid–1970s he enjoyed a brief resurgence in popularity and his records began to sell again. A whole new generation of country music fans discovered him and his old fan base had never abandoned him. However, on December 8, 1982, after his third major heart attack, Marty Robbins, one of the most diverse country artists in the history of the genre, died.

Marty Robbins was a country chameleon. Although he recorded in a variety of styles, he never ventured far from his western roots. There was accessibility to his music that was not often found in the styles of other performers. It was this familiarity that enabled him to display his many, many musical personalities.

More than any other artist, with the possible exception of Bob Wills, Robbins emphasized the western in country and western music. He had a penchant for the Old West and its glory, as he recorded many albums featuring this theme. It was a recurrent universe that he visited many times and is credited with keeping the genre alive. His fascination with the myth of the cowboy was something he never abandoned.

But there is more to his music than the western cowboy theme. He was capable of rocking his audience and influenced a number of the first generation of rockers, including Jerry Lee Lewis, Chuck Berry, and Elvis. He would have a later impact on the Eagles, the Nitty Gritty Dirt Band, Asleep at the Wheel, Commander Cody and His Lost Airmen, Code 615, the Souther-Hillman-Furay Band, and others in the country-rock vein.

He recorded albums that included Hawaiian, Caribbean and religious themes. He also laid down some of the toughest honky tonk tinged blues songs that ever graced the charts, carrying on the legacy of Hank Williams. The breadth and depth of the material that he put on vinyl was truly amazing. With his superior abilities, Robbins could have recorded in any style and come up with the best songs.

Perhaps more than any modern country artist, Robbins always remained highly visible with his numerous appearances on the big screen, television, concerts, and racing events. During times when his songs had hit a dry spell, he never suffered a lull in popularity because he turned to another facet of his multiple dimensional career. As well, his ability to successfully record and weld country with a variety of other genres endeared him to a cross-section of music fans.

He gave the world a number of great songs, including "Big Iron," "Love Me or Leave Me Alone," "I'll Go on Alone," "I Couldn't Keep from

Crying," "Pretty Words," "That's All Right," "Singing the Blues," "Knee Deep in Blues," "The Story of My Life," "White Sport Coat (and a Pink Carnation)," and "Teenage Dream" during the early part of his career. Later songs included "She Was Only Seventeen," "Stairway of Love," "El Paso," "Don't Worry," "Devil Woman," "Ruby Ann," "Begging to You," "Ribbon of Darkness," "Tonight Carmen," "I Walk Alone," "My Woman, My Woman, My Wife," "El Paso City," and "Among My Souvenir." The songs cover possibly every style of music, proving that country could be eclectic and successful in the right hands.

He made an impact on Sonny James, Johnny Cash, Patsy Cline, Jim Reeves, Johnny Horton, Brenda Lee, Hank Snow, Don Gibson, Roy Clark, Charlie Rich, Billy Dean, Clinton Gregory, the Grateful Dead, Jeanne Pruett, Stacy Dean Campbell, Shane McAnally, and Chad Austin. There is scarcely a modern artist that has not delved into the Marty Robbins songbook at one time or another in their career. His diversity as well as his powerful talents as musician and singer prove to be irresistible.

Throughout his career he worked with a number of artists, including Floyd Cramer, Bob L. Moore, William Whitney Pursell, Billy Sherrill, Richard Weize, Owen Bradley, Harold Bradley, Willie Nelson, Merle Haggard, Johnny Gimble, Hank Garland, Bobby Sykes, Farris Coursey, and James Farmer. Anyone that shared the stage with Robbins was impressed with his multiple abilities. It was difficult to play along with Robbins because of his many musical personalities and his faculty to change directions very quickly.

Marty Robbins was inducted into the Country Music Hall of Fame in October of 1982, two months before his death. He had been previously elected to the Nashville Songwriters International Hall of Fame in 1975. After his passing, the theme song to the movie *Honky Tonk Man*, starring Clint Eastwood, was released and climbed the charts effortlessly. During his career, Robbins had almost one hundred charting hits in a variety of styles, clearly indicating that he was the true country chameleon.

## Discography

*Rock'n Roll'n Robbins*, Columbia CL 2601.
*Song of the Islands*, Columbia 1087.
*The Song of Robbins*, Legacy/Columbia 976.
*Marty Robbins* [1958], Columbia 1189.
*Gunfighter Ballads and Trail Songs*, Columbia/Legacy 116.
*More Gunfighter Ballads and Trail Songs*, Columbia 1481.
*Alamo*, Columbia 1558.
*Just a Little Sentimental*, Columbia 1666.
*Devil Woman*, Columbia 1918.
*A Portrait of Marty*, Columbia 1855.

*Marty After Midnight*, Columbia 1801.
*Return of the Gunfighter*, Columbia 2072.
*Hawaii's Calling Me*, Bear Family 8840.
*Island Woman*, Columbia 2167.
*R.F.D. Marty Robbins*, Columbia 2220.
*Turn the Lights Down Low*, Columbia 2304.
*Carl, Lefty and Marty*, CBS 2544.
*What God Has Done*, Columbia 2448.
*By the Time I Get to Phoenix*, Columbia 63295.
*Saddle Tramp*, Columbia 237.
*The Drifter*, Koch 7934.
*My Kind of Country*, Columbia 62962.
*Tonight Carmen*, Columbia 63116.
*Christmas with Marty Robbins*, Columbia 09535.
*Bend in the River*, Columbia 445.
*By the Time I Get to Phoenix*, Columbia 9617.
*I Walk Alone*, Columbia 63441.
*It's a Sin*, Columbia 9811.
*Marty's Country*, Columbia 15.
*The Heart of Marty Robbins*, Columbia 2016.
*Singing the Blues*, Harmony 11338.
*Country Hymns*, Columbia 30324.
*My Woman, My Woman, My Wife*, Columbia 64066.
*The Story of My Life*, Harmony 11409.
*El Paso*, Columbia 30316.
*From the Heart*, Harmony 30756.
*Today*, CBS 64810.
*The Joy of Christmas*, Columbia 11087.
*I've Got a Woman's Love*, Columbia 31628.
*Marty*, Columbia 5812.
*Christmas with Marty Robbins* [1972], Columbia 10980.
*This Much a Man*, Decca 75389.
*Marty Robbin's Favorites*, Harmony 31257.
*Bound for Old Mexico*, Columbia 65569.
*Marty Robbins* [1973], CBS 1601.
*The Streets of Laredo*, Harmony 32286.
*Have I Told You Lately That I Love You*, Columbia 80176.
*Own Favourites*, Columbia 12416.
*Good 'n' Country*, MCA 421.
*Two Gun Daddy*, MCA 2757.
*The Double Barrelled*, CBS 88152.
*El Paso City*, CBS 81561.
*No Signs of Loneliness Man*, Columbia 33476.
*Border Town Affair*, Embassy 31563.
*Don't Let Me Touch You*, CBS 82429.
*Adios Amigo*, CBS 81871.
*The Performer*, CBS 83488.
*All Around Cowboy*, Columbia 83917.
*Marty Robbins Today*, Columbia 30816.
*With Love, Marty Robbins*, CBS 84427.
*Everything I've Always Wanted*, CBS 84816.
*Come Back to Me*, CBS 37995.

*Some Memories Just Won't Die*, CBS 38603.
*Just Me and My Guitar*, Bear Family 15119.
*Pieces of Your Heart*, Bear Family 15212.
*20th Century Drifter*, MCA 27060.
*Walking Piece of Heaven*, MCA 20395.
*Isle of the Golden Dreams*, Bear Family 18880.
*Perfect World*, Reprise 45516–2.
*Rock'n Roll'n Robbins*, Koch 7932.
*Pocket Songs: Marty Robbins*, Pocket Songs 287.
*This Much Man*, MCA Special 20446.
*Marty's Greatest Hits*, CBS 8639.
*More Greatest Hits*, Columbia/Legacy 8435.
*Greatest Hits, Vol. 3*, CBS 64591.
*The World of Marty Robbins*, Columbia 30881.
*All-Time Greatest Hits*, Columbia/Legacy 31361.
*Marty's Greatest Hits, Vol. 3*, Columbia 30571.
*The Best of Marty Robbins* [Artco], Artco 77425.
*Long, Long Ago*, CBS 39575.
*Greatest Hits, Vol. 4*, CBS 35629.
*No. 1 Cowboy*, TVT 6003.
*The Legend*, CBS 85308.
*Encore*, CBS 37353.
*Biggest Hits*, Columbia 38309.
*A Lifetime of Song (1951–1982)*, CBS 38870.
*Rockin' Rollin' Robbins*, Bear Family 15566.
*American Originals*, Columbia 45069.
*Marty* [five LP box], CBS 5812.
*Gunfighter Ballads/My Woman My Wife*, CBS 33630.
*Singin' the Hits*, CBS Special 21565.
*Ruby Ann: Rockin' Rollin' Robbins, Vol. 3*, Bear Family 15184.
*The Essential Marty Robbins: 1951–1982*, Columbia/Legacy 48537.
*Country 1951–1958*, Bear Family 15570.
*The Legendary Marty Robbins*, Sony Special Products 19206.
*Lost and Found*, Columbia 57695.
*Musical Journey to the Caribbean and Mexico*, Bear Family 15571.
*Hawaii's Calling Me*, Bear Family 15568.
*Super Hits*, Sony 67131.
*A Christmas Remembered*, Sony Special Products 21510.
*The Legendary Marty Robbins*, Sony Special 830.
*Memories in Song*, Sony Special 19163.
*Reflections*, Sony Special 16561.
*Under Western Skies*, Bear Family 15646.
*The Story of My Life: The Best of Marty Robbins*, Columbia/Legacy 64763.
*Country (1960–1966)*, Bear Family 15655.
*16 Biggest Hits*, Sony 69320.
*14 Best Hits*, Amw 15812.
*Marty Robbins Files, Vol. 2*, Bear Family 15096.
*Marty Robbins Files, Vol. 5*, Bear Family 15139.
*In the Wild West, Vol. 4*, Bear Family 15183.
*In the Wild West, Vol. 5*, Bear Family 15213.
*Marty Robbins Files, Vol. 3*, Bear Family 15118.
*In the Wild West, Vol. 3*, Bear Family 15147.

*In the Wild West, Vol. 2*, Bear Family 15146.
*Hall of Fame 1982*, King 3828.
*Live Classics from the WSM Grand Ole Opry*, Audium 8121.
*Just a Little Sentimental/Turn the Lights Down Low*, Collectables *7451.*
*Marty Robbins*, Madacy 50308.
*The Great*, Rajon 0223.
*Here's to the Ladies*, Platinum disc 3154.
*Love Songs*, Sony 92799.
*The Essential Mary Robbins*, Columbia 92569.
*Number 1 Cowboy*, CBS P15594.
*All-Time Greatest*, Curb 77425.

# BUCK OWENS (1929–2006)
## *Baron of Bakersfield*

In the 1960s, the Nashville sound dominated country music, but there was a growing disenchantment with the trappings of the style. Across the nation different movements were initiated, including one out of Bakersfield, California, that opted for a harsher, electric sound. The man responsible for this new direction became known as the Baron of Bakersfield. His name was Buck Owens.

Alvis Edgar "Buck" Owens was born on August 12, 1929, in Sherman, Texas. His family, caught in the Dust Bowl of the Great Depression, moved out west to Mesa, Arizona, in search of a better life. Owens showed an interest in music and when not performing manual labor to help the family finances, practiced his guitar and mandolin. He would eventually hone his skills and become proficient enough to play before an audience.

He landed a gig on a local radio station and hooked up with friend Theryl Ray Drifton. His promising musical career was interrupted with marriage at seventeen and fatherhood one year later. The struggle to achieve his goals had now become much more difficult than if he had remained a carefree bachelor. In 1951, he moved his family to Bakersfield, California, which proved to be a monumental decision in his career.

In Bakersfield, he found work immediately in different clubs and almost lived at the Blackboard, where he starred with the regional group, Bill Woods and the Orange Blossom Players. Once Owens had made his formal connections, he decided to put together his own group and called it the Schoolhouse Playboys. He also did much session work, backing such stars as Wanda Jackson, Sonny James and Faron Young. Later he would also play lead guitar in Tommy Collins's band.

Despite his hectic schedule and rising reputation as a first rate guitarist, mandolin player, lead singer, and important studio hired gun, like every other country artist he wanted to record his own songs. He received that opportunity in 1957 when he was signed to Capitol. His debut release, "Second Fiddle," enabled him to wax more sides, including "Under Your Spell Again," "Above and Beyond," "Excuse Me," "I Think I've Got a Heartache," "Feeling Around," and "Under the Influence of Love," all top five charters.

But more importantly was the establishment of the Bakersfield sound, a unique and distinct style that challenged Nashville. As the Nashville studios continued to release country music contaminated with pop strains, Bakersfield emitted a harsher edge that appealed to an audience who appreciated a harder honky tonk punch. Merle Haggard, Wynn Stewart, Freddie Hart and Harlan Howard were other devotees to the movement.

Howard and Owens formed Blue Book Music, a publishing company that allowed them to register the music they were collaborating on. As well, Buck hosted his own radio show and introduced the world to the then-unknown Loretta Lynn. He also formed his own group, the Buckaroos, that consisted of Don Rich, Doyle Holly and Tom Brumley. Of the three, Rich had the greatest impact on Owens' music.

Perhaps one of the most remarkable changes that he pushed onto country music was the use of Fender Telecasters that woke up everyone throughout the community. Many artists clung religiously to the acoustic instruments, but this bold move by Owens and his partner Rich created several converts. It was the electric guitar that truly separated the Bakersfield sound from other styles, especially Nashville.

On the songs "Kickin' Our Hearts Around" and "You're for Me," a strong rock and roll influence could be heard, as Owens built his group around the electric guitar, a drummer (a rarity in country music), an electric bass player and a pedal steel guitar used to maximum effect. They were daring musicians willing to withstand harsh criticism from contemporaries for their use of amplified instruments.

In the 1960s, Owens placed seventeen number one hits on the charts, including "Act Naturally," "My Heart Skips a Beat," "I've Got a Tiger by the Tail," "Buckaroo," "Waitin' in the Welfare Line," "Sam's Place," "How Long Will My Baby Be Gone?," and "Tall Dark Stranger." Almost as impressive were the venues that he and his Buckaroos played at, including Madison Square Garden and the Los Angeles Olympic Auditorium, not exactly usual arenas where country music was heard.

By the end of the decade he was a star based on his solo work, as well as duets with a number of the best female singers. For example, he recorded "Mental Cruelty" and "Loose Talk" with Rose Maddox. Later he would team up with Susan Raye and cut "We're Gonna Get Together," "Togetherness," "The Great White Horse," and "Too Old to Cut the Mustard." The latter song also included Buddy Allen, Buck's son he had with his former wife Bonnie, a marriage that had ended in divorce the previous decade.

An enterprising individual, while he was building up the musical side of his career, he was also showing that he possessed some business savvy. The formation of Buck Owens Enterprises, as well as the booking agency OMAC Artists Corporation, made him one of the most powerful persons in the field. Also, his Blue Book Music enjoyed enormous success, as his songs and those of Merle Haggard sold millions of copies. Eventually, Owens would reinvest his money in radio stations.

He continued to build his empire in Bakersfield. He opened up his own recording studio where Haggard, Wynn Stewart and Tommy Collins cut their songs. Their refreshing take on honky tonk appealed to a widespread cross-section of country music fans throughout the country as well as rock audiences (probably for its use of electric guitars). Owens would even play the legendary Fillmore West, proving that country music could be performed in any venue.

Another addition to his empire was television. In 1966, the series *Buck Owens' Ranch*, a half-hour music program, provided first rate country music entertainment. It also spread the message of the Bakersfield sound in a way that the Nashville sound was not being heard. Although the television debut was successful, it was as the host of *Hee Haw* that Owens became a superstar.

Along with co-host Roy Clark, Owens delivered authentic country music to millions of viewers every week. The popularity of *Hee Haw* was overwhelming and epitomized the peak of country music popularity throughout the early 1970s. *The Glen Campbell Show* and *The Johnny Cash Show* were other country flavored variety programs. Later on, the Mandrell sisters would host their own one hour musical variety program.

Owens' appearance on *Hee Haw* also boosted his record sales, although he was already a top selling artist. During this period, "The Kansas City Song," "I Wouldn't Live in New York City (If They Gave Me the Whole Dang Town)," "Bridge Over Troubled Water," "Ruby (Are You Mad?)," "Rollin' in My Sweet Baby's Arms," "I'll Still Be Waiting for you," "Made in Japan," and "It's a Monster's Holiday" graced the charts. He was one of the most recognizable figures in country music.

In the latter part of the 1970s his career lost some of the momentum built up during the previous fifteen years. A series of unfortunate happenings, including the cancellation of *Buck Owens' Ranch*, the death of his longtime best friend and partner Don Rich, and the fact that his once fresh sound was being copied by everyone else, contributed to his decline. He suffered from severe depression over the death of Rich, who had perished in a motorcycle accident. Owens was never the same again.

In 1975, he started to record in Nashville and his once sharp sound adopted the more lush, pop oriented treatment. A hit duet with Emmylou Harris in 1979, "Play Together Again," breathed some life into his softening sales. The reruns of *Hee Haw* enabled him to maintain a slice of popularity.

In 1980, he seriously cut back on live performances, the one side of his career that hadn't suffered a decline. He semi-retired and remained so until the late 1980s, when Dwight Yoakam coaxed him to do a show. Together they cut a fresh version of "Streets of Bakersfield" and performed on television. The new version of an old classic reached number one, prompting Owens to record and perform on a more regular basis.

However, his brief spurt of energy faded and he returned to his previous semi-retirement state. But the re-release of many of his songs on CD boosted his sales, as did the neo-traditionalists who recorded honky tonk in an electric vein, imitating Owens. Although he was not a regular performer or recorder, through the efforts of others he remained current in country music circles.

On March 25, 2006, the Baron of Bakersfield, responsible for lifting country music out of its doldrums, passed away.

Buck Owens was a country music innovator. Throughout his career he proved many times that he wasn't afraid to go against the standard practice to implement his fresh ideas. He backed up his bold statements with his playing and the many hit records he enjoyed. Also, he proved that he was an astute businessman in an industry where many musicians are usually short-changed by greedy managers, promoters and record executives.

Owens was a first class guitar player who could kick out hard driving honky tonk with the best of them. His use of the electric guitar churning out dynamic sounds was a revelation. Although not the first to use the amplified instruments on country recordings, more than anyone before him he gave his songs a powerful, rock and roll pulse that contained a much harder edged than the rockabilly of the 1950s.

Owens worked with a large number of country artists and just about anyone who passed through from the 1950s to the mid–1980s shared a stage with him. A partial list includes Dwight Yoakam, Tammy Wynette, George Jones, Merle Haggard, Marty Stuart, Tommy Collins, Wynn Stewart, Scott Joss, Roger Miller, Bonnie Owens, Johnny Cash, Ray Charles, Faron Young, Conway Twitty, and Willie Nelson. Perhaps one of his most important partners was Roy Clark, the two sharing hosting duties on *Hee Haw*. Undoubtedly, his best musical friend was Don Rich, although he worked with others, including Jerry Brightman, George French, Bobby Austin,

Ken Presley, Jay McDonald, Wayne Wilson, Mel King, Kenny Pierce, Susan Raye, Pee Wee Adams, Wayne Stone, and Allen Williams.

Since he was such a powerful figure in country music it is understandable that he was a prime influence on a number of individuals, including Marty Stuart, Dwight Yoakam, George Bedard, Gram Parsons, Stevie Moore, Radney Foster, Red Simpson, Scott Joss, Dale Watson, and many others. His decision to plug in foreshadowed the second marriage between rock and roll and country that would have an important impact on the Eagles, Linda Ronstadt, the Nitty Gritty Band, the Flying Burrito Brothers, Ozark Mountain Daredevils, and others.

One of his most important achievements was the establishment of the Bakersfield sound—a direct attack on the softening Nashville style. It took courage to defy the Nashville hold on country music, but Owens was just the man to take on the challenge. In turn, he spurred on other artists including Willie Nelson, to establish their own identity.

In 1996, Buck Owens was inducted to the Country Music Hall of Fame. It was a proper honor for someone who was such a seminal figure during the past 40 years. He was a bona fide country music star who blazed his own trail and remains a household name today because of his vast achievements as the Baron of Bakersfield.

## The Buckaroos
Circa 1960s

| *Guitar* | *Steel Guitar* | *Fiddle* | *Bass* |
| --- | --- | --- | --- |
| Buck Owens | Tom Brumley | Don Rich | Doyle Holly |
| Doyle Holly | Ralph Mooney | | |

## Discography

*Under Your Spell Again*, Capitol 1489.
*Buck Owens* [1961], Capitol T-1489.
*Buck Owens Sings Harlan Howard*, Sundazed 6101.
*You're for Me*, Sundazed 7539.
*Famous Country Music Sound of Buck Owens*, Starday 172.
*On the Bandstand*, Sundazed 6044.
*Buck Owens Sings Tommy Collins*, Sundazed 6102.
*Together Again/My Heart Skips a Beat*, Sundazed 6030.
*I Don't Care*, Sundazed 6046.
*I've Got a Tiger by the Tail*, Sundazed 6047.
*Before You Go/No One But You*, Sundazed 2353.
*Christmas with Buck Owens*, Sundazed 6162.
*Roll Out the Red Carpet*, Sundazed 6050.
*Dust on Mother's Bible*, Capitol 2497.
*The Carnegie Hall Concert* [live], Sundazed 11090.

*Open Up Your Heart,* Sundazed 6051.
*Buck Owens and His Buckaroos in Japan!* [live], Capitol 2715.
*Your Tender Loving Care,* Capitol 2760.
*In Japan* [live], Capitol 2715.
*It Takes People Like You to Make People Like Me,* Sundazed 6105.
*Sweet Rosie Jones,* Capitol 2962.
*Christmas Shopping,* Sundazed 6163.
*I've Got You on My Mind Again,* Capitol 131.
*A Night on the Town,* Capitol 2902.
*Meanwhile Back at the Ranch,* Capitol 2973.
*The Buck Owens' Buckaroos Strike Again!,* Capitol 2828.
*Anywhere U. S. A.,* Capitol 194.
*Roll Your Own with Buck Owens' Buckaroos,* Capitol 322.
*Buck Owens in London,* Capitol 232.
*Tall Dark Stranger,* Capitol 212.
*The Buck Owens: The Guitar Player,* Capitol 2944.
*Your Mother's Prayer,* Capitol 439.
*Big in Vegas,* Capitol 413.
*Kickin' In,* Curb 95340.
*Buck Owens* [1970], Capitol 574.
*A Merry Hee Haw Christmas,* Capitol 486.
*Boot Hill,* Capitol ST 550.
*Rompin' and Stompin,* Capitol ST 440.
*The Great White Horse,* Capitol 558.
*The Kansas City Song,* Capitol 476.
*Bridge Over Troubled Water,* Sundazed 6214.
*Buck Owens' Ruby and Other Bluegrass Specials,* Capitol 795.
*Merry Christmas from Buck Owens and Susan,* Capitol ST 837.
*Play the Hits,* Capitol ST 767.
*Ruby and Other Bluegrass Specials,* Sundazed 6215.
*I Wouldn't Live in New York City,* Capitol 628.
*Buck Owens Live at the Nugget,* Capitol 11039.
*Live at the John Ascuga's Nugget,* ST 11039.
*Live at the White House,* Capitol 1105.
*Too Old to Cut the Mustard?,* Capitol 874.
*Ain't It Amazing Gracie,* Capitol 11180.
*In the Palm of Your Hand,* Capitol 11136.
*Arms Full of Empty,* Capitol 11222.
*Good Old Days,* Capitol 11204.
*It's a Monster's Holiday,* Capitol 11471.
*Live at the Sydney Opera House,* Capitol 23372.
*Live in New Zealand,* Capitol 23261.
*41st Street Lonely Hearts Club,* Capitol 11390.
*Buck 'Em,* Warner Bros. 2952.
*Hot Dog!,* Capitol 91132.
*Act Naturally* [Capitol], Capitol 92893.
*Live at Carnegie Hall,* Country Music Foundation 12.
*In London,* Sundazed 1095.
*A-11,* Capitol 44295.
*Second Fiddle,* Capitol 44248.
*The Best of Buck Owens,* Capitol 2105.
*The Instrumental Hits of Buck Owens and His Buckaroos,* Sundazed 6049.

*The Buck Owens Song Book*, Capitol 2436.
*The Best of Buck Owens, Vol. 2*, Capitol 2897.
*Close-Up*, Capitol 257–2.
*The Best of Buck Owens, Vol. 3*, Capitol 145.
*Open Your Heart/Roll Out the Red Carpet/I've Got You on My Mind Again*, Capitol STCL-574.
*The Best of Buck Owens*, Capitol 830.
*Best of Buck and Susan*, Capitol 11084.
*Best of Buck Owens, Vol. 5*, Capitol 11273.
*Best of Buck Owens, Vol. 6*, Capitol 11471.
*All-Time Greatest Hits, Vol. 1*, Curb 77342.
*Rhythm and Booze*, That's Country TC 020.
*The Buck Owens Collection (1959–1990)*, Rhino R2-71016.
*All-Time Greatest Hits, Vol. 2*, Curb 77568.
*All-Time Greatest Hits, Vol. 3*, Capitol/Curb 77649.
*The Very Best of Buck Owens, Vol. 1*, Rhino 71816.
*The Very Best of Buck Owens, Vol. 2*, Rhino 71817.
*Buck Owens Story, Vol. 1*, Personality 23017.
*Buck Owens Story, Vol. 2*, Personality 23018.
*Buck Owens Story, Vol. 3*, Personality 23018.
*Half a Buck: Buck Owens Greatest Duets*, K-Tel 3582.
*Greatest Hits, Vol. 2*: The Streets of Bakersfield, Country Stars *55450*.
*Greatest Hits, Vol. 1*: Act Naturally, Country Stars *55449*.
*40 Greatest Hits*, Double 102021.
*Act Naturally* [Golden Stars], Golden Stars 5277.
*Good Old Country*, St. Clair 78252.
*Young Buck: The Complete Pre-Capitol Recordings*, Audium 8124.
*Blue Love*, Sundown 55.
*Buckaroo*, Goldies 25376.
*Country Music Legend*, Legacy 162.
*After the Dance*, Masked Weasel 301.

# JOHNNY CASH (1932–2003)
## *The Man in Black*

There has always been a rebellious nature to country music, a dark side to its multi-faceted personality. Many of the early songs were about outlaws, those desperadoes who dared to live outside the rules of proper society and because of their chosen path in life they often attracted attention. Few country singers have lived life on the edge and made a bigger impact on the music than the man in black. His name is Johnny Cash.

John R. Cash was born on February 26, 1932, in Kingsland, Arkansas. He was the son of poor cotton farmers and became acquainted with hard work as a little boy. However, music provided a place of comfort, a magical universe to escape to when the reality of life became too much to bear. As a youngster, he experienced tragedy first hand. His family moved to Dyess County, a government resettlement place, in order to survive the Mississippi River flood of 1937. The incident would later find its way into one of his songs, "Five Feet High and Rising."

The family eventually numbered seven children that put further strains on their already difficult financial situation, and music seemed their only salvation. They sang in the choir and one of Cash's brothers, Roy, formed a band, the Delta Rhythm Makers, that played on radio dates and fueled Johnny's dreams. In 1944, tragedy struck the family once again when brother Jack died in an industrial accident. It made a deep, lasting impact on Johnny.

Upon graduation, he worked a series of low paying jobs in a body shop in Detroit, and other industrial factories. He might have remained a general laborer the rest of his life, but he instead decided to enlist in the Air Force. While in the military he learned how to play the guitar and honed his skills as a songwriter. His four-year stint ended in 1954, and he moved to Memphis with his wife.

Once in Tennessee, he sold electrical appliances before taking a course on radio broadcasting. Although he met with initial frustrations when trying to build his musical career, he facilitated his efforts when he hooked up with guitarist Luther Perkins and bassist Marshall Grant. The three sounded good together and performed cover versions as well as Cash originals on a Memphis radio station.

They eventually attracted the attention of Sam Phillips, owner of Sun Records, and after a failed audition, Cash returned with a couple of gems, "Cry, Cry, Cry," and "Hey Porter." The producer liked what he heard and the cuts were released as Johnny's first singles in 1955. Perkins and Grant backed Cash on the record and were dubbed the Tennessee Two. A second single, "Folsom Prison Blues," which he had written during his service days, was released the same year and was another big hit that led to an appearance on the *Louisiana Hayride*, where he remained for a year.

Although he had made some inroads into establishing his career, it was the 1956 release of "I Walk the Line" that truly made him a star. It was both a country and pop hit. The popularity of the song meant more tour dates. Another single, "There You Go," only enhanced his popularity. His meteoric rise announced that there was a new artistic force on the scene.

In 1957, he scored with "Give My Love to Rose," adding to his burgeoning stardom, and also made his debut on the *Grand Ole Opry*. Cash, a rebel from the start, showed up dressed completely in black, a stark contrast to the cowboy regalia that others sported. Because of his penchant for the solid dark color, he was dubbed the Man in Black.

His first full album, *Johnny Cash with His Hot and Blue Guitar*, was an instant hit, as was his next single, "Ballad of a Teenage Queen." Another song, "Guess Things Happen That Way," was added to his list of chart placements. After some personal disagreements with Phillips, Cash signed with Columbia in 1958. His debut on the label, "All Over Again," continued his string of big hits.

He continued his success into the 1960s. "Don't Take Your Guns to Town," "I Got Stripes," "In the Jailhouse Now," "Ring of Fire," "Understand Your Man," "The Ballad of Iza Hayes," "It Ain't Me, Babe," "Orange Blossom Special," "The One on Your Right Is on Your Left," and "Rosanna's Going Wild" were all chart toppers. He recorded a gospel album, *Hymns by Johnny Cash*, and grinded out a relentless tour schedule, making over 300 appearances per year. In order to keep up with the hectic pace, he turned to pep pills and sank into an ever increasing drug dependency.

He started to work with June Carter, she of the famous country musical family, as early as 1961, but their relationship would not blossom until a few years later. In 1962, he toured camps in Korea playing for the soldiers to loud cheers but was brought down to earth at his Carnegie Hall date where he went over badly. It was evident that drugs and exhaustion were starting to catch up to him, but he continued to plug ahead.

In 1964, he appeared at the Newport Folk Festival and joined Bob Dylan onstage. The two entertained the crowd and Cash would call on Dylan's help later on in the decade to record an album. Johnny released the album *Bitter Tears*, a tribute to the trials and tribulations of the American Indian. However, he was near the end of the line as he teetered over the edge of self-destruction.

In 1965, he fell off that edge when state troopers in El Paso stopped him and discovered a guitar case full of pep pills. He was fined and given a thirty day suspended sentence and a stern warning. In 1966, he found himself in hot water for embarking on a magic mushroom gathering spree in the wee hours of the morning. His once promising career suffered further decline.

He was in poor health and experienced frequent blackouts. Just when it seemed that he would die, his honky tonk angel, June Carter, appeared on the scene. Although they had known each other for some time, she was now divorced from Carl Smith, and decided to rescue Cash. She helped him kick drugs and alcohol, and set his career back on track. They were married in 1968.

The rejuvenation of Johnny Cash continued into 1969, when he won six major country music awards for best male vocalist, entertainer of the year, best single, best album, outstanding service award, and (with June

Carter) best vocal group. They became the coolest couple in country music and one of the most visible. When he recorded the album *Nashville Skyline* with Bob Dylan, he became a favorite in rock circles.

The Man in Black decided to do something for inmates and recorded *Folsom Prison Blues* in Folsom Prison. Although not the first singer to record a song in front of a jailhouse setting (B. B. King had preceded him by a few years), Cash's album was highly successful. He continued the trend with *Johnny Cash at San Quentin*, which yielded the massive hit "A Boy Named Sue."

In 1969, he and his wife landed their own television show called the *Johnny Cash Show*. On the first episode Bob Dylan appeared, ensuring that a large section of the rock audience would tune in. Although the show was cancelled after a short two year run, it made a lasting impression. It was one of three country music shows on TV (the corny *Hee Haw* and *The Glen Campbell Hour* were the other two). Cash also appeared in the movie *Gunfight* staring opposite Kirk Douglas.

Cash started off the 1970s with a performance at the White House, worked with John Williams and the Boston Pops Orchestra, appeared in his own documentary, continued to enjoy chart success and seemed to be everywhere. He had conquered every form of media. By this time the Man in Black was a household name.

Although his music career came first, he also was involved in a number of community activities at home and abroad. Always an outspoken individual on many issues, he and his wife performed many concerts with the benefits going to help Native Americans. He also displayed a religious side, joining Billy Graham and making a film about his trip to the Holy Land in 1973.

Although he had trouble scoring top ten hits as the decade wore on, his fame was secure. By this point he could partake in non-serious recording sessions without jeopardizing his stardom, including his religious work. His non-musical activities kept him in the public eye.

The 1980s proved a tough decade for Cash because of a dearth of hits, but he had fun recording *The Survivors* with Jerry Lee Lewis in 1982. Later he hooked up with a bunch of country outlaws who called themselves the Highwaymen—Waylon Jennings, Willie Nelson, and Kris Kristofferson. They didn't garner any major awards for their effort, but they enjoyed working with one another.

In 1992, the Highwaymen came together again to record another album. A third release, *The Road Goes on Forever*, appeared in 1995. On a solo note, Cash left Mercury after seven years and signed with American Records. His career received a boost with his first effort, *American Recordings*, a touching collection of acoustic songs.

In 1996, he released *Unchained* featuring a guest appearance from Tom Petty and the Heartbreakers. As he had done so many years before, the crafty Cash aligned himself with rock audiences, although by this time he was seventy years old and his rockabilly days were lost in another dimension of time. But exposure on VH-1's *Storytellers* series in 1998 proved to be good for his career. In 2000, he released *Love, God, Murder*, a three-disc, greatest hits package that celebrated the wealth of his music. *Solitary Man* came out later that year.

However, the biggest news surrounding him in the 1990s was his various health problems, forcing the Man in Black to spend too much time in hospitals. On September 12, 2003, in Nashville, the revered Johnny Cash passed away. It was an international day of mourning.

Johnny Cash was a country music superstar. He overcame many obstacles to achieve his heralded status and became one of the most important figures in post World War II music circles. He developed a style that was all his own, instantly recognizable and very, very successful.

That voice—the dark masculine tone with the hint of a country accent and a heavy individuality—was always his calling card. Two notes into the song and the listener could identify it as a Johnny Cash tune. He was never mistaken for any other singer, and was undoubtedly one of the most original vocalists in the history. The friendly and soothing elements enabled him to acquire a legion of fans that didn't even like country music.

Johnny Cash was never mistaken for Jimi Hendrix. Although not a truly great axe-man, Cash had a sparse sound that when teamed with his voice created a personal musical universe. He was a man who epitomized playing a six string as a respectable endeavor. In many ways he was the opposite of the nascent slingers, since he played fewer notes, but still made an impact.

His influence covers country, pop, rock, and folk artists. A partial list includes the Mavericks, C.W. McCall, Red Sovine, Jeff Steven, John Fogerty, Curt Kirkwood, the Crook Brothers, Grace Braun, Sherrié Austin, the Wilkinsons, the Pine Valley Cosmonauts, Stompin' Tom Connors, Ike Reilly, Glen Campbell, John Denver, Jim Croce, Harry Chapin, Don McLean, Roy Clark, Willie Nelson, Kris Kristofferson, Merle Haggard, Charlie Pride, Waylon Jennings, Charlie Rich, and Bob Dylan, among others. A whole generation of newer country artists, including Garth Brooks, Ricky Skaggs, Randy Travis, Tim McGraw, Travis Tritt, Clint Black, Dwight Yoakam, and many others grew up listening to Johnny Cash.

He gave the world a number of great songs, including "Folsom Prison Blues," "I Walk the Line," "There You Go," "Don't Take Your Guns to Town," "I Got Stripes," "In the Jailhouse Now," "Ring of Fire,"

"Understand Your Man," "The Ballad of Iza Hayes," "It Ain't Me, Babe," "Orange Blossom Special," "The One on Your Right Is on Your Left," "Rosanna's Going Wild," "Daddy Sang Bass," and "A Boy Named Sue." With over a hundred singles reaching the charts he is easily one of the most successful country music artists of the last half of the century.

Johnny Cash was the youngest living artist to be elected to the Country Music Hall of Fame in 1980, a fitting honor for the singer who made country acceptable throughout the entire musical spectrum. He received hundreds of awards over the years as well as honorary degrees. With his tough, crackling voice, his unique guitar syncopation, his careful choice of material, his championing of minorities and the forgotten, the Man in Black carved out his own legend.

## Discography

*Ring of Fire: The Best of Johnny Cash*, Columbia 8853.
*The Original Sun Sound of Johnny Cash*, Sun 1275.
*Country Round Up*, Fontana 301.
*Mean As Hell*, Columbia 9246.
*Greatest Hits, Vol. 1*, CBS 2678.
*Golden Sounds of Country Music*, Harmony 11249.
*Legends and Love Songs*, Columbia 363.
*Show Time*, Sun 106.
*Singing Story Teller*, Sun 115.
*Get Rhythm*, Sun 105.
*Story Songs of the Trains and Rivers*, Sun 104.
*The Holy Land*, Columbia 9726.
*The World of Johnny Cash*, CBS 66237.
*Original Golden Hits, Vol. 1*, Sun 100.
*Original Golden Hits, Vol. 2*, Sun 101.
*Walls of a Prison*, Harmony 30138.
*The Great Johnny Cash*, Hallmark 696.
*Original Johnny Cash* [Charly], Charly 30113.
*Rough Cut King of Country Music*, Sun 122.
*Legend* [Sun], Sun 118.
*Sunday Down South*, Sun 119.
*His Greatest Hits, Vol. 2*, CBS 30887.
*The Man, the World, His Music*, Sun 126.
*Sings Hank Williams*, Sun 1245.
*Understand the Man*, Harmony 30916.
*Original Golden Hits, Vol. 3*, Sun 127.
*Starportrait*, CBS 67201.
*Give My Love to Rose*, Harmony 31256.
*Johnny Cash Songbook*, Harmony 31602.
*Magnificent Johnny Cash*, Hallmark 777.
*Original Rockabilly*, Sun 147.
*Sunday Morning Coming Down*, DCC 173.
*Mighty Johnny Cash*, Hallmark 804.

*This Is Johnny Cash*, Harmony 11342.
*Gentle Giant of Country*, Sun 6641161.
*Five Feet High and Rising (A Cash Country Collection)*, CBS 32951.
*I Forgot to Remember*, Hallmark 884.
*Kings of Country*, Musidisc 174.
*Spotlight on Johnny Cash*, Sun 01.
*At Folsom Prison and San Quentin*, Columbia 33639.
*Story of a Broken Heart*, Hallmark 897.
*Making a Legend*, Charly 18051.
*Names and Places*, Embassy 31548.
*The Unissued Johnny Cash*, Bear Family 15016.
*Johnny and June*, Bear Family 15030.
*20 Foot Tappin' Greats*, CBS 10009.
*Greatest Hits*, CBS 35637.
*Johnny Cash* [Pickwick], Pickwick 2052.
*Rock Island Line*, Hilltop 6101.
*Portrait*, CBS 64516.
*Greatest Hits, Vol. 3*, Columbia 83274.
*I'm So Lonesome I Could Cry*, Hallmark 3027.
*Encore*, CBS 37355.
*A Free Man*, CBS 85032.
*Johnny Cash*, Time Life TLCW-03.
*The Cowboys*, Ronco 2070.
*18 Legendary Performances*, Premier 1015.
*I Believe*, Supraphon/CBS 1113.3278.
*Biggest Hits*, CBS 8345262.
*Great Songs*, Astan 20086.
*The Best of Johnny Cash* [Creole], Creole 1223.
*The Sun Years* [Charly], Charly 1.
*Country Boy*, Charly 18.
*Johnny Cash*, Bellaphon 28807002.
*Up Through the Years, 1955–1957*, Bear Family 15247.
*First Years*, Allegiance D2-72926.
*Vintage Years: 1955–1963*, Rhino 70229.
*Columbia Records 1958–1986*, Columbia 40637.
*I Walk the Line* [Intertape], Intertape 500063.
*Home of the Blues*, Topline 521.
*18 Golden Hits* [Spectrum], Spectrum 85008.
*20 Greatest Hits*, Starr 2901 3001.
*Country Store*, Masterpiece 11.
*Great Country Love Songs*, Pickwick 014.
*Original Hits*, Big Country 2430712.
*Legend* [Prima], Prima 115.
*Lil' Bit of Gold*, Rhino 373002.
*1955–1958 Recordings*, Charly 146.
*Born to Lose*, Instant 5007.
*The Man in Black: 1954–1958*, Bear Family 15517.
*Greatest Hits, Vol. 2* [Country Stars], Satellite 7550.
*The Sun Years* [Rhino], Rhino 70950.
*I Walk the Line and Other Great Hits*, Rhino 70343.
*The Best of Johnny Cash* [Curb], Curb 77494.
*Many Sides of Johnny Cash*, Sony Music 19845.

*Blood Sweat and Tears*, Bear Family 155631.
*Mean as Hell*, Bear Family 155632.
*From Sea to Shining Sea*, Bear Family 155634.
*The Man in Black: 1959–1962*, Bear Family 15562.
*Come Along and Ride This Train*, Bear Family 15563.
*Collection* [Castle], Castle CCS146.
*Giant Hits*, Sony Special 15713.
*Gospel Glory*, Sony Special 21608.
*The Gospel Collection*, Columbia/Legacy 48952.
*The Essential Johnny Cash 1955–1983*, Columbia/Legacy 47991.
*Hello, I'm Johnny Cash* [Sony Special Products], Sony Special 13832.
*Hits* [1993], Sony 17570.
*Gold Collection*, Déjà vu 106.
*Super Hits*, Sony 66773.
*Back to Back*, K-Tel 3193.
*Wanted Man*, Mercury 522709.
*Personal Christmas Collection*, Columbia/Legacy 64154.
*Greatest Hits: Finest Performances*, Sun 7001.
*Lonesome Me*, Chicago Music 108.
*Folsom Prison Blues*, Charly 8101.
*Ring of Fire/Blood Sweat and Tears/Ballads of American Indians*, Sony 64812.
*Get Rhythm: The Best of the Sun Years*, Essential Gold 4257.
*Johnny Cash Sings His Best*, TeeVee 6006.
*Ultimate*, Bransounds 1505.
*Golden Hits*, Intercontinent 1002.
*The Man in Black: 1963–1969*, Bear Family 15588.
*Live*, Fat Boy 235.
*Many Sides Of: 36 All-Time Greatest Hits*, Sony 50492.
*The Best of Johnny Cash* [Columbia], Columbia 483725.
*The Christmas Spirit* [Sony Special Products], Sony Special 24082.
*Hits*, PolyGram 534665.
*I Walk the Line*, Beacon 51592.
*18 Golden Hits* [Galaxy], Galaxy 388418.
*The Rebel*, Ariola Express 01000.
*Crazy Country*, Sony 28791.
*There You Go*, Cleopatra 409.
*16 Biggest Hits*, Sony 69739.
*I Walk the Line: The Very Best of Johnny Cash*, Collectables 515.
*Man in Black: Greatest Hits*, Columbia/Legacy 65752.
*Great*, Festival 31056.
*The Very Best of Johnny Cash*, Charly 8241.
*His Greatest Hits Old and New*, Hallmark 30003.
*Ring of Fire*, Goldies 25345.
*Ballad of Ira Hayes*, Goldies 63256.
*Essential Sun Collection*, Recall 213.
*The Complete Sun Singles*, Varese 6056.
*I Walk the Line/Little Fauss and Big Halsey* [original soundtrack], Bear Family 16130.
*Original Golden Hits, Vol. 1–2*, Collectables 6425.
*Get Rhythm/Story Songs of the Trains and Rivers*, Collectables 6427.
*Singing Story Teller/Rough Cut King of Country Music*, Collectables 6431.
*Sunday Down South/Sings Hank Williams*, Collectables 6432.
*Showtime/Original Golden Hits, Vol. 3*, Collectables 6433.

*Sings I Walk the Line/Sings Folsom Prison Blues*, Collectables 6437.
*Sings the Greatest Hits/The Blue Train*, Collectables 6438.
*Greatest Hits of Johnny Cash, Vol. 1*, Platinum Disc 1498.
*Greatest Hits of Johnny Cash, Vol. 2*, Platinum Disc 1499.
*Greatest Hits of Johnny Cash*, Platinum Disc 1522.
*Best of Johnny Cash* [Castle], Castle 145.
*Johnny Cash*, Valmark 1171.
*Gold Collection* [Retro], Retro Music 4056.
*Murder*, Columbia/Legacy 65543.
*Love*, Columbia/Legacy 65544.
*God*, Columbia/Legacy 65545.
*Love, God, Murder*, Columbia/Legacy 63809.
*The Collection* [Madacy Disc 1], Madacy 5865.
*The Collection* [Madacy Disc 2], Madacy 25866.
*The Collection* [Madacy Disc 3], 25867.
*Johnny Cash: The Legend* [Double Play], Double Play 4053.
*Collection* [Madacy Disc 1], Madacy 820.
*Complete Live at San Quentin*, Columbia/Legacy 66017.
*The Legend at His Best: Ultimate Box Set and Autobiography*, Collectables 310050.
*Country Music Hall of Fame: 1980*, King 3823.
*The Sun Years, Vol. 1*, Original Sun 41005.
*A Living Legend*, TeeVee 6029.
*Best of the Best*, Federal 6548.
*The EP Collection*, See For Miles 719.
*Hymns by Johnny Cash/Sings Precious Memories*, DCC 202.
*Return to the Promised Land*, Renaissance 235.
*Very Best of Johnny Cash, Vol. 1*, Collectables 6146.
*Very Best of Johnny Cash, Vol. 2*, Collectables 6347
*Road Less Travelled: Sun Recordings*, Varese 066214.
*San Quentin to Folsom: Best of Johnny Cash*, St. Clair 132.
*The Very Best of the Sun Years*, Metro 45.
*The Legends Collection*, Dressed to Kill 581.
*Signature Series*, Direct Source 1494.
*Fabulous Johnny Cash/Songs of Our Soil*, Sony 494806.
*16 Biggest Hits, Vol. 2*, Sony 85726.
*Man in Black: Very Best of Johnny Cash*, Sony 503023.
*The Sun Years, Vol. 2*, Original Sun 41015.
*Sun Records 50th Anniversary Edition*, Direct Source 3707.
*Ragged Old Flag/Patriot*, S and P 702.
*His Sun Years*, Charly 55706.
*The Legends Collection, Vol. 1*, Dressed to Kill 291546.
*Legends Collection, Vol. 2*, Dressed to Kill 291547.
*Johnny Cash Collection* [Country Stars] 50581.
*Simply the Best*, Sony 4837259.
*Christmas with Johnny Cash*, Madacy 5054.
*Wanted Man: The Very Best of Johnny Cash*, Sony 498427.
*The Essential Johnny Cash*, Columbia 86290.
*The Man in Black: The International Johnny Cash*, Bear Family 16601.
*The Legend of Johnny Cash: The First Original Hits*, K-Tel 3515.
*Johnny Cash Sings His Best*, TeeVee 7424.
*At Folsom Prison/At San Quentin/America*, Columbia 86502.
*The Essential Sun Singles*, Varese 066332.

*20th Century Masters—The Millennium Collection: The Best of Johnny Cash*, Mercury 170217.
*Johnny Cash and Friends*, Universal International 544902.
*Cry, Cry, Cry*, Trad Line 1394.
*A Heart of a Legend*, Madacy 6494.
*A Boy Named Johnny*, Musicbank 1164.
*Classic American Voices*, Direct Source 2521.
*Artist's Choice*, Sony 90712.
*Unearthed*, American Recordings 000167902.
*Universal Masters Collection*, Universal International 981041.
*All American Country*, Universal International 5525558.
*The Songs That Made Him Famous*, Get Back 7520.
*Hey Porter*, Gusto 561.
*Cash Sings Cash*, Varese 066537.
*Life*, Columbia 91108.
*Hayride Anthology*, Cleopatra 1385.
*Original Outlaw*, Prism 1210.
*Life Goes On*, Rajon 373.
*Ultimate Christmas Collection*, Madacy 51530.
*Johnny Cash Reads the Complete New Testament*, Thomas Nelson Pub., 459.
*Traveling Cash: An Imaginary Journey*, Bear Family 16820.
*Superbilly*, Sun 1002.
*Johnny Cash and the Tennessee 2* [16 Golden Hits], Bellaphon 102.
*Johnny Cash with His Hot and Blue Guitar*, Sun 1220.
*The Fabulous Johnny Cash* [Columbia], Columbia 8122.
*The Songs That Made Him Famous*, Sun 1235.
*Greatest!*, Sun 1240.
*Songs of Our Soil*, Columbia 8148.
*Hymns by Johnny Cash*, Columbia 8125.
*Ride This Train*, Columbia 8255.
*Now, There Was a Song!*, Columbia/Legacy 66506.
*The Lure of the Grand Canyon*, Columbia 8422.
*Now Here's Johnny Cash*, Sun 1255.
*The Sound of Johnny Cash*, Columbia 8602.
*Hymns from the Heart*, Columbia 8522.
*All Aboard the Blue Train*, Sun 1270.
*Blood Sweat and Tears*, Columbia/Legacy 66508.
*The Christmas Spirit* [Columbia], Columbia 8917.
*Keep on the Sunnyside*, CBS 8952.
*I Walk the Line* [Columbia], Columbia 8990.
*Bitter Tears*, Columbia/Legacy 66507.
*Orange Blossom Special*, Columbia 9109.
*Ballads of the True West*, Columbia 62591.
*Sings the Ballads of the True West*, Columbia 838.
*Everybody Loves a Nut*, Columbia 9292.
*That's What You Get for Loving Me*, CBS 9337.
*Happiness Is You*, Columbia 62760.
*Carryin' On*, Columbia 9528.
*From Sea to Shining Sea*, Columbia 62972.
*Heart of Cash*, CSP STS 2004.
*Old Golden Throat*, CBS 63318.
*At Folsom Prison* [live], Columbia/Legacy 65955.

*Johnny Cash* [CBS], CBS 52705.
*More Old Golden Throat*, CBS 63521.
*Jackson*, CBS 9528.
*Grand Canyon Suite*, Columbia 7425.
*Hello, I'm Johnny Cash* [CBS], Columbia 943.
*At San Quentin* [live], CBS 28090/9.
*Johnny Cash Show*, CBS 64089.
*Little Fauss and Big Halsy*, Columbia 70087.
*A Man in Black*, Columbia 30550.
*I Walk the Line*, Hilltop J56097.
*International Superstar*, CBS 67284.
*A Thing Called Love*, CBS 31332.
*Christmas and the Cash Family*, CBS 31764.
*Family Christmas*, Columbia 31754.
*Johnny Cash Family Christmas*, Sony Special 24083.
*America: A 200-Year Salute in Story and Song*, Columbia 31645.
*The Gospel Road Pt. 1* [Soundtrack], CBS 65661.
*The Gospel Road Pt. 2* [Soundtrack], CBS 65662.
*The Gospel Road* [Soundtrack], CBS 32253.
*Country and Western Superstar*, CBS 68224.
*Pa Osteraker*, Columbia 32029.
*Any Old Wind That Blows*, Columbia 32091.
*Johnny Cash and His Woman*, CBS 32443.
*I Walk the Line* [CBS], CBS 70083.
*At Osteraker Prison* [live], CBS 65308.
*Junkie and Juicehead*, Columbia 33086.
*Ragged Old Flag*, CBS 32917.
*John R. Cash*, Columbia 33370.
*Riding the Rails*, CBS 88153.
*Children's Album*, CBS 32898.
*Look at Them Beans*, Columbia 34193.
*Sings Precious Memories*, Epic 33087.
*Destination Victoria Station*, CBS 150.
*Strawberry Cake*, Columbia 34088.
*One Piece at a Time*, Columbia 34193.
*Last Gunfighter Ballad*, Columbia 34314.
*The Rambler*, Columbia 34833.
*I Would Like to See You Again*, Columbia 35313.
*Gone Girl*, CBS 35646.
*Folsom Prison Blues*, Sun 140.
*I Walk the Line*, Sun 139.
*Silver*, Columbia 36086.
*A Boy Named Sue*, CBS 31827.
*Rockabilly Blues*, Columbia 36779.
*Classic Christmas*, CBS 36866.
*A Believer Sings the Truth*, CBS 38074.
*Rockabilly Blues*, Koch 7979.
*The Baron*, CBS 37179.
*Adventures of Johnny Cash*, CBS 85881.
*Inside a Swedish Prison*, Bear Family 15092.
*Survivors Live*, Razor and Tie 85609.
*Johnny 99*, Koch 7980.

*Rainbow*, CBS 26689.
*Believe in Him*, Word 47828.
*Heroes*, Razor and Tie 2078.
*Classic Cash: Hall of Fame Series*, Mercury 834526–1.
*Is Coming to Town*, Mercury 832031.
*I Love Country*, CBS 4611292.
*Water from the Wells of Home*, Mercury 834778–1.
*Boom Chicka Boom*, Mercury 842155.
*Patriot*, CBS 45384.
*The Mystery of Life*, Mercury 848051.
*Bring It Back Alive*, Realive 35.
*Country Christmas*, Laserlight 15417.
*Hey Good Lookin', Vol. 3*, Cece 66142.
*American Recordings*, American/Sony 69402.
*Unchained*, Warner 43097.
*Live and on the Air*, Double Gold 53054.
*VH-1 Storytellers* [live], Sony 69416.
*Just as I Am*, Vanguard 79530.
*American III: Solitary Man* [LP], Sony 69691.
*Christmas with Johnny Cash*, Madcy 5056.
*At Madison Square Garden*, Columbia/Legacy 86808.
*American IV: The Man Comes Around*, Universal 063339.
*The Good, the Bad and the Two Cookie Kid*, A Better Place 1–882436–0.
*Sings Folsom Prison Blues*, Get Back Italy 7512.
*Live at Town Hall Party 1958*, Sundazed 5170.
*Live at Town Hall Party 1959*, Sundazed 5171.
*A Concert: Behind Prison Walls*, Eagle 20027.
*Louisiana Hayride*, Emergent 270506.
*Get Rhythm and His Life Goes On*, Dynamic 4002.
*Country Legend, Vol. 1*, Madacy 4996.
*Country Legend, Vol. 2*, Madacy 4997.
*My Mother's Hymn Book*, American 000236202.
*Live from Austin TX*, New West 6085.
*Johnny Cash Live: Good Evenin' Asbury Park*, Hyena 9345.
*Duets*, Sony 678344.
*We the People*, Folk Era 1469.

# CHARLIE RICH (1932–1995)
## *The Silver Fox*

Like other genres, fame in country music has often been earned through patience, effort and dedication. Some seemed to have gained stardom overnight while others toiled for years before achieving the recognition they were due. One of these individuals was known as the Silver Fox. His name was Charlie Rich.

Charlie Rich was born on December 14, 1932, in Colt, Arkansas. He developed an early interest in music, but not country. As a piano player, he was driven by the hot sounds of American roots music including blues and jazz, two avenues he pursued in high school and at the University of Arkansas. He could have very well become a jazz or blues singer, however, country twang eventually won out.

His musical ambitions weren't even interrupted by a stint in the U.S. Air Force; in fact, they were bolstered. He was stationed in Oklahoma and joined the Velvetones, a pickup band that jammed on old blues and jazz standards. The lead singer in the group, Margaret Ann, would become Rich's future wife.

Upon his release from the military, he moved to Memphis, Tennessee, and played in jazz and blues clubs. He honed his musical skills and the move paid off when he was hired by Judd Phillips, brother of Sam Phillips, the man who ran Sun Records. Eventually, Rich hooked up with saxophone player Bill Justis, who also recorded for the label and wrote arrangements for the horn players.

Although he failed his initial tryout for Sun because he was still deeply involved in jazz and blues, when the company delved into rockabilly, Sam Phillips changed his mind. Rich became a session musician and could be heard on songs cut by Johnny Cash, Jerry Lee Lewis, Justis, Warren Smith, Billy Lee Riley, Carl Mann, and Ray Smith. The stable of recording stars greatly benefited from Rich's contributions.

Aside from providing solid session piano, he also wrote "Break Up" for Jerry Lee Lewis, "The Ways of a Woman in Love" for Johnny Cash, and "I'm Comin' Home" for Carl Mann. But he also had a strong desire to wax his own material and received the opportunity in 1958, cutting "Whirlwind." Although the song didn't become a smash hit, it did expand his reputation as a songwriter and establish his penchant to be a recording artist.

In 1960, his diligence paid off when "Lonely Weekends," a song he recorded himself, became a top forty hit. However, the success was only a brief taste, since none of his other cuts released graced the charts. But Rich continued to write songs knowing that sooner or later one of them would score.

In 1964, he signed with the Groove label and enjoyed a better run of success. "Big Boss Man," "Tomorrow Night" and "I Don't See Me in Your Eyes Anymore" were all minor hits. However, it seemed as if he was snake bitten because the company went bankrupt soon after, and he was left without a recording contract. Rich was frustrated because there were other artists on the scene who were much more successful and weren't as talented.

He caught on with Smash Records some time later and he was encouraged to add rock and roll elements to his country songs. Rich accepted the opportunity and released "Mohair Sam" that reached the national charts. Things were looking up for him and he enjoyed a few other hits that bolstered his sagging career.

A brief time with Hi Records produced no great hits, so he switched to Epic in 1967. With the help of Billy Sherrill, Rich reinvented himself, shedding his jazzy/blues/rock and roll image in favor of more country flavored material. The move produced moderate success with the songs "Set Me Free" and "Raggedy Ann." But, he was still a few years removed from superstardom.

It wasn't until 1972 that Rich finally tasted true stardom with the single "I Take It On Home." A year later, he released the album *Behind Closed Doors*, and life was never the same for him again. It catapulted him into the top spot in the country charts and was also a massive pop hit. The title song, "Behind Closed Doors," along with "Tomorrow Night" and "The Most Beautiful Girl," introduced him to a much wider audience.

The album *Behind Close Doors* was the monster smash that he had been waiting for his entire career. It went gold and earned him a deluge of awards, including Best Male Vocalist, Album of the Year, and Single of the Year for the title track. He also won a Grammy for Best Male Country Vocal Performance. Suddenly he was as popular as Johnny Cash, Glen Campbell, Roy Clark, Willie Nelson, Buck Owens and Kris Kristofferson in country music circles.

He continued his momentum with several other releases, including "There Won't Be Anymore," "A Very Special Love Song," "I Don't See Me in Your Eyes Anymore," "I Love My Friend," and "She Called Me Baby." He illustrated what success could do for an artist when two of his previous songs (flops released on Smash Records), "A Field of Yellow Daisies" and "Something Just Came Over Me," were re-released and became hits due to his new found status.

The country award winning entertainer of the year in 1974 continued his success in 1975 with four top ten hits, "My Elusive Dreams," "Every Time You Touch Me (I Get High)," "All Over Me," and "Since I Fell for You." While he seemed to be on the verge of conquering the music scene again, his fall from grace began. He had developed a heavy drinking habit perhaps to deal with the pressures of his new found success. His bizarre behavior at the CMA ceremony in 1975 signaled his decline.

Although he would recover and have a few hits near the end of the 1970s, throughout the 1980s he was never able to regain his old magic. In 1981, he went into semi-retirement and didn't resurface until 1992 with

*Pictures and Paintings*, a jazz album. Although he was proud to be a musician, Rich detested the limelight and preferred to remain anonymous.

He would never regain his top status. On July 24, 1995, in Hammond, Louisiana, Charlie Rich, the Silver Fox, died from a blood clot.

Charlie Rich was a country music phenomenon. His career was like the flight path of a rocket. For years he struggled to take off the launching pad as a successful recording artist but failed. Then, suddenly, with one hit album, he exploded up the charts with a burning intensity. He peaked and then began his quick descent, eventually crashing down to earth. Despite the fact that his time in the sun was brief, he made enormous contributions to the genre.

Although he wasn't the first, Rich was one of the architects of countrypolitan, a style that appealed to the urban country crowd of the 1970s. With his earnest voice he was able to blend various styles into one cohesive and very commercial sound. His blend of blues, pop, country, rock, gospel, soul, and rockabilly paved the way for the music of the last twenty years. He gave each style a boost in popularity by mixing them together.

He influenced a number of figures, including Sam Phillips, Martin Willis, Sid Manker, J. M. Van Eaton, Jimmy Wilson, Bill Abbott, Asa Wilkerson, Roland Janes, Roy Orbison, Chet Atkins, Billy Riley, Otis Jett, Al Jackson, Jr., and Stan Kesler. Many of the artists that followed in his path were never able to weld as many different genres into one cohesive sound as Rich. He was the supreme unifier.

Charlie Rich was also a country music rebel. He had specific ideas of how his music should sound and would never surrender to a different point of view. Even during his brief and immense popularity, he was never one to toe the line. From the beginning he made it very clear that he was going to make the type of music on his own terms without compromise.

He gave the world a number of treasured classics. A short list includes "Behind Closed Doors," "The Most Beautiful Girl," "Whirlwind," "Lonely Weekends," "Big Boss Man," "Tomorrow Night," "I Don't See Me in Your Eyes Anymore" "Mohair Sam," "Set Me Free," "Raggedy Ann," "I Take It on Home," "Behind Closed Doors," "Tomorrow Night," "There Won't Be Anymore," "A Very Special Love Song," "I Love My Friend," "She Called Me Baby," "A Field of Yellow Daisies," "Something Just Came Over Me," "My Elusive Dreams," "Every Time You Touch Me (I Get High)," "All Over Me," and "Since I Fell for You." Although all of the aforementioned songs were not genuine hits, they were important to Rich's career.

While he has not been elected to the Country Music Hall of Fame, Rich will likely make it to the prestigious place some day. Even though he was never a pure country artist, he enabled the style to enjoy a stunning popularity that it wouldn't have realized without his contributions. Despite his quick fall from grace, there is no denying the Silver Fox's special place in the annals of country music history.

## Discography
*Lonely Weekends*, Sun/Philips 110.
*Charlie Rich*, Groove G-1000.
*The Many Sides of Charlie Rich*, Smash 697070.
*That's Rich*, RCA Victor 7719.
*Many New Sides*, Philips 7695.
*Charlie Rich Sings Country and Western*, Hi 32037.
*Set Me Free*, Koch 25164.
*A Lonely Weekend* [Mercury], Mercury 16375.
*The Fabulous Charlie Rich*, Koch 25165.
*Boss Man*, Koch 350402.
*Time for Tears*, Sun 123.
*Behind Closed Doors*, Epic/Legacy 65716.
*The Silver Fox*, Epic 80532.
*Very Special Love Songs*, Epic 32531.
*There Won't Be Anymore*, RCA 10433.
*Tomorrow Night*, RCA 10258.
*She Loved Everybody But Me*, RCA 1489.
*Those Midnight Blues*, Hallmark 861.
*Fully Realized*, Philips 6641199.
*Charlie Rich*, Hi 32084.
*Sings the Songs of Hank Williams*, London 136.
*She Called Me Baby*, RCA 3203.
*Every Time You Touch Me (I Get High)*, Epic 80828.
*Too Many Teardrops*, Pickwick 7001.
*Original Charlie Rich*, Sun 1007.
*I Do My Swinging at Home*, Embassy 31212.
*Silver Linings*, Epic 69206.
*Favorites*, RCA 1024.
*The World of Charlie Rich*, RCA 1242.
*Take Me*, Epic 81841.
*Rollin' with the Flow*, Epic 82229.
*Big Boss Man*, RCA 2260.
*The Most Beautiful Girl*, Embassy 31653.
*I Still Believe in Love*, United Artists 30172.
*The Fool Strikes Again*, United Artists 30219.
*The Rich Collection*, Lotus 5012.
*Nobody but You*, United Artists 30284.
*Songs of Love*, Hallmark 3025.
*Once a Drifter*, Elektra 52264.
*Pictures and Paintings*, Sire 26730.
*Midnight Blues*, Quicksilver 1005.
*Early Years: Memphis Sound*, Collectables 2000.
*I'll Shed No Tears*, Hi 418.
*Unchained Melody*, Intersound 5003.
*Lonely Weekends*, Sun 6009.
*The Best Years*, Smash 67078.

*The Best of Charlie Rich*, Epic 31933.
*The Greatest*, Hallmark 839.
*Greatest Hits*, Epic 34240.
*American Originals*, Columbia 45073.
*Greatest Hits: The Best of Charlie Rich*, Epic 38568.
*The Complete Smash Sessions*, Mercury 512643.
*Charlie Rich Sings the Songs of Hank Williams Plus the R and B Sessions*, Diablo 810.
*Super Hits*, Epic 67126.
*The Very Best of Charlie Rich*, K-Tel 3578.
*Lonely Weekends: Best of the Sun Years*, AVI 5016.
*Sun Sessions*, Varèse Vintage 5695.
*Feel Like Going Home: The Essential Charlie Rich*, Columbia/Legacy 64762.
*Most Beautiful Girl: 20 Greatest Hits*, Dj Specialist 55426.
*Lonely Weekends: The Best of the Sun Years, 1958–1962*, Bear Family 16152.
*16 Biggest Hits*, Sony 69740.
*Lonely Weekends: The Very Best of Charlie Rich*, Collectables 6015.
*Classic Rich*, Sony 34727.
*Classic Rich, Vol. 2*, Epic 35624.
*Big Boss Man: The Groove Sessions*, Koch 7971.
*Early Years: Memphis Sound*, Collectables 6436.
*Lonely Weekends/Time for Tears*, Collectables 6434.
*Rich Sounds of Charlie Rich*, Platinum Disc 11512.
*Ultimate Collection*, Hip-O 157597.
*Good Old Country*, St. Clair 78182.
*Beyond Your Wildest Dreams*, Dressed to Kill 408.
*Love Songs*, Sony 62181.
*The Complete Charlie Rich on Hi Records*, Hi 250.
*The Sun Years*, Original Sun 41019.
*All-Time Greatest Hits*, K-Tel 3073.
*Back to Back*, K-Tel 3033.
*All American Country BMG Special* 46962.
*The Complete Singles Plus: The Sun Years 1958–1963*, Varese 055506.
*Country Legends*, St. Clair 6754.
*Set Me Free/The Fabulous Charlie Rich*, Edsel 8065.
*Very Best of Charlie Rich*, Prism 218.
*Country Hit Parade*, Direct Source 52712.
*Silver Fox/Every Time You Touch Me (I Get High)*, Edsel 8075.
*20 Golden Hits*, Sun 1003.
*Original Hits and Midnight Dreams*, Charly 10.
*Rebound*, Charly 52.

# GLEN CAMPBELL (1936–)
## *Rhinestone Cowboy*

During the 1960s and 1970s many country artists became household names through various mediums. Television helped boost the careers of

Johnny Cash, his wife June Carter Cash, Roy Clark and Buck Owens. There was another musician that benefited from that type of exposure and he was known as the Rhinestone Cowboy. His name was Glen Campbell.

Glen Travis Campbell was born on April 22, 1936, in Delight, Arkansas. He picked up the guitar at an early age and in the time tested method he learned the rudiments from a number of relatives. One of his uncles, Dick Bill, was the leader of a western band and Campbell performed with them during his teens. He developed a taste for the music of jazz guitarists Barney Kessel and Django Reinhardt; they became special inspirations who shaped his blossoming style.

While he honed his guitar skills on tour with his uncle's band, he sharpened his vocals abilities in the church. Later he would form his own band, the Western Wranglers, that toured all over the South playing a mixture of jazz, pop, gospel and country-tinged tunes. Sometimes Campbell played a twelve string guitar, enabling him to add special dimensions to his sound.

He relocated to California in the early 1960s and because of his easy guitar skills found plenty of session work. He backed such singers as Bobby Darin and Rick Nelson, and became a brief member of instrumental rockers the Champs, two years removed from their stone classic "Tequila." Despite the hectic schedule he found time to record his first single, "Turn Around, Look at Me," which scraped the bottom of top one hundred pop chart.

His dual career continued throughout the 1960s as he split his time between nurturing his own progress and doing session work. His single "Too Late to Worry—Too Blue to Cry" did little to improve his own situation or the cover version of Merle Travis' "Kentucky Means Paradise." During this period he appeared as a sideman with the Beach Boys, Jan and Dean, the Association, Dean Martin, Rick Nelson, and Elvis Presley, among others.

He continued this pattern throughout the rest of the decade and added Frank Sinatra, Merle Haggard, the Monkeys, and the Mamas and the Papas to his list of sideman credits. For a time it looked as if he would be a permanent member of the Beach Boys, but turned down the opportunity. Campbell might have remained an important session player for the rest of his career if he hadn't recorded John Hartford's "Gentle on My Mind." It catapulted him to the forefront and he followed with another massive seller, "By the Time I Get to Phoenix." Suddenly, he no longer needed the session work to survive and began to concentrate solely on his own career.

He had been on the cusp of recording country material for some time, starting with a cover version of Buffy Sainte-Marie's "The Universal

Soldier," and "Burning Bridges." Once he discovered the right formula for his songs, he hit gold. He would perfect his method and release a series of albums that made him a superstar.

After "Gentle on My Mind" won the Grammy for Best Country and Western Recording in 1967, he added "I Wanna Live" to his canon, as well as "Dreams of the Everyday Housewife." In 1968, he began to host his own program, *The Glen Campbell Good Time Hour*, that drew a large crowd weekly. He also recorded the top ten hits "Wichita Lineman," "Galveston," "Where's the Playground Susie?," "Try a Little Kindness," "Honey Come Back," "Everything a Man Could Ever Need," and "It's Only Make Believe." As well, he cut a couple of duets with Bobby Gentry (of "Ode to Billy Joe" fame), including "Let It Be Me" and "All I Have to Do Is Dream," cover versions from the Everly Brothers' catalog. If that wasn't enough to fuel his engine, he appeared in the films *True Grit* and *Norwood* with the Duke, John Wayne.

In the first part of the 1970s, Campbell continued to reign as one of the most popular country-pop stars, but by the end of the decade his star began to fade slightly. By then his television show had been cancelled and he wasn't racking up number one hits with such regularity as he had in the past. Despite such international smashes as "Rhinestone Cowboy," "Country Boy (You Got Your Feet in L.A.)," "Don't Pull Your Love," "Then You Can Tell Me Goodbye," and "Southern Nights," he entered a dark period of his career that included substance abuse.

Although he didn't command the same attention as he had in the past, he remained a visible performer. In the 1980s, his career was on the upswing with the release of "Faithless Love," "A Lady Like You" and "The Hand That Rocks the Cradle." They all became country hits, but more importantly he had come to terms with his drug and alcohol addiction through God's help. He recorded inspirational albums and reached the top ten at the end of the 1980s with two songs: "I Have You," and "She's Gone, Gone, Gone."

The 1990s marked a further slowdown in his career, as he no longer seemed interested in recording songs; he went into semi-retirement. One of his two major endeavors in the decade was the sponsorship of a golf tournament, the Glen Campbell Los Angeles Open, a major event on the PGA circuit. His second was the occasional performance at his theatre in Branson, Missouri. His latest appearances in the public eye have been for various arrests.

Glen Campbell is a country music icon. For a decade he was one of the biggest selling artists. He possessed the Midas touch and interested people in country music that otherwise didn't like the genre by adding a catchy pop flavor to his songs. He did as much as anyone else to promote the music on an international scale.

There was accessibility to his music that contained a definite charm. His voice and guitar playing appealed to the average person who liked a song with a good beat and good lyrics. The words to his songs were sometimes introspective but never too harsh on the preaching side. Campbell knew how to write and arrange a catchy country tune with pop dimensions.

Early in his career, he performed with a number of pop, country and rock stars as a session player. This side of his career is often overlooked because of his later success as a solo artist. However, his work on the albums of the Beach Boys, Frank Sinatra, Merle Haggard, the Association, the Mamas and the Papas, Dean Martin, the Monkeys and the Champs is an important part in the chapter of his musical life. Campbell also worked with Jim Gordon, Tommy Tedesco, Jay Migliori, Jim Horn, Jimmy Bowen, Tanya Tucker, Lew McCreary, Carol Kaye, Roy Caton, Mike Deasy, Sr., and Frank Capp, among others.

With his television show he interested audiences in country music and introduced artists that were often overlooked. Campbell's program was one of the most popular during its reign and he invaded millions of living rooms every week with his freckled-face, all–American looks, manners, and music. He helped spread the appeal of country to many corners of the globe.

Along with Johnny Cash, Bobby Goldsboro, Bobbie Gentry, Jerry Reed, Mac Davis, John Hartford, Lee Greenwood, Roy Clark, Buck Owens, Ronnie Milsap, Leon Russell, Conway Twitty, Charlie Rich, and Don Williams, he expanded the parameters of country music to include pop, rock and folk. He took his sound to middle of the road America and became a big star. Although criticized by the purists, Campbell and many of his contemporaries ensured that the genre would not wither on the vine from stagnation.

He gave the world a number of great songs. A partial list includes "Too Late to Worry—Too Blue to Cry," "Gentle on My Mind," "The Universal Soldier," "Burning Bridges," "I Wanna Live," "Wichita Lineman," "Galveston," "Where's the Playground Susie?," "Try a Little Kindness," "Honey Come Back," "Everything a Man Could Ever Need," "It's Only Make Believe," "Let It Be Me," "All I Have to Do Is Dream," "Rhinestone Cowboy," "Country Boy (You Got Your Feet in L.A.)," "Don't Pull Your Love," "Then You Can Tell Me Goodbye," "Southern Nights," "Faithless Love," "A Lady Like You," "The Hand That Rocks the Cradle," "I Have You," and "She's Gone, Gone, Gone." He was a masterful musician, writer and singer delivering a body of work that is equal to any other country music artist of his era.

He also had a huge influence on a number of groups and individuals, including Atlanta, Sam Neely, Billy Hoffman, Alabama, Alan Jackson, Brooks and Dunn, David Bellamy, George Strait, Chet Black, Garth Brooks, Randy Travis, Ricky Van Shelton, Ronnie Milsap, Tim McGraw, Ricky Skaggs, Vince Gill and Travis Tritt. As well, his style and drive made an impact on all of the session artists with which he worked.

In 2005, Campbell was elected to the Country Music Hall of Fame. Throughout his career many awards and honors have been bestowed on him for his achievements. Undoubtedly, the Rhinestone Cowboy possessed a knack for entertaining the world.

## Discography

*Big Bluegrass Special*, Capitol 1810.
*Swingin' 12 String*, Index 1002.
*Too Late to Worry, Too Blue to Cry*, Capitol 1881.
*The Astounding 12-String Guitar*, Capitol 2023.
*The Big Bad Rock Guitar of Glen Campbell*, Capitol 2392.
*Mr. 12 String Guitar*, World Pacific 21835.
*Gentle on My Mind*, Capitol 52040.
*Burning Bridges*, Capitol 2679.
*Hey, Little One*, Capitol 2878.
*A New Place in the Sun*, Capitol 2907.
*By the Time I Get to Phoenix*, Capitol 52041.
*Wichita Lineman* [Capitol], Capitol 52039.
*Galveston*, Capitol 210.
*True Grit*, Capitol 263.
*Country Soul*, Starday 414.
*Country Music Star No. 1*, Starday 437.
*Where's the Playground Susie*, Ember 5044.
*Glen Campbell: Live*, Trace 40005.
*Try a Little Kindness*, Capitol 389.
*Oh Happy Day*, Capitol 413.
*Norwood*, Capitol 475.
*The Glen Campbell Goodtime Album*, Capitol 493.
*The Last Time I Saw Her*, Capitol/EMI 733.
*Christmas with Glen Campbell*, Capitol 6699.
*Satisfied Mind*, Pickwick 3134.
*Glen Travis Campbell*, Capitol 11117.
*Glen Campbell*, Pickwick 3274.
*I Knew Jesus (Before He Was a Star)*, Capitol 11185.
*I Remember Hank Williams*, Capitol 11253.
*Houston (I'm Comin' to See You)*, Capitol 11293.
*Reunion: The Songs of Jimmy Webb*, Capitol 11336.
*Rhinestone Cowboy* [EMI], EMI 11430.
*Arkansas*, Capitol 11407.
*I'll Paint You a Song*, Pickwick 3346.
*Live in Japan*, Capitol 80288.
*Bloodline*, Capitol 11821.
*Southern Nights*, Capitol 11601.

*Live at the Royal Festival Hall*, Capitol 11707.
*Basic*, Capitol 11722.
*Highwayman*, Capitol 12008.
*Something 'Bout You Baby I Like*, Capitol 12075.
*It's the World Gone Crazy*, Capitol 12124.
*Old Home Town*, Atlantic 90016-1.
*Letter to Home*, Atlantic 90164-1.
*It's Just a Matter of Time*, Atlantic 90483-1.
*Light Years*, MCA 42210.
*No More Night*, Word 47792.
*Country Boy*, CEMA 8352.
*I Guess I Just Missed You*, 16th Avenue 70552.
*Walkin' in the Sun*, Liberty 93884.
*Unconditional Love*, Liberty 90992.
*Still Within the Sound of My Voice*, MCA 42009.
*Limited Collector's Edition*, Capitol 93157.
*Show Me Your Way*, New Haven 9250.
*Merry Christmas*, Liberty 96383.
*Favorite Hymns*, Word 701-9977-634.
*Wings of Victory*, New Haven 9253.
*The World of Glen Campbell/Live*, Trace 0400052.
*Christmas with Glen Campbell*, Capitol 12509.
*Live in London*, Bulldog 1039.
*Somebody Like That*, Capitol 97062.
*The Boy in Me*, New Haven 87537.
*Glen Campbell*, Castle 303.
*Christmas with Glen Campbell and Sonny James*, Cema Special 56623.
*Christmas with Glen Campbell* [Laserlight], Laserlight 12509.
*That Christmas Feeling* [Disky], Disky 87726.
*Branson City Limits* [live], Unison 9012.
*Home for the Holidays*, Benson 84418-7507-2.
*In Concert* [Charly] [live], Charly 8003.
*A Glen Campbell Christmas* [Unison/TNN Classic], Unison/TNN 83022.
*Glen Campbell Christmas* [EMI-Capitol Special Markets], EMI-Capitol 26235.
*Glen Campbell in Concert*, Columbia River 190037.
*The Real Men of Country*, Platinum Disc 3061.
*Glen Campbell's Greatest Hits*, Capitol 16297.
*The Best of Glen Campbell*, Capitol 11577.
*The Very Best of Glen Campbell* [Liberty], Capitol 46483.
*The Best of the Early Years*, Curb 77441.
*Classics Collection*, Liberty 94165.
*Greatest Country Hits*, Curb 77362.
*Country Gold*, Liberty 94164.
*All-Time Favorites*, Pair 1089.
*All Time Favorite Hits*, Excelsior 17987.
*All-Time Favorite Hits*, CEMA 57396.
*Greatest Hits and Finest Performances*, Reader's Digest 110.
*Ultimate*, Bransounds 41013.
*Greatest Hits Live* [Prime Cuts], Prime Cuts 2316.
*Back to Back Hits*, Cema Special 18238.
*Essential, Vol. 3*, Capitol 33834.
*Essential, Vol. 2*, Capitol 33829.

*Essential, Vol. 1*, Capitol 30288.
*Glen Campbell Live! His Greatest Hits*, LaserLight 12437.
*Jesus and Me: The Collection*, K-Tel 2037.
*Glen Campbell Collection (1962–1989): Gentle on My Mind*, Razor and Tie 2129.
*Glen Campbell: Members Edition*, United Audio 3020.
*Original Gold*, Disky 85291.
*Original Gold*, Disk 1, Disky 85292.
*Original Gold*, Disk 2, Disky 85293.
*Rhinestone Cowboy* [Cleopatra], Cleopatra 412.
*Golden Hits Live*, Intercontinent 1163.
*Capitol Years: 1965–1977*, EMI 821834.
*Greatest Hits Live* [Legacy], Legacy 044.
*20 Great Love Songs*, Disky 85614.
*Love Songs*, Gold Label 8009.
*20 Greatest Hits*, Capitol 22094.
*The Gold Collection*, Fine Tune 1141.
*Southern Nights: Greatest Hits*, Woodford 860012.
*Super Hits*, Atlantic 83374.
*Country Stars and Stripes*, Direct Source 1292.
*Star Power: Glen Campbell*, Direct Source 1461.
*Signature Series*, Direct Source 1501.
*Wichita Lineman* [BMG International], BMG 37210.
*Rhinestone Cowboy, Vol. 2*, Platinum Disc 1853.
*Glen Campbell, Vol. 1*, Platinum Disc 1854.
*Southern Nights, Vol. 1*, Platinum Disc 1852.
*All-Time Greatest Hits*, CEMA 11301–50802.
*Country Classics*, EMI Gold 6321.
*All the Best*, Capitol 41816.
*Pure Platinum*, Platinum Disc 2732.
*Ultimate Collection*, United Multi License 4049.
*Country Standards*, EMI 582650.
*Essential*, EMI 582207.
*Southern Night/Basic*, Raven 167.
*Legacy 1961–2002*, Capitol 90493.
*Country Greatest*, EMI 576044.
*Love Is the Answer: 24 Songs of Faith, Hope and Love*, Universal South 000182502.
*38 Great Performances*, Prism 2247.
*Rock Breakout Years*, Madacy 57396.
*The Very Best of Glen Campbell*, EMI 11577.

# ROY CLARK (1933–)

## *Lightning Fingers*

The 1970s spawned a large array of country entertainers who produced a wide range of styles from hard-edged honky tonk to a softer pop-oriented sound and everything in between. By this time, country artists performed all over the world and often used Nashville as a home base. They appeared in every medium available to them, including on television, on radio, on stage, and in movies. One of these multi-talented musicians was known as Lightnin' Fingers. His name was Roy Clark.

Roy Linwood Clark was born on April 15, 1933, in Meherrin, Virginia, into a musical family. Both of his parents were amateur musicians and later on in his teens he would perform with his father, because at that time he was already proficient on the banjo, guitar and mandolin. He would later add the fiddle to his instrumental arsenal. In the late 1940s he won two consecutive National Country Music Banjo Championships.

He later moved to Washington, D.C., where he continued to play in the family band that performed at local square dances as well as other events. Despite a brief respite as an athlete, by the time he had graduated from high school, he had decided to pursue a career in music. The world lost a decent boxer, but gained an excellent musician.

Because of his superior abilities, he found plenty of work in clubs and radio stations, and he became a regular on a Jimmy Dean television show called *Country Style*. He was eventually fired from the program because of tardiness, and he joined singer Marvin Rainwater's group. But Clark, who drew more applause than the star, was canned. Although his career progress seemed slow, he was determined to make it and would not quit trying until he succeeded.

In an attempt to change his luck, he moved out West and landed a spot on the George Hamilton IV television show, enhancing his damaged reputation. Later he served as the leader of Wanda Jackson's band, the country music chanteuse with the tough and tender voice. After the breakup of the band, Clark remained in Las Vegas.

He expanded his popularity when he appeared in television shows such as the *Beverly Hillbillies*, knowing full well that it was exposure on that medium that would truly make him a household name. He also landed on the *Tonight Show*, a program that he hosted on occasion, displaying his talents for a totally different audience. All of this work was a foreshadowing of his future role on the hit series *Hee Haw*, still a few years away.

Although he had clearly established himself as a live performer, the recording side of his career had suffered. He had been unable to land a contract with any of the major labels until 1963, when he finally signed to Capitol and released the single "Tips of My Fingers" that raced up the charts. Despite constantly recording new material that underlined his massive talent, none of the songs he cut in the next few years were major hits.

In 1968, he switched to the Dot label and scored with a cover version of "Yesterday, When I Was Young." But, once again it was the medium of television that revived his career. He was chosen along with Buck Owens to host a new show called *Hee Haw*. Originally designed as a country version counterpoint to the variety show *Laugh-In*, *Hee Haw* was ripe with corny humor, beautiful women, and plenty of great country music. It was this opportunity that truly made Roy Clark a household name because every week he could be seen displaying his multi-instrumental talents matching his skill level with guests Chet Atkins, Johnny Cash, Glen Campbell, Willie Nelson, his co-host Buck Owens and others. His name became synonymous with country in the minds of many who didn't even listen to or like the genre.

The widespread exposure on *Hee Haw* fueled his recording career. He put together a string of country hits that included "I Never Picked Cotton," "Thank God and Greyhound," "The Lawrence Welk–Hee Haw Counter-Revolution Polka," "Come Live with Me," "Somewhere Between Love and Tomorrow," "Honeymoon Feelin,'" and "If I Had It to Do All Over Again." Although the television show was cancelled after a short three year run, it had made a tremendous impact on his career, opening many doors for him. The reruns ensured that his popularity would remain high.

His appearance on commercials, on the syndicated version of *Hee Haw*, his songwriting and recording were all positive sides to his career. In 1976, he became the first country artist to appear in the Soviet Union. He also didn't limit his working companions to country artists; he recorded with a variety of musicians, including the Boston Pops Orchestra and Clarence "Gatemouth" Brown, the great blues virtuoso.

By the end of the decade the hits dried up and Clark's popularity waned. Despite jumping from one label to another, he could not rekindle the magic that he once possessed. As well, *Hee Haw*'s status among country fans had shrunk due to the new urban country wave that looked down upon the good humor, old timey format of the show.

Despite the fact that he no longer graced the top of the country charts, he maintained a degree of popularity as a live performer. His concerts were events, as everyone came to see the lightning fingered picker that could play all instruments with breathtaking speed and precision. He acted with Mel Tillis in the movie *Uphill All the Way* that kept his name fresh in the minds of audiences. Finally, in 1987, he became a member of the *Grand Ole Opry*, an honor long overdue.

Many of his concerts in the 1990s occurred at his theatre in Branson, Missouri, and the repackaging of his material in CD format ensured he would not be forgotten by the music buying public. He continues to record and perform sporadically.

Roy Clark is a country music superpicker. His popularity soared in the late 1960s and throughout the 1970s as a result of his appearance on the *Hee Haw* television show. His name was so closely associated with country that it seemed like he invented the genre. He has made many contributions over the years.

He is, without a doubt, one of the finest musicians to ever pick up an instrument and play country music. His level of skill has rarely been matched and he is an adept guitarist, banjoist, fiddler, and mandolin player. His speed and dexterity are reminiscent of the bluegrass fireballs Flatt and Scruggs. Clark's skill was often the highlight of the musical interlude on the TV show *Hee Haw*.

Although not a consistent maker of hits, he scored many chart placements. A partial list includes "Tips of My Fingers," "Yesterday When I Was Young," "I Never Picked Cotton," "Thank God and Greyhound," "A Simple Thing Called Love," "Magnificent Sanctuary Band," "The Lawrence Welk–Hee Haw Counter-Revolution Polka," "Come Live with Me," "Honeymoon Feeling," "Somewhere Between Love and Tomorrow," and "If I Had to Do It All Over Again." Any song he tackled was given that distinct Roy Clark stamp.

He is a genuine globetrotter and has appeared all over the world, including Russia, Canada, Australia, Europe, and the Far East, among other places. He has performed in areas where the audience had never heard of country music, much less witnessed the performance of someone as talented as Roy Clark. More than any other identity, he was always an American musician ready to make his country proud.

He has worked with a number of individuals, including Buck Owens, Richard Clarke, James Nichols, Richard Locker, Sonny Garrish, Joe Allison, Hee Haw Gospel Quartet, Johnny Cash, Kurt Garrison, Jimmy Henley, Vernon Sandusky, Hargus "Pig" Robbins, Jay Messina, Jerry Kennedy, Steve Gadd, Charlie Daniels, Alfred Brown, Sanford Allen, Billy Walker and Russell Malone. Of course, there is the entire cast of *Hee Haw*, including such personalities as Junior Sample, Minnie Pearl and Grandpa Jones.

Clarke influenced a number of the new artists, including Garth Brooks, Vince Gill, Tim McGraw, Randy Travis, Travis Tritt, Brooks and Dunn, Alan Jackson, Clint Black, Billy Ray Cyrus, David Bellamy, George Strait, and Ricky Skaggs. Anyone in the past 40 years who aspired to be a country music star stole a page from Lightning Fingers' song book. Many of the current country music stars of today grew up watching him on the show *Hee Haw*.

Roy Clark has enjoyed a rich career in country music. He is a strong candidate to be inducted into the Country Music Hall of Fame for his enormous contributions to the genre. In the 1970s, he might have been the most popular country entertainer in the world and with his lightning fingers never failed to excite the crowd.

## Discography

*The Tip of My Fingers*, Capitol 8305.
*The Lightning Fingers of Roy Clark*, Razor and Tie 82193.
*Roy Clark Guitar Spectacular*, Capitol 2425.
*Roy Clark Sings Lonesome Love Ballads*, Capitol 2452.
*Roy Clark*, MCA 20152.
*Do You Believe This Roy Clark*, Dot 25895.
*Urban, Suburban*, Dot 25863.
*Honky Tonk*, Pickwick JS 5164.
*I Never Picked Cotton*, Dot 25980.
*The Incredible Roy Clark*, Dot 25990.
*Roy Clark Country!*, Dot 25997.
*Roy Clark Live!*, Dot 26005.
*Yesterday, When I Was Young*, Dot 25973.
*The Ever Lovin' Soul of Roy Clark*, Dot 25972.
*The Magnificent Sanctuary Band*, Dot 25993.
*Come Live with Me*, Dot 26010.
*Roy Clark/Superpicker*, Dot 26008.
*Superpicker*, MCA 679.
*Roy Clark's Family Album*, Dot 26018.
*Roy Clark, Family and Friends*, Dot 2005.
*Roy Clark/The Entertainer*, Dot 2001.
*Entertainer of the Year*, Capitol 11264.
*Heart to Heart*, Dot 2041.
*Roy Clark in Concert* [live], MCA 37132.
*My Music and Me/Vocal and Instrumental*, Dot 2072.
*Banjo Bandits*, Universal Special Products 20800.
*Hookin' It*, Dot 2099.
*Labor of Love*, ABC 1053.
*Makin' Music*, One Way 22125.
*Take Me as I Am*, Pickwick 8137.
*Turned Loose*, Churchill 9425.
*Great Picks and New Traditions*, Branson Entertainment 9302.
*Live in Branson Mo. USA*, Laserlight 12135.
*My Favorite Hymns*, Intersound 9110.
*Roy Clark and Joe Pass Play Hank Williams*, Ranwood 1014.
*Branson City Limits* [live], Unison 9014.
*Live at Billy Bob's Texas*, Smith Music 5004.
*Christmas Memories*, Fine Arts 2025.
*Roy Clark Gospel: Songs of Strength, Time Life 20036.
*Roy Clark Sings and Plays Gospel Greats, Vol. 1*, Wonder Workshop 213.
*Roy Clark Sings and Plays Gospel Greats, Vol. 2*, Wonder Workshop 214.
*Superpicker/Hookin' It*, MCA 38032.
*He'll Have to Go*, Pickwick 6094.
*The Best of Roy Clark* [Dot/MCA], MCA 27015.
*Classic Clark*, Dot 2010.
*Greatest Hits, Vol. 1*, MCA 27050.

*The Best of Roy Clark*, Capitol 77395.
*Greatest Hits*, Capitol 91623.
*Ultimate*, Bransounds 1502.
*Greatest Hits*, Varese Vintage 5608.
*The Branson Sound*, Brandsounds Vol. 5, 4102.
*Greatest Hits, Vol. 2*, Varese Vintage 5842.
*The Walkin After Midnight* [Peter Pan], Peter Pan 9109.
*Roy Clark Sings and Plays Gospel Greats*, Fire Arts 2010.
*Original Artist Hit List*, Intersound 4824.
*Absolutely the Best, Vol. 1*, Fuel 2000 061276.
*The Very Best of Roy Clark*, Time Life 200352.
*Hymns from the Old Country Church*, Wonder Disc 61.
*The Very Best of Roy Clark*, Intersound 5999.
*Bluegrass: It's About Time, It's About Me*, Varese 680.

# WILLIE NELSON (1933–)
## Austin Outlaw

Although Nashville is the acknowledged capital of country music, boasting a long, colorful history, when it became too mechanical for some they searched for a different area to base their operations. For example, Buck Owens established the Bakersfield sound. Another rebel was the man who returned to his roots in Texas to establish his image as the Austin Outlaw. His name is Willie Nelson.

Willie Hugh Nelson was born on April 30, 1933, in Abbott, Texas. After his parents divorced his grandparents raised him and encouraged his musical interests. He picked up the guitar and by the time he was in his teens he had become proficient on the instrument. He played in various bands before joining fiddler Bud Fletcher's group (his sister Bobbie's husband), and remained there until he decided to serve his country. During his time in Fletcher's outfit, he had learned invaluable performance lessons, had improved his guitar as well as his songwriter skills, and assumed frontman responsibilities.

Upon his discharge from the military, he married a Cherokee girl and the couple had a daughter. After several low-paying jobs, including several as a salesman, he decided on a musical career. In order to fulfill his ambitions he talked his way into a DJ post at a local station in Waco, Texas, where he was living at the time. In 1954, he moved to Fort Worth and doubled as an entertainer in some rough honky tonk bars.

All the while he was scuffling to make a living, he was collecting the raw material for the cycle of songs that would make him famous. Already he had written "Family Bible" and "Night Life." He would cut the song "Lumberjack" for an independent label, but it didn't attract much interest and he was forced to try again. He continued to host a country radio show and work in tough bars where he developed a knack for satisfying demanding audiences.

Eventually, distressed by the lack of progress his career was making, he headed out to Nashville to try his luck there. It seemed that the change in scenery hadn't done him much good, as several record companies rejected his demos, but he did make one all-important contact in Hank Cochran. Cochran introduced him to Ray Price, who recorded "Night Life," and offered Nelson a place in his outfit—the Cherokee Cowboys.

In 1961, Nelson began to truly assert himself in country music circles. Despite the fact that he was relegated to the role of bassist in Price's band, Willie the songwriter was making waves. Patsy Cline had a hit with "Crazy," Faron Young scored with "Hello Walls," and Billy Walker took "Funny How Time Slips Away" into the top forty on the country charts. Interestingly, many of the artists that covered these songs enjoyed crossover success with them.

Although other artists recorded his songs that brought him recognition, Willie had greater ambitions. He released "The Party's Over" on Liberty Records, it was a solid hit. Later he would score again with "Willingly" and "Touch Me," both duets with his second wife Shirley Cottie. But, Nelson who for so long seemed to be destined to miss out on the big time, was left out in the cold when Liberty quit producing country tunes in the early 1960s. His once promising career that had threatened to shoot off like a rocket was grounded.

But Willie Nelson was a fighter, and he was determined more than ever to make it in the music business. Despite another failed attempt with the Monument label, he moved to RCA to try once again. For seven years he would place a string of minor hits into the charts, including "Bring Me Sunshine" in 1969. Three years later, totally frustrated by the music scene in Nashville, Nelson returned to Austin and turned his back on the industry.

In the state capital of Texas, he tried unsuccessfully to run his own farm, but music was in his blood. Since he never truly ventured far from the scene he quickly realized there was a large market for a type of anti–Nashville country sound. The opposite of the rote, plush Nashville style was a hard driving honky tonk that was stripped down to its bare essentials. Once he was able to escape his RCA contract, he signed with Atlantic and after years of struggling it was magic time for the red-headed songster.

In 1973, *Shotgun Willie* appeared in the record stores and it signaled his rise from obscure artist to national cult hero. He was the leader of the outlaw movement that turned its nose up at the entire Nashville scene. A local hero in Austin, he would amplify his popularity to echo across the country and throughout the international community.

His follow up, *Phases and Stages*, a concept album that propelled his vision of a new country—a style based on a lonesome identity with a rebellious streak—proved to be very successful. This alienation and attitude of Willie Nelson versus the world earned him a large following and by the mid-1970s Waylon Jennings, Kris Kristofferson, and Tompall Glaser had joined his crusade.

In 1975, Nelson took his barroom country style to Columbia, which gave him complete artistic freedom. The hard nosed, authentic style was best presented on *Red Headed Stranger*, which included the sparse sound of Nelson's guitar and a piano. It also contained the classic cover version of Roy Acuff's "Blue Eyes Crying in the Rain."

With the outlaw movement in full swing, it was only a matter of time before producers collected all of the solitary voices in one package to make money. The album *Wanted: The Outlaws*, featured Nelson, Waylon Jennings, Tompall Glaser and Jessi Colter, Waylon's pretty rebel wife. The record was a hit and contained "Good Hearted Woman." The mainstream country sector ignored and belittled the outlaw movement. But when the rebels won an award at the Country Music Association awards, they gained the recognition they deserved.

For the next five years, Nelson expanded his legendary status with a series of classic singles, including "Remember Me," "If You've Got the Money I've Got the Time," "Uncloudy Day," "I Love You a Thousand Ways," and "Something to Brag About." As well, he continued to deliver strong albums, including *Waylon and Willie* and *Stardust*. The latter marked a different direction since it included strings and a more pop oriented flavor. Although other artists would have suffered a lull in popularity with such a bold move, by this time Nelson could do no wrong and it only enhanced his position, providing a different dimension to his country music persona.

Because of his underground cult status and his celebrity status among hard core country fans, it was only a matter of time before Hollywood came calling. In 1979, he starred in the hit movie *Electric Horseman*. There was a raw element to his acting that borrowed from his music. It was a thrill for many to see their counter-culture hero make it as a movie star. In 1980, he played in the film *Honeysuckle Rose*. The song "On the Road Again" became another of Nelson's signature songs.

A cover version of "Always on My Mind" established him as one of the single most important country artists of the early 1980s. Johnny Cash had fallen on hard times; as had Roy Clark, Buck Owens, Glen Campbell, and many other stars of the 1970s. Whether it was the albums, or the singles such as "To All the Girls I've Loved Before," Nelson continued to cultivate his superstar status.

In 1985, he recorded *The Highwayman* album with Jennings, Cash and Kristofferson; it was a big hit. From this point on his record sales received less attention from the mainstream country audience, but his touring continued to entertain millions. Back in the 1970s he had established his July 4th Picnics, full day affairs that drew huge crowds. He also delved into charity events such as Farm Aid, a concentrated effort on helping out the hard-luck American farmer.

Although he made the news for his community projects, the spotlight truly shone on him in 1990 due to his trouble with the IRS. The federal agency presented him with a massive bill that would see much of his accumulated wealth fall into he hands of the government. Ever the rebel, Nelson dealt with the tragedy through his music and released *The IRS Tapes: Who'll Buy My Memories*. Three years later his debts were finally paid off and Nelson could concentrate once again on his musical career. The album *Across the Borderline* was a hit and marked the respect he commanded throughout the international music community. A host of artists appeared on the sessions, including Bob Dylan, Bonnie Raitt, Paul Simon, Sinead O'Connor, David Crosby and Kris Kristofferson.

He didn't slow down when he turned sixty in 1993. For the rest of the decade, he released a number of albums, including *Teatro, Night and Day, Me and the Drummer, Milk Cow Blues,* and *The Rainbow Connection*. Already an established legend, he remains the acknowledged King of Country Music. He continues to record and perform as Willie Nelson and Family.

Willie Nelson is a country music symbol. He has run a hard, long race that he has won. A gifted songwriter, he has always displayed a common sense approach to his music that appealed to a wide range of fans with many different tastes. His ability to read audiences is second to none.

Although Willie Nelson will never be confused for one of the rock and roll axe heroes, he will always be cited as a definite talent on the instrument. His sparse, redneck sound and his ability to place the right chords at the exact moment are some of his greatest qualities as a musician. He has forged his own sound on the guitar that many have imitated but never completely duplicated. He has also demonstrated his versatility, switching between acoustic and electric without really changing his style.

There is a catchy element in his voice, a soothing tone that transmits the idea that everything is going to be fine because Willie is in charge. This vocal timbre has allowed him to satisfy the soft-hearted country crowd as well as the more masculine honky tonk set. The many number one hit songs that he enjoyed proved that his phrasing style was more than just original because it was unthinkable that anyone else but he could sing "On the Road Again," and "To All the Girls I Loved Before," to name just a couple.

He has also made sure to surround himself with a talented group of musicians. A partial list includes Reggie Young, Jody Payne, Paul English, Grady Martin, Mickey Raphael, Bee Spears, Bobby Emmons, Bobby Wood, Bobbie Nelson, Ray Charles, Mike Leech, and Billy Sherrill. He also shared the stage with a cross-section of the musical community, including rocker/folk artist John Cougar Mellencamp during the Farm Aid concerts. He has performed with Johnny Cash, Lyle Lovett, Kris Kristofferson, Merle Haggard, Mickey Newbury, Townes Van Zandt, Jimmie Dale Gilmore, Waylon Jennings, David Allan Coe, Jessi Colter, Charlie Pride, Tompall Glaser, Billy Joe Shaver, Neil Young, Faron Young, Tammy Wynette, Conway Twitty and Buck Owens. Almost every country music star of the past forty years has shared a stage with Nelson at one time or another.

Many of Nelson's musical influences were rebels, including Bob Wills, Hank Williams, Sr., Ray Price, and Lefty Frizzell. In turn, the red headed stranger has made an impact on hundreds of artists from the country universe and in every style. A partial list includes Clint Black, Pat Green, Deana Carter, Trick Pony, Crooked County, Randy Travis, Travis Tritt, Garth Brooks, Brooks and Dunn, Ricky Skaggs, Tim McGraw, Stevie Ray Vaughan, Jimmie Vaughan, Doyle Bramhall, and countless others.

It was Willie Nelson more than any other individual who delivered country music from the confines imposed by the Nashville sound. He turned his back on the entire tradition to create his own brand of country music that had a serious impact on the future course of the genre. He was able to weld the best elements of several styles to create something fresh and new. His vision was shared by many artists, including Merle Haggard, Waylon Jennings, Jessi Colter, Kris Kristofferson, Tompall Glaser and David Allan Coe.

Nelson put the city of Austin, Texas, on the international music map with his brand of hard, barroom country. He spearheaded a movement that would include blues and country greats Stevie Ray Vaughan, Jimmie Vaughan, Doyle Bramhall, Lou Ann Barton, Derek O'Brien, W. C. Clarke, Denny Freeman, Michael Murphey, Jerry Jeff Walker, Doug Sahm, Commander Cody and His Lost Planet Airmen, Asleep at the Wheel, Freda and the Firedogs and John X. Reed. All would eventually make the state capital their home base.

The Willie Nelson story is that of a red haired rebel who was determined to make it in the country music business on his own terms, something he succeeded in doing beyond even his wildest imagination. When he was elected to the Country Music Hall of Fame in 1993, he was already a living legend as the Austin Rebel.

## Willie Nelson's Band
Circa 1970s

| Guitar Vocals | Piano | Percussion |
|---|---|---|
| Willie Nelson | Bobbie Nelson | Billy English |
| Jody Payne | | |
| | | |
| Harmonica | Electric Bass | Snare Drum |
| Mickey Raphael | Bee Spears | Paul English |

## Discography

*Love and Pain*, Aura 1003.
*And Then I Wrote*, Liberty 7239.
*Here's Willie Nelson*, Liberty 7308.
*Country Willie: His Own Songs*, Buddha 99676.
*Country Favorites, Willie Nelson Style*, Buddha 99698.
*Live Country Music Concert*, RCA 3659.
*Make Way for Willie Nelson*, RCA Victor 3748.
*The Party's Over*, RCA 3858.
*Texas in My Soul*, RCA 3937.
*Good Times*, RCA 4057.
*My Own Peculiar Way*, RCA 4111.
*Both Sides Now*, RCA 4294.
*Laying My Burdens Down*, RCA 4404.
*Yesterday's Wine*, Justice 1603.
*Willie Nelson and Family*, RCA 4489.
*The Willie Way*, RCA 4760.
*The Words Don't Fit the Picture*, RCA 4653.
*Shotgun Willie*, Atlantic 7262.
*Phases and Stages*, Atlantic 7291.
*Red Headed Stranger*, Columbia/Legacy 63589.
*The Sound in Your Mind*, Columbia 34092.
*The Troublemaker*, Columbia 34112.
*To Lefty from Willie*, Columbia 34695.
*Stardust*, Columbia/Legacy 35305.
*Willie and Family Live*, Columbia 35642.
*Electric Horseman*, CBS 36327.
*Sings Kris Kristofferson*, Columbia 36188.
*Pretty Paper*, CBS 36189.
*One for the Road*, Columbia 36064.
*San Antonio Rose* [CBS], Columbia 36476.
*Honeysuckle Rose*, Columbia 36752.
*Somewhere over the Rainbow*, Columbia 36883.
*Old Friends*, CBS 38013.
*Always on My Mind*, Columbia 37951.

*Tougher Than Leather*, Columbia 38248.
*Without a Song*, Columbia 39110.
*Take It to the Limit*, Columbia 38562.
*Music from Songwriter*, Monument 39531.
*Portrait in Music*, CBS 1016.
*Angel Eyes*, Columbia 39363.
*City of New Orleans*, Columbia 39145.
*Funny How Time Slips Away*, CEMA 8312.
*Me and Paul*, DCC 191.
*Half Nelson*, Columbia 39990.
*Brand on My Heart*, CBS 39977.
*Partners*, CBS 39894.
*The Promiseland*, CBS 40327.
*Island in the Sea*, CBS 40487.
*Seashores of Old Mexico*, CBS 40293.
*What a Wonderful*, Columbia 44331.
*Horse Called Music*, Columbia 45046.
*Born for Trouble*, Columbia 45492.
*Who'll Buy My Memories*, Columbia 52981.
*Across the Borderline*, Columbia 52752.
*Moonlight Becomes You*, Justice 1601.
*Healing Hands of Time*, Capitol 30420.
*Pancho, Lefty and Rudolph*, Disney 60882.
*Six Hours at Pedernales*, Step One 84.
*Just One Love*, Transatlantic 221.
*Spirit*, Island 524242.
*How Great Thou Art*, Fine Arts 9605.
*Christmas with Willie Nelson*, Unison 20037.
*All of Me*, Sony 4878732.
*Hill Country Christmas*, Fine Arts 9705.
*Willie Nelson Live*, Columbia River 1516.
*Teatro*, Island 524548.
*Life's Railway to Heaven*, Mercury 417097.
*Back to Back: Willie Nelson and Patsy Cline*, Excelsior 7201.
*Night and Day*, Free Falls 7002.
*Clean Shirt*, Sony Special 32072.
*Memories of Hank Williams, Sr.*, BSW 3252.
*Me and the Drummer*, Lockdown 1.
*Milk Cow Blues*, Island 542517.
*Good Ol' Country Singin'*, Camden 6120.
*Tales Out of Luck*, Import 55021.
*Rainbow Connection*, Island 548810.
*Country Willie*, Time Music International 1750.
*The Great Divide*, Uptown/Universal 586231.
*Is There Something on Your Mind*, Time 1749.
*Home Is Where You're Happy*, Time Music 1225.
*All of Me Live ... in Concert*, BCI 40252.
*Stars and Guitars*, Universal 170340.
*Honky Tonk Heroes*, SPV 2998
*Reunion—Can't Get the Hell Out of Town*, Bear Family 16124.
*Willie Nelson and Friends: Live and Kickin'*, Lost Highway 000045302.
*Honeysuckle Rose*, Columbia/Legacy 89259.

*Keepsake*, Sony Special Products 55611.
*Standard Time*, Sony Special Products 58164.
*To Lefty From Willie*, Sony 89255.
*Run That By Me One More Time*, Lost Highway 000061602.
*I Just Don't Understand*, Blu Mountain 90729.
*Live in Amsterdam*, BCI 45322.
*Music Legends: The Best of Willie Live*, Brentwood 40666.
*Outlaws and Angels*, Lost Highway 000279402.
*Always Will Be*, Lost Highway 2548.
*Sings for Tsunami Relief: Austin to South Asia*, Lost Highway 000440902.
*Countryman*, Lost Highway 000470602.
*Hello Walls*, Sunset 5138.
*Columbus Stockade Blues*, RCA 2444.
*Country Winners*, Pair 1007.
*The Best of Willie Nelson*, EMI America 48398.
*Spotlight on Willie Nelson*, Camden 10705.
*Shotgun Willie/Phases and Stages*, Mobile Fidelity UDCD-581.
*What Can You Do to Me*, RCA Victor 11234.
*Famous Country Music Makers*, RCA 2062.
*Country Willie* [United Artists], United Artists 410.
*Longhorn Jamboree*, Plantation 24.
*Willie and Friends*, Plantation 214.
*Before His Time*, RCA 1–2210.
*Face of Fighter*, Lone Star 4602.
*There'll Be No Tears*, United Artists 930.
*Sweet Memories*, RCA Victor 1–3243.
*Family Bible*, Songbird 3258.
*Minstrel Man*, RCA 4045.
*Blue Skies*, CBS 10025.
*Greatest Hits (and Some That Will Be)*, Columbia 37542.
*WWII*, RCA 4455.
*Willie Nelson* [10 LP Box], Columbia 3825.
*Classic Willie Nelson*, MFP 5602.
*A Song for You*, Hallmark 3127.
*Slow Down Old World*, Aura 1002.
*Help Me Make It Through the Night*, RCA 89425.
*Funny How Time Slips Away*, Collector's Series, RCA 5470.
*Sings 28 Great Songs*, Hollywood 405.
*All-Time Hits, Vol. 1*, RCA 8556-2.
*Nite Life: Greatest Hits and Rare Tracks, 1959–1971*, Rhino 70987.
*Red Headed Stranger/Sound in Your Mind*, CBS 38217.
*The Best of Willie*, RCA 56355-2.
*Early Tracks*, Rhino 70345.
*Greatest Songs*, Curb 77366.
*Yours Always*, Madacy 21562.
*20 of the Best*, RCA 5208.
*Willie*, RCA 5988-2.
*Collection*, Castle CCS178.
*20 Golden Classics*, Sound 2630512.
*Night Life*, Laserlight 15485.
*Old Time Religion*, Laserlight 12114.
*Any Old Arms Won't Do*, Sound 401262.

*Original Artist*, Fat Boy 125.
*Willie Nelson*, Fat Boy 126.
*Many Sides of Willie Nelson*, GSC 15017.
*All-Time Greatest Hits*, RCA 2695-2-R11.
*Charlie's Shoes*, Quicksilver 2.
*Starbox*, Alex Jap 394.
*Original Artist*, Fat Boy 125.
*The Early Years*, Scotti Bros. 75437-2.
*The Early Years: The Complete Liberty Recordings Plus More*, Liberty 28077.
*The Legend Begins*, Pair 1333.
*Peace in the Valley: The Gospel Truth*, Promised Land 0521.
*Greatest Hits*, K-Tel 3834.
*Super Hits*, Onyx Classix 269025.
*Gospel Favorites*, MCA Special 20784.
*Across the Tracks: The Best of Willie Nelson*, Telstar 2317.
*Pure Willie*, Jerden 7010.
*Remember Me*, Chicago Music 106.
*The Essential Willie Nelson*, RCA 66590.
*Super Hits, Vol. 2*, Epic 67295.
*Singer Songwriters*, Sony Special 21130.
*Augusta*, Sundown 80.
*Love Songs* [1995 Columbia], Columbia 477509.
*A Classic and Unreleased Collection*, Rhino 71462.
*Revolutions of Time, The Journey 1975–1993*, Columbia/Legacy 64796.
*Willie and Conway*, King 473.
*Willie Nelson, Vol. 1* [Eclipse Music Group], Eclipse Music 64705.
*Willie Nelson, Vol. 2* [Eclipse Music Group], Eclipse Music 64708.
*Golden Hits*, Intercontinent 1020.
*Crying*, Prime Cuts 2327.
*Willie Standard Time*, Sony Special 26915.
*In Concert* [live], Excelsior 2394.
*Burning Memories*, Beacon 51582.
*To Lefty from Willie/Always on My Mind/Red Headed Stranger*, Sony 65386.
*20 Golden Hits*, Galaxy 388412.
*Pure Country: Willie Nelson and Friends*, Coyote 4601.
*Blame It on the Times*, Spotlight On 132.
*Classic Willie*, BMG Special 44525.
*Broken Promises*, Intermedia 5048.
*The Best of Willie Nelson* [Camden], Camden 4877272.
*Let My Mind Wander*, Kingfisher 19.
*Original Outlaws*, BMG Special 44662.
*Double Barrel Country: The Legends of Country Music*, Madacy 5337.
*Best of Willie Nelson*, Sony 4840412.
*Nashville Was the Roughest*, Bear Family 15831.
*Back 2 Back*, Intercontinent 1201.
*16 Biggest Hits*, Legacy/Columbia 69322.
*Country Willie* [Mastertone], Mastertone 8348.
*Red Headed Stranger/To Lefty from Willie*, Columbia 494899.
*Whiskey River and Other Hits*, Flashback 75489.
*Old Friends/Funny How Time Slips Away*, Koch 8039.
*December Days*, Delta 12937.
*Building Heartaches*, Delta 12938.

*Willie Nelson* [Classic World], Classic World 9905.
*The Very Best of Willie Nelson*, Sony 65825.
*Backtracks*, Renaissance 603.
*The Best of Willie Nelson* [CEMA], CEMA Special 98876.
*Great*, Festival 31057.
*On the Road Again*, Columbia River 211100.
*A&E Biography*, Capitol 200158.
*Willie Nelson, Dolly Parton and Waylon Jennings*, Camden 6090.
*Country Legends Reunion*, Legacy 34.
*Willie Nelson, Vol. 1* [Platinum Disc], Platinum Disc 32997.
*Willie Nelson, Vol. 2* [Platinum Disc], Platinum Disc 12082.
*Singer, Songwriter*, Platinum Disc 1991 14512.
*Forever Gold*, St. Clair 5816.
*20 Golden Greats*, Cleopatra 843.
*Back to Back Hits*, EMI-Capitol 23738.
*Outlaws*, SPA 55407.
*The Gold Collection*, Fine Tune 1144.
*Country Gold: A Step Beyond*, Direct Source 6005.
*Classic Country*, Direct Source 7526.
*One Step Beyond*, Starburst 11.
*Good Old Country*, St. Clair 78152.
*Columbus Stockade Blues/December Days*, Legend 64017.
*In the Jailhouse Now/Brand on My Heart*, DCC 198.
*Love Songs* [2000 Columbia/Legacy], Sony 62183.
*Oh Boy Records Classics Presents: Willie Nelson*, Oh Boy 401.
*Willie Nelson and Eddie Rabbitt*, Madacy 848.
*On the Road Again* [Columbia River], Columbia River 1120021.
*Country Stars and Stripes*, Direct Source 1295.
*Willie Nelson* [St. Clair], St. Clair 323.
*Willie Nelson*, Direct Source 1159.
*Signature Series*, Direct Source 1500.
*Joy*, Free Falls 7016.
*All the Songs I've Loved Before*, Sony 503325.
*Certified Hits*, Capitol 34448.
*Best of Willie Nelson, Vol. 2*, Aim 3004.
*Classics Collection*, Aim 3003.
*The Legends Collection: The Willie Nelson Collection*, Legends 762.
*Midnight Country*, Dressed to Kill 0814.
*Rainbow Connection* [Radio Sampler], Island 15311.
*Georgia on My Mind*, CBS 37951.
*Night Life* [Time] Time Music International 751.
*On the Road Again* [2002], Allegro 211002.
*Greatest Hits Live in Concert*, Brentwood 60295.
*Legends*, BMG International 91097.
*Love Songs*, EMI 538851.
*Heartaches*, Prestige Elite 52.
*Country Favorites*, BMG 46973.
*The Heart of Legend*, Madacy 5149.
*Fourteen Number One Hits*, Brentwood 40251.
*RCA Country Legends*, RCA 65127.
*His Very Best*, Time Music 29.
*Absolutely the Best, Vol. 1*, Varese 061248.

*Country Classics*, EMI Gold 494922.
*Crazy: The Demo Sessions*, Sugar Hill 1073
*Legendary*, BMG 97698.
*Broken Promises*, Proper Pairs 122.
*The Essential Willie Nelson*, Columbia 86740.
*Ultimate Legend: Willie Nelson*, UMMC 4066.
*It's Been Rough and Rocky Travelin'*, Bear Family 16664.
*Platinum and Gold Collection*, RCA 52690.
*Box of Willie*, K-Tel 303.
*Great Willie Nelson, Vol. 1*, Madacy 5211.
*Great Willie Nelson, Vol. 2*, Madacy 5212.
*Singin' With Willie*, Raven 162.
*The Great Willie Nelson*, Madacy 5210.
*End of Understanding*, Fruit Tree 834.
*Face of a Fighter*, Synergy 1001.
*Things to Remember*, Fruit Tree 838.
*The Best of Willie Nelson*, St. Clair 69272.
*Songs to Remember*, Legacy 151.
*Blue Skies*, Brentwood 40984.
*Classics By Willie Nelson*, Curb 78894.
*Favorites*, St. Clair 94462.
*The Complete Ghost*, Masked Weasel 300.
*America's Troubadour*, American 192012.
*Beautiful Texas*, Bear Family 15256.
*Good Hearted Woman*, Pair 1114.
*Legend Begins/Wild and Willie*, Allegiance 72922.
*Original Artists Collector's: Willie Nelson*, Exact EX-249.
*Willie or Won't He*, Allegiance 5005.

# CONWAY TWITTY (1933–1993)

## *Uncrowned King*

There were many important contributors to country music who were either outlaws, rebels or superstars. In some instances, there were those rare performers who were all three, such as Johnny Cash and Willie Nelson. Others fit in one category or another. One individual, because of his specific talent, immense success and approach, became known as the Uncrowned King. His name was Conway Twitty.

Harold Lloyd Jenkins was born on September 1, 1933, in Friars Point, Mississippi. He learned how to play guitar at the feet of his father, a riverboat pilot who also loved country music and encouraged his son to hone his skills. Although originally from Mississippi, Twitty spent a good part of his youth in Helena, Texas, a hot center for a variety of styles including gospel, blues, and country, soaking up all of these influences and storing the information for future reference.

He pursued his double interests in music and sports—particularly baseball—concentrating his efforts on becoming either a successful country artist or a major league ballplayer. He joined his very first band before his teens—the Phillips Country Ramblers—who made a few radio appearances. But before he was forced to choose between his two major pursuits, Uncle Sam came calling. While in Korea, Jenkins kept up his musical chops performing with a few of his army buddies.

Upon his return to the United States, his baseball aspirations vanished when he heard Elvis singing about his blue suede shoes. Although his career at Sun Records wasn't exactly what he had dreamed it would be, he did write "Rockhouse," a song Roy Orbison recorded. Jenkins would later cut a single, "I Need Your Lovin'," for the Mercury label. Although it didn't go very far, his next effort, "It's Only Make Believe," for MGM Records was a huge hit.

He continued to wax pop singles that kept his name fresh to teenage audiences, including "Danny Boy," as well as "Lonely Blue Boy," and redoubled his popularity by appearing in three teen-angled movies: *Sex Kittens Go to College*, *Platinum High School*, and *College Confidential*. He also had one foot planted in country music with his songwriting abilities. When Ray Price recorded Jenkins' effort "Walk Me to the Door" it was a boost to the latter's career.

It was around this time that he changed his name to Conway Twitty, from two towns, Conway and Twitty, located in Arkansas and Texas respectively. In the early 1960s he cut a few numbers for the ABC–Paramount label that was half country and half pop. However, he was slowly moving to a purer country sound and by 1965, his songs were almost exclusively of that nature.

He switched to the Decca label and recorded from Nashville, becoming one of the many pop artists who had turned to country to solidify their career. When he wasn't performing with the Lonely Blue Boys, he cut a series of minor hits, including "Guess My Eyes Were Bigger Than My Heart," that scraped the top twenty. The height of his activities was his television program, *The Conway Twitty Show*.

In 1968, he finally scored his first number one hit, "Next in Line," which opened the flood gates. He began to churn out top charters with regularity. "I Love You More Today," "To See My Angel Cry," "Hello Darlin'," "15 Years Ago," "How Much More Can She Stand?" "You've Never Been This Far Before," "She Needs Someone to Hold Her," "The Games That Daddies Play," and "Play Guitar Play" all added to his burgeoning reputation. In a short time he became one of the best selling country male artists on the circuit.

It was also during this period that he performed many duets with Loretta Lynn. The pair sounded best on "Lead Me On," "Louisiana Woman, Mississippi Man," "As Soon as I Hang Up the Phone," and "Feelings." Their collaboration was prolific, as they recorded one album per year and a handful of top ten hits. Their efforts earned them four Duo of the Year awards from the Country Music Association, three Vocal Group of the Year honors from the Academy of Country Music and one Grammy for Best Vocal Performance by a Group.

His success continued throughout the 1970s as a solo artist and as a duet with the lovely Loretta Lynn. They were serious rivals to the duo of Tammy Wynette and George Jones, but unlike the latter pair, Twitty and Lynn didn't get married. As well, they weren't fodder for the gossip columns. Their relationship was purely professional and it allowed them to surpass Wynette and Jones, whose stormy relationship was constantly under a microscope.

During the 1980s, Twitty recorded for Elektra, mixing his own compositions with that of others. He waxed singles like "Slow Hand" that the Pointer Sisters made famous, as well as "The Rose," which Bette Middler took to the top of the charts. He covered other pop material from sources such as the Eagles, "Heartache Tonight," and the Commodores' "Three Times a Lady." He also continued to hit the charts with his own material, including "Somebody's Needin' Somebody," "I Don't Know a Thing About Love (The Moon Songs)," "Don't Call Him a Cowboy," and "Desperado Love." Later he would record "Julia" and "I Want to Know You Before We Make Love" for the MCA label.

At the start of the 1990s, Twitty could reflect on a wonderful career that had brought him much success and deserved recognition. However, on June 5, 1993, in Branson, Missouri, he succumbed to a brain aneurysm and was silenced forever.

Conway Twitty was a country staple. For 20 years he rolled out hits with such regularity that it was like a rule. He became one of the most successful artists in the annals of the genre and remains in the hearts and minds of many fans despite his passing over a decade ago. His voice, his writing talent, and his stage presence were all part of the package.

He possessed a voice that could handle any style, including pop, country, rockabilly, blues and gospel. There was a romantic element in his vocal delivery that was also soothing, mellow, and good-natured. It appealed to a cross-section of fans of different musical genres, which is an important point when celebrating Twitty's career.

He started out singing rockabilly tunes in the late 1950s, but by the end of the career had settled down and spawned pure country gold. In between, he also cut songs that were comical as well as sensuous. Perhaps more than any artist, Twitty recorded an entire wealth of material that was restricted solely to an adult audience good for when the kids had gone to bed. Although his deep, resonant voice wasn't sexually supercharged, it did contain a certain mystique that allowed him to pull it all off.

He was the acknowledged king of country-pop during the 1970s, embellishing his songs with elements of R&B, blues and rock. Although there was always a purist movement in country to retain the roots, Twitty was from the other side of the philosophical debate and believed that the genre had to merge with other styles in order to appeal to a larger audience and for the genre to grow. If the music grew stale then it would wither on the vine and die. Twitty made sure that country remained a fresh force.

He gave the world a number of classic songs, including "I See the Want to in Your Eyes," "Linda on My Mind," "Touch the Hand," "After All the Good Is Gone," "I've Already Loved You in My Mind," "Happy Birthday Darlin'," "Tight Fittin' Jeans," and "Red Neckin' Love Makin' Night." No matter the song, whether it was an original or a cover version, he added his own dimension that elevated the material to a different status.

During his illustrious career he worked with a number of artists. A partial list includes David Barnes, Jim Vienneau, Ron Treat, Mike Lawler, Vince Gill, Curtis Young, David Hungate, Eddie Bayers, Reggie Young, John Hughey, Ray Edenton, Harold Bradley, Grady Martin, Willie Nelson, Dennis Wilson and Loretta Lynn. His collaboration with one of the queens of country music ensured the continued success of the genre.

Twitty influenced artists in rock, pop and country. A partial list includes Garth Brooks, Phil Ochs, Ronnie Hawkins, Sammy Kershaw, Sammy Johns, Ricky Van Shelton, Keith Harling, Gil Grand, Steve Holy, Brooks and Dunn, Randy Travis, Ricky Skaggs, Tim McGraw and many others. Although many of the names aforementioned have enjoyed great success, none are likely to duplicate the 40 number one hits that Twitty enjoyed during his career.

In 1999, Conway Twitty was inducted into the Country Music Hall of Fame. It is unfortunate that it was posthumously, because he deserved to be honored while still alive. Nevertheless, that final deal clearly illustrated that he was one of the most important artists in the history of the genre. He truly proved that he was a superstar, the Uncrowned King.

## Discography

*Conway Twitty Sings* [MGM], MGM 3744.
*Saturday Night with Conway Twitty*, MGM 376.
*Lonely Blue Boy*, MGM 3818.

*The Conway Twitty Touch*, MGM 3943.
*The Rock and Roll Story*, MGM 3907.
*Portrait of a Fool and Others*, MGM 4019.
*Hit the Road*, MGM 4217.
*It's Only Make Believe*, Metro 512.
*Conway Twitty Sings* [Decca], Decca 74724.
*Look into My Teardrops*, Decca 74828.
*Here's Conway Twitty and His Lonely Blue Boys*, Decca 74990.
*Next in Line*, Decca 75062.
*Darling, You Know I Wouldn't Lie*, Decca 75105.
*I Love You More Today*, MCA 404.
*You Can't Take Country Out of Conway*, MGM 4650.
*To See My Angel Cry*, Decca 75172.
*Hello Darlin'* [Decca], Decca 75209.
*How Much More Can She Stand*, Decca 75276.
*I Wonder What She'll Think About Me Leaving*, Decca 75292.
*Lead Me On*, Decca 75326.
*Conway Twitty Sings the Blues*, MGM 4837.
*Shake It Up*, Pickwick 3360.
*I Can't See Me Without You*, Decca 75335.
*Conway Twitty* [Decca], Decca 5361.
*I Can't Stop Loving You*, Decca 75361.
*She Needs Someone to Hold Her*, MCA 303.
*You've Never Been This Far Before*, MCA 359.
*Clinging to a Saving Hand*, MCA 376.
*Steal Away*, MCA 376.
*Who Will Pray for Me*, MCA Special 20716.
*Never Ending Song of Love*, Coral 8006.
*Honky Tonk Angel*, MCA 406.
*I'm Not Through Loving You Yet*, MCA 441.
*Country Partners*, MCA 427.
*Star Spangled Songs*, MFP 90064.
*Linda on My Mind*, MCA 469.
*Feelin's*, MCA 2717.
*This Time I've Hurt Her More*, MCA 2176.
*Twitty*, MCA 2176.
*High Priest of Country Music*, MCA 2144.
*Now and Then*, MCA 2206.
*United Talent*, MCA 2764.
*Dynamic Duo*, MCA 2278.
*Play Guitar Play*, MCA 2798.
*I've Already Loved You in My Mind*, MCA 2293.
*Conway Twitty Country*, Decca 74913.
*Georgia Keeps Pulling My Ring*, MCA 2328.
*Honky Tonk Heroes*, MCA 2372.
*Conwaty*, MCA 3063.
*Crosswinds*, MCA 3086.
*Country Rock*, MCA 414039.
*Diamond Duo*, MCA 3190.
*Heart and Soul*, MCA 3210.
*Rest Your Love on Me*, MCA 5138.
*Mr. T*, MCA 5204.

*Dream Maker*, Electra 60182.
*Two's a Party*, MCA 3190.
*Southern Comfort*, Elektra 60005.
*Number One's* [MCA], MCA 1488.
*Lost in the Feeling*, Warner 23869.
*Merry Twismas*, Warner 23971.
*Conway's Number 1 Classics, Vol. 2*, Elektra 60209.
*Conway Twitty and Loretta Lynn*, MCA 20169.
*By Heart*, Warner Bros. 25078.
*Don't Call Him a Cowboy*, Warner 25207.
*A Night with Conway Twitty*, MCA 5817.
*Fallin' for You for Years*, Warner 25408.
*Borderline*, MCA 5969.
*Still in Your Dreams*, MCA 42115.
*Making Believe*, MCA 42216.
*House on Old Lonesome Road*, MCA 42297.
*Crazy in Love*, MCA 10027.
*Number Ones, Vol. 2*, Capitol 96679.
*Number Ones, Vol. 1*, Capitol 96293.
*Even Now*, MCA 10335.
*Country Gospel Greats*, MCA 20713.
*Final Touches*, MCA 10882.
*Sings Songs of Love*, MCA 20858.
*Crazy Dreams*, Prime Cuts 23202.
*Road That I Walk*, Prestige Elite 170.
*20 Greatest Hits*, TeeVee 6009.
*You Made Me What I Am*, Allegiance 5012.
*Conway Twitty's Greatest Hits*, MGM 3849.
*R&B '63*, MGM 4089.
*Conway Twitty* [MGM], MGM 2351006.
*15 Years Ago*, Decca 75248.
*Conway Twitty Hits*, MGM 4799.
*Conway Twitty's Greatest Hits, Vol. 1* [Decca], Decca 75252.
*Greatest, Vol. 1*, MCA 1473.
*Rock'n'Roll Story*, Contour 2870151.
*20 Great Hits*, MGM 43884.
*Greatest Hits*, Capitol 77365.
*Conway Twitty's Greatest Hits, Vol. 2*, MCA 1680.
*The Best of Conway Twitty* [MCA], MCA 2737.
*The Best of Conway Twitty, Vol. 2*, MCA 20710.
*Rock'n'Roll*, Polydor 2624031.
*The Very Best of Conway Twitty* [MCA], MCA 3043.
*I'm So Used to Loving You*, Coral 20000.
*Conway's Latest Greatest Hits, Vol. 1*, Warner 25170.
*Sings the Great Country Hits*, TVP 1010.
*Greatest Hits* [Dominion], Dominion 3293.
*Classic Conway*, MCA 1574.
*Heart and Soul/Rest Your Love on Me*, MCA 6940.
*20 Greatest Hits* [MCA], MCA 5975.
*Number Ones: The Warner Brothers Years*, Warner 2-25777.
*Greatest Hits, Vol. 3*, MCA 6391.
*Silver Anniversary Collection*, MCA 8035.

*The Very Best of Conway Twitty*, MCA 31238.
*Cross Winds/Georgia Keeps Pulling on My Ring*, MCA 6909.
*Dynamic Duo/Honky Tonk Heroes*, MCA 38011.
*Hello Darlin'/Honky Tonk Angel*, MCA 38004.
*Lead Me On/United Talent*, MCA 38003.
*Linda on My Mind/Twitty*, MCA 38008.
*We Only Make Believe/Louisiana Woman/Mississippi Man*, MCA 38002.
*The Best of Conway Twitty, Vol. 1*: Mercury 849574.
*20 Greatest Hits*, TeeVee 702.
*Rockin' Conway: The MGM Years*, Mercury 314-519958-2.
*The Final Recordings of His Greatest Hits, Vol. 1*, Capitol/Curb 77641.
*The Final Recordings of His Greatest Hits, Vol. 2*, Capitol/Curb 77642.
*Gold*, Hollywood 463.
*The Best of Conway Twitty* [Laserlight], Delta 12438.
*Country on My Mind: Hits* [Drive Archive], Drive Archive 41955.
*Super Hits*, Epic 57841.
*The Conway Twitty Collection*, MCA 11095.
*Conway Twitty and Friend*, King 1145.
*His Greatest Hits*, Laserlight 12292.
*A Bridge That Just Won't Burn*, MCA Special 20786.
*Red Neckin' Love Makin' Night*, MCA Special 22129.
*Hello Darlin'* [MCA Special Products], MCA Special 22046.
*Greatest Hits* [Special Music], Special Music 5142.
*Away Too Long*, Chicago Music 120.
*Greatest Hits: Finest Performances*, Sun 7016.
*Super Hits, Vol. 2*, Epic 57842.
*Some of My Best*, CEMA Special 56908.
*Some of My Best, Vol. 2*, CEMA Special 17611.
*At His Best*, King 487.
*More Gold*, King 481.
*All Time Favorites*, Intercontinent 1115.
*Legendary*, Intercontinent 1098.
*Classic Conway, Vol. 1*, Kingfisher 2.
*Golden Classics: 20 Classic Tracks*, Masters 4002.
*Country Classics*, Critique 15462.
*Classic Conway, Vol. 2*, Kingfisher 10.
*The Best of the Best of Conway Twitty*, Federal 6502.
*High Priest of Country Music*, Edsel 500.
*Late Great*, Simitar 5503.
*Hello Darlin'* [Sun], Sun 6011.
*Conway and Loretta Sing the Hits*, MCA Special 21016.
*Rock 'n' Roll Years*, Bear Family 16112.
*Hits* [PolyGram], PolyGram 536218.
*Revue Collection*, Revue 422.
*The Rest of the Best*, Sterling 61878.
*Best of the Early Years*, PSM 520389.
*It's Only Make Believe: The Conway Twitty Collection*, Music Club 50053.
*The Best of Conway Twitty* [Pegasus], Cleopatra 753.
*Greatest Hits, Vol. 1*, Unison V82922.
*Greatest Hits*, Platinum Disc 6752.
*Greatest Hits, Vol. 1/Greatest Hits, Vol. 1-2*, Platinum Disc 6832.

*Back to Back,* K-Tel 42562.
*Sings Elvis Presley Favorites,* Polymedia 520639.
*Double Barrel Country,* Madacy 561.
*The Ultimate Collection,* Hip-O 64724.
*20th Century Masters—The Millennium Collection: The Best of Conway Twitty,* MCA 70085.
*Very Best of Conway Twitty,* Cleopatra 2000.
*Country Music Hall of Fame: 1999,* King 3821.
*20th Century Masters—The Millennium Collection: The Best of Conway Twitty and Loretta Lynn,* MCA 112251.
*Country Gold: Only Make Believe,* Direct Source 6000.
*The Best of Country,* Direct Source 6272.
*Classic Country,* Direct Source 7533.
*Country Spotlight,* Direct Source 6171.
*The Number 1s Collection,* MCA Nashville 170152.
*Love Songs,* MCA 78400.
*Oh Boy Classics Presents Conway Twitty,* Oh Boy 404.
*20th Century Masters—The Millennium Collection: The Best of Conway Twitty, Vol. 2,* MCA 170219.
*Conway Twitty: 20 Great Hits,* Platinum Disc 21532.
*16 Biggest Hits,* Sony 85972.
*20 Classics,* Varese 066252.
*Greatest Hits,* King 1500.
*Looking Back: The Very Best of the MGM Years,* RPM 246.
*The Legend, Vol. 2,* Platinum Disc 2837.
*The Legend, Vol. 1,* Platinum Disc 2836.
*The Legend,* Platinum Disc 2839.
*Conway Rocks,* Bear Family 16670.
*Hall of Fame 1999,* Gusto 513.
*Classic American Voices,* Direct Source 2515.
*The Gospel Spirit,* MCA 000296502.
*The Platinum Collection,* Direct Source 2691.
*Rock N Roll Collection,* Universal Entertainment 554150.
*After All the Good Is Gone,* RCR 6142.
*Baby's Gone,* RCR 6152.
*The Definitive Collection,* MCA Nashville 000358102.
*World of Conway Twitty,* Karusell 551432.
*The Initial Collection,* Direct Source 4331.
*Best of Conway Twitty,* Direct Source 5182.
*Pure Country,* Sony 27420.

# WAYLON JENNINGS (1937–2002)
## *Ladies Love Outlaws*

There have been many who contributed to the outlaw-rebel movement in country music in the 1960s and 1970s. Some—Willie Nelson,

Merle Haggard, Buck Owens, Johnny Cash, and Kris Kristofferson—acquired a larger reputation than others. However, there was another lonesome desperado of the period who personified the theory that Ladies Love Outlaws. His name was Waylon Jennings.

Waylon Arnold Jennings was born on June 15, 1937, in Littlefield, Texas. He developed his guitar skills quickly and by his teens was proficient enough to play in front of an audience. His development continued when at just twelve he found work on a radio station as a DJ. His strong voice and strong personality already in evidence by his teens would serve him well during his entire career. He dropped out of school before graduation and formed his first group.

He worked a series of jobs before he relocated to Lubbock, Texas, a town of little population, oil fields, cotton and corn. It would later be known as a rock and roll center due to the exploits of its most famous native son, Buddy Holly. But when Jennings arrived there in 1954, rock and roll was just on the horizon. As luck would have it, Waylon met the soon to be illustrious Buddy Holly while working on a radio show.

The bespectacled rocker with a penchant for rockabilly and handy with a turn of phrase tutored young Waylon. They talked shop, wrote songs together and Holly was a driving force behind Jennings' debut single, "Jole Blon." In 1958, he became the bass player for the Crickets (Holly's backing band) for a brief spell. In one of the true moments of fate in music history, on February 2, 1959, at the last moment he gave up his seat on the plane in an act of kindness to the Big Bopper. The plane crashed and killed Buddy Holly, the Big Bopper, and Ritchie Valens.

Two years of depression over the death of his friend made Jennings realize that he needed a change of venue, so he moved to Phoenix, Arizona, in 1960. He didn't take long to establish himself in the western city, as he formed the Waylors soon after his arrival. They gigged often and built up a local following that earned them a recording contract with Trend, but the singles that were released didn't further his career. Another contract, with A&M, failed because Jennings wanted to record country songs, not pop material like the label executives demanded.

It wasn't until 1965 that he managed to secure another contract through connections with super picker Chet Atkins. Jennings moved to Nashville the following year and impressed many with his musical abilities. One of his first connections was Johnny Cash, a renegade of the period who had scored a stream of hits in the late 1950s and early 1960s, but had fallen victim to substance abuse by the middle of the decade.

Although Jennings' first few singles didn't muster any attention, his performance on the *Grand Ole Opry* raised eyebrows. A genuine country artist at heart, Jennings's style also contained elements of rock and roll, mainly due to his association with Buddy Holly. He was dubbed a rebel, but his greatest act of rebelliousness would surface a few years later.

With each successive release he was slowly climbing higher in the charts. While "That's the Chance I'll Have to Take" didn't place very well, his second single for RCA, "Stop the World (and Let Me Off)," rated higher. This followed a string of top twenty hits, including "Walk on Out of My Mind," "I Got You," "Only Daddy That'll Walk the Line," and "Yours Love." Although he was enjoying some success, he began to grow increasingly disenchanted with the fabricated Nashville sound. He was gravitating to a more hardcore country style.

His talent and spirit were beginning to shine through his music. With the two albums *Singer of Sad Songs* and *Ladies Love Outlaws*, he laid down the foundation for the outlaw movement. The latter yielded "Never Been to Spain" and "Delta Dawn." A collaboration with Willie Nelson, the red headed rebel who had also turned his back on Nashville, fueled Jennings's desire to deliver a more muscular sound. A new deal with RCA provided him with the opportunity to forge his own destiny.

In 1973, he released *Honky Tonk Heroes,* a pure collection of driving country numbers with many derived from Billy Joe Shaver's songbook. The hard edged sound challenged listeners, but with hits such as "This Time," "I'm Ramblin' Man," and "Rainy Day Woman" it was very hard not to like what Jennings had to offer. He had proven that a country musician could make it in the genre without being tied to Nashville.

He added to his celebrity status as a honky tonk warrior with the 1975 release *Dreaming My Dreams*, which included "Are You Sure Hank Done It This Way," a minor hit that enabled Jennings to claim the award as Country Music Association's Male Vocalist of the Year. His appearance on *Wanted! The Outlaws* featured songs from Nelson, Tompall Glaser, and Jennings' wife, the sultry Jessi Colter.

Although the record did something for the reputation of the other three, it was Jennings who benefited the most because from this point on he enjoyed stellar success. The *Waylon and Willie* album, a collaboration with his good buddy and fellow outlaw rebel Nelson, placed high on the charts. The collection of songs included one dynamite classic, "Mammas Don't Let Your Babies Grow Up to Be Cowboys." This song more than any other celebrated the outlaw-rebel figure in country music.

During the latter part of the decade and the early 1980s, Jennings scored with "Luckenbach, Texas (Back to the Basics of Love)," "The Wurlitzer Prize (I Don't Want to Get Over You)," "I've Always Been Crazy," "Amanda," and the theme "*The Dukes of Hazzard* (Good Ol' Boys)." *Dukes* was one of the most popular TV shows during its prime and Jennings only added to his popularity every week when the theme song invaded millions of homes. Bo and Luke Duke were rebels always trying to outrun the bumbling local law enforcement.

Despite Jennings' success, all was not right in his universe. In the mid-1980s, he developed a drug habit that threatened to end his career. He managed to kick his substance abuse problems and revived the falling popularity of the outlaw movement. His first attempt was the Highwaymen project that included Cash, Nelson and Kris Kristofferson. The three albums that the quartet would eventually release were well received. It proved that the outlaw movement had not died.

It seemed that his fortunes were on the rise as he moved to a new label and scored a number of hit singles, including "Rose in Paradise." The revival in his career was short lived because at the end of the decade he had fallen on hard times again and was unable to crack the top forty. The songs "Wrong," and "The Eagle" were the last two minor hits that he enjoyed.

Jennings continued to plug away and since he enjoyed a devoted fan base managed to remain a name in country music circles. He released *Right for the Time*, in 1996, and *Closing In on the Fire*, in 1998. But on February 13, 2002, in Chandler, Arizona, the renegade outlaw singer died.

Waylon Jennings was a honky tonk hero. More than any other country artist—with perhaps the sole exception of Willie Nelson—he returned to the roots of the style and as a result created a whole new movement. He was a tough, independent individual who blazed his own trail with his hard core singing and electrified, sparse playing.

Waylon Jennings possessed a unique vocal phrasing that allowed him to be a hard edged, no-nonsense singer. During his career he switched from a slick to a more honest, barer style. In the process he became a star and an inspiration to countless new artists who desired to work outside the Nashville parameters.

Jennings worked with a number of stars, including Randy Scruggs, Gary Scruggs, Duke Goff, Jack Clement, Emmylou Harris, Johnny Gimble, Chet Atkins, Bobby Wood, Jessi Colter, Johnny Cash, Willie Nelson, David Briggs, Buddy Spicher, George Jones, and Hargus "Pig" Robbins. His most famous partners were his wife Jessi Colter as well as Johnny Cash, Willie Nelson and Kris Kristofferson, the latter three being part of the Highwaymen project.

Although there were many outlaw singers, Jennings epitomized the style more than just about anyone else except his frequent partner, Willie Nelson. But others, such as Tompall Glaser, David Allan Coe, Billy Joe Shaver, Merle Haggard, Mickey Newbury, Johnny Paycheck, Hank Williams, Jr., Charlie Rich, Bobby Bare, Ray Wylie Hubbard, Guy Clark, and Jerry Jeff Walker, were inspired by Waylon's hard stance. He was the leader of the rebel group that broke away from Nashville and shocked many in the country music community.

Perhaps better than any of his contemporaries, he was able to weld different styles of music, including rock, blues and honky tonk into an acceptable package that was refreshing in country music circles. His ability to incorporate various elements into one cohesive unit underlined his talent. Although he scored many country hits, he never truly left his rock and roll roots established during his days with Buddy Holly.

In 2001, Waylon Jennings was elected to the Country Music Hall of Fame. It was an honor that in 1975 would have seemed improbable due to the nature of his rebellious stance against Nashville. However, there was no denying the incredible career that he enjoyed from his early days in radio to his rock and roll period and then on to his country music phase. He proved to the world that without a doubt, ladies love outlaws.

## Discography

*Waylon at JD's*, Bat 1001.
*Nashville Rebel*, RCA 3736.
*Don't Think Twice*, RCA Victor 4238.
*Leavin' Town*, RCA Victor 3620.
*Folk Country*, Razor and Tie 8175.
*Sings Ol' Harlan*, RCA Victor 3660.
*The One and Only Waylon*, Camden 2183.
*Love of the Common People*, Buddha 99620.
*Hangin' On*, RCA 3918.
*Jewels*, RCA Victor 4085.
*Only the Greatest*, RCA Victor 4023.
*Country-Folk*, RCA Victor 4180.
*Just to Satisfy You*, RCA 4137.
*Waylon Jennings* [Diamond], Vocalion 738873.
*Singer of Sad Songs*, RCA 4418.
*Waylon*, RCA 4260.
*Waylon*, Pair 1005.
*The Country Style of Waylon Jennings*, A&M 1006.
*The Taker*, RCA 4487.
*Ned Kelly*, United Artists 3066.
*Cedartown, Georgia*, RCA 4567.
*Good Hearted Woman*, RCA 4647.
*Ladies Love Outlaws*, RCA 4751.
*Heartaches by the Number* [Camden], Camden 2556.
*Only Daddy That'll Walk the Line*, Camden ACL 1 0306.
*Lonesome*, On'ry and Mean, RCA 4854.
*Honky Tonk Heroes*, Buddha 99619.
*The Ramblin' Man*, Buddha 99699.
*This Time*, Buddha 99669.
*Dreaming My Dreams* [DCC], DCC 161.
*Are You Ready for the Country*, RCA 11816.

*Mackintosh and TJ* [original soundtrack], RCA Victor 11520.
*Dark Side of Fame*, Camden 17019.
*Wanted! The Outlaws*, RCA 1321.
*Waylon Live*, Buddha 99640.
*Ol' Waylon*, DCC 147.
*Waylon and Willie* [US], Buddha 45862.
*I've Always Been Crazy*, RCA 12959.
*What Goes Around*, RCA 3493.
*Music Man*, RCA 3602.
*Leather and Lace*, RCA 3931.
*Black on Black*, RCA 3072.
*WW2*, Buddha 99668.
*Waylon and Company*, RCA 4826.
*Never Could Toe the Mark*, RCA 5017.
*Will the Wolf Survive*, MCA 31102.
*Sweet Mother Texas*, RCA 7184.
*Hangin' Tough*, MCA 31298.
*The Eagle*, Epic 46104.
*My Rough and Rowdy Days*, MCA 20604.
*Clean Shirt*, Epic 47462.
*Too Dumb for New York City, Too Ugly for L.A.*, Epic 48982.
*Waymore's Blues, Part 2*, RCA 66409.
*Pancho, Lefty and Rudolph*, Sony 67296.
*The Highwayman*, Sony/CBS 902296.
*Right for the Time*, Buddha 99719.
*Cowboys, Sisters, Rascals and Dirt*, RCA 63450.
*Closing In on the Fire*, Ark 21 10023C.
*Just Out of Reach*, Private I.
*The Restless Kid—Live at JD's*, Bear Family 16385.
*Big Country*, Dressed to Kill 295.
*Never Say Die: Live*, Columbia 63853.
*Back to Back*, K-Tel 3029.
*Live from Austin TX*, New West 6091.
*The Taker*, Everest 1038.
*The Best of Waylon Jennings*, RCA 4341.
*Ruby, Don't Take Your Love to Town*, Camden 2608.
*The Hits of Waylon Jennings*, RCA 42211.
*Early Years*, RCA 9561-2.
*Greatest Hits* [RCA], RCA 3378.
*Waylon Music*, RCA 41366.
*In the Beginnings*, Bulldog 1052.
*It's Only Rock'n'roll*, RCA 4683.
*Most Wanted Nashville Rebel*, RCA 43169.
*Collection's Series* [1985], RCA 5473.
*Files 1*, Bear Family 15151.
*Files 2*, Bear Family 15152.
*Files, Vol. 3*, Bear Family 15153.
*Files 4*, Bear Family 15154.
*Files 5*, Bear Family 15155.
*Files, Vol. 6*, Bear Family 15156.
*Files, Vol. 7*, Bear Family 15157.
*Files 8*, Bear Family 15158.

268    Part Five: Outlaws, Rebels and Superstars

*Files, Vol. 9*, Bear Family 15159.
*Files 10*, Bear Family 15160.
*Files 11*, Bear Family 15161.
*Files 12*, Bear Family 15162.
*Files 13*, Bear Family 15163.
*Files 14*, Bear Family 15164.
*Files, Vol. 15*, Bear Family 16165.
*Collection*, Castle 110.
*Greatest Hits, Vol. 2*, RCA 5325.
*Waylon: The Best of Waylon Jennings*, RCA 5620.
*Turn the Page*, RCA 5428.
*Burning Memories*, Castle 107.
*A Man Called Hoss*, MCA 42038.
*Country Store*, Country Store 42.
*Full Circle*, MCA 42222.
*New Classic Waylon*, MCA 42287.
*Are You Sure Hank Done It This Way?*, RCA 61139.
*White Lightning*, Laserlight 15846.
*Only Daddy That'll Walk the Line: The RCA Collection*, RCA 6299.
*Burning Memories* [Classic Sound], Classic Sound 7566.
*Thanks to Buddy*, Drive Archive 41027.
*Six Hours at Pedernales*, Rock Bottom 84.
*2Gether on 1*, RCA 94552.
*Clovis to Phoenix: The Early Years*, Zu Zazz 2021.
*Singer Songwriters*, Sony Special Products 21130.
*Super Hits* [1996], RCA 66849.
*The Essential Waylon Jennings*, RCA 66857.
*All American Country*, Collectables 9544.
*Ladies Love Outlaws* [Compilation], BMG Special 44522.
*Waylon Jennings, Vol. 2*, RCA 67716.
*Encore Collection*, BMG 44522.
*Super Hits* [1999], RCA 67660.
*Backtracks*, Renaissance 0606.
*Waylon Jennings* [Classic World], Classic World 9924.
*The Journey: Six Strings Away*, Bear Family 16370.
*Heroes*, BMG International 20273.
*The Journey: Destiny's Child*, Bear Family 16320.
*Just Out of Reach*, Private 1 646341.
*20th Century Masters—The Millennium Collection: The Best of Waylon Jennings*, MCA 170139.
*The Gold Collection*, Fine Tune 1143.
*Classic Country*, Direct Source 7529.
*Dueling Country*, Direct Source 9018.
*Good Old Country*, St. Clair 78112.
*Heartaches by the Number* [Legend], Legend 64003.
*Midnight Country*, Dressed to Kill 0816.
*Country Stars and Stripes*, Direct Source 1298.
*Ramblin' Man/This Time/Dreaming My Dreams*, BMG 82337.
*Waylon Jennings* [Platinum Disc], Platinum Disc 2108.
*Legendary*, BMG International 88169.
*Classic Country Collection*, AIM 3001.
*Honky Tonk Heroes/Ramblin' Man/Dreaming My Dreams*, Buddha 99824.

*RCA Country Legends*, Buddha 99788.
*Phase One: The Early Years 1958–1964*, Hip-O 584096.
*Abilene*, Prestige Elite 129.
*Legends*, BMG 91096.
*Don't Think Twice*, Time Music 200.
*The Complete MCA Recordings*, MCA 000092602.
*Country Legends*, St. Clair 6753.
*Red River Tribute*, Underground Sound 3.
*Early Outlaw*, Fruit Tree 835.
*Brown Eyed Handsome Man*, BMG 0632.

# MERLE HAGGARD (1937–)
## Lonesome Fugitive

Throughout the long, illustrious history of country music, trends have often ruled the course and the attitude of the performers. A classic example is the outlaw movement of the 1960s that rallied against the mechanical Nashville production. There were many who followed the path that the rebels blazed, including the man known as the Lonesome Fugitive. His name was Merle Haggard.

Merle Haggard was born April 6, 1937, in Bakersfield, California, to Okies who had fled the depressed area of dust bowl east Oklahoma. His parents were so poor that they had converted a boxcar to live in when they arrived in the Golden State. His father played fiddle, but due to his mother's strict religious stance, he didn't play in honky tonks. The music lessons were brief because Haggard's father died when Merle was only nine.

Without a strong male influence, young Merle started to run wild and despite a stint in a juvenile home, he didn't change his ways. A series of petty thefts and one major charge of attempted burglary landed him in prison, where he picked and wrote a few tunes. It was while talking to the death row inmates in San Quentin that he decided to turn a new leaf. He cleaned up his life and decided to pursue a musical career.

Although Jimmie Rodgers, Bob Wills, Lefty Frizzell, and Hank Williams were important influences on him, it was seeing Johnny Cash perform in San Quentin that truly changed Haggard's attitude. Earlier he had befriended Frizzell after seeing him perform live. Merle was released from the jailhouse in 1960, a young man trying to put his life together.

He had previously married in the late 1950s and returned to his wife. With only a high school equivalence exam and little work experience, he was imprisoned in a series of low paying jobs. His sole release came when he sang in rough bars at night, honing his skills in the dark, crowded, noisy establishments. He eventually landed a job in Johnny Burnett's band that played at the Lucky Spot, a definite improvement over the dives he had previously performed in.

Haggard made other important connections, including Fuzzy Owen, the owner of a record label, as well as Lewis Talley. Merle cut "Skid Row," but the song didn't do much for his career. However, the qualities of the venues he played in did improve and that led to more appearances. He met other personalities in the burgeoning Bakersfield community that was steadily acquiring a reputation as a solid country music center. Although Owen and Talley were vital to establishing his career, it was the friendship he struck up with Buck Owens that truly sealed his future.

The hard-edged country style known as the Bakersfield sound relied on amplification that produced a much grittier product than the lush, more pop oriented material flowing out of Nashville. There was also an exciting element of western swing to the style that was more suited to the kind of music Haggard preferred. Aside from Owens, Tommy Collins and Wynn Stewart also had an impact on Merle's direction.

In 1962, through a series of events, Haggard landed the bassist spot in Stewart's group stationed in nearby Las Vegas. Aside from playing in one of the most noted bands of the West Coast, he was also able to record a Stewart number, "Sing a Sad Song," back in Bakersfield on the Tally label, owned by Owens. The single raced to the top twenty of the charts. Although his second effort, "Sam Hill," didn't repeat the same success, "Just Between the Two of Us," a duet with Bonnie Owens (he would later marry her) the former wife of Buck, hit the top forty. However, it was the Liz Anderson (mother of Lynn Anderson) tune "All My Friends Are Gonna Be Strangers" that brought him his first top ten hit.

He signed with Capitol in 1965, a much larger company that had more power to break him than the tiny Tally label. His first single for his new company was "I'm Gonna Break Every Heart I Can" and it flopped. Haggard was not easily discouraged and recorded "Swinging Doors," a huge hit that climbed into the top five. At about this time he formed his backing band, the Strangers. For the first time in his career, he was making major progress.

The pace accelerated with the release of "I'm a Lonesome Fugitive," a number one hit. It earned him the Country Music Association award as Top Male Vocalist in 1966, and he added to his mushrooming stardom with a second CMA award, the Top Vocal Group, which he shared with Bonnie Owens. However, all of this was just the beginning because from this point on he would rule the charts.

"I Threw Away the Rose" was a smash, and then he reeled off four number one hits in a row, including "Branded Man," "Sing Me Back Home," "The Legend of Bonnie and Clyde," and "Mama Tried," which referred to his wild ways and prison record. It was at this point that his writing took on a more personal style that highlighted his experiences. Although the press could have ruined his career, if anything this honest portrayal only enhanced his spreading reputation. He also made his acting debut in the movie *Killers Three*.

A further development in his songwriting occurred with the concept album *Same Train, A Different Time*, a tribute to his hero, Jimmie Rodgers. More than paying homage to one of his early idols, Haggard displayed his deep interest in American western history and his fascination for locomotives. It was a highly personal collection of songs that proved beneficial to his career.

He continued to write and record songs that gained considerable attention for their political stance, including "Hungry Eyes," "Workin' Man Blues," and "Okie from Muskogee." The latter attacked the entire counterculture philosophy and in the heady days of the 1960s it made a serious impact. President Nixon wrote him a letter of congratulations and George Wallace begged Haggard to be part of his political campaign, but the country singer refused the offer. With the profound recognition came the awards in droves. The Country Music Association voted him as Top Male Vocalist in both 1969 and 1970, and the album *The Strangers* earned best band honors.

He continued to release controversial, personal songs, including "The Fightin' Side of Me," as well as another concept album, *A Tribute to the Best Damn Fiddle Player in the World*. It was a tip of the hat off to Bob Wills, the father of western swing, for his incredible string skills. Eventually, Haggard joined the Texas Playboys for a brief spell that spurred on a revival of the style. As well, he played on the old master's last album, *For the Last Time*.

Haggard continued to score hits throughout the 1970s and his hold on the charts never abated. He was one of the stars of the decade and it wasn't until the very end that he showed any inconstancy. He picked it up in the early 1980s, with such songs as "The Way I Am," and "Misery and Gin," tunes featured in the movie *Bronco Billy* starring Clint Eastwood.

Eventually, Haggard left MCA and signed with Epic, where he began to produce his own albums. Despite the shift in labels, he continued to deliver the hits. He sang duets with Clint Eastwood, "Barroom Buddies," and with George Jones, "Yesterday's Wine," which became a number one hit. Later he would team up with Willie Nelson and they would have a number one chart topper with "Pancho and Lefty."

Like many other country singers, his career declined around the mid–1980s when radio stations started to play the songs of the new artists such as George Strait and Randy Travis. Ironically, Haggard was a major influence on the aforementioned two as well as the entire crop of young country artists. A shift in labels didn't help him any and in 1994, he signed with Anti, known as a punk-pop label. However, his music hadn't changed and although he was no longer placing number one hits on the charts on a consistent basis, the young country musicians paid tribute to him through their songwriting that sounded very similar to Haggard's. He continues to record and perform.

Merle Haggard is one of the most stylish performers in the annals of country music. He developed a singing and playing style that Bob Wills, Jimmie Rodgers and Hank Williams influenced, but was Haggard's own. He ruled the charts for much of the latter part of the 1960s and throughout the 1970s. He reached legendary status long before he stopped enjoying great success.

His sentimental vocals always expressed an earthiness, an honesty that made him a fan favorite. He possessed an earnest appeal that became one of his purest abilities. Yet there was always a subtle confrontational element in his style that provided great tension to his more earthy side. The two worlds didn't balance each other but collided, creating an exciting and very marketable product.

He has given the world an enormous wealth of treasures, including "Sing a Sad Song," "Sam Hill," "All My Friends Are Gonna Be Strangers," "I'm a Lonesome Fugitive," "The Bottle Let Me Down," "Branded Man," "Hungry Eyes," "Working Man Blues," "Mama Tried," "Okie from Muskogee," "Soldier's Last Letter," "Someday We'll Look Back," "Daddy Frank (The Guitar Man)," "Carolyn," "Grandma Harp," "It's Not Love (But It's Not Bad)," and "I Wonder If They Ever Think of Me." With his unique vocal delivery and musicianship he gave each song a special personal touch that often reflected his dark days as a troubled youth. Although he was never proud of his checkered past, he was honest enough to tell the story through his songs.

His highly personalized style influenced a number of performers and songwriters. A short list includes John Anderson, the Bellamy Brothers, Garth Brooks, John Conlee, Rodney Crowell, Billy Dean, George Strait, Dwight Yoakam, Phil Ochs, Hasil Adkins, Joe Ely, the Flying Burrito Brothers, Gram Parsons, Kenny Chesney, Earl Thomas Conley, Alan Jackson, Ken Mellons, and Rick Ferrell. He touched many others with the Haggard magic. There was a simplicity to his songs, but also a depth that made him one of the most exciting and copied artists on the circuit.

He worked with a number of people, including Tommy Collins, Freddy Powers, Bonnie Owens, Lefty Frizzell, Glen Martin, Hank

Cochran, Leona Williams, Townes Van Zandt, Chuck Howard, Willie Nelson, Bob Wills, Dolly Parton, Casey Anderson, Wynn Stewart, Buck Owens, Lou Bradley, Abe Manuel, Jr., Chet Atkins, Bobby Wood, Ray Charles, and Kris Kristofferson. He made an impact on everyone that he worked with throughout his long career.

He was also an architect of the Bakersfield sound that demanded a grittier, more hardcore edge than the lush productions that were streaming out of Nashville. Along with Buck Owens, Wynn Stewart, Bonnie Owens, Lefty Frizzell and a handful of others, Haggard built up Bakersfield as one of the prime country music centers in the world. His string of number one hits, conceptual albums, western themes and true honky tonk power forced the style to be taken seriously as a highly personalized branch of country music.

In 1994, Haggard was inducted to the Country Music Hall of Fame, a fitting tribute to the man who did much to revitalize the genre with his polished, honest songwriting and entertaining skills. Although he has been bestowed with many awards and honors, it is the influence on the younger generation of country musicians that is the most satisfying. The Lonesome Fugitive won over many hearts with his personal life story.

## Discography

*Strangers*, Koch 4053.
*Just Between the Two of Us*, Capitol 2453.
*I'm a Lonesome Fugitive*, Capitol 22027.
*Branded Man/I Threw Away the Rose*, Koch 2789.
*Legend of Bonnie and Clyde*, Capitol 2912.
*Mama Tried*, Capitol 34974.
*Sing Me Back Home* [Capitol], Koch 4054.
*The Instrumental Sound of the Strangers*, Capitol 169.
*Pride in What I Am*, Capitol 168.
*A Portrait of Merle Haggard*, Capitol 319.
*Okie from Muskogee* [Capitol], Capitol 384.
*Same Train, Different Time* [Bear Family], Bear Family 15740.
*Same Train, Different Time* [Capitol], Capitol 223.
*Introducing My Friends, the Strangers*, Capitol 445.
*Gettin' to Know Merle Haggard's Strangers*, Capitol 590.
*The Fightin' Side of Me*, King Special 451.
*A Tribute to the Best Damn Fiddle Player*, Koch 7900.
*Honky Tonkin'*, Capitol 796.
*Hag*, Capitol 735.
*Someday We'll Look Back*, Capitol 835.
*High on a Hilltop*, Capitol 707.
*Land of Many Churches*, Razor and Tie 2158.
*Let Me Tell You About a Song*, Capitol 882.
*It's Not Love (But It's Not Bad)*, Capitol 11127.

*I Love Dixie Blues ... So I Recorded Live in New Orleans*, Capitol 11200.
*Totally Instrumental ... With One Exception*, Capitol 11141.
*A Christmas Present*, Curb 77352.
*If We Make It through December*, Capitol 11276.
*Merle Haggard Presents His 30th Album*, Capitol 11331.
*Keep Movin' On*, Capitol 11365.
*It's All in the Movies*, Capitol 11483.
*My Love Affair with Trains*, Capitol 11544.
*The Roots of My Raising* [Capitol], Capitol 11586.
*Walking the Line*, Epic 40821.
*A Working Man Can't Get Nowhere Today*, Capitol 11693.
*Ramblin' Fever*, MCA 1643.
*My Farewell to Elvis*, MCA 2314.
*Eleven Winners*, Capitol 11745.
*The Way It Was in '51*, Capitol 11839.
*I'm Always on a Mountain When I Fall*, MCA 1644.
*All Night Long*, Curb 77410.
*Goin' Home for Christmas* [Epic], Epic 38307.
*Serving 190 Proof*, MCA 3089.
*Back to the Barrooms*, MCA 31099.
*The Way I Am*, MCA 1681.
*Rainbow Stew: Live at Anaheim Stadium*, MCA 31101.
*Songs for the Mama That Tried*, Songbird 5250.
*Big City*, Epic/Legacy 65947.
*Going Where the Lonely Go*, Epic 38092.
*A Taste of Yesterday's Wine*, Epic 38203.
*Heart to Heart*, PolyGram 812138.
*That's the Way Love Goes*, DCC 180.
*Pancho and Lefty*, Epic 37958.
*It's All in the Game*, Epic 39364.
*Close-Up*, Capitol 259.
*Kern River*, Epic 39602.
*Amber Waves of Grain*, Epic 40224.
*Merle Haggard — Songwriter*, MCA 5698.
*Friend in California*, Epic 40286.
*Out Among the Stars*, Epic 40107.
*Winners*, Capitol 16303.
*Seashores of Old Mexico*, Epic 40293.
*Chill Factor*, Epic 40986.
*5:01 Blues*, Epic 44283.
*Blue Jungle*, Curb 77313.
*The Family Bible*, Curb 77363.
*Live at Billy Bob's Texas*, Salsoul 5000.
*If I Could Only Fly*, Epitaph 86593.
*Cabin in the Hills*, Madacy 1108.
*Two Old Friends*, Madacy 1107.
*Roots, Vol. 1*, Epitaph 86634.
*Like Never Before*, Hag 5.
*Ol' Country Singer*, South 6029.
*Wish I Saw Santa Claus*, Smith Music Group 7033.
*Unforgettable Merle Haggard*, EMI 63716.
*It's Not Love (But It's Not Bad)*, RCA 604.

*Chicago Wind*, Capitol 74929.
*Live from Austin TX*, New West 6090.
*Swinging Doors/The Bottle Let Me Down*, Koch 4052.
*The Best of Merle Haggard* [Capitol 1968], Capitol 46484.
*Truly the Best of Merle Haggard*, Capitol 823.
*The Best of the Best of Merle Haggard*, Capitol 11082.
*Back to the Barrooms/Way I Am*, MCA 5929.
*Songs I'll Always Sing*, Capitol 11531.
*Country Boy*, Pair 1193.
*Merle and Willie: Gospel Best*, MCA 20478.
*What a Friend We Have in Jesus*, MCA Special 20787.
*Merle Haggard's Greatest Hits*, MCA 5386.
*Goin' Home for Christmas*, Sony Special 21527.
*Epic Collection (Recorded Live)*, Epic 39159.
*His Epic Hits: First Eleven to Be Continued*, Epic 39545.
*His Greatest and His Best*, MCA 5624.
*His Best*, MCA 5573.
*The Very Best of Merle Haggard*, Capitol 46484.
*The Best of Gospel*, MCA Special 20560.
*Capitol Collectors Series*, Capitol 93191.
*More of the Best*, Rhino 70917.
*Greatest Hits of the 80's*, Epic 46925.
*The Best of Country Blues*, Curb 77368.
*The Best of Merle Haggard* [Capitol 1990], Capitol 16054.
*I Think I'll Just Stay Here and Drink*, MCA Special 22027.
*Country Pride* [Excelsior], Excelsior 17994.
*18 Rare Classics*, Curb 77490.
*The Best of the Early Years*, Curb 77438.
*Okie from Muskogee* [Pair], Pair 57246.
*A Country Christmas with Merle Haggard*, Curb 9010.
*Country Pride* [CEMA], CEMA 54720.
*The Legendary Merle Haggard*, CEMA 8354.
*The Family Bible*, Cema 9290.
*Super Hits*, Epic 53310.
*Roots of My Raising*, Delta 46129.
*Merle Haggard: Greatest Hits, Vol. 1*, Capitol/Curb 77646.
*Merle Haggard: Greatest Hits, Vol. 2*, Capitol/Curb 77647.
*Greatest Hits, Vol. 1*, Dominion 3184–2.
*Number 1 Hits*, K-Tel 3184.
*Super Hits, Vol. 2*, Sony 66772.
*Greatest Hits* [Laserlight], LaserLight 12439.
*Sing Me Back Home: Hits*, Drive Archive 41056.
*Greatest Hits* [Essex], Essex 5141.
*Super Hits, Vol. 3*, Epic 67127.
*Christmas Country Style*, CEMA Special 56722.
*20 Hits Special Collection, Vol. 1*, Curb 77760.
*Greatest Hits* [CEMA], EMI-Capitol 17678.
*The Best of Merle Haggard* [Laserlight], Laserlight 12584.
*Lonesome Fugitive: The Merle Haggard Story*, Razor and Tie 82059.
*Untamed Hawk: The Early Recordings of Merle Haggard*, Bear Family 15744.
*It's Been a Great Afternoon*, MCA 20304.
*Greatest Hits: Finest Performances*, Sun 7015.

*24 Greatest Hits*, TeeVee 703.
*Today I Started Loving You Again* [King], King 1434.
*Vintage Collections Series*, Capitol 33838.
*Classics*, Sun 7026.
*The One and Only*, Intercontinent al 1100.
*Down Every Road*, Capitol 35711.
*Today I Started Loving You Again* [Kingfisher], Kingfisher 1.
*The Fightin' Side of Me*, King 1460.
*More Great #1 Hits*, Special Music 5219.
*Silver Wings*, Kingfisher 5.
*Golden Classics: 23 Classic Tracks*, Masters 4001.
*Country Classics, Vol. 2*, Critique 15460.
*Always Wanting You*, Kingfisher 9.
*Sings Story Songs*, Koch 1463.
*This Is for You*, Sony Special 28124.
*Okie from Muskogee* [Sun], Sun 6010.
*My Best*, Simitar 5504.
*Misery and Gin*, Kingfisher 13.
*Super Hits/Super Hits, Vol. 2/Super Hits Vol. 3*, Sony 65376.
*Legendary Performer*, Beacon 51593.
*This Is Merle Haggard*, Music Club 50046.
*Back 2 Back*, Intercontinent 1191.
*16 Biggest Hits*, Legacy/Epic 69321.
*I'm a Lonesome Fugitive* [Compilation], CST 55447.
*I'm a Lonesome Fugitive/Branded Man*, EMI 96854.
*Strangers/Swinging Doors*, EMI 96856.
*Yesterday's Wine (1981–1988)*, Edsel 549.
*Twelve Number 1 Hits, Vol. 1*, Platinum Disc 6742.
*Twelve Number 1 Hits, Vol. 2*, Platinum Disc 8922.
*A&E Biography*, Capitol 20304.
*For the Record: 43 Legendary Hits*, BNA 67844.
*Country Music Hall of Fame*, King 3812.
*20th Century Masters—The Millennium Collection: The Best of Merle Haggard*, MCA 112110.
*Best of the 90's, Vol. 1*, Curb 7796.
*Best of the 90's, Vol. 2*, Curb 77967.
*The Ultimate Collection*, Hip-O 541345.
*The Best of Country*, Direct Source 5962.
*Country Gold: Workin' Man*, Direct Source 6001.
*Dueling Country*, Direct Source 9044.
*Branded Man*, King 1481.
*Good Old Country*, St. Clair 78282.
*Super Hit Set*, King 3513.
*Best of the Best Gospel*, Federal 6545.
*Greatest Hits* [Legend], Legend 64013.
*20 Number One Hits*, Varèse 066164.
*Oh Boy Classics Presents: Merle Haggard*, Oh Boy 402.
*5:01 Blues/Chill Factor*, DCC 207.
*Elvis Favorites*, Universal 112071.
*New Light Through Old Windows*, 7-N Music 77008.
*Merle Haggard*, St. Clair 324.
*Stars over Bakersfield: Early Recordings*, Import 55418.

*Greatest Hits* [Madacy], Madacy 1747.
*Lonesome Fugitive: Live*, Town Sound 70570.
*Merle Haggard: 20 Great Hits*, Platinum Disc 2154.
*Hurtin'*, Capitol 34454.
*Prison*, Capitol 34453.
*Cheatin'*, Capitol 34455.
*Drinkin'*, Capitol 34452.
*In Concert*, Aim 1070.
*Oh Boy Classics Presents: Merle Haggard Again*, Oh Boy 407.
*Train Whistle Blues, Vol. 5*: Classic Railroad Songs, Rounder 1153.
*20 Greatest Hits*, Capitol 34482.
*21 Years of Super Hits*, Double Play 4066.
*My Love Affair with Trains/The Roots of My Raising*, Beat Goes On 544.
*The Peer Sessions*, Audum 8152.
*Best of Merle Haggard*, Columbia 191042.
*Hag/Let Me Tell You About a Song*, Beat Goes On 548.
*The Fugitive*, Prism 929.
*Classic American Voices*, Direct Source 2517.
*Walkin' Man Blues*, Acrobat 104.
*Award Winning Gospel Hits*, Compenda 8.
*Everybody Has the Blues*, RCA 602.
*Sing Me Back*, RCA 603.

# KENNY ROGERS (1938–)

## *The Gambler*

The explosion of country music in the 1970s featured a number of male contemporary stars. Some of them, like Johnny Cash, had started out singing rockabilly. Others struggled for a long time before they made it big, including Charlie Rich. In the mid 1970s, another singer began to gain increasing popularity as he racked up one number one hit after another to race ahead of the pack. He was known as the Gambler. His name is Kenny Rogers.

Kenneth Donald Rogers was born on August 21, 1938, in Houston, Texas. Rogers grew up poor along with his seven siblings, but he discovered music, which provided solace. He taught himself to play guitar and fiddle, but it was his voice that would earn him superstar status in country music circles. In high school, he joined his first group, called the Scholars, which managed to wax three singles, including "Kangeqah."

After graduating from high school, he released two singles, "We'll Always Fall in Love Again" and "For You Alone," on a local, independent label. Later he released "That Crazy Single" that earned him a spot on

*American Bandstand*. Although he had made progress with his musical career, he decided to give college a try. He took courses in music and commercial art before dropping out and joining the Bobby Doyle Three, a jazz combo. Rogers played bass in the group and remained long enough to record one album, *In a Most Unusual Way*. He left the Bobby Doyle Three fold and joined the Kirby Stone Four. He would later moonlight playing on a session that included Mickey Gilley's hit single "Is It Wrong."

Rogers concentrated on his solo career, releasing a few singles on the Mercury label, but it proved to be a dead end. The New Christy Minstrels provided a much better opportunity and he joined the group in 1966. His stint with the outfit was brief—one year—before he, Mike Settle, Terry Williams and Thelma Lou Camacho all left to form the First Edition. With the addition of drummer Terry Jones, the group found success with the singles "Just Dropped In (to See What Condition My Condition Was In)," "Ruby, Don't Take Your Love to Town" and "Reuben James." The group's repertoire (eventually billed as Kenny James and the First Edition) consisted of country, pop and mild psychedelic overtones. "Something's Burning" was the group's last significant big hit. However, they enjoyed their own syndicated television show.

The hits dried up even after they switched to Rogers' own label, Jolly Rogers. In 1974, Kenny left the group for a solo career and a year later the First Edition called it quits. At this point, Rogers had been in the music business for nearly twenty years and his success had been fleeting. His financial situation at the time was precarious, as his label went bankrupt.

Never one to quit, he signed to a major label and concentrated on middle of the road material with a strong country flavor. His first single, "Love Lifted Me," did well, but it was the song "Lucille" that really put him on the map. Suddenly, in 1977, Rogers seemed to be everywhere. "Lucille," the number one country hit of the year, had strong crossover appeal. The man who had waited for 20 years to gain success could now do no wrong.

From 1977 and for the next half dozen years, he established his legend. He dominated the charts with five number one country hits, including "Love or Something Like It," "The Gambler," "She Believes in Me," "You Decorated My Life," and "Coward of the County." He had major duet hits with Dottie West, "Every Time Two Fools Collide," "All I Ever Need Is You," and "What Are We Doin' in Love." He also teamed up with Kim Carnes on "Don't Fall in Love with a Dreamer," with Sheena Easton on "We've Got Tonight" and Dolly Parton on "Islands in the Stream." His name meant an instant hit no matter his singing partner.

But his success didn't stop with gold or platinum albums and singles. He also made a splash on television and the movies with such worthwhile material as *Six Pack* (a TV show) and the films *The Gambler* and *Coward of the County*. Both were major hits and he even starred in them. He hosted his annual Christmas television show that drew high ratings. Kenny Rogers was by now a household name.

After he scored with the song "Lady," the hits started to dry up in the mid–1980s. He did enjoy some success with "Crazy," "Real Love," "Morning Desire," "Tomb of the Unknown Love," and "Make No Mistake, She's Mine," a duet with Ronnie Milsap. His last big hit was the 1989 release "The Vows Go Unbroken (Always True to You)." Despite falling on hard times, he had enjoyed a long period in the spotlight.

Although his musical career waned in the 1990s, he remained popular through charity work, concerts and his very own fast food restaurants. He seemed to be everywhere with his television specials, movies and photography, and the self-publication of two books of his photos. He continued to record but never came close to the same mega success he enjoyed in the late 1970s and early 1980s. He continues to record and perform.

Kenny Rogers is a country music winner. Although it took him a very long time to achieve superstar status, once he arrived he was there to stay. For six years, he was undoubtedly the number one superstar, outshining Johnny Cash, Glen Campbell, Roy Clark, George Jones and a host of his contemporaries. Perhaps only Dolly Parton could claim the same high plateau that Rogers reached in the late 1970s. It is this period in his career that will forever be remembered by fans.

Kenny Rogers had a tailor made style for the material he recorded and it was this formula that was the secret to his enormous success. He never tried to be something he wasn't as a singer and although he didn't possess the greatest pipes, his voice had a soothing element that millions found comforting. The familiarity in his voice went a long way toward establishing his power on the charts.

He was very much a man of the times and that is perhaps why it took him so long to make it in the music business. In the late 1970s and early 1980s the public demanded exactly what he had to offer. It was a perfect match of supply and demand and this simple business formula allowed him to race to the top of the charts. Time favors the prepared man and Rogers had learned the business through and through as a member of the New Minstrel Singers and the First Edition.

His golden era of the late 1970s is the period that influenced a large number of artists. A short list includes Travis Tritt, Atlanta, Alabama, Alan Jackson, Brooks and Dunn, Clint Black, David Bellamy, Garth Brooks, George Strait, Ricky Van Shelton, Randy Travis, Ronnie Milsap, Tim McGraw, Vince Gill and Dwight Yoakam, among others. But his country-pop overtones had an effect on numerous singers outside of country music.

As part of the New Minstrel Singers, the First Edition, as a solo artist or part of a duet, he had numerous hits. A partial list includes "Coward of the County," "Lady," "Ruby, Don't Take Your Love to Town," "Reuben James," "Lucille," "The Gambler," "She Believes in Me," "Heed the Call," "Sunshine," "Islands in the Stream," "Crazy," "Real Love," "Morning Desire," "Tomb of the Unknown Love," "Make No Mistake, She's Mine," and many others. Even today his biggest hits are instantly recognizable and take the listener back to a specific time period. Many people grew up humming "Coward of the County," "The Gambler," and "Lucille." They became a staple of daily American life.

Rogers worked with a number of individuals including Bergen White, Jim McKell, Randy Dorman, Farrell Morris, Jim Horn, Shane Keister, Mills Logan, Pat Bergeson, George Tidwell, Brent Maher, Lisa Silver, Cindy Reynolds Wyatt, John Willis, as well as members of the New Christy Minstrels and First Edition. But he will be best remembered for his solo work as much as anything else.

Kenny Rogers is one of the most important contemporary male country music stories of the modern era. He spent years struggling and when he did find a formula for success it was a very rich one indeed. The period he spent as a relatively unknown singer were the dues he was paying. The Gambler knew how to play his cards.

## Discography

*The First Edition*, Reprise 6276.
*Ruby Don't Take Your Love to Town*, Reprise 6352.
*Fools*, Reprise 6429.
*Something's Burning*, Reprise 6385.
*Tell It All Brother*, Reprise 6414.
*Transition*, Reprise 2039.
*Backroads*, Jolly Roger 5001.
*Planet Texas*, Reprise 4–27690.
*The Ballad of Calico*, Reprise 6426.
*Monument*, Jolly Rogers 5004.
*Rollin*, Jolly Rogers 5003.
*Love Lifted Me*, EMI America E2–48401.
*Daytime Friends*, EMI America E2–48406.
*Kenny Rogers*, United Artists 689.
*Love or Something Like It*, United Artists 30194.
*The Gambler* [EMI], EMI America E2–48404.
*Every Time Two Fools Collide*, United Artists 30170.
*Kenny*, Razor and Tie 2041.
*Gideon*, Razor and Tie 2042.
*Shine Out*, Radar 24037.
*Christmas* [EMI], EMI America E2–46558.
*Lady*, Liberty 30334.

*Ruby*, MFP 50514.
*Share Your Love*, Razor and Tie 2049.
*Love Will Turn You Around*, EMI America E2-48407.
*We've Got Tonight*, Razor and Tie 2050.
*Eyes That See in the Dark*, RCA 6088.
*What About Me*, RCA 85043.
*Once Upon a Christmas*, RCA 85307.
*Heart of the Matter*, RCA 7023.
*Love Is What We Make It*, Liberty 51157.
*Short Stories*, Liberty 51170.
*They Don't Make 'Em Like They Used To*, RCA 5633-2.
*I Prefer the Moonlight*, RCA 6484-2.
*Christmas in America*, Reprise 2-25973.
*Something Inside So Strong*, Reprise 2-25792.
*Yes, No, Maybe*, Cypress 14166-0132-2.
*Love Is Strange*, Reprise 2-26289.
*Some Prisons Don't Have*, Warner 26740.
*Back Home Again*, Reprise 2-26740.
*Lucille*, Special Music 57251.
*Heart to Heart* [RCA], RCA 1046.
*If Only My Heart Had a Voice*, Warner 24490.
*Timepiece*, 143/Atlantic 82698.
*Country Songs*, MCA 913.
*Pieces of Calico Silver*, MCA 944.
*The Gift*, Magnatone 108.
*Across My Heart*, Magnatone 116.
*Branson City Limits* [live], Unison 9009.
*Christmas from the Heart*, Dreamcatcher 1.
*She Rides Wild Horses*, Dream Catcher 4.
*Christmas Greetings*, Capitol 27287.
*X-Mas*, Disky 87731.
*Christmas Wishes from Kenny Rogers*, Delta 21730.
*There You Go Again*, Dream Catcher 6.
*The Way It Used to Be*, Direct Source 5043.
*A&E Live by Request*, Dreamcatcher 7.
*Sing You a Sad Song*, Starburst 1043.
*Calico Silver*, Kala 2041.
*For the Good Times*, Musicbank 1165.
*Ruby, Don't Take Your Love to Town*, Planet Media 1126.
*Back to the Well*, Import 90129.
*Heart of the Matter*, Castle 699.
*Back to the Well*, Dream 8.
*If Only My Heart Had a Voice*, Castle 819.
*Back to the Well*, Sanctuary 129.
*Christmas with Kenny*, Rio Creek 3001.
*American Classic Songbook*, Artemis 1795.
*Water and Bridges*, Capitol Nashville 63614.
*HBO Presents Kenny Rogers*, Liberty 8344.
*Vows Go Unbroken (Always True to You)*, Reprise 22828.
*Christmas Without You*, RCA 9070-4-R52.
*Star Collection*, WEA 24012.
*Singles Album*, United Artists 30263.

*Classics*, United Artists 30235.
*Ten Years of Gold* [EMI-Capitol Special Markets], EMI America 48047.
*Greatest Hits* [Evergreen], Evergreen 9056.
*Greatest Hits* [EMI America], EMI America 7–4600.
*Greatest Hits* [SND], SND 56.
*20 Greatest Hits* [EMI America], EMI America 46106.
*The Best of Kenny Rogers* [Breakaway], Breakaway 100.
*Duets*, Capitol 46595.
*15 Greatest Hits*, MCA 5895.
*25 Greatest Hits*, EMI America 46673.
*Kenny Rogers with Kim Carnes*, Capitol 92802.
*Breakout*, Pair 1238.
*Lucille and Other Classic*, Pair 57251.
*All Time Greatest Hits, Vol. 2*, MCA Special 22056.
*Greatest Hits* [RCA], RCA 31311.
*Hits and Pieces*, MCA 943.
*Featuring the Songs of Kenny Rogers and First Edition*, MCA Special 22011.
*20 Great Years*, Reprise 2–26711.
*Greatest Country Hits*, Curb 77358.
*At Their Best*, Hollywood 410.
*The Best of Kenny Rogers and the First Edition*, Huub 55042.
*The Very Best*, Quicksilver 5056.
*Love Songs* [MCA], MCA Special 22039.
*The Best of Kenny Rogers* [CEMA], CEMA 57683.
*All Time Greatest Hits, Vol. 1*, MCA Special 22055.
*Every Time Two Fools Collide: The Best of Kenny Rogers and Dottie West*, EMI-Capitol 56838,
*20 Greatest Hits* [Big Country], Big Country 30215.
*Early Years*, Essex 4801.
*60's Revisited*, MCA 942.
*Ultimate*, Bransounds 7620.
*Christmas Wishes*, CEMA Special 18226.
*Greatest Hits* [Prime Cuts], Prime Cuts 1346.
*Anthology*, Alex VSOP148.
*The Best of Kenny Rogers* [Capitol], Capitol 35779.
*Sweet Music Man*, CEMA 9187.
*Kenny Rogers* [Eclipse], Eclipse Music 64703.
*Golden Hits*, Intercontinent 1012.
*Greatest Hits* [Hip-O], Hip-O 40016.
*All-Time Greatest Hits*, CEMA 1130–15015.
*Greatest Hits, Vol. 1*, Public Music 9012.
*Decade of Hits*, Warner 46571.
*20 Golden Hits*, Galaxy 388411.
*Songs You Know By Heart*, Beacon 51590.
*Revue Collection*, Revue 420.
*King of Country*, Javelin 104.
*For the Good Times* [SMS], Planet 1008.
*Original Hits*, Master Tone 303.
*Good Time Liberator*, Mastertone 8349.
*With Love* [1998], Madacy 371.
*Original Gold*, Disky 85386.
*Original Gold Disc One*, Disky 85387.

*Original Gold Disc Two*, Disky 85388.
*Through the Years* [Disc 1], BX 207.
*Through the Years* [Disc 2], BX 0821.
*Through the Years* [Disc 3], BX 0920.
*For the Good Times* [Cleopatra], Cleopatra 456.
*Through the Years: A Retrospective*, Capitol 33183.
*A&E Biography* [live], Capitol 98755.
*Love Collection* [1999], Madacy 1177.
*Classic Love Songs*, Crimson 209.
*Through the Years*, Golden Sounds 85206.
*The Greatest Hits: 1983–1988*, Music Club 371.
*Love Songs* [Madacy Box], Madacy 8643.
*Love Songs* [Madacy Box Disc 2], Madacy 8642.
*Love Songs* [Madacy Box Disc 1], Madacy 8641.
*All the Hits and All New Love*, EMI 520778.
*Endless Love*, Empire Music 410.
*Simply the Best*, Disky 86004.
*Kenny Rogers*, Liberty E2-48402.
*First Hits*, Legacy 92.
*Solid Gold*, Cleopatra 745.
*Forever Gold*, St. Clair 5823.
*Always in Love*, Madacy 1637.
*Hearts on Fire*, Madacy 325.
*Heart to Heart* [Madacy], Madacy 326.
*Kenny Rogers and Friends*, Madacy 327.
*Classics from the Heart*, Madacy 328.
*Collector's Edition* [two disc], Madacy 3471.
*Collector's Edition* [single disc], Madacy 3459.
*Always and Forever*, Madacy 495.
*The Gold Collection*, Fine Tune 1142.
*The Best of Love* [box], Madacy 486.
*Classic Country*, Direct Source 7525.
*Dueling Country*, Direct Source 9021.
*Platinum Series*, D-3 3330.
*Good Old Country*, St. Clair 78122.
*With Love* [2000], Madacy 866.
*The Best of Kenny Rogers and the First Edition*, Edeltone 172182.
*Superstar*, Dressed to Kill 390.
*The Love Collection* [2000 Madacy Box], Madacy 1177.
*Greatest Hits*, Columbia River 190044.
*Love Songs, Vol. 2*, Capitol 27516.
*Greatest Country Hits, Vol. 2*, Curb 78704.
*Greatest Country Hits, Vol. 3*, Curb 78705.
*For the Good Times* [Direct Source], Direct Source 5042.
*For the Good Times, Vol. 2*, Platinum 2389.
*Signature Series*, Direct Source 1493.
*Best Inspirational Songs*, Curb 77952.
*The Best of Kenny Rogers* [Madacy], Madacy 3124.
*Songs of Love*, Madacy 483.
*Ten Years of Gold* [Madacy], Madacy 3126.
*The Gambler* [Dreamcatcher], Dreamcatcher 902.
*Always Leaving*, Starburst 1039.

*The Legends Collection: The Kenny Rogers Collection*, Legends 768.
*Love Songs* [Madacy], Madacy 50484.
*Collection*, Madacy 25864.
*Kenny Rogers Love Songs*, Capitol 753694.
*Kenny Rogers*, Columbia River 190045.
*Kenny Rogers*, Laserlight 21770.
*For the Good Times*, Park South 900006.
*The Gambler*, Originals 631327.
*The Heart of a Legend*, Madacy 5484.
*Kenny Rogers*, Columbia River 191047.
*Country Classics*, EMI Gold 6322.
*Kenny Rogers*, Direct Sound 1029.
*Sunshine, Vols. 1–2*, Platinum Disc 2467.
*Classic American Voices*, Direct Source 2529.
*Beginnings of an Icon*, American Legends 100112.
*Classic Love Songs*, Double Play 4071.
*The Greatest*, Rio Creek 3000.
*The Hits and More*, Goldies 25437.
*Unchained Melody*, Disky 24889.
*20th Century Masters—The Millennium Collection: The Best of Kenny Rogers*, Hip-O/Geffen 000103702.
*Hits Collection*, MCA 18230
*Anthology*, Cleopatra 1370.
*Country Greatest*, EMI 576040.
*42 Ultimate Hits*, EMI 98794.
*Country Legends*, St. Clair 6752.
*Buried Treasure*, Sanctuary 37499.
*Something's Burnin'*, Masked Weasel 309.
*This Is Gold*, Disky 902059.

# *Bibliography*

Acuff, Roy. *Roy Acuff's Nashville*. New York: Perigee Books, 1983.
Allen, Bob. *George Jones: The Life and Times of a Honky Tonk Legend*. New York: St. Martin's Press, 1996.
\_\_\_\_\_. *Waylon and Willie*. New York: Flash Books, 1979.
Arnold, Eddy. *It's a Long Way from Chest*. New York: Pyramid Books, 1976.
Atkins, John. *The Carter Family*. New York: Old Time Music, 1973.
Barthel, Norman. *Ernest Tubb: The Original E. T.* Oklahoma: Rowland, 1984.
Bego, Mark. *I Fall to Pieces: The Music and the Life of Patsy Cline*. Hollbrook, Massachusetts: Adams Media Corp, 1995.
Black, Bob. *Come Hither to Go Yonder: Playing Bluegrass with Bill Monroe*. Illinois: University of Illinois Press, 2005.
Brown, Jim, and Matin Melhuish. *George Jones: Why Baby Why*. Indiana, New York: Quarry Music Books, 2000.
Campbell, Glen, and Tom Carter. *Rhinestone Cowboy: An Autobiography*. New York: St. Martin's Press, 1995.
Carlin, Richard. *The Big Book of Country Music: A Biographical Encyclopedia*. New York: Penguin, 1995.
Carter Cash, June. *From the Heart*. New York: St. Martin's Press, 1988.
Cash, Johnny, and Patrick Carr. *Cash: The Autobiography*. San Francisco: Harper, 1997.
Clark, Roy. *My Life in Spite of Myself*. New York: Simon and Schuster, 1994.
Cross, Wilbur, and Micheal Kosser. *Conway Twitty Story: An Authorized Biography*. New York: Doubleday, 1986.
Cusic, Don. *Eddy Arnold: I'll Hold You in My Heart*. Nashville: Ruthledge Hill Press, 1997.
Daley, Dan. *The Nashville Music Machine: Unwritten Rules of the Country Music Business*. New York: Overlook Hardcore, 1997.
De Marco, Mario. *Ken Maynard: The Fiddling Buckaroo*. Publisher Unknown. 1979.
Donleavy, Kevin. *Strings of Life: Conversations with Old-Time Musicians from Virginia and North Carolina*. Blacksburg, Virginia: Pocahontas Press, 2004.
Dunkleburger, A.C. *Queen of Country Music: The Life Story of Kitty Wells*. Nashville, Tennessee: Ambrose Printing, 1977.
Emery, Ralph. *The View from Nashville*. New York, William Morrow, 1998.
\_\_\_\_\_, with Patsi Bade Cox. *Fifty Years Down a Country Road*. New York: William Morrow, 2000.
Enns, Chris. *The Cowboy and the Senorita: A Biography of Roy Rogers and Dale Evans*. San Ramon, California: Falcon, 2004.
Erbsen, Wayne. *Rural Roots of Bluegrass, Songs, Stories and History*. Charlotte, North Carolina: Native Ground Music, 2003.

Eron, Judy. *Charlie Rich (Rock's Popstars)*. New York: Children's Press, 1975.
Escott, Colin. *Conway Twitty: The Rock 'n' Roll Years*. Germany: Bremen, 1986.
\_\_\_\_, George Merritt, and William MacEwen. *Hank Williams: The Biography*. New York: Little Brown, 1995.
\_\_\_\_, and Vince Gill. *The Grand Ole Opry: The Making of an American Icon*. New York: Center Street Publisher, 2006.
George-Warren, Holly. *The Singing Cowboy: Gene Autry's Wild Ride*. New York: Oxford University Press, 2006.
Green, Douglas B. *Singing in the Saddle: The History of the Singing Cowboy*. Nashville, Tennessee: Vanderbilt University Press, 2005.
Haggard, Merle, and Tom Carter. M*erle Haggard's My House of Memories: For the Record*. New York: HarperEntertainment, 2002.
Hall, Doug. *The Real Patsy Cline*. Dallas, Texas: Quarry Press, 1998.
Hemphill, Paul. *Lovesick Blues: The Life of Hank Williams*. New York: Penguin, 2006.
Hill, Fred. *Grass Roots: An Illustrated History of Bluegrass and Mountain Music*. Lincolnton, North Carolina: Academy Books, 1981.
Hume, Martha. *Kenny Rogers, Gambler, Dreamer, Lover*. New York: New American Library, 1980.
Jennings, Waylon, and Lenny Kaye. *Waylon: An Autobiography*. New York: Warner Books, 1998.
Jones, George. *I Lived to Tell It All*. New York: Dell, 1997.
Jones, Margeret. *Patsy: The Life and Times of Patsy Cline*. New York: Da Capo Press, 1999.
Jones, Timothy Edward. *Country Conversations: Timeless Stories from the Legends of Country Music*. Washington, D.C.: PublishAmerica, 2006.
Kingsbury, Paul, Ed. *Encyclopedia of Country Music: The Ultimate Guide to the Music*. New York: Oxford University Press, 1998.
Knight, Peggy. *My 33 Years Inside the House of Cash: A Special Tribute to My Closest Friends: Johnny, June, and Mother Maybelle*. Nashville, Tennessee: Premium American Press, 2004.
Koon, George William, and Bill Koon. *Hank Williams: So Lonesome*. Mississippi: University of Mississippi Press, 2002.
Lynn, Loretta. *Coal Miner's Daughter*. New York: Warner Books, 1976.
\_\_\_\_, and Patsi Bale Cox. *Still Woman Enough: A Memoir*. Boston, Massachusetts: Hyperion, 2002.
Malone, Bill C. *Singing Cowboys and Musical Mountaineers: Southern Culture and the Roots of Country Music*. Athens, Georgia: University of Georgia Press, 2003.
\_\_\_\_. *Stars of Country Music: Uncle Dave Macon to Johnny Rodriguez*. Chicago: University of Illinois Press, 1975.
Mansfield, Brian. *Remembering Patsy*. Nashville, Tennessee: Rutledge Hill Press, 2003.
McGee, Marty. *Traditional Musicians of the Central Blue Ridge: Old Time, Early Country, Folk and Bluegrass Label Recording Artists, with Discographies (Contributions to Southern Appalachian Studies)*. North Carolina: McFarland, 2000.
McWhorter, Frankie, John R. Erickson, and Lanny Fiel. *Cowboy Fiddler in Bob Wills' Band*. Denton, Texas: University of North Texas Press, 1997.
Miller, Bill. *Cash: An American Man*. New York: CMT, 2004.
Nassour, Ellis. *Honky Tonk Angel: The Intimate Story of Patsy Cline*. New York: St. Martin's Books, 1994.
Palmer, Jack, and Robert Olson. *Vernon Dalhart: First Star of Country Music*. Littleton, Colorado: Mainspring Press, 2004.

Piazza, Tom. *True Adventures with the King of Bluegrass.* Nashville, Tennessee: Vanderbilt University Press, 1999.
Porterfield, Nolan. *Jimmie Rodgers: The Life and Times of America's Blue Yodeler.* Illinois: University of Illinois Press, 1992.
Pruett, Barbara J. *Marty Robbins: Fast Cars and Country Music.* Lanham, Maryland: Scarecrow, 1990.
Pugh, Ronnie. *Ernest Tubb: The Texas Troubadour.* North Carolina: Duke University Press, 1996.
Rodgers, Carrie and Cecil Williamson. *My Husband Jimmie Rodgers.* Nashville: Country Music Foundations, 1975.
Rorrer, Clifford Kinney. *Charlie Poole and the North Carolina Ramblers.* North Carolina: Tar Heel Printing, 1968.
Rothel, David. *The Singing Cowboys.* London, England: W.H. Smith Publishers, 1981.
Russell, Tony, and Bob Pinson. *Country Music Records: A Discography, 1921–1942.* New York: Oxford University Press, 2004.
Schlappi, Elizabeth. *Roy Acuff: The Smoky Mountain Boy.* New York: Pelican, 1978.
Sheldon, Ruth. *Bob Wills: Hubbin It.* Nashville: Country Music Foundation, 1995.
Smith, Richard D. *The Life of Bill Monroe, Father of Bluegrass.* New York: Da Capo, 2001.
Snow, Clarence Eugene, Jack Owenbey, and Robert Burris. *The Hank Snow Story (Music in American Life).* Illinois: University of Illinois Press, 1994.
Stanfield, Peter. *Horse Opera: The Strange History of the 1930s Singing Cowboy.* Illinois: University of Illinois Press, 2002.
Streissguth, Micheal. *Eddy Arnold: Pioneer of the Nashville Sound.* New York: Schirmer Books, 1997.
Thomson, Graeme. *Willie Nelson: The Outlaw.* London, England: Virgin Books, 2006.
Tilton, Jeff Todd. *Old-Time Kentucky Fiddle Tunes.* Kentucky: University Press of Kentucky, 2001.
Townsend, Charles. *San Antonio Rose: The Life and Music of Bob Wills.* Illinois: University of Illinois Press, 1986.
Tribe, Ivan M. *The Stonemans: An Appalachian Family and the Music That Shaped Their Lives (Music in America).* Illinois: University of Illinois Press, 1993.
Turner, Steve, and Rex Linn. *Johnny Cash: The Life, Love and Faith of an American Legend—The Authorized Biography.* New York: Blackstone Books, 2005.
Urbanski, Dave. *The Man Comes Around: The Spiritual Journey of Johnny Cash.* Columbus, Ohio: Relevant Books, 2003.
White, Raymond E. *King of the Cowboys, Queen of the West: Roy Rogers and Dale Evans.* New York: Popular Press 3, 2006.
Wiggins, Gene. *Fiddlin' Georgia Crazy: Fiddlin' John Carson His Real World and the Real World of His Songs.* Illinois: University of Illinois Press, 1986.
Wills, Bob. *King of Western Swing.* New York: Hal Leonard Corporation, 1997.
Wills, Rosetta. *The King of Western Swing: Bob Wills Remembered.* New York: Watson-Guptill Publications, 2000.
Wolfe, Charles. *Classic Country.* New York: Routledge, 2000.
\_\_\_\_\_. *A Good-Natured Riot: The Birth of the Grand Ole Opry.* Nashville: Vanderbilt University Press, 1999.
Zwonitzer, Mark, and Charles Hirschberg. *Will You Miss Me When I'm Gone? The Carter Family and Their Legacy in American Music.* New York: Simon and Schuster, 2004.

# Index

Numbers in *bold italics* indicate pages with main entries.

A., Johnny 201
Abbott, Bill 232
Acuff, Roy 15, 30, *54–60*, 65, 70, 73, 115, 141, 142, 171, 247, 285, 287
Acuff, Roy, and His Smokey Mountain Boys 49, 50, 55
Adair, Smith "Hezzy" 128
Adams, Pee Wee 216
Adams, Teddy 101
Adcock, Eddie 95, 109, 135
Addington, Maybelle 28, 29
Adkins, Hasil 272
Alabama 238, 279
Albright, Oscar 18, 20
Alguier, Danny 101
Allen, Buddy 214
Allen, Deborah 183
Allen, Red 95
Allen, Rex 70
Allen, Sanford 243
Allison, Joe 243
Alvin, Phil 127
Anderson, Bill 57, 127
Anderson, Casey 273
Anderson, David 127
Anderson, John 197, 272
Anderson, Lee 101
Anderson, Liz 270
Anderson, Lynn 161, 165, 172, 180, 183, 188, 194, 270
Andrews, Jim 111
Andrews, Joe 101
Andrews Sisters 113
Anglin, Jack 171
Ann-Margret 230
Arkin, Steve 109, 135
Arkins, Bobby 109
Armstrong, Louis 42, 44
Arnold, Eddy 22, 51, 57, 66, 70, 74, *88–93*, 285, 287
Arnspiger, Norman 97, 101
Ashley, "Tom" Clarence 9

Ashlock, Jesse 100, 101
Asleep at the Wheel 100, 115, 208, 249
The Association 235, 237
Atkins, Chet 34, 41, 65, 75, 86, 87, 115, 127, 164, 198, *199–205*, 232, 242, 263, 265, 273
Atkins, Jim 199
Atlanta 201, 238, 279
Atlanta Symphony Orchestra 200
Austin, Bobby 215
Austin, Chad 209
Austin, Lonnie 33, 34
Austin, Sherrie 189, 222
Autry, Gene 6, 45, 50, 52, 53, 56, 58, 62, 63, 65, *67–72*, 76, 77, 78, 91, 116, 137, 167, 197, 286
*Avalon Time* 73

Baez, Joan 30
Bailey, DeFord 16, 49
Baker, Billy 110
Baker, Bob 69
Baker, Kenny 110
Ball, E.C. 30
Ball, Orna 30
Bandy, Moe 45, 57
Bare, Bobby 200, 265
Barker, Danny 194
Barrett, Bill 20
*Barn Dance* 63
Barnes, David 258
Barnes' H.M. Blue Ridge Ramblers 100
Barnett, Mandy 183
Barton, Lou Ann 183, 194, 249
Bascom, Texas Rose 157
Basie, Count 98
Bate, Alcyone 18, 19, 20
Bate, Buster 18, 19, 20
Bate, Humphrey 10, *17–20*, 26, 28, 30, 49, 157
Baugus, Scottie 110
Baum, Clyde 128

Bayers, Eddie 149, 258
Bayes, Coy 160
Beach, Freddy 128
Beach Boys 235, 237
Bean, Mumford and His Itawambians 9
Beasley, Larry 109
The Beatles 91, 203
Beaumont, Tex 150
Beck, Jeff 86
Bedard, George 216
Bellamy, David 238, 243
Bellamy Brothers 150, 272, 279
Bennett, Tony 125
Benny, Jack 125
Bergeson, Pat 280
Berle, Milton 89
Berline, Byron 95, 108, 110
Bernard, Junior 101
Berry, Chuck 100, 148, 208
*Beverly Hillbillies* 121, 122, 134, 241
Big Bopper 263
Big D Jamboree 142
Big Sandy and His Fly-Rite Boys 100, 127
Bill, Dick 235
Bine, Doug 95
Bird's Kentucky Corn Crackers 9
Black, Bob 109
Black, Chet 238
Black, Clint 222, 243, 279
Blackwell, Curtis 110
Blake, Norman 95
Blancett, Bertha 157
Blessing, Faye 157
Blue Grass Boys 34, 96, 106, 107, 108, 111, 112, 118, 119, 133, 134
Blue Grass Champs 38
Blue Ridge Playboys 95
Blue Shadows 122
Blue Sky Boys 26
Bluegrass Alliance 122
The Bluegrass Cardinals 95
Blueground Undergrass 108
Boatright, Bobby 101
Bobby Doyle Band 278
Boggs, Noel 101
Boling, Daniel Jack "Beanpole" 128
Bond, Johnny 45, 64, 70, 87
Boone, Pat 74, 91
Boone, Shirley 74
Boone County Jamboree 85
Boston Pops Orchestra 221, 242
Botet, Andy "Bijou" 108
Bowen, Jimmy 237
Bowers, Bryan 30
Bowers, James Gar 108
Bowlin, Robert 110

Bowman, Billy 101
Bowman, Charlie 9
Box, Bill 110
Boyd, Bill 65
Boyd's, Bill Cowboy Ramblers 95
Bradley, Harold 115, 143, 195, 209, 258
Bradley, Lou 149, 273
Bradley, Owen 115, 128, 188, 201, 209
Bradshaw, Curly 111
Brady, Pat 78
Bramhall, Doyle 249
Brashear, Alex 101
Braun, Grace 222
Breau, Lenny 201
Brewer, Teresa 125
Briggs, Billy 101
Briggs, David 265
Brightman, Jerry 215
The Brinkley Brothers 9
Brock, Carlos 110
Brooks, Garth 22, 51, 127, 150, 222, 238, 243, 249, 258, 272, 279
Brooks and Dunn 238, 243, 249, 258, 279
Brown, Alfred 243
Brown, Clarence "Gatemouth" 242
Brown, Dorwood 97
Brown, Ella 158
Brown, Frank "Hylo" 122, 136
Brown, Junior 201
Brown, Milton 65, 97
Browne, Jann 195
Brown's Ferry Four 85
Bruce, Ed 197
Brumley, Tom 213, 216
Bruner, Cliff 95
Bryant, Felice 56
Buchanan, Frank 110
*Buck Owens' Ranch* 214
The Buckaroos 213, 217
Buffalo Bill 51
Bumboat Billy and the Sparrow 9
Burgess, Wilma 158
Burke, Pete 144
Burnett, Johnny 270
Burnett and Rutherford 9
Burnette, Smiley 68
Burrows, Earl 194
Burson, Polly 157
Burton, James 195
Bush, Johnny 142, 143, 144
Butler, Carl 57
Butler, Larry 195
Butrum, Hillous 125, 128
Byrd, Billy 115, 116
Byrd, Jerry 128
Byrd, William Lewis 128

Camacho, Thelma Lou 278
Campbell, Archie 199
Campbell, Glen 41, 65, 87, 139, 198, 222, 231, *234–240*, 242, 247, 279, 285
Campbell, Jimmy 110
Campbell, Stacy Dean 209
Canova, Judy 158
Capp, Frank 237
Carlisle, Bill 54, 199
Carlisle, Cliff 45
Carnes, Kim 278, 282
Carolina Wildcats 132
Carrigan, Jerry 195
Carson, Billy Raymond 139
Carson, Fiddlin' John 5, 9, 10, *11–14*, 28, 35, 199, 287
Carson, John Kong 13
Carson, Martha 158
Carter, A.P. 10, *28–31*, 158, 159, 160, 161, 163, 164, 165, 166, 167, 177, 178
Carter, Anita 161, 164, 165, 178
Carter, Billy 101
Carter, Deanna 249
Carter, Ezra 164
Carter, Helen 161, 164, 165, 178
Carter, Janette 160
Carter, Joe 160
Carter, Maybelle 28, 29, 157, 158, 159, 160, 161, *163–167*, 170, 174, 177, 178, 199, 286
Carter, Sara (Dougherty) 28, 29, 31, 157, 158, *159–163*, 164, 165, 166, 174, 177, 178
Carter, Wilf 45, 50, *60–63*, 70, 82
The Carter Family 5, 9, 10, 11, 28, 29, 30, 31, 32, 38, 106, 120, 158, 159, 160, 161, 162, 163, 164, 166, 285, 287
Carter Sisters 178, 179, 199
Cash, Jack 219
Cash, Johnny 7, 29, 65, 70, 75, 87, 115, 127, 139, 141, 158, 164, 178, 179, 180, 189, 198, 202, 209, *218–229*, 230, 231, 235, 237, 242, 243, 247, 248, 249, 255, 263, 265, 277, 279, 285, 286, 287
Cash, June Carter 29, 158, 161, 164, 165, 170, 176, *177–180*, 195, 215, 220, 235, 285, 286
Cash, Roy 219
Cather, Willa 170
Caton, Roy 237
Chadbourne, Eugene 201
Chambers, Kasey 45
The Champs 235, 237
Chance, Floyd Taylor "Lightnin'" 128
Chapin, Harry 222
Charles, Ray 39, 215, 249, 273
Charleton, Buddy 116
Cherokee Cowboys 116, 142, 143, 246

Chesney, Kenny 272
Chicken Chokers 16
Christian, Gene 110
Christianson, Laurie 194
Chuck Wagon Gang 49
Church, Porter 110
Clapton, Eric 86
Clark, Guy 197, 265
Clark, Lefty 128
Clark, Roy 34, 41, 65, 87, 127, 139, 197, 202, 209, 214, 215, 222, 231, 235, 237, *240–245*, 247, 249, 279, 285
Clarke, Richard 243
Clarke, W.C. 249
Clayton, Lee 197
Clement, Jack 265
Clements, Vassar 110
Cline, Charlie 110
Cline, Patsy 12, 74, 158, 161, 165, 170, 172, 176, 177, *180–187*, 188, 191, 208, 246, 249, 285, 286
Cochran, Hank 182, 194, 246, 272–273
Cochran, Tammy 189
Code 615 208
Coe, David Allen 197, 249, 265
Coleman, Keith 101, 144
Collins, Tommy 96, 212, 214, 215, 216, 270, 272
Colter, Jessi 197, 247, 249, 264, 265
Commander Cody and His Lost Planet Airmen 65, 208, 249
The Commodores 257
Como, Perry 89, 90, 91, 125, 200
Compton, Paul 128
Conley, Earl Thomas 272
Conley, John 272
Conniff, Ray 206
Connors, Stompin' Tom 222
*The Conway Twitty Show* 256
Cooke, Jack 110
Cooley, Spade 77, 100, 192–193
Coon Creek Girls 157
Cooper, Gary 207
Cooper, Stoney 57
Cooper, Wilma Lee 157
Copas, Cowboy 182
Coryell, Larry 201
Cottie, Shirley 246
Country Crooked 249
The Country Gentlemen 95, 108C
Country Style 241
Countryman, Vicki 194
Coursey, Farris 115, 128, 209
Cousey, Farris 115
Cousin Jody 16, 26
Covay, Don 194
Cox, Bill 45

Cramer, Floyd 115, 144, 182, 200, 209
Crase, Noah 109, 135
Crisp, Ray 58
Criswell, Clyde "Chris" 128
Crittenden, Zeke 128
Croce, Jim 222
Crockett, Davey 74
The Crook Brothers 18, 19, 115, 222
Crosby, Bing 90, 98
Crosby, Bob 91
Crosby, David 248
Cross, Hugh 25, 26, 27, 40, 41
Crowe, J.D. 135
Crowell, Rodney 272
Crownover, Gene 101
Crudup, Arthur "Big Boy" 206
Cryel, L.C. 129
Crystal Springs Ramblers 95
Cumberland Highlanders 135
Cupp, Dana 109, 135
Cuviello, Johnny 101
Cyrus, Billy Ray 243

Dacus, Smokey 98, 101
Daffan Ted 65, 95, 96
Daily, H.W. "Pappy" 147
Dalhart, Vernon 5, 9, 10, *20–23*, 116, 197, 286
Dane, Eric 201
Daniels, Charlie 243
Daniels, Vic 110
Darin, Bobby 235
Davis, Betty 158
Davis, Cleo 109
Davis, Dale 194
Davis, Danny 201
Davis, Don 129
Davis, Gail 157
Davis, Jimmie 45
Davis, Lynn 175, 176, 177
Davis, Mac 237
Davis, Randy 109
Davis, Skeeter 30, 115, 158, 161, 172, 180, 183
Day, James Clayton "Jimmy" 129, 142, 143
Dean, Bernice 157
Dean, Billy 209, 272
Dean, Jimmy 241
Deasy, Mike, Sr. 237
The Delmore Brothers 9, 15, 30, 45, 85
Delta Rhythm Kings 219
Dennis, Richard Paul 128
Denver, John 222
Dere, David 109
Desert Rose Band 108
DeVaney, Yvonne 194
Dexter, Al 65, 96

The Dickel Brothers 16, 34
Dickens, Casey 101
Dickens, Hazel 30
Dickens, Little Jimmy 57, 149, 206
The Dillards 122
Dillman, Dwight 109
DiMucci, Dion 127
Dixie Chicks 116, 165, 172, 180
The Dixie Clodhoppers 9
Dixie Dewdrop 16
*Dixie Early Birds Show* 171
Dixie Gentlemen 95
Dixie Sacred Singers 15
Dixon, Willie 202
The Dixon Brothers 57
Dobson, Dubert 140
Dr. Havler's Traveling Show 54
*Dr. Quinn, Medicine Woman* 179
Dr. Smith's Champion Hoss Hair Pullers 9
Dore, Florence 189
Dorman, Randy 280
Dove, Ronnie 115
Drake, Bill 129
Drake, Jack 115, 116
Drake, Pete 115, 143
The Drifter 207
Drifting Cowboys 85, 124, 125, 142
Drifton, Theryl Ray 212
Drumright, Joe 108
Drusky, Roy 171
Duke, Bo 265
Duke, Luke 265
Dukes of Hazzard 189, 264
Duncan, Bill 110
Duncan, Glenn 101, 110
Duncan, Tommy 97, 98, 99, 100, 101, 102
Dunkin, Allen M. 128
Dunn, Ronnie 116
Duvall, Robert 179
Dylan, Bob 30, 179, 202, 220, 221, 222, 248

The Eagles 208, 216, 257
Eanes, Jim 109, 122, 136
Earl Scruggs Revue 134, 135, 136
East Texas Serenaders 95
Easton, Sheena 278
Eastwood, Clint 53, 209, 271
Eatson, Connie 158
*Eddy Arnold Time* 90
Edenton, Ray 87, 115, 129, 195, 258
*Edgar Bergen–Eugene McCarthy Show* 167
Ellington, Duke 98, 100
Ellis, Tony 109
Elrod, Jimmy 109, 110

Ely, Joe 150, 197, 272
Elza, Charles "Little Darlin'" 122, 136
Emmons, Buddy 115, 116, 142, 144, 202, 249
England, Ty 57
English, Paul 249, 250
Ernest V. Stoneman and the Blue Ridge Corn Shuckers 39
Ernest V. Stoneman and the Dixie Mountaineers 39
Ernest V. Stoneman and the Stoneman Family 39
Etheridge, Floyd 109
Evans, Dale 6, 50, 77, 78, 79, 116, 157, 158, *167–170*, 174, 285, 287
Everly, Don 85
Everly, Ike 85
Everly, Phil
Everly Brothers 56, 86, 87
Ewing, Tom 110

Fairchild, Barbara 158
Fargo, Donna 172
Farmer, James 209
Farr, Hugh 78
Farr, Karl 78
Farrar, Jay 30
Feagan, Mike 110
Fender, Leo 86
Ferguson, Bob 201
Ferguson, Dave 100
Ferguson, Joe 101
Ferrell, Rick 272
Field Brothers' Medicine Show 67
Fields, Monroe 109
First Edition 278, 279, 280, 282, 283
The Five Pennies 135
Flatt, Lester 30, 34, 41, 87, 96, 106, 108, 109, *118–123*, 133, 134, 135, 136, 199, 243
Fletcher, Bud 245
Flores, Rosie 194, 195
Flying Burrito Brothers 216, 272
Fogerty, John 222
Foggy Mountain Boys 120, 133
Foley, Betty 74
Foley, Red 49, 50, 70, *72–75*, 113, 171, 174, 199
Foley, Sue 194
Foran, Dick 69, 76
Ford, Tennessee Ernie 86, 87
Forester, "Sally Ann" Wilene 106, 111
Forrester, Howdy 57, 58, 109, 122, 136
Forrester, Joe 108
Forty-Niners 175
Foss, Joe and His Hungry Sand-Lappers 9
Foster, Billy Joe 110

Foster, Radney 216
The Four Virginians 16, 41
Fowler, Bob 110
Fraley, J.P. 26, 100
Francini, Tony 128
Franklin, Aretha 177
Franks, Randall "Randy" 110
Franzese, Pat 194
Freda and the Firedogs 249
Freeman, Denny 249
French, George 215
Friedman, Kinky 197
Frizzell, Lefty 45, 57, 65, 96, 115, 120, 134, 249, 269, 272, 273
Fruit Jar Drinkers 15
Fuller, Blind Boy 39
Fulmer, Eulon E.B. 128
Fulson, Duke 100

Gadd, Steve 243
Garcia, Benny 101
Garland, Hank 182, 209
Garren, Amos 108
Garrish, Sonny 243
Garrison, Kurt 243
Gasaway, Gene 101
Gaster, Marvin 16
Gately, Connie 110
Gayle, Crystal 161, 165, 170, 172, 177, 180, 183, 188, 189
Gentry, Bobby 237
Georgia Old Time Fiddler's Association 24
Georgia Wildcats 25, 41, 85, 86
Gerrard, Alice 158
The Ghost Rockets 122
Gibson, Clifford 45
Gibson, Don 56, 200, 209
Gibson/Miller Band 91, 127
Gilewitz, Richard 122
Gill, Vince 149, 238, 243, 258, 279, 286
Gillette, Lee 87
Gilley, Mickey 96, 278
Gilmore, Jimmie Dale 249
Gimble, Johnny 66, 101, 144, 209, 265
*Girl of the Golden West* 21
Glaser, Jim 201
Glaser, Tompall 197, 247, 249, 264, 265
*Glen Campbell (Good Time) Hour* 214, 221, 236
Gobble, Ruby 157
Godfrey, Arthur 89, 181
Goff, Duke 265
Goldsboro, Bobby 237
Good, Dorothy 158
Good, Mildred 158
Goodman Wendell 193

Gordon, Jim 237
Graham, Billy 221
Grand, Gil 258
*Grand Ole Opry* 5, 6, 10, 15, 16, 18, 19, 37, 49, 50, 55, 56, 57, 58, 61, 64, 73, 74, 75, 81, 82, 89, 106, 113, 114, 115, 119, 120, 124, 125, 132, 133, 134, 142, 147, 164, 171, 172, 178, 181, 182, 199, 206, 207, 208, 219, 242, 263, 286, 287
Grandpa Jones 16, 85, 86, 243
Grant, Claude 43, 46
Grant, Jack 43, 46
Grant, Marshall 219
Grateful Dead 209
Graves, Burkett "Uncle Josh" 122, 136
Graves, Ernest 110
Gray, Billy 87, 138, 139, 140
Green, Doug 109, 110
Green, Jack 115
Green, Pat 249
Green, Yates 110
Greene, Richard 110
Greenwood, Lee 237
Gregory, Clinton 57, 209
Gregory, Hubert 16
Grier, Lamar 109
Griffin, Rex 45
Grishaw, Edward "Zeb Turner" 129
Grishaw, James Cecil "Zeke Turner" 129
Guthrie, Jack 70
Guthrie, Woody 30, 45
Guy, Buddy 87

Haggard, Merle 45, 100, 127, 149, 198, 209, 213, 214, 215, 222, 237, 249, 263, 265, *269-277*, 286
Haley, Bill and the Comets 7, 74, 100
Hamel, Dave "Pappy" 74
Hamilton, George 127
Hamilton, George IV 241
Hammond, Lorraine "Lee" 158
Happy-Go-Lucky Boys 119
Happy Trails 77, 168
Harkreader, Fiddlin' Sid 14, 15, 16
Harling, Keith 258
Harman, Buddy 182, 201
Harman, Murray, Jr. 202
Harris, Bonnie Gray 157
Harris, Clyde "Boots" 128
Harris, Emmylou 30, 177, 180, 215, 265
Harris, R.C. 109
Hart, Freddie 213
Hart, James 20
Harte, Roy 87
Hartford, John 135, 235, 237
Harvey, Roy 33, 34
Hawkins, Hawkshaw 182

Hawkins, Ronnie 7, 258
Hawkins, Ted 24, 25, 27, 40
Hay, George D. 6, 18, 49, 124
Haynes, Walter 143
Head, Ray "Keno" 116
Headley, Fisher and His Aristocratic Pigs 9
Heckle, Texas Bob 206
*Hee Haw* 26, 198, 214, 215, 221, 241, 242, 243
Hee Haw Gospel Quartet 243
Helms, Don 125, 128
Helton, Ernest 43
Hembree, Mark 109
Hendrix, Jimi 86, 87, 135, 201, 222
Henley, Jimmy 243
Herron, Herman 129
Hi-Flyers 95
Hicks, Buddy 110
Hicks, Jack 109
Hill, Cameron 101
Hill, Charles 128
Hill, Faith 172, 180, 183, 189
Hill, Goldie 158
Hill, Tommy 129
Hillman, Chris 108, 122
Hirt, Al 200
The Highwaymen 221
*HMS Pinafore* 21
Hoffman, Billy 238
Hofner, Adolph 95, 100
Hogan, Kelly 183
Holden, Bill 109
Holley, Joe 100, 101
Hollow Rock String Band 34
Holly, Buddy 91, 263, 264, 266
Holly, Doyle 213, 216
*Hollywood Barn Dance* 76
Holmes, Clent 128
Holy, Steve 258
Homer and Jethro 178
Hometown Boys 40
*Hooperman* 65
Hoosier Hotshots 73
Hope, Bob 89, 125
Hopkins, Sam Lightnin' 107
Hoppers, Lonnie 109
Horn, Jim 237, 280
Horton, Johnny 65, 96, 209
House, Son 107
Howard, Chuck 273
Howard, Harlan 182, 194, 213, 216
Hubbard, Ray Wylie 265
Huff, Leon 100, 101
Huffmaster, Raymond 109
Hughey, John 258
Hungate, David 258

Hunt, Prince Albert 95
Hurt, Mississippi John 45, 107
Husky, Roy M. "Junior" 58
Hutchens, Doug 109
Hutcherson, Burt 18

Innis, Louis 58, 129

Jack and His Texas Outlaws 76
Jackson, Al, Jr. 232
Jackson, Alan 238, 243, 272, 279
Jackson, Aunt Molly 157
Jackson, Lula 157
Jackson, Thomas Lee "Tommy" 129, 143
Jackson, Wanda 7, 74, 137, 158, 161, 165, 170, 176, 177, 180, *192-196*, 212, 241
Jagger, Mick 91
James, Don 110
James, Skip 107
James, Sonny 194, 209, 212, 239
Jan and Dean 235
Janes, Mary 127
Janes, Roland 232
Jarrell, Tommy 122
Jarrett, Millard 128
Jefferson, Blind Lemon 39
Jennings, Waylon 41, 100, 115, 116, 127, 149, 197, 198, 200, 201, 221, 222, 247, 248, 249, *262-269*, 285, 286
Jerrolds, Wayne 110
Jett, Otis 232
Jezzro, Jack 201
Jim and Jenny and the Pinetops 30, 108
Jim and Jesse 95
*Jimmy Dean Show* 37
Jimmy Rodgers Entertainers 43
*The Johnny Cash Show* 214, 221
Johns, Sammy 258
Johnson, Big Jack 45, 70
Johnson, Blind Willie 39
Johnson, Bob 109
Johnson, Charles "Little Jody Rainwater" 122, 136
Johnson, Clifton "Sleepy" 97, 101
Johnson, Courtney 135
Johnson, Earl 13
Johnson, Enos 110
Johnson, Eric 201
Johnson, Johnny 116, 122, 136
Johnson Mountain Boys 108
Jones, Billy Jean 125
Jones, Bob 110
Jones, Ernest Carl "Wimpy" 128
Jones, Frank 65
Jones, George 57, 65, 74, 96, 97, 100, 115, 116, 127, *146-156*, 215, 257, 265, 271, 279, 285, 286

Jones, Red 41
Jones, Skip 89
Jones, Terry 278
Joplin, Janis 177, 194
Jordan, Vic 109
The Jordanaires 182
Joss, Scott 100, 215, 216
The Judds 180
Justis, Bill 230

Kaye, Carol 237
Keister, Shane 280
Keith, Bill 108, 109, 135
Kelley, Irene 189
Kelso, Millard 101
Kennedy, Gregg 109
Kennedy, Jerry 243
Kenton, Stan 66
The Kentuckians 106
Kentucky Pardners 119
Kerr, Anita 158
Kershaw, Sammy 127, 150, 258
Kesler, Stan 232
Kessel, Barney 235
Kiker, Harry 27
Kilgore, Merle 178
Kincaid, Bradley 106
King, B.B. 221
King, Mel 216
King, Pee Wee 56
King, Pee Wee Golden West Cowboys 89
Kingston Trio 30
Kirby, Pete (Bashful Brother Oswald) 55, 58
Kirby Stone Four 278
Kirk, Eddie 87
Kirkwood, Curt 222
Klugh, Earl 201
Knopfler, Mark 201, 202
Koehler, Ester "Violet" 157
Krauss, Alison 95
Krise, George "Speedy" 175
Kristofferson, Kris 127, 197, 221, 222, 231, 247, 248, 249, 250, 263, 265, 273
Kurtis, Jan 116
Kuykendall, Mark 109

Laine, Franky 125
Lair, John 16, 41
Lair, Johnny's, Cumberland Ridge Runners 73
Lambert, Curly 122, 136
Lambert, Tag 101
Landers, Jake 110
lang, k.d. 82, 161, 172, 180, 183, 189
Lange, Evelyn "Daisy" 157

Lanham, Roy 87
Lansford, Sonny 101
Last Forever 30
Lauderdale, Jim 150
*Laugh-In* 242
Law, Don 65, 87, 143
Lawler, Mike 258
Layne, Bert 24, 25, 26–27
Layne's Bert Mountaineers 41
Ledford, Lily Mae 157, 175
Ledford, Minnie 157
Ledford, Rose 157
Lee, Albert 195, 201
Lee, Brenda 209
Lee, Frankie 57
Leech, Mike 249
Leggett, Walter 18, 20
Leiber, Jerry 194
Lester, Bobby Joe 110
Lewis, Curly 140
Lewis, Doc 101
Lewis, Jerry Lee 7, 75, 208, 221, 230
Lewis, Ralph 110
Lewis, Wayne 110
Liebert, Billy 87
Light Crust Doughboys 97
Lilly, Everette 122, 136
Lindbergh, Charles 21
Lineburger, Dan 109
Linneman, Billy 87
Little Walter 19
Lloyd, Jack 101
Locker, Richard 243
Logan, Mills 280
Lohman, Dale 128, 129
Lonely Blue Boys 256, 259
Lost Valley Brazos Boys 116
Loudermilk, John D. 56
*Louisiana Hayride* 124, 147, 171, 172, 219, 229
Louvin, Ira 57, 127
Louvin Brothers 56
Love, John 41
Loveless, Patty 176
Lovett, Lyle 249
Lowinger, Gene 110
Lunceford, Jimmie 98
Lunsford, Lynwood 135
Lyle, Rudy 108, 109
Lynn, Judy 158
Lynn, Loretta 115, 158, 161, 165, 170, 172, 176, 177, 183, *187–192*, 194, 195, 198, 202, 213, 257, 258, 260, 261, 262, 286
Lynn, Oliver Moonshine 188
Lynne, Shelby 183
Lynyrd Skynyrd 45

Macon, Dorris 15
Macon, Uncle Dave 5, 10, *14–17*, 26, 35, 49, 55, 132, 141, 286
*Madame Butterfly* 21
Maddox, Rose 158, 213
Magness, Tommy 109
Maher, Brent 280
Mainer, Wade 135
Malone, Russell 243
Mamas and the Papas 235, 237
Mandrell, Barbara 116, 161, 165, 170, 172, 176, 180, 189
Mandrell, Louise 116, 177
Mandrell Sisters 183, 214
Manker, Sid 232
Mann, Carl 230
Manuel, Abe, Jr. 273
Maphis, Joe 87, 88
Martin, Benny 58, 108, 110, 122, 136
Martin, Dean 90, 91, 235, 237
Martin, Glen 272
Martin, Grady 115, 195, 249, 258
Martin, Jimmy 30, 95, 106, 110
Martin, Thomas 129
Mason, Brent 149
Mathews, Neal 195
The Mavericks 127, 183, 222
Mayfield, Edd 110
Maynard, Jimmy 110
Maynard, Ken 45, 50, *51–54*, 65, 68, 70, 167, 285
Maynard, Kermit 52
Mays, Mexican Charlie 128
McAlpin, Vic 194
McAnally, Shane 209
McAuliffe, Leon 98, 99, 100, 101
McBay, Billy 101
McBay, Bobby 101
McBride, Laura Lee 101
McCall, C.W. 222
McCormick, Neal "Pappy" 129
McCoury, Del 95, 108, 110
McCreary, Les 237
McDonald, Jay 216
McDonald, Rusty 101
McDowell, Mississippi Fred 107
McEntire, Reba 172, 180, 183, 188
McGhee, Kirk 15, 16, 49
McGhee, Paul 101
McGhee, Sam 15, 16, 49
The McGhee Brothers 9, 15
McGraw, Tim 222, 238, 243, 248, 258, 279
*McHale's Navy* 172
McKell, Jim 280
McKinney, Dean 101
McKinney, Evelyn 101

McLean, Don 222
McMichen, Clayton 9, 24, 25, 26, 27, 40, 41, 88, 199
McMillan, Terry 149, 201
McNally, Zeb 101
McNatt, Speedy 89
McNeely, Larry 57
McNett, Bob 125, 128
McPeake, Curtis 109
McTell, Blind Willie 39
McWhorter, Frankie 101
McWilliams, Elsie 45
Meadows, Joe 110
Medlin, Greasy 91
Mellencamp, John Cougar 249
Mellons, Ken 272
*Merry-Go-Round Show* 171
Messina, Jay 243
Metzel, Bob 110
Midler, Bette 257
Midnight Ramblers 105
Migliori, Jay 237
Millard, Tommy 111
Miller, Lost John 132
Miller, Roger 96, 142, 143, 215
Mills Brothers 140
Milsap, Ronnie 237, 238, 279
Minnie Pearl 125, 158, 243
Mitchell, Guy 125, 206
The Monkees 235, 237
Monroe, Bill 6, 15, 16, 26, 41, 87, 95, 96, *104–112*, 118, 119, 121, 132, 133, 135, 199, 285, 287
Monroe, Birch 105, 108
Monroe, Charlie 105, 111, 119
Monroe, James 105, 109, 110
Monroe Brothers 34, 105, 112
Montana, Patsy 45, 70, 157, 158, 175
Montana Slim *see* Carter, Wilf
Montgomery, Johnny 109
Montgomery, Melba 57, 147, 149, 151, 158, 165, 170, 172
Moody, Clyde 109, 119
Mooney, Ralph 195, 216
Moonshine Kate 11, 13
Moore, Bob L. 201, 209
Moore, Scotty 86, 87
Moore, Stevie 216
Moore, Tiny 101
Moratto, Jim 109
Morgan, George 91
Morrell, Tommy 101
Morris, Dale 110
Morris, Farrell 280
Morris Brothers 132
The Morrison Family 9
Mott, Tiny 101

Mouldin, Bessie Lee 109
Moultrie, Cois "Pee Wee" Elmo 128
Mountain Boys 41
Mountjoy, Monty 101
Mullican, Moon 96
Murphey, Michael 249
Murray, Anne 62, 82
Music Village 193
Myrick, Weldon 195

Nashville Bluegrass Band 108
Nashville Grass 121
Nation, Ann 158
*National Barn Dance* 6, 49, 68, 73, 74, 105
National Country Music Banjo Championships 241
Neely, Sam 201, 238
Nelson, Ken 65, 138, 194
Nelson, Bobbie 245, 249, 250
Nelson, Rick 235
Nelson, Willie 7, 41, 70, 75, 86, 100, 116, 127, 139, 141, 142, 143, 144, 182, 189, 194, 197, 198, 209, 215, 216, 221, 222, 231, 242, *245–255*, 258, 262, 264, 265, 267, 271, 273, 285, 287
The New Christy Minstrels 278, 279, 280
The New Lost City Ramblers 16, 34
Newbury, Mickey 197, 249, 265
Newman, Johnny C. 70
Newman, Ray and His Boys 95
Newport Jazz Festival 200, 220
Nichols, Bob 76
Nichols, James 243
Nichols, Junior 140
The Nite Owls 95
Nitty Gritty Dirt Band 30, 58, 122, 208, 216
Nixon, Richard 271
Nolan, Bob 76, 78
Norred, R.D. "Sonny" 128
Norris, Fate 24, 25, 26, 27, 40
Norris, Land 13
North Carolina Ramblers 10, 33, 34, 35
Northern Lights 108
Notting Hillbillies 201
Numerov, Bruce 109

O'Brien, Derek 249
Ochs, Phil 258, 272
O'Connor, Sinead 248
O'Daniel, W. Lee 97, 98
O'Day, Molly 158, 161, 165, *174–177*
Old and in the Way 95, 108
Orbison, Roy 56, 232, 256
Osborne, Roland "Sonny" 108

Osborne Brothers 96, 108
Owen, Fuzzy 270
Owens, Bonnie 214, 215, 270, 272, 273
Owens, Buck 7, 34, 41, 65, 86, 100, 116, 127, 149, 198, *212–218*, 231, 235, 237, 242, 243, 245, 247, 249, 263, 270, 273
Owens, Texas Ruby 175
Ozark Jubilee 74
Ozark Mountain Daredevils 216

Page, June 105
Paige, Tommy "Butterball"
Parker, Andy 65
Parker, Carolyn "Little Caroline" 128
Parker, Colonel Tom 81, 178
Parker, Fess 74
Parnell, Lee Roy 100
Parsons, Gram 216, 272
Parth, Johnny 13
Parton, Dolly 161, 170, 172, 176, 180, 183, 189, 194, 273, 278, 279
Party Timers 193
Pass, Joe 244
Paul, Les 199
Paycheck, Johnny 142, 148, 150, 197, 265
Payne, Jody 249, 250
Payne, Leon 151
Payne, Rufe (Tee-Pot) 124
Payne, Skip 109
Pearl, Minnie 125, 158, 243
Pedigo, Ben 109
Peer, Ralph 9, 11, 28, 29, 36, 43, 45, 159, 164
Pendleton, Buddy 110
Pennington, Robert Lee "Buddy" 109, 128
Perkins, Carl 7, 75, 139
Perkins, Luther 219
Perkins, Tommy 101
Perryman, Lloyd 78
Petty, Tom, and the Heartbreakers 222
Phelps, Jackie 109
Phillips, Judd 230
Phillips, Sam 219, 220, 230, 232
Phillips Country Ramblers 256
Pierce, Jack 43, 46
Pierce, Kenny 216
Pierce, Webb 45, 171
Pike, Fred 41
Pine Valley Cosmonauts 222
Pitney, Gene 151
Pointer Sisters 257
Poole, Charlie 10, 13, 22, *32–35*, 132
Poole, Charlie and His Carolina Ramblers 105, 287
Porter, Bill 201
Porter, Jimmy 128

The Possum Hunters 18, 19, 157
Potter, Dale 110, 129
Powers, Billy E. 122, 136
Powers, Freddy 272
Presley, Elvis 7, 45, 75, 81, 86, 91, 107, 147, 164, 178, 179, 193, 195, 196, 200, 206, 208, 235, 256
Presley, Ken 216
Presson, Nonnie 26, 34, 41
Price, Bill 110
Price, Joel 108
Price, Ray 57, 65, 74, 96, 97, 116, 125, 127, *141–146*, 149, 246, 249, 256
Pride, Charlie 74, 139, 200, 222, 249
*Prince Albert Show* 73
Pruett, Felton 128
Pruett, Jeanne 209
Pruett, Samuel K. 128
Puccini 21
Puckett, Riley 5, 10, 22, 24, 25, 26, 27, *39–42*, 199
Pursell, William Whitney 143, 209
Pyle, Pete 109

Rager, Mose 85
Rainwater, Marvin 241
Raitt, Bonnie 248
Randall, Jack 69
Raphael, Mickey 249, 250
Rausch, Leon 101
Raye, Don 194
Raye, Susan 216
Rector, Red 108
Red Clay Ramblers 30
Reddy, Helen 190
Reed, Jerry 87, 201, 202, 203, 237
Reed, John X. 249
Reed, Ramona 101
Reese, Vernon Toby 116
Reeves, Jim 22, 65–66, 74, 91, 209
Reilly, Ike 222
Reinhardt, Django 235
Remington, Herb 101
Renfro Valley Barn Dance 73, 74
Reno, Don 108, 120, 133
Reno and Smiley 122
Reynolds, Bronson "Brownie" 122
Rhees, Glen 101
Rhodes, Curly 58
Rhodes, Leon 116
Rice, Hoke 24, 27, 41
Rich, Charlie 74, 127, 139, 198, 209, 222, *229–234*, 237, 265, 277, 286
Rich, Don 213, 214, 215, 216
Richardson, Larry 108
Riddle, Jimmy 57, 58
Riley, Billy 232

Riley, Billy Lee 230
Rimes, LeAnn 170, 172, 177, 180, 183, 189, 194
Ritter, John 65
Ritter, Tex 6, 45, 50, 52, *63–67*, 69, 70, 73, 87, 116, 137, 167, 192
Rivers, Jack 87
Rivers, Jerry 125, 128
Robbins, Hargus "Pig" 115, 143, 201, 243, 265
Robbins, Marty 6, 22, 70, 74, 115, 139, 198, *205–212*, 287
Roberts, Kenny 45
Robins, Butch 109
Robinson, Billy 129
Robinson, Carson J. 9, 22
Robinson, Jessie Mae 194
Rocky Mountaineers 76
Rodgers, Carrie 113, 287
Rodgers, Jesse 45, 127
Rodgers, Jimmie 9, 11, 12, 22, 29, 31, 38, 40, 41, *42–47*, 56, 62, 67, 71, 76, 80, 82, 84, 91, 96, 104, 106, 112, 113, 114, 115, 116, 123, 124, 126, 137, 197, 269 , 271, 272, 287
Rodriguez, Johnny 197
Rogers, Kenny 116, 189, 198, 199, *277–284*
Rogers, Roy 6, 45, 50, 52, 53, 58, 62, 65, 69, 70, *76–79*, 157, 158, 167, 168, 169, 170, 197, 285, 286, 287
Ronstadt, Linda 172, 183, 189, 216
Roosevelt, Franklin Delano 69
Rorer, Posey 33, 34
Rose, Billy 109
Rose, Clarice 194
Rose, Fred 55, 56, 57, 124, 125, 129, 175
Rose, Wesley 56
Ross, Lee 101
Rothman, Sandy 109
Rowan, Peter 108, 110
Rowe, Louise 101
Rush, Otis 87
Russell, Johnny 57, 115
Russell, Leon 237
Rutherford, C.C. 14

Sahm, Doug 249
Sainte-Marie, Buffy 235
Salyers, South 110
Sample, Junior 243
Sandusky, Vernon 243
Sandy, Leslie 109, 110
Sapp, Johnny 116
Satherly, Art 99
Saylor, Lucky 110
Schoolhouse Playboys 212
Schuffert, Braxton 128

Schultz, Arnold 105
Schwarzenegger, Arnold 53
Sciaky, Carla 158
Scott, Fred 69
Scruggs, Earl 30, 34, 41, 58, 87, 96, 106, 108, 119, 120, 121, 122, 123, *132–136*, 199, 243
Scruggs, Gary 265
Scruggs, Randy 58, 265
Seals, Shorty 128
Sears, Dawn 194
Seckler, Curly 120, 122, 133, 136
Settle, Mike 278
Seven Foot Dilly and His Hot Pickles 9, 16, 27
The Shadows 201
Shamblin, Eldon 101
Shaver, Billy Joe 197, 249, 264, 265
Sheehan, Oscar 109
Shepherd, Audrey Mae 124, 125
Shepherd, Jean 172
Shepherd Brothers 85
Sherrill, Billy 194, 209, 231, 249
Sholes, Steve 201
Shook, Jerry 115, 195
Shook, Loren Otis "Jack" 129
Shore, Dinah 89
Short, Johnny 116
Shumate, Jim 110, 119, 122, 133, 136
Shuping, Garland 135
Silver, Lisa 280
Simon, Paul 248
Simpson, Red 216
Sims, Benny 122, 136
Sinatra, Frank 91, 235, 237
Sir Douglas Quartet, 127
*Six Pack* 279
Sizemore, Herschel 108
Skaggs, Ricky 122, 149, 222, 238, 243, 249, 258
Skelton, Red 73
The Skillet Lickers 10, 24, 25, 106
Skyle's, Bob, Skyrockers 954
Smith, Arthur 49
Smith, Bessie 42
Smith, Bobby 110
Smith, Cal 115, 116
Smith, Carl 91, 178, 220
Smith, Charlie 110
Smith, Connie 183, 200
Smith, Odell 33, 34
Smith, Ray 230
Smith, Roger 109
Smith, Sammi 197
Smith, Warren 230
Smith, William Elon 128
Smokin' Grass 108, 135

Smook, Jim 109
Snead, Earl 109
Snow, C.E. 203
Snow, Hank 45, 50, 62, 70, *79–84*, 115, 195, 200, 209, 287
Sonnier, Jo-El 150
Sons of the Pioneers 76, 77, 78, 79
The Souther-Hillman-Furay Band 208
Sovine, Red 96, 222
Spacek, Sissy 189
Spears, Bee 249, 250
Spencer, Tim 76, 78
Spicher, Buddy 110, 265
Sprague, Carl T. 22
Squires, Mark 110
Stafford, Jo 125
Stallone, Sylvester 53
Stamper, Art 110
Stampley, Joe 45, 57, 127
Stanley, Carter 110
Stanley, Harold "Red" 110
Stanley, Ralph 95
Stanley Brothers 106, 108, 120, 133
Starrett, Charles 76
Steagall, Red 100
Steven, Jeff 222
Stevenson, Guy 109
Stewart, Billy 140
Stewart, Golden 16
Stewart, Redd 56
Stewart, Travis 110
Stewart, Wynn 96, 213, 214, 215, 270, 273
Stoker, Hugh Gordon 195
Stokes, Lowe 24, 27, 40
Stoller, Mike 194
Stone, Oscar 18, 19, 20
Stone, Wayne 216
Stoneman, Donna 37, 38
Stoneman, E.V. "Pop" 5, 10, 28, *35–39*
Stoneman, Jim 37, 38
Stoneman, Roni 37, 38
Stoneman, Scotty 37, 38
Stoneman, Van 37, 38
Story, Carl 109
Stover, Don 109
Strait, George 100, 116, 238, 243, 272, 279
Strehli, Angela 194
Stricklin, Al 98, 99, 101
Stringbean 16, 26, 106 108
Stripling, Chuck 108
Strzelecki, Henry 201
Stuart, Joe 109, 110, 122, 136
Stuart, Marty 215, 216
Stuart, Uncle Am 9
Studdard, Chester 116

Summey, Clell 54
Sykes, Bob 209
Sykes, Ernie 109

Talley, Lewis 270
Tanner, Arthur 24, 25, 27
Tanner, Elmo 56
Tanner, Gid 10, 13, *23–27*, 28, 199
Tanner, Gid and His Skillet Lickers 9, 26, 30, 40, 157
Tanner, Gordon 24, 25, 27
Tarzan 52
Tate, Clarence "Tater" 109, 110, 135
Taylor, James 148, 149
Taylor, Koko 177
Taylor, Merle "Red" 110
Taylor, Rufus "Puddin'" 128
Taylor, Sue Williams 128
The Taylor Brothers 9
Tedeschi, Susan 194
Tedesco, Tommy 237
Tennessee Crackerjacks 54
Tennessee Mountain Boys 171
Tennessee Two 219, 227
Terry, Arnold 110
Terry, Gordon 110
Terry, Sonny 39
The Texans 64, 66
Texas Troubadours 114, 115, 117
Thawl, Willie 129
Thomas, "Slim" 129
Thompson, Cecil 91, 135
Thompson, Hank 86, 96, 116, *137–141*
Thompson, Hank, and the Brazos Valley Boys 65, 137, 138, 139, 141, 193
Thompson, Jack 109
Thompson, Luke 91, 135
Thompson, Shorty, and His Rangers 199
Thorogood, George 124, 127
*Those Stonemans* 37
*Three's Company* 65
Thurmond, Garry 110
Tidwell, George 280
Tierney, Louie 101
Tierney, Marcel 101
Tillis, Mel 74, 127, 242
Tillman, Floyd 65, 96
Tillotson, Johnny 70
Todd, Mary 15
Todd, Winston "Red" 128
Tomlins, Gene 101
*Tonight Show* 241
Travis, Merle 49, 50, *84–88*, 137, 139, 140, 149, 200, 235
Travis, Randy 127, 150, 222, 238, 243, 249, 258, 272, 279
Treat, Ron 258

Trick Pony 127, 249
Trigger 77, 168, 169
Tritt, Travis 222, 238, 243, 249, 279
Tubb, Ernest 45, 49, 65, 70, 74, 80, 96, *112–118*, 120, 134, 137, 141, 149, 190, 191, 285, 287
Tubb, Justin 115
Tucker, Sophie 56
Tucker, Tanya 116, 172, 180, 183, 194, 237
Tullock, English P. "Cousin Jake" 122, 136
Tune Wranglers 95
Turner, Bernice Hillburn 128
Turner, Doyle 129
Tuttle, Wesley 65, 87
Twain, Shania 172, 180, 183, 189
Twitty, Conway 127, 141, 149, 189, 198, 215, 237, 249, *255–262*, 285, 286

Uncle Tupelo 30
Ungar, Jay 13

The Vagabonds 49
Valens, Ritchie 263
Van Damme, Jean-Claude 53
Vandivier, Uncle Pendleton 105
Van Eaton, J.M. 232
Vanover, Carl 110
Van Shelton, Ricky 238, 258, 279
Van-Springsteen, Alice 158
Van Zandt, Townes 249, 273
Vaughan, Jimmie 249
Vaughan, Stevie Ray 249
Velvetones 195, 230
Vienneau, Jim 258
Vipperman, Johnny 110
Virginia Reelers 11, 12, 13
Voss, Jane 172, 183

Wakely, Jimmy 49
Walker, Bill 195
Walker, Billy 243, 246
Walker, Cindy 157
Walker, Frank 9
Walker, Jerry Jeff 197, 249, 265
Wallace, George 271
Waller, Fats 56
Walton, Stanley 18, 19, 20
Wariner, Steve 150, 201
Warren, Paul 122, 136
Watson, Dale 216
Watson, Doc 30
Watson, Gene 149, 150
Watts, Howard "Cedric Rainwater" 106, 108, 119, 122, 128, 133, 136
Watts, Wilmer and the Lonely Eagles 9
Wayne, Curtis 194

Wayne, John 53, 70, 236
Webb, Brenda Gayle 188
Webb, Jay Lee 188
Webster, Jimmy 129
Weeks, Anson Orchestra 168
Weems Swing Band 27
Weissberg, Eric 135
Weize, Richard 58, 195, 209
Welch, Gillian 30
Wells, Kitty 54, 73, 158, 165, *170–174*
West, Dottie 158, 172, 278, 282
West, Kitty 181
West, Wesley Webb 87
West Texas Cowboys 95
West Virginia Snake Hunters 9
Westbrooks, Bill "Cousin Wilbur" 108
*Western Caravan* 206
Western Wranglers 235
Weston, Dick 76
Whalen, June 98, 101
Whalen, Kermit 101
White, Bergen 280
White, Bob 101, 140
White, John 22
White, Joy Lynn 45
White, L.E 110
White, Roland 110
Whiteman, Paul Orchestra 56
Whitley, Keith 150
Whitley, Ray 63, 85
Whitten, Mike 24, 25, 27
Whittier, Henry 35
Widener, Jimmie 87, 101
The Wilbur Brothers 115, 188
Wilburn, Teddy 115
Wilder, Laura Ingalls 170
Wilkerson, Asa 232
Wilkinson, Jimmy 128
The Wilkinsons 222
Williams, Allen 216
Williams, Andy 90, 91
Williams, Benny 110
Williams, Blake 109
Williams, Don 237
Williams, Hank, Jr. 126, 265
Williams, Hank, Sr. 6, 10, 12, 22, 34, 44, 45, 55, 56, 57, 59, 70, 74, 87, 96, 97, 104, 112, 115, 117, *123–132*, 141, 142, 143, 146, 149, 150, 154, 155, 175, 197, 208, 223, 233, 234, 244, 249, 250, 269, 272, 286
Williams, John 221
Williams, Leona 273
Williams, Terry 278
Williams, Tex 85–86
Williams, Velma 129
Williamson, Cecil 175
Williamson, Joe 175

Williamson, Skeets  175
Williamson, Sonny Boy I  19
Williamson, Sonny Boy II  19
Willis, Charles Ray "Skeeter"  129
Willis, James "Guy"  129
Willis, John Victor "Vic"  129
Wills, Billy Jack  101
Wills, Bob  6, 25, 26, 34, 45, 65, 66, 74, 87, 95, 96, *97–104*, 116, 137, 139, 150, 193, 208, 249, 269, 272, 273, 286, 287
Wills, Bob, and His Texas Playboys  96, 98, 99, 102, 104, 271
Wills, John  280
Wills, Johnny Lee  98, 100, 101
Wills, Johnny Lee and His Boys  100
Wills, Luke  101
Wills, Martin  232
Wills, Tex  109
Wills Fiddle Band  97
Wilson, Dennis  258
Wilson, Frank  9
Wilson, Jimmy  232
Wilson, Wayne  216
Wise, Chubby  106, 109, 122, 129, 136
Wiseman, Lulu Belle  175
Wiseman, Mac  96, 108, 109, 120, 121, 122, 133, 136, 175, 176
Womack, Lee Ann  116, 172, 180, 183
Wonder, Stevie  39
Wood, Bobby  249, 265, 273
Wood, Woody  101
Woodie, Ephraim, and the Henpecked Husbands  9
Woodlieff, Norman  33, 34

Woods, Bill, and the Orange Blossom Players  212
Wooten, Art  109, 122, 136
Woodward, Mabel Strickland  158
Wray, Link  87
Wright, Bobby  172
Wright, Charles "Indian"  129
Wright, Chely  189, 194
Wright, Doyle  109
Wright, Johnny  171
Wright, Louise  171
Wright, Michelle  194
Wyatt, Cindy Reynolds  280
Wyble, Jimmy  101
Wynette, Tammy  148, 149, 151, 154, 161, 165, 170, 172, 176, 180, 183, 188, 190, 194, 215, 249, 257

Yarbrough, Rual  109, 135
Yates, Bill  109
Yearwood, Trisha  161, 170, 172, 177, 180, 183, 189
Yoakam, Dwight  150, 215, 216, 222, 272, 279
York, William Herbert "Lum"  128
Young, Curtis  258
Young, Faron  96, 212, 215, 246, 249
Young, Neil  249
Young, Reggie  249, 258
Young, Vern  109
Youngblood, Jack  110

Zincan, Joe  58, 143